Politics and the Past

WORLD SOCIAL CHANGE
Series Editor: Mark Selden

Politics and the Past

On Repairing Historical Injustices

Edited by
John Torpey

ROWMAN & LITTLEFIELD PUBLISHERS, INC.
Lanham • Boulder • New York • Oxford

ROWMAN & LITTLEFIELD PUBLISHERS, INC.

Published in the United States of America
by Rowman & Littlefield Publishers, Inc.
A Member of the Rowman & Littlefield Publishing Group
4720 Boston Way, Lanham, Maryland 20706
www.rowmanlittlefield.com

P.O. Box 317, Oxford OX2 9RU, United Kingdom

British Library Cataloguing in Publication Information Available

Library of Congress Cataloging-in-Publication Data

Politics and the past : on repairing historical injustices / edited by
John Torpey.
    p. cm. — (World social change)
   Includes bibliographical references and index.
   ISBN 0-7425-1798-5 (cloth : alk. paper) — ISBN 0-7425-1799-3 (pbk. :
alk. paper)
    1. Reparations. 2. Intergenerational relations. 3. Ethnic relations.
4. Restorative justice. I. Torpey, John C. II. Series.
KZ6785 .P65   2003
364.6'8—dc21   2002013569

Printed in the United States of America

♾ ™ The paper used in this publication meets the minimum requirements of
American National Standard for Information Sciences—Permanence of Paper for
Printed Library Materials, ANSI/NISO Z39.48-1992.

Contents

Preface and Acknowledgments

This book contains a variety of chapters that address the problem of repairing past injustices. It explores the meaning of the extensive talk in recent years of "reparations" and of other approaches to "coming to terms with the past." The contributors' fields of expertise span the disciplines of sociology, history, political science, law, art history, and museum curating. The authors—many of them leading commentators on reparations politics—seek to provide perspectives on the origins of the contemporary trend toward dealing with past wrongs, the dynamics of reparations politics, and the consequences of struggles for reparations in a variety of contexts around the world.

In the introductory chapter 1, I offer a framework for understanding both the broad field of reparations politics and the nature and significance of the main types of reparations claims that have been raised so far.

The chapters in part 1 seek to make sense of the recent wave of atonement and reparation from sociological and historical perspectives. In their contribution, sociologists Jeffrey K. Olick and Brenda Coughlin examine the origins of what they call "the politics of regret," arguing that the spread of concern with past injustices is a symptom of the decline of the nation-state as a force for social self-understanding. Alan Cairns, a political scientist, considers the variety of historical tributaries that have fed into the larger stream of efforts to "come to terms with the past." In his chapter, Elazar Barkan, a historian of reparations politics, argues that there has been a major shift in the morality of international relations and that, as a result, many new possibilities have emerged for redress of previous wrongs. Part I concludes with the reflections of Roy L. Brooks, a legal scholar, concerning a theory of reparations that addresses both the features of successful claims for reparations and the variety of forms of redress.

Part II of this book offers chapters covering reparations claims-making. First, sociologist Dalton Conley assesses the historical sources of black economic disadvantage and the extent to which reparations may be expected to ameliorate the relevant inequities. In her chapter, historian of Japan Laura Hein details the upwelling of efforts to call the Japanese government to account for its misdeeds during World War II and the relatively limited success of those efforts. From their vantage point as direct participants, two scholars deeply enmeshed in the world of museums, Ruth B. Phillips and Elizabeth Johnson, discuss the process of negotiating new relationships between those once unapproachable temples of high culture and the populations whose cultures are on display. Next, political scientist Sharon F. Lean explores the relatively meager reparations programs that have been created in response to the atrocities of the generals in Latin America and their importance for reconciliation among citizens in these countries. Rhoda E. Howard-Hassmann, a sociologist of development and of human rights, casts doubt on the argument that the West is responsible for the disastrous state of much of Africa today, but nonetheless argues that apologies for wrongdoing and various forms of economic assistance from the more prosperous countries of the world would be desirable. R. S. Ratner, William K. Carroll, and Andrew Woolford analyze the dynamics of treaty making between indigenes and majority governments in British Columbia, arguing that while the demand for return of Aboriginal lands to their previous owners is morally and politically appropriate, this process may lead to the creation of a new elite that may or may not pursue the best interests of their band (tribe). Finally, Stef Vandeginste, a Belgian legal researcher, outlines the various attempts to provide reparations for the victims of the 1994 Rwandan genocide, including recourse to the traditional *gacaca* ("front-porch") forms of justice.

The book closes with the reflections in part III about the current transformation of the relationship between history and the law, of which the spread of reparations politics is an element. Henry Rousso, a French historian of the memory of World War II, argues that the trial of Maurice Papon symbolizes a dramatic shift of orientation in the prosecution of World War II–related misdeeds. This shift, from state-initiated prosecutions based on *raison d'état* to cases initiated by private parties in pursuit of their own political goals, reflects the weakening of states in general and of the republican sensibility in France in particular. In the book's final chapter, historian Charles S. Maier considers the function of the "re" words that make up reparations politics—"retribution, reparation, remembering, recording, reconciliation." He also explores the tasks of the truth commission, the historian, and the judge, respectively. He argues that while both the historian and the judge—in contrast to the truth commission—must seek to understand motivation in order to assess responsibility, the historian's main contribution is to rescue the formerly voiceless from the obscurity of the past. That, too, is a mode of repairing historical injustice, and an important one indeed.

Some of the essays in this book were first presented at a symposium titled

"Politics and the Past: On Repairing Historical Injustices" that I organized in late February 2000 under the auspices of the Institute for European Studies and the Peter Wall Institute for Advanced Studies at the University of British Columbia in Vancouver. I am deeply grateful to Sima Godfrey, the Director of the Institute for European Studies, and to Ken MacCrimmon, Director of the Peter Wall Institute, for their support on that occasion. The Peter Wall Institute also generously supported an Exploratory Workshop in November 2001 that brought together some of the contributors to this volume for further discussion of the themes examined herein.

Funding for my research on the issues addressed in the book has been provided by the University of California Institute on Global Conflict and Cooperation, the University of California Center for German and European Studies, and the University of British Columbia.

Finally, I would like to thank Sharon Lean and Jeanne Batalova for their research assistance, Christine Webster and Caroline Ford for their translation of the Vandeginste and Rousso essays, respectively, and Joseph Tan for his help in preparing the manuscript for publication.

Introduction

Politics and the Past

John Torpey

The pursuit of reparations and apologies by many groups for a wide array of past injustices has in recent years become a major preoccupation of the one-time victims (or their descendants), of their societies more broadly, and of scholars studying social change as well. "[T]he world does appear to be caught up," Nigerian author Wole Soyinka has said, "in a *fin de millénaire* fever of atonement."[1] Indeed, so pervasive is this phenomenon that "coming to terms with the past" in contemporary politics has extensively supplanted the elaboration of visions of the future. The mood of post-totalitarian caution—of what Jürgen Habermas has called "enlightened bewilderment"[2]—was reflected in the comments of a participant at the 2002 Porto Alegre alternative "summit" on globalization. The Brazilian novelist Moacyr Scliar argued that the absence of any grand future plan emanating from the meeting could be explained as follows: "The political horrors of the twentieth century taught us that it's better we don't leave here with a magic formula."[3] The declining trust in alternative visions of society indicated in these remarks, coupled with the simultaneous upsurge of concern with memory, history, and "coming to terms with the past," suggest that the lessons of twentieth-century history have facilitated a shift from the labor movement's traditional rallying cry of "don't mourn, organize" to a sensibility that insists we must "organize to mourn." This book explores the background and consequences of this shift.

Despite the ways in which the preoccupation with past crimes and atrocities may mirror the eclipse of visionary modes of imagining the future, it also promotes attention to the once-neglected suffering of victims and bears witness to an enhancement of their status vis-à-vis the perpetrators of injustices. The spread and growing recognition of claims for reparations calls sharply into question the age-old idea, articulated by Thucydides in the "Melian dialogue," that "the standard of justice depends on the equality of power to compel . . . [;] the strong do what they have the power to do and the weak accept what they have to accept."[4]

In truth, this realist position has been eroding since at least the nineteenth century. Among the many aspects of the French Revolution to which he objected, Edmund Burke excoriated the revolutionaries' efforts "to chastise men for the offenses of their natural ancestors"; according to Burke, "corporate bodies are immortal for the good of the members, but not for their punishment. Nations themselves are such corporations."[5]

A century later, however, Friedrich Nietzsche set out to assess what he regarded as the debilitating consequences of the "historical fever" in which his contemporaries were gripped. Notwithstanding a corrosive condemnation of the outsized cultivation of history, which he regarded as detrimental to "life," Nietzsche recommended a "critical" history that illuminated the degree to which "living and the practice of injustice are synonymous": "For since we happen to be the products of earlier generations, we are also the products of their blunders, passions, and misunderstandings, indeed, of their crimes; it is impossible to free ourselves completely from this chain."[6]

Immediately after World War II, the existentialist philosopher Karl Jaspers extended this argument to the crimes of the Nazis in his stirring effort to encourage his fellow Germans to assume political responsibility and make reparation for those atrocities.[7] More broadly, Jaspers's student Hannah Arendt wrote in the early postwar years, "We can no longer simply afford to take that which was good in the past and simply call it our heritage, to discard the bad and simply think of it as a dead load which by itself time will bury in oblivion. The 'subterranean' stream of Western history has finally come to the surface and usurped the dignity of our tradition."[8] In many of his writings, Jürgen Habermas has reiterated the theme of the continuity of national traditions and the corresponding need to "come to terms with the past."[9]

The posture toward the past adopted by Nietzsche, Jaspers, Arendt, and Habermas became, in effect, the official self-understanding of postwar West Germany. That stance, in turn, has contributed mightily to the worldwide spread of Holocaust consciousness and set a standard of reckoning with the past that others have been forced to confront.[10] The concern to come to terms with many pasts has advanced arm in arm with the proliferation of Holocaust consciousness in many parts of the world.[11] In this sense, those who claim that the Holocaust has drained the life out of other commemorative projects are mistaken; the situation is the reverse of what they claim. Without the Holocaust as standard and model, other projects oriented to coming to terms with the past would not have been as successful.[12] Indeed, in view of the remarkable spread of demands to face up to the once subterranean past, one might well say that "we are all Germans now" in the sense that all countries (and many other entities as well) that wish to be regarded as legitimate confront pressures to make amends for the more sordid aspects of their past and, often, to compensate victims of earlier wrongdoing.[13]

In the remainder of this introductory chapter, I offer a framework for understanding the worldwide spread of reparations politics at the dawning of the new millennium. As in the book itself, this introduction emphasizes "reparations" in the narrow sense as a response to past injustices, while viewing reparations politics as a broader field encompassing "transitional justice," apologies, and efforts at "reconciliation" as well.

DEFINING REPARATIONS

Let us begin by defining some terms. Clear definitions will help to circumscribe the conceptual terrain explored in these chapters, although the contributors themselves do not necessarily hew to any consistent usage. Perhaps the most frequently used single term connected with many of the efforts to "come to terms with the past" is that of "reparations." Generally speaking, the term refers to compensation, usually of a material kind and often specifically monetary, for some past wrong. The prominence of this term derives from the signal importance of Holocaust-related compensation in stimulating the concern to come to terms with past injustices elsewhere. Claims for reparations have spread in parallel with the diffusion of Holocaust consciousness, at least among political and intellectual elites, in precincts far distant from the mainly European sites of the Jewish *Shoah*. A widespread Holocaust consciousness, in turn, has been the water in which reparations activists have swum, defining much of the discourse they use to enhance their aims.

Some people use the term "reparations" synonymously with that of "restitution." Like the former term, the latter can be interpreted expansively to include a variety of ways of making amends.[14] There are difficulties with using the terms "reparations" and "restitution" interchangeably, however. Even if the dictionary allows for a broad interpretation, the term "restitution" tends to suggest a more narrow concern with the return of specific items of real or personal property, whereas the term "reparations" has come to suggest broader and more variegated meanings. It is telling, for example, that studies of the problems connected with the return of land to blacks in South Africa and to Indians in the northeastern United States both speak of restitution rather than reparations, while Karl Jaspers and others speak of reparation without specifying the modalities of repair.[15]

To be sure, the term "reparations" is widely thought to imply *monetary* compensation per se, but this need not be its only meaning, and many would insist that the term has much broader connotations. For example, Priscilla Hayner suggests that the term "encompasses a variety of types of redress, including *restitution, compensation, rehabilitation, satisfaction, and guarantees of nonrepetition.*"[16] As a student of truth commissions, Hayner has in mind contexts in which the wrongs in question were human rights violations of recent vintage. What is striking, however, is that the term "reparations" has come to be applied to a great diversity of historical settings and alleged wrongs. In many of these cases, much more is at stake than the return of, or compensation for, concrete items of property, as suggested by the more limited term "restitution."

The shift in meaning is captured nicely by certain remarks in the study that underlies the Civil Liberties Act of 1988, which sought to recompense Japanese Americans for their internment in the United States during World War II. That study, *Personal Justice Denied*, noted that the Japanese American Evacuation Claims Act of 1948 "attempted to compensate for the [internees'] losses of real and personal property" but made no attempt to compensate for the stigma, deprivation of liberty, or psychological impact of exclusion and relocation.[17]

An important feature of contemporary reparations politics is to give much greater weight to psychic harms and "trauma" than was the case in the period up to and immediately following World War II.[18] This shift reflects the "triumph of the therapeutic" in realms far removed from individual psychology, as well as the transformation of the concept of trauma from a purely physical to a predominantly mental construction.[19]

In contrast to restitution, then, the notion of reparations points to attempts to make up for egregiously and unjustly violated selves and for squandered life chances, rather than to efforts to compel the return of goods per se. The spread of human rights ideas in the post–World War II era has fueled the sense that such wrongs, no matter how acceptable they may have been deemed at the time they were committed, may now be said to have been illegitimate and must be compensated or redressed accordingly. Because it has come to cover this broad class of wrongs, the term "reparations" has emerged as the most widely used term to refer to processes of coming to grips with past injustices.

The term "reparations," which has of course been around for a long time, has also come to be applied to a much wider range of claimants since World War II. Before that epochal conflagration, the term referred to a fine among *states*. Once hostilities had ceased, the winners of the war insisted that the losers had caused the conflict and the resulting damages and that they should be compelled to compensate the countries that had suffered in the process. Reparations were thus a relatively unambiguous and tangible form of "victor's justice" and were resented accordingly. The indemnities imposed on Germany by the triumphant Allies after World War I are the most notorious example. Yet the reparations demands of the Great War Allies remained anchored in the tradition that states, and states only, were the sole legitimate subjects of international law (the "law of nations") until World War II.

That state of affairs has changed dramatically with the burgeoning of the human rights paradigm in response to the carnage of World War II.[20] Since that time, individuals and subnational groups have been endowed with "standing" in international law in a series of UN documents and international covenants. This shift arose in part because, in addition to making war *bianca* on other countries, the Nazis also made a separate, undeclared war on the defenseless Jews as well as on other groups (e.g., the handicapped, homosexuals, Gypsies). As a result, and despite long-standing debate about whether Jews constitute a "nation," the assault on the Jews eventually gave them a kind of legal standing in international law (quite apart from the existence of Israel), setting an important precedent for other groups to lay claim to a similar status.

The human rights instruments promulgated by the United Nations after World War II were drafted to ensure that human beings would not, in the future, exercise their barbarous impulses on others without the latter having a juridical leg to stand on—especially when the perpetrator was the victim's own government. Human rights talk, the curtailment of the strong "Westphalian" notion of sovereignty, and the rising status of the individual as a subject of international law have gone hand in hand. In turn, reparations— "making good again," to translate literally the German term *Wiedergutmachung*—have been an essential complement to the spread of human rights ideas. This is because reparations help to make the notion of human rights seem real and enforceable in the absence of a global police force empowered to back rights claims with armed might.

MAPPING REPARATIONS POLITICS

Connected as it is etymologically to the word "repair," the term "reparations" has come to suggest activities oriented to repairing frayed or torn relations handed down from the past. Yet the modalities of repair are manifold. The repair of rent social relations may involve trials of perpetrators, purges, truth commissions, rehabilitation of those wrongly convicted of crimes, monetary compensation, social policies designed to rectify inequalities rooted in unjust past social arrangements, memorials, changes in school history curricula, and more. Following Pierre Bourdieu, it may be useful to conceptualize the various phenomena connected with reparations politics not as a mélange of isolated cases, but as a *field* of related activities.

As has already been noted, the term "reparations" is used to discuss claims for mending past wrongs that are themselves extremely varied, running the gamut from specific human rights abuses against individuals such as unjust imprisonment and torture to such diverse social systems as plantation slavery, apartheid, and colonialism. Yet viewing reparations politics as a field helps us to grasp the ways in which, far from each of the groups in question pursuing their own narrow concerns, the various kinds of reparations politics share a common language and outlook concerning the importance of the past in moving forward in the present day.

As figure I.1 suggests, the broad field of reparations politics can be conceived of as a series of concentric circles. These circles progress from a "core" of what has come to be known as "transitional justice" (typically involving criminal trials, political purges, and truth commissions) through reparations and restitution of a material kind, to apologies and statements of regret, and finally to a concern with "collective memory" and with processes that one might refer to as the pursuit of a "communicative history"—that is, a history oriented toward mutual agreement by the various parties that participate in re-writing historical narratives on the basis of a claim that they are (most) directly affected by the history in question. In part this conceptualization reflects the chronological development of reparations politics during the past two decades or so; in part it represents an analytical grid

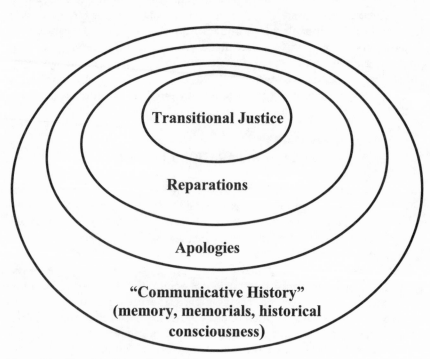

Figure I.1. Mapping Reparations Politics

distinguishing "ideal types" of activities germane to coming to terms with the past that may, in practice, be found lumped together.

At the core of the field are those activities associated with "transitional justice" in what might be called its classic sense. Here the perpetrators of the injustices in question comprise a more or less definable group and are, generally speaking, still alive. Punishment of misdeeds or at least illumination of the circumstances of their commission—rather than compensation for the victims—is the focus of the activity of repair.

In contrast, reparations in the narrow sense of material compensation steers concern away from evildoers and, instead, in the direction of victims and also of *beneficiaries*. Whether those who suffered the alleged wrongs are still alive becomes a major bone of contention in the struggle for reparations; the further away in time one gets from the commission of the acts for which compensation is sought, the thornier the problems of repair become. Even if they are dead, however, there may be present-day beneficiaries of past arrangements who may be said to owe reparations.

Apologies and statements of regret involve exchanges of sentiments between perpetrators and victims, whether the interaction takes place between surviving members of either group or their descendants.[21] Apologies may or may not be accompanied by material compensation. They are a more purely symbolic exercise, even if it is also often true that monetary payments are chiefly symbolic in nature.

Finally, efforts to commemorate past suffering and to get the history straight are increasingly contentious, despite having the least direct impact on public policy. This aspect of reparations politics, the search for a "communicative history," involves scrutiny and revision of school textbooks, the erection of commemorative plaques and memorials, and the search for a past about which all the (putative) participants can agree.

Transitional Justice

The idea of transitional justice (or "transitology," as it is sometimes known, with tongue firmly in cheek) arose in connection with the demise of military dictatorships in Latin America and, hard on the heels of the outgoing generals, the collapse of Communist regimes in the Soviet Union and Eastern Europe and of the apartheid regime in South Africa.[22] The writings in this genre have sought to make sense of the global trend toward democratization that swept far-flung parts of the world in the closing third of the twentieth century.[23] The chief activities associated with transitional justice have been trials and purges of perpetrators and collaborators, as well as the instauration of truth commissions.[24] As a general rule, the misdeeds for which a reckoning is sought are atrocities and wrongs committed against individuals, principally in the form of what the United Nations has codified in recent years under the heading of "gross violations of human rights."[25]

The conceit underlying transitology is that there is a generic "transition to democracy" (or at least one "from authoritarianism"). Yet the particular type of rule that is being left behind, and the variety of paths away from undemocratic rule, make a very big difference in determining what kind of transitional justice will occur.[26] For example, one of the most insightful analysts of the legacy of communism in the East bloc, Tina Rosenberg, has noted that there were important similarities but also major differences between the transitions in the former Soviet bloc and those in Latin America.

Rosenberg deftly distinguished between the "criminal regimes" that had ruled the Communist countries and the "regimes of criminals" under the generals in Latin America. Her analysis of Communist regimes owed much to the view of those such as Vaclav Havel that everyone in the Communist countries bore their share of complicity in the persistence of the political order. Accordingly, Rosenberg suggested that it was more difficult to envision trials of "collaborators" in such countries than it would be in the case of brutal regimes run by relatively small groups of *responsables*.[27]

Yet such trials were blocked, at least initially, in those cases where the transition from violent rule was a bargain negotiated among political elites. The leaders of the old regime were not likely to lay down their guns if they would soon find themselves facing criminal trials; hence, amnesty was the order of the day.[28] The subsequent efforts to prosecute former Chilean strongman Augusto Pinochet revealed that not everyone accepted these bargains, which were hammered out by elites in their final hours. Still, coming to terms with the past in Latin American and East European societies has chiefly involved a sort of collective agreement to move on, either because that was the deal that permitted the transition to more democratic forms of rule or because there was no obvious way to prosecute any but a few big fish. As Sharon F. Lean has pointed out, demands for and payments of monetary reparations have been relatively limited in the Latin American cases.[29] Although one cannot say for sure, this situation may be also in part a function of the rather weak echo of the Holocaust in that part of the world.[30]

Against the background of the spreading worldwide preoccupation with righting historical injustices, however, the main difficulty with the transitional justice paradigm has been its foreshortened time horizons, its tendency to view the past as having begun only the day before yesterday. Dominated as this approach has been by lawyers, political scientists, and human rights activists, the disproportionate attention to regime changes of the very recent past is perhaps not surprising.

In contrast to the historical shallowness of the transitional justice paradigm, many of the historical injustices for which repair and reckoning have been demanded in recent times involve wrongs that occurred or had their origins far in the past and in societies with venerable liberal credentials. These demands for repair of the subterranean past concern heinous regimes and actions that may stretch back hundreds of years or they may impugn political and social orders whose flaws for particular groups have only recently grown politically salient. Demands for repair of the legacies of these pasts recall the important lesson, once taught us by Barrington Moore, that even liberal democratic societies were born in fire and blood.[31] Campaigns for attention to, and repair of, these past wrongs also highlight that for some groups, even in liberal democratic societies of long standing, dispossession was the rule and the promise of equal treatment was chimerical until only yesterday—or, indeed, remains so to the present day.

The theoretical premises underlying the transitional justice model thus distort our understanding both of authoritarianism and of liberal democracy. The model takes the self-characterization of liberal societies too literally to accommodate the insistence of various groups that they have been denied the equality that such societies claim to afford their citizens. As Aristide Zolberg has pointed out, "Despite the usage popularized by Washington-area political scientists, authoritarianism should not be thought of as a distinct regime type but, rather, as an element of political process shared by many different systems of rule and associated with a variety of socioeconomic formations."[32]

Thus, recently "authoritarian" regimes are not the only ones seeking a reckoning with the past, as the "transitional justice" literature tends to imply. Liberal democracies also face demands for repair arising from instances of past abrogation of the universalistic ideas on the basis of which they claim legitimacy. At the same time, compared to regimes based more on force than persuasion, such efforts at repair demonstrate the greater inclination and ability of liberal democracies to respond to demands to mend a rent social and political fabric.

Reparations

Largely because of the publicity given to the Truth and Reconciliation Commission (TRC), the transition from *apartheid* to "nonracialism" in South Africa has bulked very large in the transitional justice literature. Yet the case of South Africa parts company with those of other recent regime transitions in a manner that leads us straight into the problem of reparations in the material sense.

The TRC has come to be the darling of many advocates of coming to terms with the past in societies leaving behind a despotic form of rule. It appeared to many observers to get beyond the shortcomings of trials in bringing out more of the truth than would have been possible in adversarial proceedings concerned with assigning guilt. The TRC thus famously traded justice for truth—an exchange deeply resented by many of those who had been victimized by the state security forces or the families of those victims. As in some of the Latin American cases,[33] the TRC was also empowered through its Committee on Reparation and Rehabilitation to provide limited compensation to the victims of gross human rights abuses at the hands of the state.

But here the similarities with the Latin American and East European regimes end. The apartheid regime was not simply another brutal regime, but a species of the genus colonialism. As Mahmood Mamdani has pointed out, "Where the focus is on perpetrators, victims are necessarily defined as the minority of political activists; for the victimhood of the majority to be recognized, the focus has to shift from perpetrators to beneficiaries. The difference is this: whereas the focus on perpetrators fuels the demand for justice as criminal justice, that on beneficiaries shifts the focus to a notion of justice as social justice."[34] In other words, the TRC neglected "the link between conquest and dispossession, between racialised power and racialised privilege, between perpetrator and beneficiary"[35]—in a word, the enduring legacy of inequality that the apartheid system and its predecessors had left in its wake.

Along with violations of human rights in violent regimes, colonial conquest and expropriation have come to constitute major sources of demands for reparations. Indeed, the language of reparations broadens out here from the paradigm case of reparations for the Jewish (and other) victims of the Nazis into rhetoric available for groups that have undergone very different kinds of historical injustices.

In an earlier essay on this theme,[36] I argued that there were two principal types of reparations claims, paralleling the variants suggested by Mamdani. There I called these two types of reparations claims "commemorative" and "anti-systemic," reflecting the difference between specific abuses committed against individual persons and systemic abuses leading to group-based inequalities in the present.

The decisive issue in this distinction is the extent to which economic disadvantage in the present is relevant to the claim for reparations. Even if current economic circumstances are taken into account in the design of a reparations program, economic inequality is not essential to commemorative reparations claims.[37] In contrast, such inequality *is* at the heart of the matter for those demanding anti-systemic reparations. In connection with this difference, I argued in that earlier discussion that commemorative reparations were essentially the end of the matter for many who sought or received them, whereas those making anti-systemic reparations claims were typically connected to broader movements for egalitarian social change. For them, the pursuit of reparations tends to be but one strategy in a larger project designed to promote equality.

Here I wish to refine that earlier schema somewhat, as suggested in figure I.2. Whereas my previous formulation may have suggested that the two types of reparations claims were to be understood as being mutually exclusive, they should in fact be regarded as endpoints on a continuum. Many who seek reparations of the commemorative sort also see what they are doing as helping to ensure the growth and survival of democracy and the rule of law or, perhaps, as part of the struggles to end sexual violence, torture, and impunity. In that sense, they are operating in an anti-systemic fashion. Still, economic inequality remains less central to their concerns than human rights in the liberal sense. The continuum relating commemorative and anti-systemic reparations claims is indicated by the "east–west" axis in figure I.2. The distinction has been re-phrased according to the meaning assigned in various reparations claims to money, to the extent that it plays a role at all. Reflecting this distinction, the endpoints on the continuum are now designated as either "symbolic" or "economic."

In addition to clarifying the relation between commemorative/symbolic and anti-systemic/economic reparations claims, I want to elaborate further the nature of the claims being made. Here the key consideration concerns the extent to which past injustices are regarded by the claimants as having contributed to the destruction of a culture and the role of reparations in repairing the damages said to have been inflicted on a culture. This aspect of reparations claims making bears witness to the heightened significance of "culture" in recent politics. More specifically, the notion of "rights" to "one's culture" has emerged as an important aspect of multicultural discourse and its recognition of previously disregarded groups.[38]

This cultural dimension of reparations claims making is indicated by the "north-south" axis in figure I.2. The poles of this continuum run from reparations claims arising from expropriation of land and objects viewed as having deep cultural significance, at one end, to unjust takings that are specifiable in a more mundane legal sense, albeit perhaps retroactively so. Let me now explicate the diagram, which seeks to capture more effectively than my previous efforts the variety of reparations claims currently afoot around the globe.

As indicated in the lower left of figure I.2, symbolic reparations are those given to or sought by those groups who were victimized and forced to perform forced labor by the Axis powers during World War II; those of Japanese ethnicity unjustly interned in North America during the war; and recent victims of "gross violations of human rights." The claims are in many ways analogous to the sorts of civil liabilities that might be brought against firms accused of wrongdoing, except that the responsible parties are usually states. (The fund recently created by the German government to compensate World War II–era forced and slave laborers was a joint government–industry under-

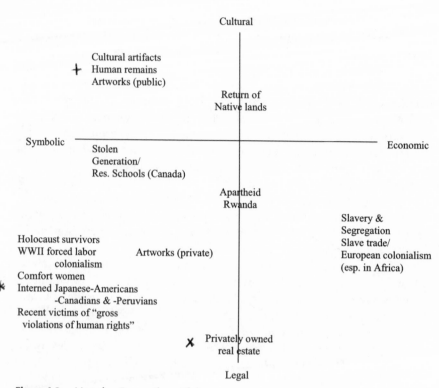

Figure I.2. **Mapping Reparations Claims**

taking, but the terms were largely hammered out under official government auspices.)

The claims are not generally justified in terms of any alleged cultural destruction but in terms of the direct damage sustained by the victims. The harms for which compensation are sought are chiefly psychological rather than physical, although of course physical injuries may underlie the claims as well.[39] The main point is that the harms in question were carried out directly on the bodies of the persons to be compensated, rather than their descendants or heirs.

The restitution of artworks to private owners falls near to these kinds of harms, in the sense that their expropriation was unjust but without great spiritual value to a national or religious community. The return of such artworks is often largely a symbolic matter, as the person(s) reclaiming them may simply give them (back) to a museum for public display, rather than profiting from their re-acquisition or even just holding them privately.[40]

When the artworks in question came not from private hands but from state-run institutions, however, the problem becomes much more complex,

and perceptions of injustices by one country or community toward another come into play. The inflammation of national feelings shapes decisions about what is just with regard to artworks plundered during wartime.[41] Hence, claims for restitution of artworks stolen from public institutions tend to be
+ evaluated more in cultural than in purely legal terms, as indicated in the diagram.

Restitution of real property lies further toward the "economic" end of the continuum concerning the meaning of money because such properties are more likely to have a use value or a market value, or both, that can be reappropriated by the owners of wrongly expropriated property or their heirs. However, Charles S. Maier notes that, as with artworks, "many private owners [of real estate] ask only for nominal recognition of earlier ownership and donate the property for public uses."[42] In any case, precisely because of its mundane qualities, privately owned real estate expropriated by a nefarious regime is less likely to excite the passions associated with the illegitimate tak-
X ing of cultural artifacts and is thus located at the "legal" end of the continuum concerning the importance of cultural reconstruction in reparations politics.

Let us now move to the opposite end of this continuum. Cultural artifacts, along with human remains, have long been housed in museums of anthropology and natural history. They have been widely seen as essential for the pursuit of scientific knowledge or the advancement of public understanding of the groups from which they were taken (or, perhaps, by whom they were given).

Ruth B. Phillips and Elizabeth Johnson note that cultural artifacts often were collected by those most sympathetic to the peoples with whom Europeans came into contact, and that such collectors often sought to defend these peoples from obliteration by encroaching outsiders.[43] Yet the perception has spread in recent years that even such sympathetic views had a paternalistic quality about them, and that in any case the basic relationship involved was one of racial domination.

The result has been an accelerating shift toward negotiating new relationships between the museums and the communities from which originated the artifacts and remains that the museums display or house. One prominent legislative effort to regulate these new relationships came with the 1990 Native American Graves Protection and Repatriation Act (NAGPRA) in the United States. With that act, "mainstream respect for the dead was formally extended to Indians," an outcome that took cognizance of the traditional American respect for freedom of religion and its abrogation with regard to indigenous populations.[44] In 1992, Canada followed the NAGPRA precedent when the "Task Force on Museums" issued guidelines regulating the disposition of cultural objects held in Canadian museums.[45]

Despite these changes in the relations between museums and North Amer-

ican Aboriginal populations, however, the pleas of the Greeks for the return
of the Elgin Marbles (the friezes from the façade of the Parthenon) by the
British Museum have so far fallen on deaf ears.[46] This may have something to
do with the fact that the objects in question are often said to have been sold
"fair and square" by the overlord in Athens at the time, the Turkish pasha.
One suspects, however, that the Greeks' lack of success also has something
to do with the perception that the British and the Greeks share a common
("Western") culture, whereas European settler societies and indigenous
groups are increasingly viewed as inhabiting an impassable divide, as a result
of which putatively indigenous groups are regarded as having a stronger
claim to the return of their cultural artifacts.

The identity-based politics of recent years have tended to draw the divide
between conqueror and Aborigine more sharply. This is perhaps under-
standable insofar as the route to redress of historical injustices based in race
and ethnicity involves the reassertion, as the grounding of claims for such
redress, of precisely those categories of difference on the basis of which the
earlier wrongs were perpetrated. The assimilationist ideals of yesteryear have
been tarnished as the subterranean history of relations between indigene and
invader have been brought to light. To be sure, some of the intruders upheld
an ideal of common citizenship consistent with liberal principles, which
require the de-emphasis of difference in favor of what people hold in common.[47] Yet it has recently been argued persuasively that the assimilationist
policies toward Aboriginals in the settler states of North America and Australia were ultimately designed to eliminate the indigenous population in
order to make their land available for appropriation by white settlers.[48]

Hence, it is somewhat perplexing that the claims of those supporting the
movement for reparations in Australia have focused chiefly on the "stolen
generation," those Aboriginal children who were forcibly removed from
their families and placed in the homes of white Europeans in an effort to
transform them into Euro-Australians, with relatively little focus on land
claims. The Stolen Generations Inquiry, officially known as the National
Inquiry into the Separation of Aboriginal and Torres Strait Islander Children
from Their Families,[49] sought to investigate the laws and policies under
which these removals—and attendant physical and sexual abuse—took place.

In one of the Inquiry's most striking conclusions, it found that the Australian government had committed "genocide" in its use of these practices. The
rationale underlying this finding was that the practices in question fulfilled
the clause in the Genocide Convention (1948) according to which "forcibly
transferring children of the group to another group" constitutes an act of
genocide. As Chris Cunneen has pointed out, in addition to the physical and
emotional harms that were inflicted, much of what is deemed to have been
wrong about the removal of Aboriginal children concerned the loss of cultural rights and opportunities.[50]

The situation in Canada with regard to residential schools for Aboriginal children is quite similar. The comparable practice of forcibly introducing indigenous children into state- and church-run schools is what led to the Canadian national effort to make amends for past wrongs. That effort is outlined in the 1998 report *Gathering Strength: Canada's Aboriginal Action Plan*, which is "designed to renew the relationship [of the federal government] with the Aboriginal people of Canada."[51]

The Action Plan follows up on the recommendations of the report of the Royal Commission on Aboriginal Peoples.[52] Its "Statement of Reconciliation: Learning from the Past" calls for special attention to the cultural distinctiveness of indigenous populations: "Diverse, vibrant Aboriginal nations had ways of life rooted in fundamental values concerning their relationships to the Creator, the environment, and each other, in the role of Elders as the living memory of their ancestors, and in their responsibilities as custodians of the lands, waters and resources of their homelands." The grounding of the claims for reparations by Aboriginal peoples in Australia and Canada stress the cultural damage they have sustained under these policies of forced assimilation. Hence, both are located closer to the "cultural" end of the "north–south" axis in the diagram, though not as high as land claims, which typically carry a heavier burden of cultural loss even than practices of forced assimilation. Ancestral lands are usually said to be at the center of indigenous ways of life by those seeking their return.

Yet both culture and economics were involved in the encounter between indigene and European settler, and both, according to *Gathering Strength*, had often been ignored in the past: "The assistance and spiritual values of the Aboriginal peoples who welcomed the newcomers to this continent too often have been forgotten."[53] The cultural dimension of the demand for the return of traditional lands is connected to the claim that they represent spaces that have been inhabited by the groups in question for long periods before the arrival of European settlers and that those spaces have a special spiritual significance as the repository of ancient ancestors and traditional wisdom.[54] The immemorial past and groups thought to be connected to it have acquired an enormous symbolic authority in rootless, cosmopolitan societies caught up in the modern capitalist whirlwind of "creative destruction."[55]

Nonetheless, the chief aspect of the demands for the restitution of land is the economic viability of Aboriginal communities and their right to control their own resources. This is the significance, for example, of a recent agreement between the Canadian province of Quebec and the Cree Nation, which "gives Indians management of their natural resources [and] recognizes their full autonomy as a native nation."[56] Demands for the return of lands are a prominent element of politics in North America and the antipodes, of course, but they can be found in less obvious places as well. Notably, a number of groups in Southern Africa have recently launched a campaign for the restitution of lands to indigenous groups in South Africa, Namibia, and Zimbabwe.[57] Claims to the control over land as well as to fishing rights and other rights of usufruct in natural resources are at the heart of these discussions. Hence, these claims are located closer to the "economic" end of the continuum concerning the meaning of money than are the reparations sought in connection with the stolen generation, the inmates of residential schools, and the like.

R. S. Ratner and his colleagues advance an unusual and innovative perspective in the debate over the land claims advanced by indigenes against the majority in settler societies.[58] The authors are sympathetic to the demand for the return of the lands taken from Aboriginals by European interlopers in the process of white settler colonization. In comparison to the situation in the United States and in most of Eastern Canada, however, relations in British Columbia between First Nations and the majority are complicated by the lack of any treaty basis for the earlier expropriations, to which recourse might now be had to sort out claims of ownership. The prevailing doctrine that the lands were *terra nullius* ("empty land") may have made the confiscation of land easier at the time, but that legal theory (also deployed in the British conquest of Australia) has led to a situation in which new arrangements must be negotiated against the backdrop of a "Fourth World" movement with considerably greater power than would have been the case, say, before 1960. Around that date, colonialism in traditional form, whether external or internal, became less and less defensible, violating as it did the norms of national autonomy that European political development had done so much to promote.[59]

Some observers have objected to these land claims because of the record of corruption and malfeasance that has been compiled by some Aboriginal governments.[60] In a realist vein, Ratner and his colleagues accept that First Nations control over land and other resources may lead not to the restoration of putatively indigenous ways of doing things, but rather to the creation of "comprador bourgeoisies" (analogous to those that had emerged from independence in the postcolonial Third World) that are prone to corruption and abuse of power.

The authors insist, however, that such wrongdoing has little to do with the predispositions of Indians per se and is, instead, a phenomenon that arises with all elites not subject to strict accountability. Ratner and his co-authors see no plausible moral alternative to the return of native lands in British Columbia and elsewhere, but they also appreciate that this may have problematic consequences to the extent that, in the absence of appropriate constraints, such resources may enable new indigenous elites to exploit their newly privileged positions.

The rationale for returning indigenous lands is connected to the fact that, generally speaking, First Nations populations define the bottom rung of the racial order, and their condition constitutes the most glaring violation in Canadian society of the norm of equal citizenship.[61] The indignities and inequalities suffered by natives in Canada thus occupy a place on the public agenda analogous to that of blacks in the United States. The two groups share the historical condition of having been forcibly subjected to white European domination, but here the similarities end. Although indigenes were subordinated as a result of conquest on their home grounds, blacks were subjugated through forced migration and enslavement on lands distant from their origins.

These differences in the processes of subordination generate different kinds of reparations politics in the present. Whereas Indians and other indigenes can lay claim to "their" original homelands, black Americans have recourse primarily to recompense for the ways in which their treatment has violated self-proclaimed American norms of freedom and autonomy. Blacks cannot (and, given the current condition of much of Africa, likely would not) lay claim to their original territories. In pursuing reparations, black Americans must rely on the prospect that the foreshortened opportunities available to them will pique the conscience of the broader American populace and spur deep social change, as occurred during the Civil Rights Movement.

In view of their relatively greater population share, as well as of the fact that slavery has been widely seen as so fundamental an abrogation of the deep rhetorical commitment to freedom in the United States, the problems of the black population have generally superseded those of indigenes in the American national consciousness. The persistent inequalities suffered by blacks in the United States continue to be the subject of anguished and often passionate debate.[62]

In recent years, affirmative action—which many would regard as the appropriate approach to dealing with inequities rooted in past injustices—has fallen from political favor. The result has been a renewed call among many, especially in the black intelligentsia, to seek reparations for those inequalities. The relationship between the declining political support for affirmative action and the demand for reparations is enunciated straightforwardly by Robert Westley in his analysis of reparations for black Americans: "Affirmative action for Black Americans as a form of remediation for perpetuation of past injustice is almost dead," and it is thus necessary to "revitalize the discussion of reparations."[63]

In the case of reparations for black Americans, the material dimension of reparations is clearly paramount. At this point, there is no possibility of claiming that reparations will help those directly subjected to enslavement, the historical crucible out of which the diminished status of blacks in American society is generally said to have developed.[64] As a result of this historical distance from the "scene of the crime," so to speak, some reparations advo-

cates argue that it would be more desirable to assert that the inequalities suffered by blacks today are a product of the more recent history of legal
segregation ("Jim Crow"), through which many people still alive actually
lived. But the main concern of all of these commentators and groups is with
the economic inequalities suffered by blacks in contemporary America.

There is nonetheless a cultural dimension of the demand for reparations,
which is why I have located the claim for reparations for black Americans
nearer to the middle along the "North–South" axis. In his prominent book
on the subject of reparations, *The Debt: What America Owes to Blacks*, Randall Robinson, a leading advocate of reparations for black Americans, bases
a considerable portion of his argument on the notion that the experience of
enslavement deprived blacks of their African cultural heritage.[65]

Despite the potential for galvanizing blacks behind a reparations agenda,
however, insistence on the cultural dimension of reparations arguably makes
the goal more difficult to reach. Emphasizing the cultural separateness of
blacks seems likely to send the campaign for reparations down a political
blind alley. To the extent that the wrongs for which redress is sought are
chiefly economic and that material improvement in the lives of black Americans is the primary aim of those who support the movement for reparations,
it may be best to focus on economic harms in mounting the case.[66]

Employing the language of reparations in this case offers advantages but
entails disadvantages as well. Supporters of reparations for blacks often point
to the precedent set by the reparations paid to Jews for their Holocaust-
related suffering, as well as to persons of Japanese descent for their unjust
internment during World War II. These cases do, indeed, raise questions
about why blacks might not similarly demand compensation for the wrongs
to which they have been subjected and for their uncompensated contributions to the wealth of the contemporary United States.

Yet despite the intentionally incendiary manner in which he makes the
point, David Horowitz is not incorrect to argue that payment to Holocaust
survivors and interned Japanese Americans is a different matter than compensation to those who are ("merely") the descendants of slaves, rather than
themselves the victims of atrocities.[67] Some things are true even if David
Horowitz says them. The point here is that the focus has to be shifted from
perpetrators to *beneficiaries*, as Mamdani suggested with regard to South
Africa.

Moreover, to the extent that Americans have come to associate the term
"reparations" with monetary payments to individuals, such a goal would
seem likely to be a political nonstarter. Although many reparations activists
actually seek such measures as college scholarship funds, small business
loans, and educational programs designed to call greater attention to the history of racial oppression in America, for the uninitiated the use of the term
"reparations" tends to conjure up images of monetary payouts that would

have to be rather large to make any significant impact on individual blacks. In addition, the idea of individual payments raises eyebrows among those potentially responsible for the resulting tax burden. Some of the estimates of what would be owed for back wages, lost opportunities, and the like are, not surprisingly, astronomical sums. The prospect of individual payments to black Americans, in the manner of the funds recently developed by the German government to compensate those exploited as slave labor under the Nazis, therefore seems dim. Again, however, such payments are not universally the objective of the supporters of reparations for black Americans.

As in the cases of "internal colonialism" in the United States and South Africa, although cultural loss plays a part in demands for reparations for classical "overseas" colonialism, the economic gains to be had from reparations are clearly the central consideration. Most such demands have emanated from Africa. This is in part because other regions of the formerly colonized world, especially Latin America, attained their independence long ago and thus have weaker grounds for claiming that European colonizers are the source of their problems.

A number of Latin American countries, especially Brazil, were also major beneficiaries of the slave trade, further weakening its claims to be a mere victim of colonialism. Thus contemporary Africa alone can be said to have suffered both from a colonial rule that ended but recently and from having been turned "into a warren for the commercial hunting of black skins," to use Marx's pungent phrase.[68]

Finally, as a result of decolonization, the colonizers have been largely driven from the continent or were subordinated to large non-white majorities in the transition to independent rule in the middle third of the twentieth century. Hence, there are relatively few outstanding land claims as such, although pressure on whites to return the valuable lands they own and farm has been a major issue in recent Zimbabwean politics. Thus, Africans have made demands for reparations, but those demands have had relatively little to do with land claims per se.

The pursuit of "reparations" for Africa took wing in 1992, when the Organization for African Unity (OAU) impaneled a "Group of Eminent Persons" in Abuja, Nigeria, "to explore the modalities and strategies of an African campaign for restitution similar to the compensation paid by Germany to Israel and to survivors of the Nazi Holocaust."[69] The group's work has not borne much fruit, in part because it was closely tied to the career of the then president of Nigeria, Moshood Abiola,[70] who was subsequently arrested by his successor, Sanni Abacha, and died soon thereafter under mysterious circumstances.

The discussions at the meeting were also complicated because the participants could not decide whether the chief cause for complaint was slavery or colonialism. One of the participants, the prominent author and historian Ali

Mazrui, focused primarily on slavery in his later written remarks about the campaign. Mazrui acknowledged the role of Africans in the slave trade, but argued that the chief beneficiaries were Americans and Europeans, who therefore had a responsibility to compensate Africans for the damage done them.

In particular, he proposed the idea of a "skills transfer" designed to make up for "what may well be the most devastating consequence of Black enslavement and African colonization—the enormous damage to Black and African capacities for self-improvement as compared with other societies."[71] This proposal suggested a way around the knotty problem of the form that reparations should take, avoiding any hint that it would come in direct monetary form.

The presence at the meeting of a participant from Tunisia pointedly raised the difficulty, however, concerning the major "cause of action" underlying a potential campaign for reparations for Africa. Should reparations be sought for the ravages to the continent caused by slavery or, as the Tunisian delegate proposed, for the damage caused by European colonialism? As Wole Soyinka has remarked, a campaign directed against colonialism would "require a totally different orientation and strategy, [and] would expand to embrace the indigenes of both North and South America, Australia, and New Zealand."[72] Clearly, this was not the appropriate approach for those concerned to make good on the depredations of the Atlantic slave trade in sub-Saharan Africa, as opposed to redressing the consequences of colonialism.

Even assuming that the principal "cause of action" turns out to be colonialism, Rhoda E. Howard-Hassmann has raised substantial doubts that such reparations can be said to be owed.[73] From the vantage point of one who has written about economic development in Ghana, she explores the claim that "Europe underdeveloped Africa"[74] and finds it wanting—not least on logical grounds. To put her argument briefly, there could be many reasons for the impoverished condition of contemporary Africa, and there is no way to determine with certainty that colonialism (or slavery) was the main cause of this situation.

Despite her difficulties with the arguments underlying claims for compensation for past wrongs, Howard-Hassmann agrees with the proponents of reparations that the current state of Africa demands assumption of responsibility by the West for its part in the current disastrous state of affairs on the continent.[75] Such measures could include "debt relief, a special development fund, and improvement of access to international markets," as proposed at the recent UN Conference on Racism in Durban, South Africa.[76]

Assumption of greater responsibility by the international community—which is to say by its wealthiest and most powerful members—for the plight of Africa and the Third World has been the objective of the various branches of the "Jubilee 2000" movement for debt relief for the poor countries of the globe. The movement has had some limited successes; in 2001, for example, wealthy creditor nations wrote down the debt of eighteen of the world's poorest countries, most of which were in Africa. Recently, the movement's South African branch, in collaboration with nongovernmental organizations (NGOs) and local South African political organizations, has launched a campaign to demand reparations from European companies and banks that profited from apartheid, especially those in Switzerland.[77] We thus come full circle: the model of "commemorative" claims pioneered by the victims of the Holocaust and the language and strategies it generated are being deployed by activists seeking reparations for the consequences of the internal colonialism of the apartheid regime. Nothing could demonstrate better the fundamental coherence of the variety of reparations claims being raised around the world today, regardless of differences in their locales and in the types of injustices for which they seek recompense.

Indeed, the circle is even tighter than it at first appears. According to a recent report, the new non-white majority government of South Africa is now facing land claims from the country's own indigenous populations, collectively known as the Khoisan (formerly the "Bushmen" and "Hottentots"). At a conference in early 2001, representatives of thirty-six groups speaking for South Africa's original inhabitants asserted that all those who had come after themselves had destroyed their cultures and ways of life. They were "slaughtered by colonists, oppressed by the apartheid regime and marginalized under the country's young democracy." In response, they are demanding recognition as a separate nation and return of their lands. They are troubled that the current land restitution laws refer only to properties confiscated after 1913, at which point South Africa began to operate as a sovereign country beyond British overlordship.[78] In the age of reparations, the complexities of the South African situation are myriad, to put it mildly.

Finally, in addition to broader demands for reparations for the damage done by slavery and colonialism, such claims have been raised in response to the role of the more powerful countries and institutions of the world in connection with the 1994 genocide in Rwanda. As the OAU put it in its 2000 special report assessing the genocide in Rwanda, "The international community must be made to understand the need for reparations for its complicity in the calamities of the past decade."[79] The question of Western responsibility for the killings in Rwanda has become the subject of heated debate, frequently tied to the figure of Canadian general Romeo Dallaire and his unheeded calls for reinforcements in the critical hour. A striking feature of this discussion is the extent to which the West is held to be responsible for the killings committed, after all, by Rwandans.[80]

The discussion of responsibility for the genocide thus curiously reprises the colonialist perception that Africans lack agency of their own. Yet in contrast to the cases of colonialism and slavery, the sufferings of the Rwandans were largely self-inflicted, as most people are unlikely to fail to see. The case for reparations from "the international community" seems correspondingly shakier. Still, there is precedent for holding persons and (by extension) countries accountable for acts of *omission* rather than those of commission, as would be the case with demands for reparations to Rwanda by Western powers. As John Dower has noted, the Tokyo Tribunal sentenced General Matsui Iwane to death for his failure to prevent atrocities by his troops at Nanking in 1937.[81]

The campaign for reparations from other countries and international institutions has had relatively little issue. This is in part because the Rwandans must be cautious about antagonizing many of their biggest donors. Nonetheless, there have been extensive efforts to come to terms with the past within Rwanda itself. However, the large number of victims and the paltry means available to compensate them hamper these efforts. Demands for reparations in the Rwandan case present many perplexities stemming from the fact that both the so-called *genocidaires* and the ultimately victorious Rwandan Patriotic Front, which now holds power in the country, committed human rights abuses for which the United Nations has mandated a formal right to reparation.

Similarly, the dilemma of whether reparations should be directed toward individuals or toward the reconstruction of Rwandan society and infrastructure plagues efforts to meet the crying needs of a society that has undergone a tremendous catastrophe. To make matters worse, the large number of perpetrators has overwhelmed the judicial system, despite the recourse that has been had to traditional (*gacaca* or "front-porch") forms of justice. The International Criminal Tribunal for Rwanda (ICTR), meanwhile, seems a rather distant reality for most Rwandans.[82]

In sum, it is difficult to locate Rwanda on the grid in figure 2.1 because money will have both symbolic and economic meanings for those who receive it. What is clear is that cultural loss plays little role in the claim, primarily because the genocide was essentially an indigenous phenomenon—even if it could have been prevented or stanched by bystanders who did nothing.

Apology and Regret

Perhaps the best the Rwandans can expect is some sort of apology for being left by the world's most powerful to twist in the wind. Samantha Power has noted that Bill Clinton offered an apology—or, more accurately, a "carefully hedged acknowledgment"—for the West's failure to stop the massacres in Rwanda in 1994.[83] Power's qualification of "the Clinton apology" points to the high importance that may be accorded to the precise wording of statements of apology and regret in contemporary reparations politics but also to the ways in which "talk is cheap." Indeed, without some sort of monetary compensation to go along with an apology, many will be inclined not to take such apologies very seriously.

At the same time, compensation without apology is likely to be dismissed on the grounds that "it's not about the money," and any suggestion that it is may be regarded as cheapening the sufferings of the individuals in question, which are said to be beyond price. This is the situation, for example, in the case of the so-called comfort women or military sexual slaves of the Japanese government during World War II.[84] The apologies of the Japanese government have so far been less than full throated, and the reparations offered have been made available through the Asian Women's Fund, a private institution.

Without an unvarnished statement of apology by the government in conjunction with putting money where its mouth is, the Japanese government is unlikely to satisfy the demands of the comfort women.[85] As Roy L. Brooks has noted, corporations settle claims against them every day with offers of monetary compensation without any corresponding admission of wrongdoing.[86]

Nicholas Tavuchis has provided the most nuanced and insightful analysis of the social alchemy worked by apologies. He argues that there are profound differences between apologies at the individual level and those at the collective level, and that there can be no assumption that the latter works in the same way as the former. This is in part because "an authentic apology cannot be delegated, consigned, exacted, or assumed by the principals, without totally altering its meaning and vitiating its moral force."[87] Whether apologies are important to the individuals who are members of groups that have been wronged in the past is likely to vary widely from person to person.

The importance of these statements has grown so much in recent years, however, that Jeffrey K. Olick and Brenda Coughlin argue that the "politics of regret" is the signature of our age. In a subtle analysis, they argue that the rise of regret is a product of "the transformation of temporality and historicity that is tied up with the decline . . . of the nation-state" and its project of integrating and assimilating disparate groups.[88] That is, while it once went without saying that the state should turn "peasants into Frenchmen," whatever the costs to "their culture," states can no longer ignore the subterranean histories of the many groups submerged or oppressed in the "nation-building" process and who now seek apologies and reparations for their forcible incorporation into the modern world system. Olick and Coughlin's discussion of the politics of regret links up directly with the changes taking place in historiography and in historical representations of "the nation."

Judging and Making Sense of the Past

Debates over representations of history and over the voices that constitute history have been a major aspect of history writing since the 1960s, when labor and social historians began to insist on a new "history from below." The historians of postcolonialism pushed this agenda forward by asking: "Can the Subaltern Speak?" This bubbling activity has brought to light new voices that had previously suffered what the English Marxist E. P. Thompson once called "the enormous condescension of posterity."[89] Much of this historiography has unearthed the subterranean elements of the once-cozy national narratives to which Arendt called attention.

Yet the diversity of groups whose pasts have been resurrected gave rise to a fragmentation of the traditional objects of history that went hand in hand with the turn toward network theories of society, mirroring the world of computers on which these ideas were banged out. The trends also echoed the transformation of one big audience for mass media into a minutely divided series of market niches. The result of these various currents has been a shift in history writing from a focus on state and class to a nearly obsessive mantra of "race, class, gender, and sexuality" as the cornerstones of a new understanding of the world.

These tendencies are also reflected in the commemorative practices that have undergone a similar upward revaluation in public and intellectual circles. In contrast to the era around World War I in the North Atlantic world, at least, the commemorative acts of governments today have little to do with heroic myths of national sacrifice and greatness. Rather than celebrating conquest and triumph, monuments must now acknowledge the forgotten, the mistreated, the enslaved, and the murdered. As Paul Goldberger has recently pointed out, moreover, since Maya Lin's Vietnam Veterans Memorial, it has become de rigueur to commemorate individuals rather than a mass, as was done at Gettysburg, for example.[90]

As a result of the swelling attention to the iniquitous past that has followed from these various changes, historians have more frequently been asked to leave their studies to play an unfamiliar (though often rather lucrative) role as expert witnesses and members of commissions of inquiry into potentially actionable histories. Yet not all historians have been comfortable assuming this role—not because it means leaving the familiar confines of the ivory tower, but because they question the purposes served by the pursuit of the past.

For example, the prosecution of a very elderly Maurice Papon arose against the background of changing perceptions of France's role in World War II and a greater understanding during recent years of the complicity of the Vichy regime in the persecution of the Jews.[91] Henry Rousso shows, however, that the prosecution of Papon represents a remarkable shift from attention to crimes defined by the state to a focus on crimes against Jews. Recent judicial actions concerning World War II perpetrators thus "did not occur because of a *raison d'État*, but because of a will to render justice to the victims, in the name of a 'duty to memory' whose objective was the perpetuation of memory against all forms of forgetting, considered in this perspective as a new crime." According to Rousso, the trial bore witness to a troubling "desacralization of state authority and of traditional French national sentiment" in favor of strengthened group identities "in a country that has always in large part denied them."[92]

The pressures for coming to terms with the pasts of particular groups do, indeed, reflect a rising attentiveness to the concerns of victims as they define themselves, rather than to offenses understood to have been committed against the citizenry as a whole. Rousso is doubtful about the attendant commingling of judicial and scholarly purposes, arguing that the issue is unclean. In contrast, Maier argues that the roles of historian and judge share important similarities. Both must ultimately arrive at plausible narratives based on the motivations of actors, though of course the judge must ultimately decide and perhaps punish.

Despite the prosecutorial tone of much of the relevant historiography, the drift in recent years has been toward a much greater attentiveness to the voices of the previously voiceless. Maier thus shares the view of Alan Cairns regarding the tremendous significance of the emergence into the light of the formerly subterranean.[93] Maier argues that, ultimately, "the projects of reparation, remembering, and reconciliation involve the right to tell histories and have them listened to respectfully." This has led to efforts by various interested parties who have sought to repair deep-rooted international rifts by drafting histories that win the assent of "both sides" in past conflicts. For example, Polish and German historians and history teachers have tried to develop textbooks telling the story of their twentieth-century relations "in mutually acceptable accounts."[94] Indeed, the contents of history textbooks have become a major focus of both public controversy and scholarly inquiry.[95] The fracas regarding the degree of recognition and contrition for World War II atrocities in Japanese junior high history texts is an excellent case in point.

While the term "reconciliation" is bandied about in many of the discussions of coming to terms with the past, perhaps the best that can be said about it is that previously divided groups will come to agree on a mutually satisfactory narrative of what they have been through, opening the way to a common future.[96] With luck, what they do with that future will be a matter of bargaining, negotiation, and compromise—the mundane business of politics.

In the meanwhile, the teaching of history, the contours of "collective memory," and the character of "historical consciousness" have become major subjects of concern among certain segments of academia and the wider public.[97] These concerns are fueled in part by demands from legislators for new "standards" in history education that often appear to be veiled orders to reinstitute a consensus historiography now long since beyond retrieval. Yet these are also the concerns of specialists who pursue the past—or at least the memory of it—as a sort of glue undergirding collective identities. Under these circumstances, as Peter Novick has argued, the past comes to serve the purposes of group cohesion.[98]

Kerwin Lee Klein has commented caustically that the preoccupation with memory comes to the fore "precisely because it figures as a therapeutic alternative to historical discourse."[99] The critical historiography that Nietzsche recommended to us must remain open to contestation and thus cannot well serve the interests of those in need of a particular image of the past that remains frozen for future generations. The scholarly pursuit of the past can be *political*, and hence contribute to revealing the subterranean aspects of the past, but it fails if it becomes *politicized*, subservient to narrowly political interests.[100]

CONCLUSION

In a certain sense, the concern with coming to terms with and repairing the unquiet past is not new. All politics is always and inevitably about the past to some degree. What matters is the horizon against which the past is viewed: how forward-looking is the political pursuit of the past? The question is one of balance and of how to draw inspiration from the past in the face of the entirely appropriate and desirable recovery of its uglier, previously subterranean features. We need to be aware, as we seek to mend the damage from the past, that a politics of the past may crowd out or replace a vision of progress. There will be continued cause for controversy over the facts of past history and over their relation to current inequalities and injustices. For now and in the foreseeable future, however, these efforts to repair the injustices of the past form an important part of the search for justice in the present.

NOTES

1. Wole Soyinka, *The Burden of Memory, The Muse of Forgiveness* (New York: Oxford University Press, 1999), 90.

2. Jürgen Habermas, "Vorwort," *Die postnationale Konstellation: Politische Essays* (Frankfurt: Suhrkamp, 1998), 7. My translation.

3. See Simon Romero, "Brazil Forum More Local Than Worldly," *New York Times*, February 7, 2002, at www.nytimes.com/2002/02/07/international/americas/07BRAZ.html (accessed July 20, 2002).

4. Thucydides, *The Peloponnesian War*, trans. Rex Warner (New York: Penguin, 1954), 402.

5. Edmund Burke, *Reflections on the Revolution in France*, edited with an introduction by Conor Cruise O'Brien (New York: Penguin Books, 1969 [1790]), 246–47.

6. Friedrich Nietzsche, "On the Use and Disadvantage of History for Life," in

Unmodern Observations, ed. William Arrowsmith (New Haven, Conn.: Yale University Press, 1990), 102–3.

7. Karl Jaspers, *Die Schuldfrage: Von der politischen Haftung Deutschlands* (Munich: Piper, 1987 [1946]). Jaspers's important text finally has been re-issued in English; see *The Question of German Guilt*, trans. E. B. Ashton (New York: Fordham University Press, 2001).

8. Hannah Arendt, "Preface to the First Edition," *The Origins of Totalitarianism* (New York: Harcourt, Brace, 1973 [1951]), ix. The passage continues, presciently, "This is the reality in which we live. And this is why all efforts to escape from the grimness of the present into nostalgia for a still intact past, or into the anticipated oblivion of the future, are vain."

9. See various essays in *Eine Art Schadensabwicklung*, which collects Habermas' contributions to the so-called *Historikerstreit*. For Habermas' appreciation of Jaspers's *Schuldfrage*, see the essay on Jaspers in Jürgen Habermas, *Philosophische-politische Profile* (Frankfurt: Suhrkamp, 1971), 110.

10. For a discussion of Jaspers's text and Habermas' appropriation of its main themes, see Anson Rabinbach, "The German as Pariah: Karl Jaspers' *The Question of German Guilt*," in his *In the Shadow of Catastrophe: German Intellectuals between Apocalypse and Enlightenment* (Berkeley: University of California Press, 1997), 129–65. For the divergent responses to the Nazi past in the two Germanys that emerged from the defeat of the Third Reich, see Jeffrey Herf, *Divided Memory: The Nazi Past in the Two Germanys* (Cambridge, Mass.: Harvard University Press, 1997). For an analysis of the efforts to come to terms with the past in postwar Germany and Japan that finds the latter wanting in comparison with the former, see Ian Buruma, *The Wages of Guilt: Memories of War in Germany and Japan* (New York: Meridian, 1994).

11. See Peter Novick, *The Holocaust in American Life* (Boston: Houghton Mifflin, 1999), and Daniel Levy and Natan Sznaider, *Erinnerung im globalen Zeitalter: Der Holocaust* (Frankfurt, Germany: Suhrkamp, 2001).

12. One of the more incendiary attempts to claim that the Holocaust has robbed attention to other crimes of the past—in this case, from those of Communism—was Stéphane Courtois, introduction to *The Black Book of Communism: Crimes, Terror, Repression*, by Stéphane Courtois et al., trans. by Jonathan Murphy and Mark Kramer (Cambridge, Mass.: Harvard University Press, 1999), 23.

13. See, for example, the recent announcement that several orders of the Roman Catholic Church in Ireland would compensate many victims who had been abused, sexually and otherwise, in church-run schools during the twentieth century. The announcement is reported in Brian Lavery, "Religious Orders Offer $110 Million to Irish Sex Abuse Victims," *New York Times*, February 1, 2002, national edition, A3. The notion that "we are all Germans now" paraphrases Nathan Glazer's *We Are All Multiculturalists Now* (Cambridge, Mass.: Harvard University Press, 1997). To put the relative importance of reparations politics in some perspective, however, it is perhaps worth noting that the *New York Times* described a session on "the politics of apology" chaired by Archbishop Desmond Tutu and Elie Wiesel at the 2002 World Economic Forum in New York as "likely to stir at least curiosity." See Serge Schmemann, "Rich and Powerful Gather at Elite Forum on Economy," *New York Times*, January 31, 2002, national edition, A10.

14. See, for example, Elazar Barkan, *The Guilt of Nations: Restitution and Negotiating Historical Injustices* (New York: Norton, 2000).

15. Marj Brown et al., *Land Restitution in South Africa: A Long Way Home* (Cape Town, South Africa: Idasa, 1998); Paul Brodeur, *Restitution: The Land Claims of the Mashpee, Passamaquoddy, and Penobscot Indians of New England* (Boston, Mass.: Northeastern University Press, 1985); Karl Jaspers, *The Question of German Guilt*; and Stef Vandeginste's chapter in this volume.

16. Priscilla Hayner, *Unspeakable Truths: Confronting State Terror and Atrocity* (New York: Routledge, 2001), 171.

17. *Personal Justice Denied: Report of the Commission on Wartime Relocation and Internment of Civilians*, foreword by Tetsuden Kashima (Seattle: University of Washington Press, 1997 [1983]), 12.

18. See Martha Minow, *Between Vengeance and Forgiveness: Facing History after Genocide and Mass Violence* (Boston: Beacon Press, 1998), 61ff.

19. Here I am borrowing the title of Phillip Rieff's *The Triumph of the Therapeutic* (New York: Harper & Row, 1966). For a skeptical view of the advantages of this triumph in American life, see Eva S. Moskowitz, *In Therapy We Trust: America's Obsession with Self-Fulfillment* (Baltimore, Md.: Johns Hopkins University Press, 2001). On the transformation of the concept of "trauma" from a physical to a mental notion, see Ian Hacking, *Rewriting the Soul: Multiple Personality and the Sciences of Memory* (Princeton, N.J.: Princeton University Press, 1995). See also Allan Young, *The Harmony of Illusions: Inventing Post-Traumatic Stress Disorder* (Princeton, N.J.: Princeton University Press, 1995).

20. Michael Ignatieff has noted that the post–World War II advance of the human rights paradigm was an important aspect of the twentieth century, belying those who would see the century as an unmitigated disaster. See Michael Ignatieff, *The Rights Revolution* (Toronto, Canada: Anansi, 2000), and *Human Rights as Politics and Idolatry*, ed. Amy Gutmann (Princeton, N.J.: Princeton University Press, 2001).

21. It is questionable, however, whether any meaningful apology can be made by those not directly involved in the acts for which an apology is now offered. See Nicholas Tavuchis, *Mea Culpa: A Sociology of Apology and Reconciliation* (Stanford, Calif.: Stanford University Press, 1991), 49.

22. See Guillermo O'Donnell, Philippe C. Schmitter, and Laurence Whitehead, eds., *Transitions from Authoritarian Rule: Prospects for Democracy* (Baltimore, Md.: Johns Hopkins University Press, 1986); Neil J. Kritz, *Transitional Justice: How Emerging Democracies Reckon with Former Regimes* (Washington, D.C.: United States Institute of Peace Press, 1995); A. James McAdams, *Transitional Justice and the Rule of Law in New Democracies* (Notre Dame, Ind.: University of Notre Dame Press, 1997); Jon Elster, "Coming to Terms with the Past: A Framework for the Study of Justice in the Transition to Democracy," *European Journal of Sociology* 39 (1998): 7–48; and Ruti Teitel, *Transitional Justice* (New York: Oxford University Press, 2000). On the complexities of "transitional justice" in Europe immediately following World War II, see also István Deák, Jan T. Gross, and Tony Judt, eds., *The Politics of Retribution in Europe: World War II and Its Aftermath* (Princeton, N.J.: Princeton University Press, 2000). For an incisive analysis of the various ways in which societies have dealt with past atrocities, see Heribert Adam, "Divided Memories: Confronting the Crimes of Previous Regimes," *Telos* 31 (1999): 87–108.

23. See Samuel Huntington, *The Third Wave: Democratization in the Late Twentieth Century* (Norman, Okla.: University of Oklahoma Press, 1991).

24. Of the increasingly vast literature on truth commissions and commissions of historical inquiry, see A. James McAdams, *Judging the Past in Unified Germany* (New York: Cambridge University Press, 2001); Antjie Krog, *Country of My Skull: Guilt, Sorrow, and the Limits of Forgiveness in the New South Africa* (New York: Three Rivers Press, 1999); and the recent comprehensive study by Hayner, *Unspeakable Truths.*

25. Much of this is owing to the work of the Dutch jurist Theo van Boven, who was Special Rapporteur on these matters to the UN Sub-Commission on Prevention of Discrimination and Protection of Minorities. See for example Theo van Boven et al., eds., *Seminar on the Right to Restitution, Compensation, and Rehabilitation for Victims of Gross Violations of Human Rights and Fundamental Freedoms* (Utrecht, The Netherlands: Studie- en Informatiecentrum Mensenrechten, Netherlands Institute of Human Rights, 1992).The so-called van Boven principles have since been superseded by the "Bassiouni principles" as the determinative UN guidelines in this area. See "The right to restitution, compensation and rehabilitation for victims of gross violations of human rights and fundamental freedoms: Final report of the Special Rapporteur, Mr. M. Cherif Bassiouni, submitted in accordance with Commission resolution 1999/33," E/CN.4/2000/62, January 18, 2000, at www.unhchr.ch/Huridocda/Huridoca.nsf/0/42bd1bd544910ae3802568a20060e21f/$FILE/G0010236.doc (accessed July 20, 2002).

26. On this point, see Huntington, *The Third Wave.*

27. Tina Rosenberg, *The Haunted Land: Facing Europe's Ghosts after Communism* (New York: Random House, 1995), 397–407. For Havel's analysis of the social underpinnings of Communist regimes, see his essay "The Power of the Powerless," in *Living in Truth*, ed. Vaclav Havel (London, U.K.: Faber and Faber, 1987 [1978]), 36–122.

28. See Huntington, *The Third Wave.*

29. See Sharon F. Lean, "Is Truth Enough? Reparations and Reconciliation in Latin America" in this book; see also Hayner, *Unspeakable Truths*, chapter 11.

30. See Ilan Stavan's remarks at the conference "Third World Views of the Holocaust," held at Northeastern University, April 18–20, 2001, at www.violence.neu.edu/Ilan.Stavans.html (accessed July 20, 2002).

31. Barrington Moore, Jr., *The Social Origins of Dictatorship and Democracy: Lord and Peasant in the Making of the Modern World* (Boston, Mass.: Beacon Press, 1966).

32. Aristide Zolberg et al., *Escape from Violence: Conflict and the Refugee Crisis in the Developing World* (New York: Oxford University Press, 1989), 255.

33. See Hayner, *Unspeakable Truths*, 7, and Sharon Lean's essay in this book.

34. Mahmood Mamdani, "Degrees of Reconciliation and Forms of Justice: Making Sense of the African Experience" (paper presented at the conference "Justice or Reconciliation?" at the Center for International Studies, University of Chicago, April 25–26, 1997), 6; quoted in Hayner *Unspeakable Truths*, 164.

35. Mahmood Mamdani, "A Diminished Truth," in *After the TRC: Reflections on Truth and Reconciliation in South Africa*, ed. Wilmot James and Linda van de Vijver (Athens, Ohio: Ohio University Press, 2001), 59.

36. John Torpey, "'Making Whole What Has Been Smashed': Reflections on Reparations," *Journal of Modern History* 73, no. 2 (June 2001): 333–58.

37. See, for example, Hayner's description of the reparations program in Chile, in *Unspeakable Truths*, 172–73.

38. See especially Will Kymlicka, *Multicultural Citizenship: A Liberal Theory of Minority Rights* (New York: Oxford University Press, 1995); Kymlicka, ed., *The Rights of Minority Cultures* (New York: Oxford University Press, 1995); for a vigorous (though in some respects intemperate) rejoinder to Kymlicka and his allies, see Brian Barry, *Culture & Equality* (Cambridge, Mass.: Harvard University Press, 2001).

39. On the nature of the harms experienced by the "comfort women," see Yamashita Yeong-ae, "The Re-Discovery of the 'Comfort Women' Issue in Korea" (paper presented at the symposium on "Comfort Women of World War II: Their Suffering Must Not Be Forgotten," University of British Columbia, January 18, 2002), 4–5. For a detailed treatment of the comfort women, see Yoshimi Yoshiaki, *Comfort Women: Sexual Slavery in the Japanese Military During World War II*, trans. Suzanne O'Brien (New York: Columbia University Press, 2000 [1995]).

40. Minow, *Between Vengeance and Forgiveness*, 100–111 and 184 n. 77.

41. On this issue, see Barkan, *The Guilt of Nations*, chap. 4.

42. Charles S. Maier, "Overcoming the Past? Narrative and Negotiation, Remembering, and Reparation: Issues at the Interface of History and the Law," p. 297 in this book.

43. Ruth B. Phillips and Elizabeth Johnson, "Negotiating New Relationships: Canadian Museums, First Nations, and the Negotiation of Repatriation," in this book.

44. Barkan, *The Guilt of Nations*, 171.

45. Quoted in Phillips and Johnson, "Negotiating New Relationships," p. 156 in this book.

46. For a recent intervention in the controversy, see "Return the Parthenon Marbles," *The New York Times*, February 2, 2002, editorial, at www.nytimes.com/2002/02/02/opinion/_02SAT3.html (accessed July 20, 2002).

47. On this point, see Barry, *Culture & Equality*, chap. 3.

48. See Patrick Wolfe, "Land, Labor, and Difference: Elementary Structures of Race," *American Historical Review* 106, no. 3 (June 2001): 866–905.

49. *Bringing Them Home: Report of the National Inquiry into the Separation of Aboriginal and Torres Strait Islander Children from Their Families (NISATSIC)* (Sydney, Australia: Human Rights and Equal Opportunity Commission, 1997), available at www.austlii.edu.au/au/special/rsjproject/rsjlibrary/hreoc/stolen/.

50. Chris Cunneen, "Competing Discourses on Reparations: Human Rights, Aboriginal People and the Australian Government" (paper presented to the conference, "Into the 21st Century: Reconstruction and Reparations," organized by the International Third World Legal Studies Association and the Community Peace Program, School of Government, University of the Western Cape, in Cape Town, South Africa, 4–6 January 2001) (*Third World Legal Studies Journal*, forthcoming).

51. The document can be found at www.ainc-inac.gc.ca/gs/chg_e.html (accessed July 21, 2002).

52. The RCAP report is discussed at length in Alan Cairn's contribution to this book, "Coming to Terms with the Past."

53. "Gathering Strength," at www.ainc-inac.gc.ca/gs/chg_e.html (accessed July 21, 2002).

54. See Arthur J. Ray, *I Have Lived Here Since the World Began: An Illustrated History of Canada's Native Peoples* (Toronto, Canada: Lester Publishing, 1996). For two skeptical views of Indian claims regarding the spiritual significance of specific lands, see Tom Flanagan, *First Nations? Second Thoughts* (Montreal, Canada: McGill-Queen's University Press, 2000), and Fergus Bordewich, *Killing the White Man's Indian: The Reinvention of Native Americans at the End of the Twentieth Century* (New York: Doubleday, 1996).

55. The phrase is Joseph Schumpeter's characterization of capitalism in chap. 7 in *Capitalism, Socialism, and Democracy* (New York: Harper & Brothers, 1942), but it is also an apt characterization of Marx's understanding of capitalism as reflected in *The Communist Manifesto*.

56. Rhéal Séguin, "Cree, Quebec Sign Historic Deal," *The Globe and Mail* (Toronto), February 8, 2002.

57. See the press release of the South African Reparations Movement (SARM), "Launch of South African Reparations Movement," Johannesburg, South Africa, October 25, 2000, in the author's possession. The official launch took place in December 2000. The SARM is considerably more "culturalist" in orientation than other efforts concerning reparations for Africa; for example, the first of the principles to which its constituent organizations subscribe is the "reclamation of our African identity, in which are enshrined the values of equitable sharing." See also the press release of the SARM, "First National Reparations Congress: Namibian, Zimbabwean, Khoi, San, Griqua and Korana Indigenous Reparations Leaders Featured," Johannesburg, South Africa, January 12, 2002, in the author's possession. The Congress took place in Johannesburg during February 1–3, 2002.

58. R. S. Ratner, William K. Carroll, and Andrew Woolford, "Wealth of Nations: Aboriginal Treaty Making in the Era of Globalization," in this book.

59. For a discussion of the importance of the end of colonialism for subsequent politics, see Geoffrey Barraclough, "The Revolt against the West," chap. 6 in his *An Introduction to Contemporary History* (New York: Penguin, 1967 [1964]); on the concept of internal colonialism, see Robert Blauner, *Racial Oppression in America* (New York: Harper & Row, 1972); an updated version is available in Blauner, *Still the Big News: Racial Oppression in America* (Philadelphia, Pa.: Temple University Press, 2001).

60. The charge of corruption is one among the litany of objections mounted in chap. 6 in Flanagan, *First Nations? Second Thoughts*.

61. It is of course true that many Canadian political theorists have been arguing against this notion of "equal citizenship" for a number of years; indeed, theories of minority group rights have been Canada's chief export on the international market of ideas in recent years. In addition to the works of Will Kymlicka cited in note 38 in the preceding endnotes, see the writings of Charles Taylor and James Tully. For an approach that takes issue with the paradigm of group rights and the "nation-to-nation" vision it supports, see Alan C. Cairns, *Citizens Plus: Aboriginal Peoples and the Canadian State* (Vancouver: University of British Columbia Press, 2000).

62. For one (relatively optimistic) assessment of racial progress since the mid-1960s, see Orlando Patterson, *The Ordeal of Integration: Progress and Resentment in America's "Racial" Crisis* (New York: Basic/Civitas, 1997).

63. Robert Westley, "Many Billions Gone: Is It Time to Reconsider the Case for Black Reparations?" *Boston College Law Review* 40, no. 1 (December 1998): 429, 432. Similarly, University of San Diego law professor Roy Brooks's support for reparations is presumably connected to his negative evaluation of the consequences of integration for blacks; see his *Integration or Separation? A Strategy for Racial Equality* (Cambridge, Mass.: Harvard University Press, 1996). See also Roy Brooks, ed., *When Sorry Isn't Enough: The Controversy over Apologies and Reparations for Human Injustice* (New York: NYU Press, 1999).

64. Tocqueville's pessimistic analysis of the consequences of the overlap between slavery and color remain relevant here. See pt. II, chap. 10 in Alexis de Tocqueville, *Democracy in America*, vol. 1, trans. George Lawrence and ed. J. P. Mayer (Garden City, N.Y.: Anchor Doubleday, 1969). For a valuable assessment of Tocqueville's pessimism, see George Fredrickson, "Race and Empire in Liberal Thought: The Legacy of Tocqueville," in *The Comparative Imagination: On the History of Racism, Nationalism, and Social Movements* (Berkeley: University of California Press, 1997), 98–116.

65. See Randall Robinson, *The Debt: What America Owes to Blacks* (New York: Dutton, 2000). For a scathing review, see John McWhorter, "Against Reparations," *The New Republic* (July 23, 2001): 32–38; also at www.thenewrepublic.com/072301/mcwhorter072301.html (accessed July 21, 2002).

66. This appears to be the approach taken by the lawyers who have been planning to launch a lawsuit against the U.S. government for reparations; see "Forum: Making the Case for Racial Reparations," *Harper's* (November 2000): 37–51.

67. See David Horowitz, "Ten Reasons Why Reparations for Slavery Are a Bad Idea for Black People—and Racist Too," *Salon.com*, May 30, 2000, at www.salon.com/news/col/horo/2000/05/30/reparations/ (accessed July 21, 2002); for a response, see Robert Chrisman and Ernest Allen, Jr., "Ten Reasons: A Response to David Horowitz," *The Black Scholar* 31, no. 2 (Summer 2001); also at www.umass.edu/afroam/hor.html (accessed July 21, 2002).

68. Karl Marx, "The Genesis of the Industrial Capitalist," chap. XXIII, vol. 1 of *Capital* in *The Marx-Engels Reader*, ed. Robert Tucker, 2nd ed. (New York: Norton, 1978), 435.

69. Ali A. Mazrui, "Who Should Pay for Slavery?" *World Press Review* 40, no. 8 (August 1993): 22.

70. See Barkan, *The Guilt of Nations*, 302.

71. Mazrui, "Who Should Pay for Slavery?" 23.

72. Wole Soyinka, "Reparations, Truth, and Reconciliation," in *The Burden of Memory*, 44–46.

73. Rhoda Howard-Hassmann, "Moral Integrity and Reparations for Africa," in this book.

74. The reference is to a book of considerable influence among those seeking reparations for Africa, namely, Walter Rodney's *How Europe Underdeveloped Africa* (Washington, D.C.: Howard University Press, 1972).

75. For an assessment of "The Third World's Third World," see Paul Kennedy, *Preparing for the Twenty-First Century* (New York: Vintage, 1993), 211ff.

76. Howard-Hassmann, p. 209 in this book.

77. Nacha Cattan, "Restitution Attorneys Plan Lawsuits Backing 3rd World Debt Relief," *The Forward* (November 30, 2001). See also Jubilee 2000 South Africa, "Apartheid-Caused Debt: The Role of German and Swiss Finance" (available online at www.sacc-ct.org.za/j2ksa/contents.html or from Aktion Finanzplatz Schweiz, www.aktionfinanzplatz.ch (accessed September 18, 2002); authored by Mascha Madörin and Gottfried Wellmer, with a contribution by Martine Egil and originally published in German by Bread for the World, Stuttgart, in February 1999). In June 2002, a group whose lead lawyer was Ed Fagan jumped the gun on the plans of Jubilee 2000 when it filed a $50 billion class action suit against Citigroup, UBS, and Credit Suisse on behalf of victims of South African apartheid; see BBC News, "Apartheid Victims File Suit," June 19, 2002, available at: news.bbc.co.uk/hi/english/world/africa/newsid_2054000/2054898.stm (accessed September 18, 2002).

78. Mike Cohen, "Indigenous S. Africans Demand Rights," *Associated Press*, April 1, 2001.

79. Special report of the International Panel of Eminent Personalities to Investigate the 1994 Genocide in Rwanda and the Surrounding Events, issued July 7, 2000, Executive Summary $68; the report was previously found at www.oau-oua.org/Document/ipep/ipep.htm, but it appears that this URL has not survived the recent transition from the Organization for African Unity to the African Union.

80. For two representative positions in the debate, see Alan J. Kuperman, *The Limits of Humanitarian Intervention: Genocide in Rwanda* (Washington, D.C.: Brookings Institution Press, 2001), and Samantha Power, "Bystanders to Genocide," *The Atlantic Monthly* (September 2001), at www.theatlantic.com/issues/2001/09/power.htm (accessed July 21, 2002). Kuperman's sober analysis reads like an apology for the failure of the outside powers to intervene, while Power's indictment of U.S. foreign policy bears remarkable similarities to that advanced by those who see the United States (and Britain) as responsible for the deaths of many Jews at the hands of the Nazis. The chief prosecutor here is David Wyman in his *The Abandonment of the Jews: America and the Holocaust, 1941–1945* (New York: The New Press, 1998 [1984]). For critiques of this position, see Peter Novick, chap. 3 in *The Holocaust in American Life*, and William D. Rubinstein, *The Myth of Rescue: Why the Democracies Could Not Have Saved More Jews from the Nazis* (New York: Routledge, 1997).

81. John Dower, *Embracing Defeat: Japan in the Wake of World War II* (New York: Norton/The New Press, 1999), 459.

82. See Stef Vandeginste, "Victims of Genocide, Crimes against Humanity, and War Crimes in Rwanda: The Legal and Institutional Framework of Their Right to Reparation," in this book.

83. See Power, "Bystanders to Genocide."

84. See the discussion in Laura Hein, "War Compensation: Claims against the Japanese Government and Japanese Corporations for War Crimes," in this book.

85. On these demands, see the Violence against Women in War Network Japan, at www1.jca.apc.org/vaww-net-japan/e_new/index.html (accessed July 21, 2002).

86. See Roy L. Brooks, "Reflections on Reparations," in this book.

87. Tavuchis, *Mea Culpa*, 49.

88. See Jeffrey K. Olick and Brenda Coughlin, "The Politics of Regret: Analytical Frames," in this book.

89. See Maier, "Overcoming the Past?" in this book.

90. Paul Goldberger, "Requiem: Memorializing Terrorism's Victims in Oklahoma," *The New Yorker* (January 14, 2002): 91.

91. The seminal work unearthing the independent French role is Michael R. Marrus and Robert O. Paxton, *Vichy France and the Jews* (New York: Basic, 1981).

92. Henry Rousso, "Justice, History, and Memory in France: Reflections on the Papon Trial," in this book.

93. See Cairns, "Coming to Terms with the Past," in this book.

94. Donald Shriver, *An Ethic for Enemies: Forgiveness in Politics* (New York: Oxford University Press, 1995), 91; see also Minow, *Between Vengeance and Forgiveness*, passim.

95. For a recent discussion, see Yasemin Soysal, "Teaching Europe," *OpenDemocracy* at www.opendemocracy.net/forum/document_details.asp?CatID = 106&Doc ID = 886&DebateID = 217 (accessed July 21, 2002).

96. For a sober-minded discussion of "reconciliation," see Susan Dwyer, "Reconciliation for Realists," *Ethics and International Affairs* 13 (1999): 81–98.

97. See Peter Stearns, Peter Seixas, and Sam Wineburg, eds., *Knowing, Teaching and Learning History: National and International Perspectives* (New York: New York University Press, 2000), and Laura Hein and Mark Selden, eds., *Censoring History : Citizenship and Memory in Japan, Germany, and the United States* (Armonk, N.Y.: M.E. Sharpe, 2001); note the recent rise in importance of Maurice Halbwachs's seminal studies of the social foundations of collective memory, collected in Lewis Coser, ed., *Maurice Halbwachs: On Collective Memory* (Chicago, Ill.: University of Chicago Press, 1992); see also the writings of Jörn Rüsen, such as *Zerbrechende Zeit: Über den Sinn der Geschichte* (Cologne, Germany: Böhlau, 2001).

98. See Novick, *The Holocaust in American Life.*

99. Kerwin Klein, "On the Emergence of *Memory* in Historical Discourse," *Representations* 69 (Winter 2000): 127–50.

100. I borrow these terms from Charles Maier, "A Surfeit of Memory? Reflections on History, Melancholy and Denial," *History and Memory* 5, no. 2 (Fall–Winter 1993): 136–51.

I

Historical and Theoretical Considerations on the Spread of Reparations Politics

1

The Politics of Regret
Analytical Frames

Jeffrey K. Olick and Brenda Coughlin

Only under certain historical circumstances does frailty appear to be the chief characteristic of human affairs.

—Hannah Arendt, *The Human Condition*

In the past several years, major world newspapers have run front-page stories reporting apologies and other expressions of regret by world leaders. Examples include Pope John Paul II's remarks about both the Church's treatment of Galileo and Catholic individuals' behavior during World War II; British Prime Minister Tony Blair's acknowledgment of an English role in the Irish potato famine; U.S. President Bill Clinton's public consideration of an official apology for slavery; and an official (though limited) Japanese recognition of wartime atrocities in Nanking and elsewhere. A variety of redress movements have demanded—and, frequently enough, won—material reparations for numerous historical injustices. We have also seen widespread acceptance of a "universal human rights" paradigm, with concrete institutional manifestations like the expanded powers of international tribunals to prosecute war crimes, as well as the growth of trans- and nongovernmental "watchdog" organizations. And from South Africa to Latin America, Guatemala, Central and Eastern Europe, postauthoritarian governments have placed an open discussion of the past at the heart of their legitimation efforts.

In many places in the world today, the past is very much present on the public agenda, but it is more often a horrible, repulsive past than the heroic golden ages so often the part of public discourse in previous centuries. Political legitimation depends just as much on collective memory as it ever has, but this collective memory is now often one disgusted with itself, a matter of "learning the lessons" of history more than of fulfilling its promise or remaining faithful to its legacy. Observing this transformation, we identify a new principle of legitimation, which we call the *politics of regret*. We include under this rubric the variety of practices with which many contemporary societies confront toxic legacies of the past. Many analysts distinguish apology, reparation, and criminal prosecution, among others, as distinct genres of retrospective practice.[1] While the differences among these types are many and important, here we are concerned with what they have in common.

Recent literature offers two distinct frames for understanding the politics of regret: a philosophical-jurisprudential discourse centered around the concept of universal human rights and a comparative political study of regime transitions now often referred to as transitology. These two frames are well developed and ubiquitous, yielding much insight into varieties of contemporary political regret and problems faced by practitioners. Nevertheless, they are often less interested in explaining what is unique and new about regret as a political principle, either denying its novelty or seeing it merely as the result of contingent historical events (most often Nuremberg or the transformations of 1989 or both).

In contrast, we seek here to explore ideas for a genuinely developmental sociohistorical account of political regret.[2] Where has the politics of regret come from? What social structural and cultural developments have made it possible, and which developments does it, in turn, make possible? In order to answer these questions, it is necessary to re-theorize the historical dimensions of this phenomenon. In what follows, we begin by looking more closely at the two dominant frames just mentioned to evaluate their fitness for this sociohistorical task. We then explore a number of other theoretical resources that we believe provide better tools for understanding the politics of regret historically. In particular, we place the politics of regret in the context of a more general consciousness of progressive temporality that is a central, constitutive feature of modernity and is implicated in a variety of major institutional transformations over centuries. This exploration of theoretical resources, it should be clear, is a framework for ongoing research, not its end product. We conclude this chapter by describing the directions this research is taking.

MORAL PHILOSOPHY AND THE DISCOURSE
OF UNIVERSAL HUMAN RIGHTS

The first analytical frame available for understanding the politics of regret is a philosophical-jurisprudential discussion about universal human rights.[3]

Philosophers of the Enlightenment and their revolutionary political counterparts in France and the United States often articulated theories in terms of basic guarantees to which human beings, merely by virtue of being human, had a legitimate claim. At the time, obviously, there were important minor exceptions, variously including women, Africans, the nonpropertied, and so forth! But the relevant point for our purposes is that these arguments were made in terms of *"human* rights," often illustrated by demonstrating what Modern Man has in common with his "natural" ancestor. Basic humanity, in this account, remains basic humanity throughout the transition to civilization, though this history can be presented alternately as one of gradual perversion (e.g., Rousseau) or realization (e.g., Hegel).

Despite some tentative formulations in the late nineteenth century and later in the wake of World War I, it was not until after World War II that a discourse on "universal human rights" became quite so dominant a frame in world politics. Since then, with a special gaze directed at the Nuremberg Tribunals, human rights entrepreneurs have pushed to develop international legal and political instruments for guaranteeing universal human rights and have pressured governments both to improve their records and to deal harshly with other states that do not.[4] In the immediate aftermath of World War II, the most important early achievement of this movement was the Universal Declaration of Human Rights of 1948. Since then, numerous nongovernmental agencies, such as Human Rights Watch and Amnesty International, have become vibrant institutional forces on the world stage.

Accompanying this advocacy work have been efforts to articulate these claims of universality in theological, philosophical, and jurisprudential terms. A significant academic literature on universal human rights has grown alongside the political work. Here the goal is to specify and elaborate the concept, to argue for its importance, and to demonstrate its necessity. R. H. Tawney describes the basic principle this way: "The essence of all morality is this: to believe that every human being is of infinite importance, and therefore that no consideration of expediency can justify the oppression of one by another." "But," Tawney adds, "to believe this it is necessary to believe in God."[5] Not all—perhaps not even most—human rights advocates would agree with this last deduction, but Tawney and others, in our opinion, rightly point out that the discourse of universal human rights—even its philosophical versions—often takes on a tone of irrefutable conviction. The task for such work, as a result, is most often exegetical or a matter of identifying conceptual and political obstacles.

One of the most important philosophical works in this vein, though it does not center on the universal human rights trope, is Karl Jaspers's *Die Schuldfrage* (translated as *The Question of German Guilt*).[6] Within a discussion about German collective responsibility for National Socialist crimes, Jaspers articulates four distinct varieties of guilt (criminal, political, moral, and metaphysical), each of which entails different forms of accountability. Indeed, the German case—and the precedents established at Nuremberg— remain an important touchstone for the human rights literature.

The important points here, however, are that Jaspers's articulation of metaphysical guilt is strongly connected to the concept of original sin and that he sees the question of guilt in many ways as a permanent part of the human condition. A more recent example along these lines is Donald Shriver's *An Ethic for Enemies: Forgiveness in Politics,*[7] which outlines a principle of forgiveness—founded in Christian ethics—as the basis for peace in human affairs.

On the jurisprudential side, efforts aim at solving practical dilemmas. One good example is the discussion surrounding the case of former Chilean president Augusto Pinochet. What are the relevant jurisdictional limits? What role should the passage of time play (e.g., should there be a statute of limitations on crimes against humanity)?[8] What value do such limits have? At a more general level, both philosophers and legal theorists have debated the age-old question of utility versus right: Do we pursue former leaders after they relinquish power if doing so will make others in similar circumstances hesitate to go peacefully? Indeed, this issue of principle versus consequence (which we will discuss later in Max Weber's terms of an "ethic of conviction" versus an "ethic of responsibility") is a central question for theorists of human rights: Are we morally obliged to pursue human rights as a principle regardless of whether doing so decreases the likelihood of realizing them in practice, or is it acceptable to do business with dictators if doing so will improve political realities?

Many theorists in the tradition of universal human rights have sought to specify the psychological, social, cultural, and political costs of failing to prosecute perpetrators.[9] They do so in reaction to those (ranging from Friedrich Nietzsche to Henry Kissinger) who argue that amnesty and forgetting are the only ways to ensure peace. There is a difference, human rights advocates argue, between peace and temporary quiescence, and many such theorists speak in terms of a Freudian return of the repressed.

For all its evocative language and practical success, however, this frame has two major deficiencies. First, it tends to be ahistorical. This is not to say that it does not offer a historical account of itself—quite the contrary, many participants in this discourse expend considerable energy specifying the lineage of the concept. A recent compilation of readings includes "sources" as wide ranging as the Bible, Epictetus, the Magna Carta, the English Bill of Rights, Immanuel Kant, Karl Marx, Woodrow Wilson, and Frantz Fanon.[10]

However, tracing the lineage of a concept and specifying its developing role in changing social circumstances are not the same things. The lineage, moreover, often takes on Hegelian overtones: "The History of the world," Hegel wrote, "is none other than the progress of the consciousness of Freedom." And so it is with universal human rights. The lineage of universal human rights thus does not truly historicize the concept—for indeed, from this perspective, the concept is transhistorical—but focuses on its realization in practice and on "the coming to consciousness of itself" of the principle (Hegel).

According to the standard account, human rights, after all, are universal, which means not only that they are applicable all over the world but that they are valid principles for evaluating past societies as well. Missing, however, is an explanation of the historical circumstances that make it possible—and necessary—to think universalistically.

In addition (and often as result of its ahistoricism), the literature on universal human rights is frequently unscientific, violating conventional distinctions between normative and empirical concerns. The question of why such rights exist in some places and not in others—the identification of conditions of possibility—is solely at the service of increasing and solidifying claims on behalf of the idea.[11] In many respects, for all its talk of the value of unique cultures and rights to self-determination, the philosophical-jurisprudential literature on universal human rights commits the same conceptual sins its practitioners reject in modernization theory (i.e., assuming only one unilinear and teleological model of moral and social development).

The strong position on human rights dismisses historical or cross-cultural contextualization as either theologically unacceptable (i.e., to see the universality of human rights as contingent on kinds of social organization is to deny what makes us all human) or philosophically dangerous (i.e., sociological contextualization leads directly down a slippery slope to cultural relativism, thus vitiating the concept's legitimacy claim in practical politics).

These issues have been fought out partly under the rubric of a so-called Asian values debate, in which critics charge that the human rights concept illegitimately universalizes what are in fact specifically Western values. The Western preference for liberal individualism, critics claim, is no more inherently universal than putative Asian preferences for collectivism. Criticisms of this and other sorts resulted in the 1993 Bangkok Declaration, an explicit response to documents like the 1948 Universal Declaration of Human Rights (and to the more recent politics carried out under its banner), which questioned the prioritizing of rights over duties and individuals over collectivities.[12]

As Jürgen Habermas and others argue, however, the stark dichotomy between universal human rights and Asian values acts as a straitjacket: For it *is* possible to entertain doubts raised by critics of universal human rights without capitulating to the apparent relativism of the Asian values position.[13] Our own call to investigate the historical conditions of possibility of universal human rights, therefore, should not be read as an embrace of moral relativism. Rather, it is part of an effort to make the politics of human rights more supple conceptually, indeed to recognize the socio-historical achievement this frame of reference represents. Focusing on historical conditions of possibility, in sum, reframes the question as a sociological rather than philosophical one.[14]

The discourse of universal human rights is tied directly to a politics of regret because its advocates believe that only gestures of reparation, apology, and acknowledgment can restore the dignity of history's victims and can deter new outbreaks of inhumanity. The retrospective gaze of this discourse is thus part of an anticipation of the future. Hannah Arendt puts this most eloquently when she binds forgiving and promising:

> The two faculties [forgiving and promising] belong together in so far as one of them, forgiving, serves to undo the deeds of the past, whose "sins" hang like Damocles' sword over every new generation; and the other, binding oneself through promises, serves to set up in the ocean of uncertainty, which the future is by definition, islands of security without which not even continuity, let alone durability of any kind, would be possible in the relationships between men.[15]

Nevertheless, this argument remains at a philosophical level. Arendt does offer some considerations on the rise of the "politics of pity" after the French Revolution and on the unique conditions for the *Vita Activa* after the Holocaust, but the appeal of regret here, as elsewhere in the discourse on universal human rights, remains general.[16] The question remains of *why* the wave of regret is taking place now, however salutary these theorists see that wave or however much advocates celebrate its triumphs.

TRANSITOLOGY

The second major frame for analyzing public apology is work, particularly by political scientists, that has come to be known as "transitology."[17] Following the demise of authoritarian regimes in Latin America in the 1980s and the breakup of the Soviet Union following 1989, social scientists, legal scholars, and politicians alike have focused a great deal of their attention on problems of "transitional justice." How do new regimes deal with the legacies of their predecessors' past misdeeds? What solutions—including show trials, "political justice," "lustration," compensation, truth and reconciliation commissions, general amnesties, memorialization, and organized amnesia—are most likely to provide a solid foundation for a peaceable future? Who is responsible for the crimes of the past, and what does that responsibility entail? What are its limits? Where legal scholars and politicians debate solutions normatively, social scientists observe the various choices and attempt to correlate them with differences in circumstances.

One of the earliest entries in this tide of studies is Samuel Huntington's *The Third Wave*.[18] There Huntington lays out a number of basic empirical issues, raising questions of the correlation among various transition variables and possible outcomes. In his analysis of post-1989 transitions, Huntington places great emphasis on the timing and personnel involved in the changes. Were old elites agents of the change or objects of it? Did old elites remain in power, hand it over peacefully, or resist violently? Did the transformation come at the beginning of an international wave, and did the particular country and its leaders advocate the transformation or resist it? All of these factors, according to Huntington, contributed to the nature of the posttransition settlements.

Perhaps the most important goal of transitology is *typological*. Another work in this vein, by Claus Offe, reveals this goal in its title: *Varieties of Transition*.[19] A major three-volume compilation edited by Neil Kritz[20] consists of case studies of the transition process and the solutions offered in a variety of cases, most prominently from Eastern Europe and Latin America. Another recent book—sitting at the borderline between the philosophical-juridical and transitological frames (as does the Kritz volume)—is called *Human Rights in Political Transitions: Gettysburg to Bosnia*.[21]

Several other volumes have drawn comparisons between American Reconstruction after the Civil War and recent transitions in Latin America and Eastern Europe. A number of other studies have compared Japan and Germany, many of them returning to the theory of shame-versus-guilt cultures Ruth Benedict advanced fifty years ago.[22] We will return as well to Benedict's theory, but for its historical rather than typological dimensions.

In such inquiries, many scholars argue that the questions of transitions from authoritarian regimes are not just widespread in the modern world, but perennial ones, facing every society that has developed principles of justice based on anything more abstract than instantaneous retribution. In a programmatic statement for contemporary studies of transitional justice, for instance, Jon Elster uses an example from Ancient Greece to demonstrate this permanence.[23] In *The Constitution of Athens*, Aristotle describes an agreement between the Athenian oligarchs (the so-called three thousand) and the democrats in exile at Piraeus, drawn up under Spartan supervision. Most remarkable here was a provision that granted a general amnesty for everyone but the top leadership, who were nevertheless to become immune from prosecution once they had rendered their accounts. "A striking feature of the Athenian reconciliation treaty," Elster writes, "is that so many of the general themes of justice in the transition to democracy are already found in the very first well-documented instance."

One major difference between the Athenian case and contemporary ones, however, is the scope and purpose of reconciliation. In Athens, as Donald Shriver has pointed out, vengeance was indeed limited for the purpose of preserving the community, but this did not lead to a universal human ethic against vengeance per se.[24] Quite the contrary at Nuremberg or in the current debate concerning jurisdiction over Pinochet. In contrast to ancient Athens, where the concern was largely for the continuity of the community, and to the age of heroic nationalism, where even the slightest vacillation was rejected as blasphemous,[25] today a great number of cases demonstrate a willingness to admit historical mistakes and even to try to make up for them.

Central to this new politics of regret is a more general moralization of political conflict.[26] While the idea of "just war" is ancient, for instance, contemporary definitions are rather strict in comparison to earlier ones, and contemporary remedies are rather different. Premodern conflicts were often understood as contests between kings, who did not necessarily hold each other morally responsible for their conquests or defeats. And when acts of war *were* seen as illegitimate (for instance when Charles V's armies sacked Rome in the sixteenth century), this involved the *personal* honor and responsibility of the king rather than the obligation of one people to another (in the sack of Rome, for example, most of the soldiers were foreign mercenaries and the battlefield was not the object of the conflict, which was between a Spanish king and a French king).

Solutions to premodern conflict most often involved bribes, trades, marriages, territorial transfers, and the like, but rarely expressions of remorse, reparation to civilian victims, reeducation, or prosecution of "war crimes." And while premodern blood feuds may have been born out of moral indignation, there are stark differences between premodern and modern political conflict and between blood feuds and collective responsibility. Thus, while there are earlier precedents and models for reparation and apology, regret as a *sine qua non* of postconflict peace building, we argue, is a preeminently modern phenomenon; indeed, in many ways, the principle of political accountability defines contemporary politics.

In sum, principles of political justice, vengeance, compensation, and so forth have been around as long as there has been law: they were central in the Athenian example; they were present in the code of Hammurabi; they were formalized as principles of an international "system" by Hugo Grotius in 1625; and they have played out in twentieth-century institutions. According to transitologists, the more cases we can include in our models, the clearer will be our typologies and the better our predictions. Many important works in this tradition therefore adduce cases from widely divergent times and places into one vast model of transition. Where the transitology frame is to be admired for its analytical clarity and scientific impulse, however, its "variables" approach removes much of the context from the analysis, erasing the peculiarities of specific cases. In this literature, virtually any case is grist for the analytical mill.

In what sense can we speak of a transition to democracy in both ancient

Athens and modern Hungary? In what sense can we speak of problems of restitution as comparable in Rwanda and Argentina? The very meaning of the terms and the units of analysis can be radically different, not just in the conditions or orders in which universal variables operate. The transitology frame is thus no more help than the philosophical-jurisprudential frame in answering the question: Why regret, why now? Seeing the problems of transitional justice as basically perennial is to miss the profound ways in which both the questions and the answers have changed over the course of history.

THE HISTORICAL SOCIOLOGY
OF POLITICAL REGRET

How can we explain this proliferation of collective regret?[27] One account emphasizes the postmodern demise of legitimating narratives: Within societies, disenfranchised groups produce alternative historical narratives that call elites to account for historical wrongs; across societies, subjugated peoples in the periphery challenge the arrogance of the center. Other accounts point to the morally shattering experiences of total war and genocide in the twentieth century: The Holocaust was a decisive refutation of the idea of progress and makes us all guilty, or, as Walter Benjamin argued so persuasively, World War I destroyed the bases of genuine experience, ending all claims to innocent national purpose (of course, more commonly the myth of the war experience stoked an even more bellicose nationalism).[28]

Still others point to the role of the mass media: Aryeh Neier, for instance, has argued that a decisive moment in the development of principles of political justice was the emergence of war correspondents in the mid-nineteenth century, who were able to present the horrors of modern warfare to their readers at home.[29] In another important statemer... ...ich we will discuss shortly, Michel-Rolph Trouillot argues that the apologetic state extrapolates from the apologetic liberal individual; in a sort of inversion of Habermas, Trouillot could be said to be arguing for a colonization of the system by the life world![30]

Nevertheless, most of these theories, while intriguing, seem to us to be merely descriptive or partial. They share a presumption that the emergence of regret is only a symptom of modernity (or of its demise)—perhaps an interesting result or window, but not at the heart of the process. In contrast, in the remainder of this chapter, we will explore resources for a more general developmental account that places regret at the center of modernity.[31] We argue that important efforts outside of sociology suffer from a lack of attention to social-structural and cultural developments understood sociologically. We find leads for a sociological account of memory and regret in different theoretical traditions, ranging from Emile Durkheim and Norbert Elias on differentiation and density to Weber and Habermas on rationalization.

In what follows, we review these and others as resources for a theory of political regret, but ultimately give our greatest attention to a theory that attends to historical transformations in temporal perceptions leading to a rise in "historical consciousness." This perspective, we argue, places memory and regret properly at the center of the sociological account of modernity.

REGRET AND RESPONSIBILITY

Two central questions for a sociohistorical theory of regret concern the ways in which regret is modern and the ways in which modernity is regretful. Beginning with the first, we can turn to William James for some basic considerations. In his *Principles of Psychology*, James writes: "An act has no ethical quality whatever unless it be chosen out of several all equally possible."[32] Perhaps we might modify this just a bit by adding that the *perception* of alternative possibilities is important as well. And precisely this is what has developed to a radically different order in modern societies: Modernity makes the individual master of his fates and opens up to him a range of possibilities; at the same time, it also introduces a clearer sense of personal and collective responsibility, both theoretically in terms of philosophical and legal principles and practically as it involves him in matters of politics and war. Only under these conditions can one be aware of, and thus regret, not having acted otherwise, and only thus can one be held accountable—in all the senses of that word—for one's own acts of commission and omission as well as for acts committed "in one's name." This is as true for contemporary collectivities and their agents as it is for individuals.

In many ways, the problem of collective regret is synonymous with the problem of collective memory and, indeed, of collectivity per se. In premodern societies, the space between individual and collective experience was easily bridged. In complexifying societies, however, people from different milieus congregate in urban settings, leaving behind both their earlier contexts and to some degree their earlier selves; the labors of life are more highly differentiated than in rural households; classes and guilds and interest groups form. Hence, the bases of agreement, the bonds of commonality, are much less obvious, requiring vast new efforts and conceptual frameworks.

This is, of course, a Durkheimian account. Missing from many cultural accounts of collective regret, as we already hinted, is a sense of the social-structural transformations just mentioned, the kinds Durkheim highlighted in his argument about the rise of individualism. Also important here are Durkheim's ideas about the growing functional requirements for contractual obligation and consistency in increasingly interlocked commercial societies. For instance, the idea of reparations, we hope to show in future work, is strongly based on an extrapolation of tort law and other institutions for generating consistency in commercial relations (e.g., insurance). This is one reason why Japan, whose cultural resources and identity might (and do) work against participating in the politics of regret, has made some gestures (albeit reluctantly): Reparation of past injustice maintains restitutive norms essential for contemporary forms of international commerce.

But a social-structural account such as this can describe more than just a commercial order (to which the current discourse on reparations is sometimes reduced). In Elias's account, for instance, increasingly dense networks of relations give any single action a wide and unforeseeable circle of implication. As a result, actors need to temper violent outbursts, whose ultimate outcomes are impossible to predict. Indeed, one could explain the recent wave of apology as recognition of the long chains of consequence for one's actions. This is the kind of argument Arendt makes about forgiveness:

> [M]en . . . have known that he who acts never quite knows what he is doing, that he always becomes "guilty" of consequences he never intended or foresaw, that no matter how disastrous and unexpected the consequences of his deed he can never undo it, that the process he starts is never consummated unequivocally in one single deed or event, and that its very meaning never discloses itself to the actor but only to the backward glance of the historian. . . . The possible redemption from the predicament of irreversibility—of being unable to undo what one has done though one did not, and could not, have known what he was doing—is the faculty of forgiving. . . . Without being forgiven, released from the consequences of what we have done, our capacity to act would, as it were, be confined to one single deed from which we could never recover.[33]

Elias employs a similar logic, though highlighting the novelty of this condition. For him, the court society, with its complexly stylized ritual, in which a subtle gesture can lead to social (or even real) death, is the paradigm of contemporary civilization. The actors who constitute (and are constituted by) highly complex interaction orders by necessity have highly developed superegos, agencies of self-restraint. Combining Arendt and Elias, then, one can see how apology becomes a necessary part of the modern interaction ritual, as Erving Goffman described it. This works close-up (personal regret) as well as at a distance (collective regret) because the same principle governs both, which are, in Elias's terms, merely facets of the same figuration.[34]

SHAME CULTURE VERSUS GUILT CULTURE REVISITED

Perhaps it would be useful, in this context, to revisit what is by now a quite old and much-criticized theory of regret—the distinction, originally the anthropologist Ruth Benedict's, between a shame culture and a guilt culture.[35] This theory has been rightly criticized for its strong notions of national character and for the suspicion that the argument implies only Westerners are morally developed. Nevertheless, as with many dismissed older theories, there is more there than remains of it in our intellectual collective memory.

According to Benedict and others in this tradition, shame cultures are characterized by high and connected degrees of visibility and conformity. In such societies, the most dangerous transgression is to draw attention to oneself; one avoids doing so through strict conformity to complex social rituals. The most important quality, in such a society, is a reputation for correct social performance. Everything depends on protecting appearances, and failure to do so produces a feeling of shame analogous to the feeling of shame produced by nakedness in public. Such societies require a high degree of self-discipline and frequently demand priority of the group over the individual. The reward for conformity in such a society is security and predictability. Behavioral norms in such societies, moreover, are quite group- and context-specific, unique cultural forms that are rarely transposable.

In contrast, guilt cultures are characterized by the private judgment of individual consciences, heard as internal voices rather than felt as external gazes. Individuals in such cultures are individually responsible to generalized norms. Guilt, in this account, does not destroy the individual; rather it forms the foundation of the moral person. Internalizing social norms, as Sigmund Freud emphasized, is part of the process of individuation, not the elimination of the individual.

This distinction is obviously quite overdrawn. We find instances of both guilt and shame in most societies; characterizing a society as fundamentally one or the other is clearly a distortion.[36] Nevertheless, the theory does provide some important insights into the history of regret: Although Benedict's argument is based primarily on a psychological reading of a national character, she contextualizes her reading within a historical and structural frame.

In Japan, for example, a feeling of indebtedness, known as *on*—pervasive in Japanese political and social structure, according to Benedict—serves as a support mechanism for a thoroughly hierarchical political system. Each individual is under obligation to someone above them, culminating in the Emperor or the Shogun (feudal lord) in premodern history. *On*, more akin to debt than guilt, is therefore depicted by Benedict as the glue of a social system dependent on the primacy of the homogenous group. In contrast, we may recall Friedrich Nietzsche's argument in *The Genealogy of Morals* that the history of Western morality is the transformation of debt into guilt. Guilt, extrapolating from Benedict's account, is inherently more universalistic because it is founded on (and founds) structural heterogeneity.

For all its ethnocentrism, the attempt to articulate different historical paths to, and structural conditions of, guilt and shame is a clear advance over the ethical universalism and transhistoricism of the universal human rights paradigm. Made more supple by refining its concept of national character with Elias's less essentialist notion of national habitus (an inherently historical phenomenon) revives some of this theory's usefulness in explaining the wave of regret. Moreover, it is not necessary to assume that the politics of regret involves all guilt and no shame.

We are reminded, though, how much questions of political ethics are rooted in the duality of emotion and social structure. The politics of regret is a feature of high social-structural and cultural capacities for both shame and guilt. One advantage of revising this approach by reading it through Elias is that doing so shows us how both guilt and shame are products of highly developed social structures[37] and that both can result in a politics of regret, but that the politics of regret takes different forms in different places.[38] Most important, however, this approach shows the central relationship between guilt and universalism, a connection missing from important sociological accounts of universalization, discussed in the next two sections.

THE RATIONALIZED WORLD AND THE ETHIC OF RESPONSIBILITY

In order to understand the relation just discussed between political ethics and social structure, there is no more useful place to turn than Max Weber.[39] Discussions of transition within the philosophical-jurisprudential frame, as we saw, pose a stark choice between retribution and utility, just deserts, and peace at all costs. In the abstract, there are good reasons for defending each of these and long traditions of doing so. But in practice, they often become mere justifications for less admirable positions: On the one hand, the victim's lust for revenge; on the other, the perpetrator's self-serving haste to bury misdeeds. Excluding the victim's lust for revenge and the perpetrator's self-interested amnesia, however, does not solve the problem. According to Weber, then, the absolute terms of the debate—dogma versus opportunism—are not really supple enough to respect the different positions in which equally serious parties advocate different solutions (e.g., purge versus amnesty) as well as see different criteria (e.g., principle versus consequence) as ethical guides. Particularly in his essays on science and politics as vocations, Weber articulated a subtler, and more historical, distinction between what he called an "ethic of conviction" and an "ethic of responsibility."

This was no mere exercise in political ethics: The distinction, it is often forgotten, rests on a profoundly historical account of the conditions of possibility for the two principles. Indeed, Weber connected his preference for an ethic of responsibility over an ethic of conviction with his wider historical account of the rationalization and disenchantment of the world. For Weber, an ethic of conviction, though perhaps admirably motivated, fails to recognize the contribution of science in the modern rationalized world. In this context, science means acknowledging the inescapability of value conflict and that ends and means are not integrally connected.

For a follower of an ethic of conviction, the ought does not depend on feasibility, and this kind of a position thus denies the realistic framework of science. In contrast, the ethic of responsibility embraces the ethical irrationality of the world and recognizes that realizing values in politics often involves a so-called "pact with diabolical powers." Weber is careful—this is not dogma versus opportunism or even ethical policy versus realpolitik. Responsibility is an ethical principle, not the absence of one. But it opts for compromise and small steps in the pursuit of political values. Responsibility lies between conviction and realpolitik.

While Weber unpacked this argument in general terms, it is important to remember that he developed it immediately following his work on the war guilt question in "negotiations" over the Treaty of Versailles and in reaction to revolutionary parties in Germany in 1918, who were ready to accept the war guilt thesis out of pacifist and other convictions. Weber rejected these positions as blind to necessity, feasibility, and consequence and exhorted students to understand the ethical obligation of the politician to be "responsible."

Again, this is not a call to realpolitik, which would imply no ethical principle, but a call to pursue whatever value one advocates in a manner sensitive to the possibilities of realizing it and to the relativity, rather than absolute hierarchy, of possible outcomes. The ability to recognize this relativity of values and the distinction between means and ends characteristic of the rationalized, scientific worldview is possible only at a certain moment in history.

Following Weber, then, regret based on an ethic of conviction seems to be a premodern residue, unless one justifies the regret in terms of its consequences. Weber himself rejected the pacifist voices calling for Germany to accept the war guilt clause (as if Germany had a choice) because he thought this was irresponsible—that is, a rejection of the consequences in favor of the principle. The question remains whether it is ever possible, in Weber's framework, to have a responsible politics of regret.[40]

APOLOGY AS UNIVERSAL NORMS OF JUSTICE

Habermas provides another argument—generically related to Weber's—potentially useful for explaining the recent wave of regret within a developmental account.[41] According to Habermas, modern collective identity has involved a shaky balance between two products of modernization: universalism and particularism. Universalism refers to ideas of freedom and democracy that are central features of Enlightenment thinking, but these ideas have been pursued, for the most part, through the particularism of nation-states—structures that have also developed during modernization. For the most part, these two principles have remained in balance to produce what Habermas calls "conventional identity." Fascism, according to Habermas' scheme, finds its organic form of nationalistic identity by embracing particularism at severe cost to universalism.

In contrast, Habermas would like to see communal identities form on the basis of universalistic principles alone. In the case of Germany, and by extension elsewhere, this should take the form of a "constitutional patriotism," in which a "post-conventional" identity is founded on rational principles and embodied in democratic legal structures. For Habermas, universalism is the great achievement of modernity. Habermas' developmental theory analogizes psychological theories of moral development and the social history of legal norms.

According to psychologists like Jean Piaget and Lawrence Kohlberg, the younger child seeks direct rewards and avoids punishment and only the older child is able to follow abstract rules; according to Kohlberg, only rational Western men of a particular level of education are able to behave in a universalistic fashion, and only a very few individuals are able to do so consistently. For Habermas, who "reconstructs" historical materialism, the history of society is a learning process, the ultimate achievement of which is a rational (and so, universal) norm of justice. Thus, one could infer from this theory that the recent wave of regret is a result of the triumph of universalistic principles of justice, principles built not only on reciprocity and restitution but on the horror of past failures.

One problem with Habermas' account is that it does not provide a good explanation for allegiances based on constitutional patriotism. Emotionally, motivating communal feelings on rationalistic principles is difficult. Indeed, for Habermas, the sense of community that requires Germans to accept responsibility for National Socialism is, in important ways, pre- or extra-rational. This must be the case, because historical consciousness for Habermas is not, strictly speaking, a rational principle of identification. For Habermas, the reason to remember the Holocaust is that doing so is a promise to the universalistic future, to put it in Arendt's terms.

Attaching a theory of guilt to a Habermasian account of the progress of universal norms may help us see regret as the central indicator of the rationalization process. But the inherent teleology of the account, it seems to us, does not get us all that much further than the Hegelianism of the Universal Human Rights frame. The process remains rather disembodied.

Certainly, Habermas does tie his account of the evolution of norms to more traditionally materialist concerns on the one hand, and to Weberian notions of rationalization on the other. Nevertheless, such approaches seem to us to leave out the most important, and directly relevant, feature of modernity's trajectory—temporality, more specifically the profound transformation in the experience of time that characterizes modernity, the German word for which (*Neuzeit*) literally means new time. Where the theoretical perspectives just enumerated provide important background considerations, it seems to us that the rise of historical consciousness crystallizes what is fundamental to the modern regretful experience. In the remainder of this chapter, we theorize the outlines of this process.

THE RISE OF HISTORICAL CONSCIOUSNESS

Regret is a form of historical consciousness. "Historical consciousness," however, is by no means a universal and monolithic phenomenon. While storytelling and "constitutive narration"[42] have been important features of collective identity for as long as people have reflected on and symbolized their sociation, certain important transformations from the late Middle Ages through the modern era have effected a major shift in the experience of temporality and modes of reflection on it.

Broadly speaking, there has been a move from predominantly circular-oral to linear-written forms of historicity.[43] The acceleration of change and standardization of time measurement associated with, and definitive of, the modern era produced a growing distinction among past, present, and future. Increased mobility, lengthened life courses, and greater social differentiation demanded new conceptual and existential frames for grasping this now extended spatiotemporal horizon. History and memory, as many scholars have pointed out, became central exactly when they seemed to be losing their salience, their unproblematic presence and importance for everyday life.[44]

With these developments, the redemptive eschatology of religious doctrine made less and less sense just when the political dominance of the Church was declining. Where in religious worldviews redemption or apocalypse was always a potential part of the present, the secular experience of development created a sense of the human future. The future was understood not as immanent in the present—the pervasive possibility of apocalypse—but as a long horizon of expectation stretching out beyond the space of present experience. Each individual moment is thus merely one in a long chain of becoming. The fundamental sameness of cyclical time became the perpetual progress of linear time. In turn, the present appeared more and more distinct from the past, which became a "foreign country."[45]

Through the seventeenth and eighteenth centuries, a wide variety of new experiences and events produced an awareness of the "noncontemporaneity of the contemporaneous" as well, a perception that simultaneously existing places and groups could be relatively more or less "advanced."[46] This was tied up with the development of grand historical schemes, be they evolutionary (i.e., history is gradual improvement), revolutionary (i.e., history progresses through radical breaks), or devolutionary (i.e., history is progressively dehumanizing). Indeed, the modern historical profession was born within this philosophical frame, intending to reveal how such grand programs manifested themselves in the world. Nevertheless, professional history eventually became a basis for rejecting not only particular grand schemes, but the very idea of grand schemes at all: historicism (belief in accounts of the progressive stages of history) begat historism (belief in the uniqueness of every historical culture and the randomness of history) as it encountered the incommensurable details of each time and place it studied (though sometimes the process worked the other way, just to keep things complicated!).

These new understandings of time and history were matched at the personal level by an increase in the sense of one's own experience of change: A life begun in the cyclical temporality and relative uniformity of agrarian cultures could now end in the polyglot world of the industrial city. In the modern world, the past was thus no longer felt to be immediately present but was something that required preservation and recovery.

In the nineteenth century in particular, Romanticism was just one expression of a growing fervor for commemorating, and multifarious forms for doing so proliferated, including coins, medals, postage stamps, statuary, monuments, among others. Perceptions of a memory crisis—born of the feeling that the past was perpetually slipping away, moving further and further out of reach—led to interest in the organic and psychological bases of memory, to new forms of self-narrative ranging from autobiography to psychoanalysis, and to the popularization of genealogy and similar practices.

Coupled with the demands for greater social coordination for the ever-complexifying market society (enabled by the gradual accumulation of capital from about the fifteenth century on), these ideological and existential transformations fed the development of the modern nation-state. This new institutional form not only enabled ever more centrally located rulers to ward off external threats, but provided mechanisms for extracting the necessary resources for doing so from their ever-larger territories. The nation-state, however, sought to provide not just these material benefits, but existential ones as well.

While the classical sociologists of the late nineteenth century worried over the decline of religious-based solidarity, national leaders developed identitarian doctrines to replace the existential security lost with the decline of religious salvationism. New nationalist eschatologies sought to link past, present, and future together in redemptive narratives that answered the dislocations of modernization while also producing an extraordinary commitment to themselves and their projects. In these efforts, history and memory took on crucial roles. As Eric Hobsbawm has pointed out, nation-states in the nineteenth century became the purveyors par excellence of "tradition," be it long standing or thoroughly new (but always invented). This was the heroic period of the mnemonic nation, which entailed triumphalist historiography to underwrite often belligerent ethnocentrism: the nation was an ancient essence whose historical path to power was inevitable.[47]

At their height in the nineteenth century, European states supported a new kind of memory—a homogeneous memory of the nation—at the same time that this new kind of memory made possible a new kind of state. At this point, the past became a central occupation and preoccupation, not only providing substance for shared allegiance to the state but legitimating the "empty, homogeneous time" of the state over other less "progressive" temporalities.[48] In this "Age of Historicism" professional custodians of the past sought to ground identity through "objective" accounts of "the way it actually was," as the famous historians' dictum puts it, while states and societies produced a wide variety of inquiries into, and representations of, the common past. Memory was the handmaiden of nationalist zeal, history its high counsel.[49]

The age of ideology can thus be seen as the attempt to replace that one monolithic principle with a number of new monolithic principles: within each nation according to its own character, among the nations according to competing principles of difference. But while it may be possible to be the only articulated monolith available, the very existence of more than one such candidate begins to undermine the monolithic principle itself. The very secular basis of the appeal to a unified national identity based on a collective memory in the presence of difference makes it a very unsteady place to stand.

The hope for a unitary collective memory of the nation-state in the nineteenth century was thus a task doomed from the start, indeed from much earlier. The hysterical fever with which that memory was pursued in the late nineteenth century merely testifies to the profound insecurity out of which the attempt grew. European society became too complex from the Middle Ages on to support one monolithic principle of legitimation.

From World War I on, the possibility of "constitutive narratives" has been in a state of crisis. As Benjamin put it, "never has experience been contradicted more thoroughly than strategic experience by tactical warfare, economic experience by inflation, bodily experience by mechanical warfare, moral experience by those in power."[50] The cataclysm of 1914 to 1918, in Benjamin's account, left people not only without the conditions for telling stories but without communicable experiences to tell. Nevertheless, just as the effects of war were felt more brutally than ever among civilian populations, the tasks of consolation were made more public than ever before. As a result, the historian George Mosse has written, "The memory of the war was refashioned into a sacred experience which provided the nation with a new depth of religious feeling, putting at its disposal ever-present saints and martyrs, places of worship, and a heritage to emulate."[51] Part of this was a massive democratization of the cult of the dead. While the war experience did result in pacifism in some quarters, however, in most places it did not.

World War I indeed created new attitudes toward both the present and the past. Nevertheless, according to many theorists of memory, the Holocaust produced an even more decisive "crisis of representation" in Western cultures. "We are dealing," writes Saul Friedlander, "with an event which tests our traditional conceptual and representational categories, an 'event at the limits.'"[52] There is the oft-quoted remark of Theodor Adorno that to write lyric poetry after Auschwitz is barbaric; doing so would in some way be to make it beautiful, no matter how melancholic the form.[53] By extension, many have portrayed the Holocaust as challenging the validity of any totalizing view of history. What unifying meaning is to be found there or in its wake? Which of the great "metanarratives" of so-called Western civilization—be they of progress or decline—contain such an unassimilable set of events and experiences?

Memory of war, and indeed memory per se, has often been understood in new ways since 1945. While some authors make the Holocaust the turning point, others see in it merely one last and most horrible stage in a development already underway—one that includes recognition of the horrors of colonialism, two world wars, racism, environmental damage, and so on—on the road to postmodernity. Indeed, questions of time and memory have been at the center of postmodernism, which in principle rejects, and in practice often plays with, "conventional" notions of linear and uniform time.

In the second half of the twentieth century, the development of electronic means of recording and transmitting information has led to changes not only in the ways we remember but in how we conceive of memory, with possibly radical—though not yet fully realized—implications for social organization and identity. As the postmodern cultural critic Andreas Huyssen argues, mnemonic practices in the late twentieth century are attempts "to slow down information processing, to resist the dissolution of time in the synchronicity of the archive, to recover a mode of contemplation outside some anchoring space in a world of puzzling and often threatening heterogeneity, non-synchronicity, and information overload."[54] In other words, new information technologies have decontextualized memory so that images and even physical remnants of diverse ages are experienced simultaneously and even physically side by side, as when we go from period to period while moving from room to room in a museum, from shelf to shelf in a library, or from channel to channel on television.

CONCLUSION

The politics of regret, then, is no mere fad, no simple offshoot of more important developments. It appears to be the major characteristic of our age, an age of shattered time and shifting allegiances, indeed of skepticism toward allegiances at all. Trouillot asks as we have here: Why so many apologies now?[55] In Trouillot's account, the wave of apologies at the political level expresses the triumphant extrapolation of the liberal individual to the collective level: the rhetoric of collective identity, he argues, has copied the integrative tools of the modern individual. Clearly, we disagree with this argument. First, it is certainly less true today than it was a hundred years ago that we anthropomorphize collective identities (or if we do this now, it is more the individual suffering posttraumatic stress or multiple personality syndrome that we extrapolate rather than the sober figure of psychological health). And it is only now that these identities and their spokespersons have become regretful.

Second, there is nothing at all triumphant about this grasp by collectivities for human character: where earlier the king literally embodied the unity of the nation, the problem of memory has emerged at exactly that point when the problem of the collectivity has reached its peak. Memory and regret are not the result of the integration of the collectivity but of the impossibility of this in an age of competing claims, multiple histories, and plural perceptions. Furthermore, to see the state as taking on the character of the individual is to miss the ways in which the state acts precisely as a surrogate for the individual—what the state commemorates and compensates, we do not have to. For us, the rise of regret in all its forms is a sign of the failure of the state to generate adequate psychological defense mechanisms, not of the state's success in doing so. Trouillot has the order of logic reversed: the confessional individual mimics the regretful state, not the other way around—or at the least they are codetermined phenomena.

In sum, the appropriate frame for explaining the recent rise of regret is a historical-sociological one that sees regret as part of the transformation of temporality and historicity that is tied up with the decline, rather than the triumph, of the nation-state. In contrast to the moral philosophers of universal human rights, we thus see the contemporary wave of regret as an embedded social product and not as the coming into self-consciousness of a world-historical idea. It may indeed be appropriate and desirable, but like all moral codes and practices, it is socially conditioned. In contrast to the transitologists, we resist seeing transition outcomes as combinatorial solutions to perennial problems. The very meanings of the terms and social identities of the possible players are historical, rather than logical, constructs.

The question is now how to specify this account of regret. Our considerations here, it should be clear, are a mere prolegomenon to a detailed empirical study of the moments and mechanisms in which regret has developed into this fundamental feature of late modern life. As we have seen, such an account will need to focus on commercial, political, legal, as well as conceptual developments, none of which should be seen as inevitable despite the developmental trajectories outlined here. In addition to determining possible turning points within these developments (e.g., the 1919 Treaty of Versailles, which in many ways introduced the modern notion of war guilt), one must investigate the changing institutional mechanisms for encouraging regret, which include not just the idea of a community of nations and universal human rights, but new ideas for restitution, reparation, apology, redress, and historical inquiry, as well as the trans- and nongovernmental organizations that we discussed at the beginning of this chapter. Producing this kind of historically situated account, we hope, will help us to see present debates as about neither historical necessities nor strategic options, but as a form of consciousness particular to our moment.

NOTES

Address correspondence to Jeffrey K. Olick, Department of Sociology, Fayerweather Hall, Columbia University, New York, NY 10027, jko5@columbia.edu. Earlier versions of this chapter were presented at a conference on "Utopia, Violence, Resistance," Center for Historical Analysis, Rutgers University, April 2000; Department of Sociology, University of Washington, April 2001; and Department of Sociology, Rutgers University, September 2001. The authors thank John Torpey, Charalambos Demetriou, Omer Bartov, Matt Matsuda, Charles Tilly, Debra Minkoff, Kurt Lang, Steve Pfaff, and Karen Cerullo for these opportunities to discuss our ideas or for their advice.

   1. See for example, Priscilla B. Hayner, *Unspeakable Truths: Confronting State Terror and Atrocity* (New York: Routledge, 2001); Neil J. Kritz, *Transitional Justice: How Emerging Democracies Reckon with Former Regimes* (Washington, D.C.: United States Institute of Peace Press, 1995); Martha Minow, *Between Vengeance and Forgiveness: Facing History after Genocide and Mass Violence* (Boston, Mass.: Beacon, 1998); Claus Offe, *Varieties of Transition: The East European and East German Experience* (Cambridge, Mass.: MIT Press, 1997); Ruti Teitel, *Transitional Justice* (New York: Oxford University Press, 2000).
   2. Norbert Elias, one of our central inspirations, carefully distinguishes between evolutionary and developmental theory. Norbert Elias, *The Civilizing Process: Socio-genetic and Psychogenetic Investigations*, trans. Edmund Jephcott (Oxford, U.K.: Blackwell Publishers, 1994 [1939]). For Elias, the physical world changes mostly very slowly, the biological somewhat faster through "evolution," and the social much more quickly through "development." This distinction between evolution and development is the foundation on which Elias refutes charges that his account of "the civilizing process" partakes of the sins of nineteenth–century evolutionism: develop-

ment has none of the connotations of necessity inherent in evolutionist accounts. By extension, we wish to avoid the frequently overt teleological tone of accounts in which the politics of regret reflects the supposed moral maturation of Western societies (and, by extension, their superiority over other less developed societies). See our discussion of the so-called Asian values debate in note 13.

3. While the literature is vast, a selection of these ideas can be found in Belgrade Circle, *The Politics of Human Rights* (London, U.K.: Verso, 1999); Jack Donnelly, *International Human Rights* (Boulder, Colo.: Westview Press, 1998); Micheline Ishay, *The Human Rights Reader: Major Political Writings, Essays, Speeches, and Documents from the Bible to the Present* (New York: Routledge, 1997); Paul Gordon Lauren, *The Evolution of International Human Rights: Visions Seen* (Philadelphia: University of Pennsylvania, 1998); Michael J. Perry, *The Idea of Human Rights: Four Inquiries* (New York: Oxford University Press, 1998); Geoffrey Robertson, *Crimes Against Humanity: The Struggle for Global Justice* (New York: New Press, 2000); Henry J. Steiner and Philip Alston, *International Human Rights in Context: Law, Politics, Morals* (New York: Oxford University Press, 1996).

4. The Nuremburg Tribunals do indeed form a central frame of reference for most subsequent efforts. Nevertheless, as Peter Maguire and Gary Bass, among others, have demonstrated, the road to Nuremburg was long and varied. Peter Maguire, *Law and War: An American Story* (New York: Columbia University Press, 2000); Gary Jonathan Bass, *Stay the Hand of Vengeance: The Politics of War Crimes Tribunals* (Princeton, N.J.: Princeton University Press, 2000).

5. R. H. Tawney, *Commonplace Book*, ed. J. M. Winter (Cambridge, U.K.: Cambridge University Press, 1972).

6. Karl Jaspers, *Die Schuldfrage: Zur politischen Haftung Deutschlands* (Munich: Piper, 1965 [1946]).

7. Donald W. Shriver, *An Ethic for Enemies: Forgiveness in Politics* (New York: Oxford University Press, 1995).

8. For a discussion of the numerous parliamentary debates in the Federal Republic of Germany on this issue, see Karl Jaspers, *Wohin treibt die Bundesrepublik? Tatsachen, Gefahren, Chancen* (Munich: Piper, 1966), and Helmut Dubiel, *Niemand ist frei von der Geschichte: Die nationalsozialistische Herrschaft in den Debatten des deutschen Bundestages* (Munich: Carl Hanser Verlag, 1999).

9. For the German case, see especially Theodor Adorno, "What Does Coming to Terms with the Past Mean?" in *Bitburg in Moral and Political Perspective*, ed. Geoffrey Hartman (Bloomington: Indiana University Press, 1986 [1959]), 114–29; Alexander Mitscherlich and Margarethe Mitscherlich, *The Inability to Mourn: Principles of Collective Behavior*, trans. Beverly R. Placzek (New York: Free Press, 1967); Herman Lübbe, "Der Nationalsozialismus im deutschen Nachkriegsbewußtsein," *Historische Zeitschrift* 236 (1993): 579–99, and Gesine Schwan, *Politics and Guilt: The Destructive Power of Silence*, trans. Thomas Dunlap (Lincoln: University of Nebraska Press, 2001 [1997]).

10. Ishay, *The Human Rights Reader*.

11. We will outline some of these conditions in the section on "The Historical Sociology of Political Regret"; see also note 27 in this note section.

12. Jürgen Habermas, "Remarks on Legitimation through Human Rights," in *The*

Postnational Constellation: Political Essays, trans. and ed. Max Pensky (Cambridge, Mass.: MIT Press, 2001), 113–29; Lynda S. Bell, Andrew J. Nathan, and Ilan Peleg, eds., *Negotiating Culture and Human Rights* (New York: Columbia University Press, 2001).

13. On the one hand, Habermas argues, "Asiatic societies . . . deploy positive law as a steering medium in the framework of a globalized system of market relations. They do so for the same functional reasons that once allowed this form of law to prevail in the Occident over the older guild-based forms of social integration. . . . Asiatic societies cannot participate in capitalistic modernization without taking advantage of the achievements of an individualistic legal order." On the other hand, he suggests, "the [Western] understanding of human rights must jettison the metaphysical assumption of an individual who exists prior to all socialization and, as it were, comes into the world already equipped with innate rights." As a result, "The choice between 'individualist' and 'collectivist' approaches disappears once we approach fundamental legal concepts with an eye toward the dialectical unity of individuation and socialization processes." Habermas, *The Postnational Constellation*, 124, 126.

14. Mamdani similarly highlights the historical development of what he calls "rights talk" in the case of Africa. He traces the present-day opposition of "culture" and "rights" to forms of rule adopted during the late colonial period and the transformation of these forms after independence. He thus argues that South African apartheid was not an exceptional form of rule, but rather a generic one in Africa, parallel to the indirect rule of the colonial state. See Mahmood Mamdani, *Citizen and Subject: Contemporary Africa and the Legacy of Late Colonialism* (Princeton, N.J.: Princeton University Press, 1996).

15. Hannah Arendt, *The Human Condition* (Chicago, Ill.: University of Chicago Press, 1958), 237.

16. Arendt's writings have served more as a source for the human rights discourse than she herself did as a participant in the accompanying movement.

17. Major works in this tradition, some of which we discuss later on, include Timothy Garton Ash, "The Truth about Dictatorship" in *New York Review of Books*, vol. 45, no. 3 (February 19, 1998), 35–40 ; John Borneman, *Settling Accounts: Violence, Justice, and Accountability in Post Socialist Europe* (Princeton, N.J.: Princeton University Press, 1997); Jon Elster, "Coming to Terms with the Past," in *European Journal of Sociology* 39 (1998): 7–48; Hayner, *Unspeakable Truths*; Carla Alison Hesse and Robert Post, *Human Rights in Political Transitions: Gettysburg to Bosnia* (New York: Zone Books, 1999); Samuel P. Huntington, *The Third Wave: Democratization in the Late Twentieth Century* (Norman, Okla.: University of Oklahoma Press, 1991); Kritz, *Transitional Justice*; A. James McAdams, *Transitional Justice and the Rule of Law in New Democracies* (Notre Dame, Ind.: University of Notre Dame Press, 1997); Minow, *Between Vengeance and Forgiveness*; Guillermo A. O'Donnell and Philippe C. Schmitter, *Transitions from Authoritarian Rule: Tentative Conclusions about Uncertain Democracies* (Baltimore, Md.: Johns Hopkins University Press, 1986); Guillermo A. O'Donnell, Philippe C. Schmitter, and Laurence Whitehead, *Transitions from Authoritarian Rule: Comparative Perspectives* (Baltimore, Md.: Johns Hopkins University Press, 1986); Offe, *Varieties of Transition*; Tina Rosenberg,

The Haunted Landscape: Facing Europe's Ghosts after Communism (New York: Random House, 1995); and Teitel, *Transitional Justice*. Some of these works participate in both the universal human rights literature and the transitional justice literature, which are often inextricable in practice.

18. Huntington, *The Third Wave*.

19. Offe, *Varieties of Transition*.

20. Kritz, *Transitional Justice*.

21. Hesse and Post, *Human Rights in Political Transitions*.

22. Ian Buruma, *The Wages of Guilt: Memories of War in Germany and Japan* (New York: Farrar, Straus, Giroux, 1994).

23. Elster, "Coming to Terms with the Past."

24. Shriver, *An Ethic for Enemies*.

25. Eric Hobsbawm, *Nations and Nationalism since 1780: Programme, Myth, Reality* (New York: Cambridge University Press, 1990).

26. The relationship between political contests and religious crusades is a problematic one. In one sense, religious and political matters were indistinguishable in earlier periods. But in another sense, political disputes—involving land and sovereignty—were often seen as rather mundane contests between kings and were thus devoid of the moral overlay of religious crusades. In the modern period, religion and politics are separated by secular states, at least in the letter of the law. Yet political contests now often take on the moral vocabulary and righteous tone of religious crusades, while religious contests employ the instruments of politics.

27. In identifying "the politics of regret," we are making both a quantitative and a qualitative claim, though the former is perhaps more difficult to substantiate than the latter. Do people apologize more frequently now than in earlier epochs? This is not exactly what concerns us. In the first place, we argue that the nature of apology as an act differs greatly in the modern world. Second, we are claiming that apology has entered the political realm, where it was not previously present. Our assertion that this is the case is, at this point, anecdotal and based on our reading of discourse surrounding post-conflict settlements from different eras; but we believe it would bear up to a rigorous quantitative analysis. While there are cases of political apology before the modern era and before the last twenty years, moreover, they were, we hypothesize, comparatively rare and of a qualitatively different sort. See Roy L. Brooks, *When Sorry Isn't Enough: The Controversy Over Apologies and Reparations for Human Injustice* (New York: New York University Press, 1999).

28. Walter Benjamin, "The Storyteller," in his *Illuminations*, trans. and ed. Hannah Arendt (New York: Schocken, 1969), 84.

29. Aryeh Neier, *War Crimes: Brutality, Genocide, Terror, and the Struggle for Justice* (New York: Times Books, 1998) see also Luc Boltanski, *Distant Suffering: Morality, Media and Politics* (Cambridge, U.K.: Cambridge University Press, 1999).

30. Michel-Rolph Trouillot, "Abortive Rituals: Historical Apologies in the Global Era," *Interventions: A Journal of Postcolonial Studies* 2, no. 2 (Spring 2000): 171–86.

31. In the process, we bring classical concerns of sociological theory into greater contact with the concerns of social theorizing outside of sociology: while the concept of collective memory comes from sociology, within sociology its study is considered a special interest of the sociology of culture or the sociology of knowledge; outside

of sociology (in history, literary criticism, anthropology, and elsewhere), in contrast, the concept has attracted some of the most fertile theoretical minds and has become a central preoccupation at the highest levels. See especially Maurice Halbwachs, *On Collective Memory*, trans. and ed. Lewis A. Coser (Chicago, Ill.: Chicago University Press, 1992 [1925]); Eric Hobsbawm and Terence Ranger, eds., *The Invention of Tradition* (Cambridge, U.K.: Cambridge University Press, 1983); Andreas Huyssen, *Twilight Memories: Marking Time in a Culture of Amnesia* (New York: Routledge, 1995); Jacques Le Goff, *History and Memory*, trans. Steven Rendall and Elizabeth Claman (New York: Columbia University Press, 1992); Pierre Nora, *Realms of Memory: The Construction of the French Past*, trans. Lawrence D. Kritzman (New York: Columbia University Press, 1996 [1984]); Richard Terdiman, *Present Past: Modernity and the Memory Crisis* (Ithaca, N.Y.: Cornell University Press, 1993); Yosef Yerushalmi, *Zakhor: Jewish History and Jewish Memory* (Seattle: University of Washington Press, 1982); Jeffrey K. Olick and Joyce Robbins, "Social Memory Studies: From 'Collective Memory' to the Historical Sociology of Mnemonic Practices," *Annual Review of Sociology* 24 (1998): 105–40.

32. William James, *The Principles of Psychology* (Cambridge, Mass.: Harvard University Press, 1981 [1890]).

33. Arendt, *The Human Condition*, 233, 237.

34. Erving Goffman, *Interaction Ritual: Essays on Face-to-Face Behavior* (New York: Pantheon, 1967). Later on, we discuss an argument that the apologetic state mimics the apologetic individual. In contrast, we will argue, in a similar way to our statement here, that the two are co-determined.

35. Ruth Benedict, *The Chrysanthemum and the Sword: Patterns of Japanese Culture* (Boston: Houghton Mifflin, 1989 [1964]).

36. Just to complicate matters, a recent book by Father Robert Drinan, a major human rights activist, is called *The Mobilization of Shame*. Father Robert F. Drinan, *The Mobilization of Shame: A World View of Human Rights* (New Haven, Conn.: Yale University Press, 2001).

37. In perhaps surprising ways, the Benedict account reinforces Habermas' position in the Asian values debate that "Asiatic societies . . . cannot participate in capitalistic modernization without taking advantage of the achievements of an individualistic legal order."

38. One should note here that despite Benedict's argument that Germany is a guilt culture and Japan is a shame culture, apology pervades everyday discourse in Japanese culture. See Nicholas Tavuchis, *Mea Culpa: A Sociology of Apology and Reconciliation* (Stanford, Calif.: Stanford University Press, 1991), however, for a typology of apology.

39. Max Weber, "Politics as a Vocation," in *From Max Weber: Essays in Sociology*, trans. and ed. H. H. Gerth and C. Wright Mills (New York: Oxford University Press, 1946), 77–128; Wolfgang Schluchter, *Paradoxes of Modernity: Culture and Conduct in the Theory of Max Weber* (Stanford: Stanford University Press, 1996).

40. Jeffrey K. Olick, *The Value of Regret? What Can We Hope For after Conflict, and for Whom?* (Department of Sociology, Columbia University, n.d.).

41. Jürgen Habermas, *Between Facts and Norms: Contributions to a Discourse Theory of Law and Democracy* (Cambridge, Mass.: MIT Press, 1996).

42. Robert N. Bellah et al., *Habits of the Heart: Individualism and Commitment in American Life* (Berkeley: University of California Press, 1985).

43. Clearly, this distinction, like Benedict's between shame and guilt cultures, is overdrawn. There are examples of linear thinking in premodern societies, as there are of cyclical temporalities in complex societies. This claim is based on a generalization of dominant tendencies.

44. Patrick Hutton, *History as an Art of Memory* (Hanover, N.H.: University Press of New England, 1993); Reinhart Koselleck, *Futures Past: On the Semantics of Historical Time*, trans. K. Tribe (Cambridge, Mass.: MIT Press, 1985); Le Goff, *History and Memory*; Nora, *Realms of Memory*.

45. David Lowenthal, *The Past Is a Foreign Country* (New York: Cambridge University Press, 1985).

46. Koselleck, *Futures Past.*

47. Eric Hobsbawm, "Introduction: Inventing Traditions," in *The Invention of Tradition*, ed. Hobsbawm and Ranger.

48. Walter Benjamin, "Theses on the Philosophy of History," in *Illuminations*, 261.

49. Olick, "Social Memory Studies."

50. Walter Benjamin, "The Storyteller," in *Illuminations*, 84.

51. George L. Mosse, *Fallen Soldiers: Reshaping the Memory of the World Wars* (New York: Oxford University Press, 1990), 7.

52. Saul Friedlander, *Probing the Limits of Representation: Nazism and the "Final Solution"* (Cambridge, Mass.: Harvard University Press, 1992), 2–3.

53. Theodor W. Adorno, "Cultural Criticism and Society," in *Prisms*, trans. Samuel Weber and Sherry Weber (Cambridge, Mass.: MIT Press, 1981), 34.

54. Huyssen, *Twilight Memories*, 11.

55. Trouillot, "Abortive Rituals."

2

Coming to Terms with the Past

Alan Cairns

I n the mid-nineteenth century, Thomas Babington Macaulay, described by Robert Fulford as perhaps the "most popular historian of all time," wrote history as if "the main purpose of past events had been to create the society of which Macaulay was a member." "The general effect of this . . . narrative," he wrote in one work, "will be to excite thankfulness in all religious minds, and hope in the breasts of all patriots. For the history of our country during the last hundred and sixty years is eminently the history of physical, of moral, and of intellectual improvement."[1]

THE LEGACY OF THE TWENTIETH CENTURY

Macaulay's past is not ours. "Coming to terms" with our past is not a celebration of great achievements, but rather the reverse: a moral and intellectual grappling with past behavior that gives cause more for shame than for pride, ranging from great evils such as the Holocaust to lesser actions fueled by arrogance and insensitivity. In most cases, the relevant past, with the important exceptions of the slave trade, slavery, and colonialism, is the twentieth century so recently left behind. Given this focus on past events that have marred our conscience, the following discussion is necessarily a somewhat dispiriting exercise. In fact, one of the difficulties in coming to terms with the past is the nightmare nature of the realities we are trying to understand and explain.

Commentators have outdone themselves in searching for an evocative phrase to capture the essence of the previous century. To Yehudi Menuhin, the twentieth century "raised the greatest hopes ever conceived by humanity,

and destroyed all illusions and ideals."[2] "Our century," according to a
French student of Communism, "has outdone its predecessors in its blood-
thirstiness.... Ours is the century of human catastrophes."[3] "Our century,"
stated the Soviet writer Vasily Grossman, "is the century of the greatest violence ever committed against human beings by the state."[4] To François Furet
it was "the cruel century from which we are now emerging, filled with the
suicidal violence of its nations and regimes."[5]

While some authors have found rays of sunlight amidst the torrent of cruelties humans inflicted on each other, most would agree with Robert Conquest that it was a "ravaged century."[6] Even Jürgen Habermas, who
identified three markedly positive features—the defeat of fascism, decolonization, and the elaboration of the welfare state—nevertheless reminded his
readers of the "gruesome features of a century that 'invented' the gas chamber, total war, state-sponsored genocide and extermination camps, brain-
washing, state security apparatuses, and the panoptic surveillance of entire
populations. The twentieth century 'generated' more victims, more dead soldiers, more murdered civilians, more displaced minorities, more torture,
more dead from cold, from hunger, from maltreatment, more political prisoners and refugees, than could ever have been imagined. The phenomena of
violence and barbarism mark the distinctive signature of the age."[7]

Although individuals may succeed in not looking back and some nations
may deny or obfuscate their complicity in orchestrating tragedy, the human
species as such cannot escape troubling bouts of memory. We misconceive
our relation to the past if we think the only relevant pasts are national
pasts—German, Japanese, or South African, only that and nothing more—
and "our" past is sufficiently unblemished that we can hold our heads up
high. "Yes" and "no." It is true that national pasts differ in their contribution to "our bloodstained century of violence."[8] However, the perpetrators
all belong to the human race. We cannot avoid the understanding that if we,
in whatever little corner of the world we inhabit, have been bit players in
inflicting cruelties on our fellows, we nevertheless belong to the same
humanity as those whose actions horrify us. All pasts in that large sense are
also *our* pasts.

Scarcely a week goes by without mention of a claim for redress from some
group, a denial or acceptance of responsibility by some government, or a
report on the issuing of an apology—most recently and unexpectedly
"Memory and Reconciliation: The Church and the Faults of the Past," a
lengthy document issued by the Vatican going back two thousand years.[9]

Even Canada, which gets little attention in the competitive annals of state
cruelties and victimizations of their own peoples, is not immune from pressures to come to terms with particular pasts. In the last two decades, claims
for redress, apology, and the revision of history came from Japanese Canadians with respect to their World War II relocation and detention (a settlement

was reached); Chinese Canadians for redress of the imposition of the Head Tax on Chinese immigrants; the World War I detention of about five thousand Ukrainian Canadians; the World War II detention of Italian Canadians; the refusal of permission to land at Vancouver to a shipload of intending immigrants from India in 1914 (the *Komagata Maru* incident); the hanging of the Métis leader Louis Riel in 1885; the relocation of Inuit to the High Arctic in the 1950s; the sexual and physical abuse of Aboriginal students in Church-run residential schools; and the removal of Doukhobor children from their parents in the 1950s: the list is not exhaustive.

Although the specifics of the various claims for attention, recognition, and redress in Canada vary, the claimants employ a common language—of being dishonored, denigrated, cast out, stigmatized, and publicly humiliated. At a minimum, they seek an official recognition that they were unjustly treated and merit a serious apology from the majority society.[10]

If our confidence in the future is weak, one reason is that we are at an unusual moment in human history in which grappling with the past is a priority issue on the agenda of dozens of contemporary states. Coming to terms with the past is, of course, an everyday reality for governments, even in normal times. Every agenda of every cabinet meeting—no matter what the policy area—confronts the question of how to respond to the inheritance of past policies and of how to maneuver through the minefield of past decisions.

My focus is more somber. The relevant past for this chapter is not the routinized past of everyday living, but its drastic, often terminal interruption by the Holocaust, by the Gulag archipelago, by World War II atrocities, and by the internal colonialism that marginalized indigenous peoples in Canada. We do not lack for examples. A more comprehensive coverage, beyond the scope of this chapter, could add apartheid, the slave trade, slavery, colonialism, the Chinese assault on Tibetan culture, and recent slaughters in Rwanda, the Sudan, and the former Yugoslavia.

Given the tortured road to the present, Timothy Garton Ash's observation seems almost platitudinous: "The question of what nations should do about a difficult past is one of the great subjects of our time."[11] John Torpey agrees but rephrases Ash with a more positive observation: "Broadly stated, the various movements for reparations for past injustices bespeak the dawning of a new phase in relations between states and the groups that they have victimized historically."[12] The emergence and contagious proliferation of the rhetoric of coming to terms with the past, of redress, and of apologies— often for events prior to the lives of both speakers and listeners—suggest both a sympathetic climate and aggrieved, formerly silent groups to take advantage of it.

Focusing on the evils of yesterday in a search for apologies and redress is sometimes criticized for distracting us from the positive future ventures we could collectively undertake. A different criticism decries the victim psychology that it fosters in the claimants, to the detriment of a sturdy self-help. Yet others argue that it encourages an opportunistic making of claims, regardless of their merit, for the potential rewards are high.

The preceding critiques no doubt contain some truth. Only the naive would assume that a complex and messy process of coming to terms with the past would be without drawbacks. However, a more positive assessment has greater credibility. The issue did not come from nowhere. Coming to terms with the past is on the agenda of so many states because Germany, Japan, and the Axis powers lost World War II; because the racial hierarchies that sustained empires have been overthrown; because Communist dictatorships have collapsed; because the internal colonialism over indigenous peoples is on the defensive; and because, as a consequence of the preceding, millions of people now have a voice, which they employ to draw attention to past theories and practices that were instruments of their own or their predecessors' subordination and often of their death. Seen in this light, coming to terms with the past is an extremely positive development. The Holocaust would not be an issue if Hitler's imagined thousand-year Reich had emerged from World War II.

Humankind will continue to create new pasts, which will burden future generations. Nevertheless, coming to terms will have an unaccustomed priority on our agenda for the next few decades because we are involved in a wrenching transition from "the most terrible century in Western history," in Isaiah Berlin's phrase,[13] to a successor world still in the making. From this perspective, coming to terms with the past is a positive transitional phenomenon.

"Coming to terms with the past" is not a simple concept. At a minimum, it means seeing the behavior of our predecessors, and sometimes of our earlier selves, in terms of its consequences for contemporary generations. This may include trying those responsible for shameful acts and punishing them if found guilty. It includes apologizing to the victims, or their successors; paying reparations; and providing symbolic recognition by plaques and memorials. Where the victims and the perpetrators or their successors live in the same society, it involves seeking reconciliation between those who have to live together in spite of past injustices.

THE INTELLECTUAL TASK

Coming to terms with the past is a complex set of actions and behavior on many fronts. To find the proper voice to confront the realities of what we have done to each other in the twentieth century is not easy. The subject lends itself to a sermon, to a cry of pain, to accusations against the perpetrators of countless cruelties, to sympathy with the victims, and to the false claim of exceptionalism—"I (we) could not have acted thus and thus!" As Eric Hobsbawm appropriately observed, judgment is easy. "It is understanding that comes hard."[14] The subject is daunting and the literature is vast. What follows, therefore, is simply one person's attempt to provide one out of many possible perspectives as a way of understanding the special nature of our relation to the conduct of our predecessors in "our" country, whatever it may be, and in other countries, with all of whom we share a common humanity.

Of the many vantage points that could have been chosen for a subject whose complexities are close to paralyzing, I have largely restricted my focus to an "intellectual" coming to terms with the past, on the premise that getting the past straight is a prerequisite to the larger, messier task of a political coming to terms. "Whatever else is necessary [to learn from history]," Daniel Goldhagen writes, "an accurate and properly interpreted history has to be available."[15] The distinction between the intellectual and the political is not intended to deny that the intellectual task is itself permeated with and driven by the understanding that published research is a form of political influence. Further, governing elites themselves commission research and set up committees of inquiry in order to educate the society and enlarge the knowledge base for their own decisions. Nevertheless, an intellectual coming to terms is a discrete part of the larger enterprise that deserves separate examination.

A Change in Human Sensibility

If there is, as I argue, a broad change in human sensibility in the past half a century, a large part of the explanation lies in the profound structural transformations in the global community of states and in citizen–state relations. Failed attempts at empire-building by Nazi Germany and militaristic Japan—followed by the Nuremberg and Tokyo war crimes tribunals—had convulsive effects on the international system. Not only did these attempts leave successor generations in the defeated Axis powers with a burden of history that Germany has struggled to manage and that Japan has been unable to manage, but they contributed to the disappearance of the European empires that controlled much of the non-Western world until the middle decades of the twentieth century.

The display of barbarism at the heart of European civilization weakened imperial self-confidence and stimulated nationalist critiques by colonial intellectuals of their subject status. The delegitimation of empire, which led to the creation of more than one hundred new states, eroded the Eurocentric worldview on which empire had rested. Europeans lost their status as *The Lords of Human Kind*, in V. G. Kiernan's evocative phrase.[16] In this postimperial world, South Africa, whose ideology of apartheid offended the emergent international morality of antiracism, could not survive its stigmatic designation as a pariah state. The majority-based successor government employed the Truth and Reconciliation Commission as a key instrument for coming to terms with a racially divided past in the transition to a universal suffrage democracy.

The ideology of national independence that carried the day in overseas colonies against faltering imperial powers inevitably spread in a modified form to systems of internal colonialism in which white settler regimes in Australia, Canada, the United States, New Zealand, Scandinavia, and elsewhere wielded paternal authority over indigenous peoples. Previously, a de facto imperialist international, in which each European empire, simply by its existence, supported the assumption that undergirded the others—that it was right and proper for the few who were white to rule over the many who were not—gave a derivative legitimacy to domestic wardship over indigenous peoples in settler colonies. The collapse of the overseas empire undermined the legitimacy of internal empire. The end of an empire in India and Nigeria meant that internal wardship for Canadian Indians and Australian Aborigines was no longer sustainable.

Yesterday's spirit of the times, which had made racial hierarchies part of the natural order, was replaced by a new *Zeitgeist*. The change in sensibility is neatly captured in Hedley Bull's contrast between the "old Western-dominated international order . . . associated with the privileged position of the white race," and the impact of Third World states that "have overturned the old structure of international law and organization that once served to sanctify their subject status." In the old international order, the "international society of states was at first exclusively, and even in its last days principally, one of white states; non-white peoples everywhere, whether as minority communities within these white states, as majority communities ruled by minorities of whites, or as independent peoples dominated by white powers, suffered the stigma of inferior status." In the postimperial international community, "the equal rights of non-Western states to sovereignty, the rights of non-Western peoples to self-determination, the rights of non-white races to equal treatment, non-Western peoples to economic justice, and non-Western cultures to dignity and autonomy [are embodied] . . . in conventions having the force of law."[17]

The postimperial heterogeneity of the contemporary international society of states, the processes that led to it, and the imperial past from which it is an escape have transformed the moral, intellectual, and legal environment of both global and domestic politics. The imperialist consortium of those who had thought they had a natural entitlement to rule was initially displaced by a Third World majority of ex-colonies in the United Nations General

Assembly, which proceeded to transform the normative order by which the external conduct and domestic behavior of states were judged.

This Third World refashioning of the international order was subsequently reinforced by an indigenous "international" composed of "indigenous peoples [who] occupy an encapsulated status as disempowered and dispersed subjects of a larger political entity."[18] Indigenous peoples, now defined as belonging to a Fourth World, quickly established an international presence, and skillfully wielded the language of anticolonialism to relax the grip of settler majorities over their lives. They confronted settler societies with massive claims for restitution, for the return of dispossessed lands, and for redress in Canada for the efforts at forced assimilation in residential schools.[19] Supplementary redress claims in Canada focus on sexual and physical abuse in residential schools.[20] In Australia widespread adoption into white families was a deliberate instrument of assimilation, for which financial redress is sought.[21]

The collapse and breakdown of empire spread to Yugoslavia and the Soviet Union, followed by the freeing of the former satellite states of East and Central Europe. The latter confronted Tina Rosenberg's "Haunted Land," haunted by the "ghosts of communism,"[22] or by what Vaclav Havel called the "monstrous heritage" of shattered lives and amorality.[23] Finally, in Latin America and the Iberian peninsula, dictatorships and military regimes were replaced by democracies,[24] leaving newly democratic regimes to confront difficult transitions, often in the presence of the still strong military, police, and security forces that had been instruments of oppression and perpetrators of the atrocities of the previous regime.

Nazism, fascism, communism, Japanese militarism, rule by junta, and domestic and overseas imperialism—some of which claimed to have a handle on a predestined future—had all reinforced the idea that millions, in fact hundreds of millions, were properly ruled by others, and in extreme cases were expendable on the road to utopia. That age of racially defined hierarchies of leaders and subjects, of master races and backward peoples, and of vanguard elites and proletarian masses has been succeeded by the age of rights, by the norm of racial equality, and by cultural pluralism.

Millions have emerged from the sidelines of history in which they or their predecessors had been subjects, not citizens; voiceless; treated with contempt; considered unworthy of self-rule; stigmatized; and in some cases slaughtered. Their emergence gives voice to New Zealand Maori, Jews, Korean comfort women, black South Africans, African Americans, relatives of the disappeared in Argentina, and countless others. That many of them would use their newly liberated voices to protest their past maltreatment and to seek apologies and reparations may not have been inevitable, but given the multiple settings in which the collapse of the old order occurred and the contempt from which so many had suffered, a blanket of silence would have been an implausible outcome.

Given the reinforcement of a contagion factor—"This is the way we are now!"—coming to terms with the past has emerged as a major political problem throughout the international community. This global context of a series of rejected and repudiated pasts permeates all the particular settings within which struggles over history have taken place. All the participants know that their struggles are duplicated in countless other settings.

INTRODUCTION TO FOUR CASE STUDIES

One component of coming to terms with the past, the intellectual task previously mentioned, is the scholarly recovery and interpretation of historical facts, including the identification of who did what to whom. Academic research of this nature is not an alternative to apology, compensation, or the punishment of perpetrators. It has its own independent justification. It has the virtue of unexpectedly appearing as a result of the passion of individual scholars impelled by the prosaic, yet noble, goal of finding out what happened.

Three works of private scholarship, to be discussed in the proceeding, are good examples. Their appearance was unpredictable; they were privately undertaken; they were infused with passion; and they add to our understanding. The fourth, a Royal Commission report, differs in origin and style from the three examples of private scholarship, but it, too, was driven by passion and had as one of its goals the transformation of the historical consciousness of Canadians.

The comments on the three books and one Royal Commission report known as the *Report of the Royal Commission on Aboriginal Peoples* (the RCAP *Report*) that follow do not imply that they are the last words on their subject. There is never a last word on megadeaths, on mass cruelties, or on brutal insensitivities and their perpetrators. They are, however, serious public attempts to come to terms with particular pasts. They deserve our attention not because they are unique—other equally instructive choices could have been made—or because their analysis is unquestionably the best available (we lack consensus on this), but because they provide lessons in the contributions of scholarship and research to our collective self-understanding. That the three books were written by individuals—six authors for *The Black Book*—is a reassuring reminder that the scholarly role is not incompatible with passionate engagement with profound moral issues that challenge our humanity.

Neither do the four snapshots that follow deal with comprehensive attempts to come to terms with particular pasts—which would have to include other scholarly contributions; the behavior of governments; the political mobilization of victims; the psychological world of the accused, past or present; and other phenomena essential to a rounded analysis. Rather, they are episodes in which a book, or in the Canadian case, a royal commission *Report* is the vehicle or instrument for an intellectual coming to terms with the past.

DANIEL GOLDHAGEN'S *HITLER'S WILLING EXECUTIONERS: ORDINARY GERMANS AND THE HOLOCAUST* (1996)

Daniel Goldhagen, the American son of a Holocaust survivor, received a Harvard Ph.D. in 1993. The published English version of his revised thesis, which focused on the Holocaust—"the most shocking event of the twentieth century"[25]—received very negative reviews from German scholars.[26] The book was subsequently translated into German, which led to a tour of German cities involving five panel discussions and one television debate with German specialists on the subject.

The tour generated immense crowds. There were twenty-four hundred people in the audience in the Munich Philharmonic Hall, and it was stated that the Olympic stadium could have been filled. The discussion tour was a "triumphal procession" for Goldhagen. He and his book met with "overwhelming public sympathy" in Germany, despite its message, which was a "damning argument regarding Germans and the darkest parts of their cultural heritage."[27] Both the English and German versions generated an extraordinary, long-lasting and passionate debate in the German press, including a lengthy response from Goldhagen.[28]

Goldhagen's thesis was that "ordinary Germans" undertook the task of killing Jews with enthusiasm and sadistic brutality. They believed in the rightness of their actions. They mocked their victims and engaged in excessive brutality. They were influenced, he argued, by an "eliminationist anti-semitism."[29] They were, however, not puppets. The "perpetrators," he insisted, "lived in a moral world of contemplation, discussion, and argument."[30] They could have refused to kill.[31] The killings of men, women, children, the sick, and the healthy were often face-to-face. They were neither mediated by bureaucratic distance nor undertaken by faceless Eichmanns signing orders. These ordinary Germans were "Hitler's willing executioners." Goldhagen received the Democracy Prize of the *Blätter für deutsche und internationale Politik* (*Journal of German and International Politics*) for his book. The speech honoring Goldhagen at the awards ceremony was delivered by Jürgen Habermas, probably the most influential German social theorist of the post–World War II era. In an elaborate eulogy, delivered in full awareness that the Goldhagen thesis had been sharply criticized by German specialists, Habermas thanked and congratulated Goldhagen for providing "a powerful stimulus to the public conscience of the Federal Republic."[32]

Goldhagen was not a lonely outsider seeking to break down a wall of indifference or denial. His book and lecture tour followed a major historians' debate in the mid-1980s about the meaning of and responsibility for the Holocaust, analyzed in Charles Maier's *The Unmasterable Past*.[33] His and the book's reception, including the initial personal criticisms, the critiques by German historians, and the subsequent public accolades, simply confirmed the seriousness with which the German public, the German government, and the academic community after an initial postwar hiatus have confronted the German past in the Nazi period.

Although Goldhagen congratulated Germany as "the country that has succeeded best at dealing honestly with the least savory part of its past,"[34] it nevertheless would have been astonishing if the debate with its attendant passions had not occurred. Goldhagen was attacking the work of serious German scholars. He was young. He was American. He wrote as a social scientist, while most of the German contributors to Holocaust understanding were historians. He explicitly accused German scholarship of evading what he saw as a central question: What "induced ordinary Germans to kill unarmed, defenseless Jewish men, women, and children by the thousands, systematically and without pity"?[35] He implied that as a non-German he could address issues that German scholars avoided. Finally, his book dealt with tortured issues of German identity and its relation to a shameful past. Habermas was right in suggesting that Goldhagen made a significant contribution to perhaps the most difficult issue to confront Germans since World War II.

IRIS CHANG'S *THE RAPE OF NANKING: THE FORGOTTEN HOLOCAUST OF WORLD WAR II* (1997)

Daqing Yang puts *The Rape of Nanking* into context in the matter-of-fact statement that the controversy over Nanking, now entering its fourth decade, "has become one of the longest-running historical controversies in East Asia."[36] Chang, whose grandparents miraculously escaped from Nanking as Japanese soldiers were arriving and whose parents fled China after World War II and ultimately ended up in the United States, wrote *The Rape of Nanking* because to have such a carnage neglected and forgotten appalled her. She was terrified that those whose lives had been taken from them might also be deprived of the posthumous recognition of their cruel fate[37] and that

Nanking might remain the "Forgotten Holocaust." The frequent denial that the massacre ever happened, the trivialization of the number killed, and, in general, what she saw as "the deliberate attempt . . . to distort history most . . . strongly confirmed in me the need for this book."[38]

Her book is a testament to remembering and a recovery of the past. In addition to massive sales and multiple translations, the author was active on the scholarly conference circuit and on book-signing tours. The book delivers an almost unbearable narrative and analysis of the Japanese occupation of Nanking, China, in December 1937. Massive killings of a variously estimated 260,000 to more than 350,000 noncombatants[39] and the rape of 20,000 to 80,000[40] were described in scenes of brutality straight out of Breughel, what the author calls "an orgy of cruelty seldom if ever matched in world history."[41] This was a *"public* rampage . . . in full view of international observers."[42] The death toll in six weeks of uncontrolled savagery surpassed the combined death toll of Hiroshima and Nagasaki.[43]

Yet attempts to get a Japanese translation of *The Rape of Nanking* have foundered. The official Japanese admission of responsibility has been guarded and oblique. The military reaction at the time to the orgy of rape, which it was feared would sully Japan's reputation, was the establishment of military brothels staffed with "comfort women." About two hundred thousand women, mainly from Korea, were removed from their homes and subsequently organized into military brothels. About three-quarters of these women died as a result of their forced sexual exploitation.[44] Until a decade ago, the Japanese government claimed the women were volunteer camp followers recruited by private enterprise. This explanation collapsed when archival material discovered in 1991 confirmed that the army set up the brothels.

The symbolism of Hiroshima and Nagasaki[45] and a tightly controlled education system[46] contribute to the self-definition of many Japanese as victims of World War II, not as perpetrators of atrocities. International politics also enters into the silence. Neither the People's Republic of China (PRC) after the Communist victory nor the government of Taiwan insisted on reparations, fearing that to do so would damage their trade relations with, and undermine their desire for political recognition from, Japan. According to Joshua Fogel, the PRC government strategically exploits the atrocity to extract benefits from Japan.[47] The Cold War inhibited the United States from pursuing the issue with the Japanese government.[48]

The amnesia within Japan is not monolithic. There are numerous courageous exceptions, including the occasional veteran, although they sometimes pay a heavy price in death threats, intimidation, and even attempted assassination.[49] The Japanese left frequently raises the issue of Japan's war guilt. Also, Japanese scholarship exposing Nanking is not as miniscule or nonexistent as Chang suggests.[50] On the whole, however, the contrast with Germany remains profound.[51] There is no Japanese equivalent to the very public German debate about the Holocaust, in which the starting point is that the Holocaust happened. By contrast, in Japan, in spite of many scholarly Japanese accounts of Nanking by "progressives," they have not vanquished the "revisionists," who deny or explain it away. The revisionists are more concerned with reinforcing national pride than with respect for historical scholarship that sullies the reputation of the Japanese people.[52]

Iris Chang could not conceivably have had the kind of tour and reception that Goldhagen received in Germany. Within Japan, the Nanking events are still contested. In January 2000, a right-wing Japanese conference took place on the theme "The Verification of the Rape of Nanjing: The Biggest Lie of the Twentieth Century."[53]

The Japanese case is an extraordinary example of forgetting, suppression, or denial by significant and influential groups in the population, given the fact that fifty thousand Japanese soldiers were obviously eyewitnesses of their own behavior. The Japanese press at the time reported the killings,[54] and the documentary evidence is massive and irrefutable. More generally, John W. Dower suggests that millions of servicemen had at least heard of or seen brutal atrocities by the imperial army.[55] Furthermore, in his prize-winning book *Embracing Defeat*, Dower points out that by 1946, as a flood of returning soldiers arrived, Japanese at home "were already . . . exposed to a steady flow of information concerning the shocking range of atrocities committed by the imperial forces in China, Southeast Asia, and the Philippines, as well as against Allied prisoners generally."[56]

Whatever the explanation that can be offered—cultural, political, the shock of defeat—for the facts that Nanking is still contested in Japan, that the responsibility of the military for organizing brothels of comfort women was officially denied for half a century, and that government apologies have been oblique and low key—the reputation of Japan has suffered.

STÉPHANE COURTOIS ET AL., *THE BLACK BOOK OF COMMUNISM* (1999; ORIG. FRENCH, 1997)

"Communism has been the great story of the twentieth century."[57] Making sense of this "'tragedy of planetary dimensions,' the most colossal case of political carnage in history"[58] will be one of the major intellectual tasks of the twenty-first century. The authors of *The Black Book* were motivated by the fact that the crimes of Communism were underresearched compared to Nazi crimes.[59] There is no overall equivalent to the Nuremberg or Tokyo war crimes tribunals. In contrast to ex-Nazis, there is little or no stigma in being an ex-Communist. Hardly any of the responsible officials have been punished. And, of course, there are still Communist regimes in power.

The book's purpose was to serve as a memorial. "There is a moral obligation to honor the memory of the innocent and anonymous victims of a [Communist] juggernaut that has systematically sought to erase even their memory."[60] The contributors are ex-Communists or former fellow travelers.[61] As they look back, they encounter not only Lenin and Stalin, but their former selves as well. As the lead author reports, "Some of the contributors to this book were not always strangers to the fascinations of Communism."[62] Their self-assigned task is to present "a balance sheet of . . . Communism's human costs" based on the best evidence available.[63]

The time is appropriate for such an undertaking for, even admitting the continuing presence of nominally Communist regimes in China, North Korea, and Cuba, Communism has become yesterday's experiment. It now has a beginning, a middle, and an end. Since its justification always resided in the future it was to achieve, and that future has vanished, Furet argues that "Communism is completely contained within its past."[64] It ended, he suggests, "in a sort of nothingness."[65]

The Black Book covers all countries that have experienced Communist rule since the 1917 October revolution. At its high point, Communist governments ruled one-third of humankind on four continents. The diligent reader is "rewarded" with a veritable catalog of cruelty, prison camps, random terror, incompetent policies, and massive death tolls attributed to the major actors—Russia and China—and to such lesser examples as Bulgaria, Ethiopia, North Korea, and Cambodia. The latter make their own contribution to our understanding with the reminder that Communism was a species of globalization, able to implant itself in diverse national settings whenever a messianic elite could seize power and employ the coercive state apparatus to sustain it.

Cambodia, albeit a short-lived player in the annals of Communism, serves as a revealing example of a dystopia. A figure of two million dead, albeit followed by a question mark, is the estimated toll for Cambodia of the bizarre policies of Pol Pot and the Kampuchean Communist Party.[66] The attempt to "implement total Communism in one fell swoop"[67] carried the faith in human engineering to new heights of folly and tragedy. At a minimum, one in seven or more plausibly one in four or five of the population died.[68]

The significant role of the Communist Party in French politics has made any analysis of the Soviet, or more broadly Communist, record a deeply divisive issue in France. Communism captured the enthusiasm and support of much of the intellectual classes in the West, nowhere more so than in France. No Soviet atrocities, from labor camps to purges, were without intellectual defenders in the West. No illusion, such as the humanity of Stalin, was too difficult for a cadre of Western intellectuals to imbibe.

In the early fifties, Jean-Paul Sartre could find no "evidence of an aggressive impulse on the part of the Russians in the last three decades"[69] and claimed that Soviet citizens were completely free to criticize the system, and did so "more frequently and more effectively than us."[70] Tony Judt argued with an abundance of evidence that French intellectuals in support of Communism could only be explained by a "will to ignorance," an unquenchable "desire to believe well of a system that daily provided you with nothing but evidence against itself."[71]

The Black Book also generated controversy by overtly comparing Nazism and Communism, not to the advantage of the latter, with a death toll three to four times greater than the 25 million death toll of Nazism. This comparison inflamed various sensitivities by appearing to devalue the claimed unique and ineffable horror of the Nazi genocide of Jews. The debate even divided the authors of the book, with the authors of the chapters on Russia and China disassociating themselves from several of Courtois' "bolder conclusions."[72]

The Black Book confirms the analysis/confession of the authors of *The God That Failed* (1949). That book's authors, Arthur Koestler, Richard Wright, Andre Gide, and three others, reported their loss of faith while Communism was still a going concern and before Khrushchev's "secret" speech of 1956 on the crimes of Stalin to the Twentieth Party Congress.[73] That speech may be, as Furet suggests, "the twentieth century's most important text in the history of Communism,"[74] and it was a major contributor to the erosion of faith in the Communist idea. *The Black Book*, one might say, finishes the job.

Individual confessions by contemporary Koestlers would be redundant now that the Communist record is on public display. The overall death toll of the Communist experiments for the future is estimated at 85 million to 100 million.[75] Official sources admit a death toll of 20 million in the "Great Leap Forward" in China (1959–1961)[76] that precipitated the "most murderous famine of all time, anywhere in the world."[77] Other estimates range up to 43 million.[78] Tiananmen Square, where about 1,000 died, was almost trivial by comparison.

As the book's message sank in with the French public, "an apparently dry academic work became a publishing sensation, the focus of impassioned political and intellectual debate,"[79] and a best-seller. As was true of *Hitler's Willing Executioners* and *The Rape of Nanking*, *The Black Book* describes scene after scene of extravagant cruelties and humiliations almost lustfully inflicted on helpless victims.

The book is written as a memorial to millions of victims. Its political purpose is not to confront a state with its crimes, as in Japan and Germany, but to confront a once potent ideology and its believers, which at one time included a significant portion of the intellectual community of the West, with the consequences of their belief. The book is aimed in part at Western intellectuals who persisted in defiantly misunderstanding the Soviet system up until the very end. They were a goodly number. Furet, who was himself once a believer, suggests that "if we were to put together all the famous European authors who, at one time or another during the twentieth century, were Communists or pro-Communists, we could constitute a Who's Who of philosophy and literature."[80]

Courtois argues that these duped or deluded intellectuals "should be held accountable as accomplices in the bloody politics of the purges."[81] In *Political Pilgrims*, Paul Hollander presents the views of credulous Western intellectuals on Soviet Communism, including such luminaries as George Bernard Shaw, Beatrice and Sidney James Webb, Sartre, Edmund Wilson, and numerous others. Even the purge trials of the 1930s, which led to the liquidation of approximately 690,000 people,[82] were positively assessed by a cadre of Western intellectuals.[83] As Hollander observes, "the credulousness of Western intellectuals . . . remains somewhat daunting," even when all the contextual factors are considered.[84] For example, at the time of widespread famine in the Soviet Union in 1931, Shaw saw "no evidence of food shortages in . . . the first class restaurant . . . his considerate hosts" took him to.[85] Fifty years later, the Reverend Dr. Billy Graham saw "no evidence of religious repression,"[86] as his hosts kept him away from Baptists in prison camps.

The gullibility of Western intellectuals over the Soviet system was duplicated for China, as Simon Leys shows in *Chinese Shadows*.[87] In both China and Russia that gullibility was skillfully manipulated by varying versions of Potemkin villages—show pieces, false fronts, and facades as instruments of deception. Hollander, whose *Political Pilgrims* is subtitled "Travels of Western Intellectuals to the Soviet Union, China, and Cuba," described the book's contents as "an inquiry into half a century of political daydreaming."[88] *The Black Book* and Hollander remind us that coming to terms with the past involves more than governments. It also includes explaining and judging the past role of intellectuals in providing support for regimes whose atrocities reveal an inhumanity of staggering proportions.

REPORT OF THE ROYAL COMMISSION ON ABORIGINAL PEOPLES (1996)

Report of the Royal Commission on Aboriginal Peoples[89] (RCAP *Report*) is the Canadian example of public introspection, duplicated elsewhere,[90] over the past treatment of minority indigenous populations in settler countries and of the search for a new social contract.

The five volumes and over thirty-five hundred pages of the RCAP *Report* were based on extensive public hearings and on probably the most elaborate research program ever undertaken concerning the relations between indigenous peoples and a majority settler society. Four of the seven commissioners were Aboriginal, including the co-chair, Georges Erasmus, and the RCAP

Report was clearly written from an Aboriginal perspective. Although the RCAP *Report* focused on Aboriginal peoples in Canada and its commissioning and publication responded to Canadian realities, it should also be seen as the Canadian component of the politicization of indigenous peoples in the Fourth World reacting against systems of internal colonialism. While the 800,000 self-identifying Aboriginal peoples in Canada are only a fraction of 1 percent of the global total of some 300 million indigenous peoples,[91] the Canadian example reveals the themes and rhetoric common to indigenous people elsewhere, who have been equally marginalized, dispossessed, and treated with contempt.

Historically, the external world of European empire up until the middle of the twentieth century sustained a view of the relations between peoples that justified treating Indians, the only Aboriginal people singled out for special legislative treatment in Canada, as wards. Conversely, the end of empire knocked out the props that had sustained the marginalization of minority indigenous peoples in settler societies. The RCAP *Report*, accordingly, is a document of anti-colonialism that is, among other things, a major attempt to revise and challenge dominant views of the Canadian past.

The *Report* in a way is a Canadian version of a truth commission, calling the non-Aboriginal majority to account. The first volume, which is devoted to history from an Aboriginal perspective, presents a litany of abuses, coercions, and insensitivities. Four categories of mistreatment are highlighted— the physical and sexual abuse in residential schools and the assimilation goals they pursued; the inequitable treatment of Aboriginal veterans of both world wars; the forced relocations of Aboriginal communities that often led to disastrous results; and the cultural aggression of the Indian Act, which banned certain cherished customs and provided the legislative framework for a system of internal colonialism. These, however, are little more than supporting evidence for a larger portrayal of the stigmatization of a people and of the policies that presupposed cultural backwardness, which assumed an incapacity for self-rule and which were aimed at a future goal of assimilation when Aboriginality would be but a memory.

Overall, the RCAP *Report* portrays a cultural assault on Aboriginal peoples, especially status Indians,[92] by the Canadian state. To read the relevant historical chapters is to be taken on an emotionally wrenching journey through a past that is a historical storehouse of mistreatment, deception, arrogance, dispossession, coercion, and abuses of power by governments acting on behalf of the majority society. The RCAP *Report* singles out for denunciation the Indian Affairs Branch's mismanagement and irresponsible paternalism, which belied the government's trusteeship responsibility for its wards. The chapter on "Relocation of Aboriginal Communities" concludes that "some past grievances are too great to ignore,"[93] a conclusion difficult to challenge.

Canadian history is broken down into three contact stages, "Contact and Co-operation"; "Displacement and Assimilation"; and the contemporary period, "Negotiation and Renewal," all of which follow the precontact setting of "Separate Worlds." "Displacement and Assimilation" documents the relegation of Aboriginal peoples to the sidelines. In numerous areas, the *Report* describes the non-Aboriginal majority, by its disregard and self-centeredness, inflicting both deliberate and accidental harm on Aboriginal peoples; acting as masters; disrupting Aboriginal, especially Indian, ways of life; and ignoring their wishes—on the grounds that wards are properly subject to the benevolent rule of those who are in charge. Rights that Indian peoples thought were protected by treaties were ignored or trivialized, and reserve lands were reduced to the benefit of the settler majority.

The authors of the RCAP *Report* share with Goldhagen, Chang, and the multiple contributors to *The Black Book* a desire to get certain historical facts on record, and in effect to write history from below—from the perspective of the subjugated and maltreated. They all agree that one component of coming to terms with the past is a revised understanding of what happened in the past. Unlike the other books discussed previously, however, the RCAP *Report* was also designed to be a major state paper to facilitate the harmonious co-existence of Aboriginal and non-Aboriginal peoples in a revised Canada based on a multinational vision.

The RCAP *Report* was policy driven. It argued for a public apology as part of a new Royal Proclamation leading to reconciliation and rapprochement based on a "great cleansing of the wounds of the past."[94] The need for healing is a recurrent theme.[95]

The documentation of past abuses of power and the demands for redress and apology to which they led did not exhaust the uses of the past. History was also a vehicle to describe a golden age in the early contact years when relations were nation to nation, and treaties were the instruments to regulate the relationship. The RCAP *Report*'s constitutional vision for the future was to return to a contemporary version of that relationship embodied in a future multinational Canada.

In that new arrangement, the Canadian nation or the non-Aboriginal nation—the *Report* was not clear on the distinction between the two—was to provide massive support for several decades to build sixty to eighty Aboriginal nations. One of the major justifications for the proposed breakthrough to a better future was the "ethical responsibility of the majority society and its governments to redress past injustices."[96] The RCAP *Report* is the major presentation from an Aboriginal perspective since Confederation in 1867. Its overriding theme is an extended plea for the majority society and its governments to come to terms with the past.

These four case studies of Germany and the Holocaust, Japan and the Nanking massacre, the destructive consequences of political rule informed by communist theory, and Canada and its treatment of Aboriginal peoples all appeared within a few years of each other. The authors want cruelties and barbarities recalled and recorded. They give voice to the formerly voiceless and to the dead. Their simultaneous emergence responds to and reflects a contemporary climate of opinion that puts the past on trial.

CONCLUSION: HOW ARE WE TO THINK OF IT ALL?

Coming to terms with the past is usually understood as applying to particular countries grappling with individual pasts: appropriately so, because our pasts are primarily national pasts, and the perpetrators of what we now see as injustice are normally past or present state actors. Thus, individual states are typically called on to apologize and to pay reparations. The search for a political resolution of most of the issues concerned with coming to terms with the past takes place within individual states (although international tribunals are increasingly active), even if the victims are elsewhere.

Habermas points out that Goldhagen did not provide explanations of German behavior in terms of universals or regularities. Rather, he wrote of a particular cultural context, of "very specific traditions and mentalities."[97] His explanation, therefore, is appropriately specific. He sought to explain why Germans did what they did, which then provides German citizens and governments with the opportunity to learn from the catastrophe, to take remedial action to prevent a recurrence, and to undertake appropriate forms of apology and redress.[98] Goldhagen's answer to those who asked why he wrote *Hitler's Willing Executioners* is appealing in its simplicity. "The twofold answer is simple: To improve knowledge of the past by providing a true account and the best interpretation of the Holocaust and of the people who perpetrated it of which I am capable. To allow all people who wish to do so to derive meaning from the past by affording them the opportunity to confront this knowledge openly and honestly."[99] The "passion of his inquiry," focusing on the role of ordinary Germans in the Holocaust, explains the remarkable resonance of his work for German audiences.[100]

Iris Chang tried to do the same for the Japanese, without, however, achieving a similar resonance with Japanese audiences. Other authors who seek to hold the wounds of apartheid up to the light and explain how such a system came to be in South Africa or to explain and criticize the survival of Jim Crow race relations in the United States as Gunnar Myrdal did in *An American Dilemma*[101] are attempts to engage the consciences of their readers with uncomfortable facts. These particular explanations, always presented with moral fervor, are essential contributions to all versions of coming to terms that are specific to a particular country.

However, as particular explanations multiply as to why this people, or that people, or yet another people almost appear to have engaged in a competition to be in the top ranks of perpetrators of cruelty, a larger and troubling message comes through. If so many people in so many different countries could engage in abhorrent practices, then so could we. None of us has a guaranteed immunity against a collective breakdown in morality, a point strongly made by Iris Chang.[102] We are all subject to the spirit of our times and of our country, albeit not total prisoners of it. Civility is always fragile, and in the right circumstances, it will bend and shatter. Opportunists and collaborators are ubiquitous, even for the most tyrannical regime. All Czechs, argued Vaclav Havel, were at least mildly complicit in the former Communist regime, if only as the price of getting along.[103]

There is, therefore, in addition to particular explanations of the behavior of a particular people and its government and its particular victims, a more abstract or universal level, tied to no country, where humankind—bearing all the wounds inflicted in a ravaged century on millions of victims—is seen, as it were, from a mountaintop. From this vantage point, where national distinctions have faded, we do not see the corruption of the Czech character of which Havel speaks, or the German perpetrators of the Holocaust, or the Japanese rape of Nanking, or the Soviet engineers of the Gulag archipelago, or the Canadian or Australian formulators of the Aboriginal policies of settler states that suppressed indigenous cultures. We see instead the human condition, independent of national context, in the light of what we now know. We can only sadly agree with Takashi Yoshida that "the obvious lesson of the [Nanjing] Massacre, and the Holocaust [is] . . . that no part of humanity is immune to such pathological violence."[104] Mark Eykholt concurs with his admission that "inhuman behavior and advanced civilization are not exclusive categories."[105] We look back on authors from earlier eras who saw the history of particular countries or of humanity as a progressive ascent, and we recognize sadly that their confident voices speak to us from an earlier world of innocence that we can scarcely fathom. That world is gone.

We are differently circumstanced. Master narratives of progress are now on the shelves. We look back with uneasiness and ahead without confidence. Some of the voices we hear are those of victims—voices that formerly were silenced by the juggernauts of those who were in control. We speak and listen out of a different sensibility. We are children of a different spirit of the times—in our definitions of acceptable and unacceptable behavior and in the values we bring to our judgments. We understand why it is now easier to construct dystopias than utopias. We look back on atrocities we can scarcely comprehend. And then we realize with regret that Hitler's willing executioners were ordinary men, as well as being Goldhagen's ordinary Germans, and that the Japanese soldiers who ran amok in Nanking were also standard human beings, as were all the other violators of human dignity, and also all the victims. The legacy of the twentieth century with which we all must come to terms is that while it may have been some "they" who did "it," "they" are part of "us."

Coming to terms with the past means trying to confront the past with honesty and integrity. Typically, this means seeing history from below as a corrective supplement to elite versions. This means recognizing and inserting the voiceless and the forgotten into history. It nearly always means recognizing that the realities of the past and in most cases our interpretation of them were biased in favor of those who were in charge—governments—and, in democratic societies, the majorities they represented. For example, until the recent explosion of abuse cases in the courts and books, especially *A National Crime* by John S. Milloy,[106] the official image of residential schools in Canada was benign. There was, so to speak, an official party line assiduously promoted by governments and the churches responsible for running the schools, which portrayed a benevolent paternalism in the service of uplift. The reality of underfunding, of sexual and physical abuse, and of what was experienced by many students as a cultural assault was kept from public view by the marginalization of Aboriginal peoples.

Martin Malia employs the helpful phrase "retrospective affirmative action . . . fulfilling our 'duty of remembrance' to all the oppressed of the past"[107] to describe the responsibility of scholars. Our obligation is to do on a grander scale, especially for those who can speak no more, what Victor Klemperer, a German Jew and a professor of literature, did for himself and for posterity in *I Will Bear Witness, 1933–1941: A Diary of the Nazi Years*.[108] Saved from the concentration camps because his wife was a Protestant, his diary of daily life in the Third Reich as a Jew was faithful to Leopold von Ranke's instruction to historians to tell it as it really was. If we try to do likewise, we give at least limited recognition to the legions of the dead whose lives were so easily disposed of in the service of someone else's ideology or fantasy.

Iris Chang was bearing witness, as was Daniel Goldhagen. Chang's book "started out as an attempt to rescue [the] victims from more degradation by Japanese revisionists and to provide my own epitaph for the hundreds upon thousands of unmarked graves in Nanking."[109] As Goldhagen notes, this approach requires us not to reduce the slaughtered to mere numbers, not to depersonalize the dead behind the statistical precision of four hundred killed here, ten thousand murdered elsewhere, but always to remember that "to the killers whom they faced, the Jews were people who were breathing one moment and lying lifeless, often before them, the next."[110] To remind ourselves of the latter—that it was ten thousand individual lives that were ended in all their variety of young, old, male, female, healthy, sick, the terrified, and the defiant—is a moral obligation.

The RCAP *Report* was an official version of bearing witness, given the special mantle of legitimacy that attaches to a Royal Commission, a legitimacy that was reinforced by the extensive quotations from the massive public hearings it held. *The Black Book of Communism* was also bearing witness with its scholarship. "The historian," states Courtois, "can speak on behalf of those who have had their voices silenced as a result of terror."[111] When asked why we should study the history of yesterday's actually existing Communism, Courtois speaks of "our sense of duty to history. A good historian leaves no stone unturned. [Nothing] . . . should hinder the historian from engaging in the quest for knowledge, the unearthing and interpretation of facts, especially when those facts have been long and deliberately buried in the immense recesses of government archives and the conscience of the people."[112]

A phrase that I find helpful is "democratizing the past." We cannot, of course, restore actual democracy to particular pasts in which it was glaringly absent for all or a portion of society. We can, however, try to give a democracy of equal recognition to the marginalized or victimized of the past. Although scanty records and shortened lives may preclude much of the detail more abundantly present for the wealthy and powerful, we can show them a concern they did not get from their contemporaries. We can give to those whose human dignity was routinely disregarded, too often to the point of rape, torture, and massacre, the tribute of significant and sympathetic inclusion in our historical accounts, and we can provide the best explanation we can offer of how they came to be victims.

Democratizing the past means challenging official party lines that ignore or explain away or trivialize mass cruelties. This role might be likened to an academic Amnesty International. Scholars from outside have a particularly crucial role in documenting, analyzing, and recording oppression, especially by surviving totalitarian governments for whom democratizing their recent past by their own scholars would not go unpunished. Martin Malia argues that the intellectual poverty and distortions of scholarship in the Soviet era mean that contemporary Russian scholarship is heavily dependent on previous Western scholarship to understand the former Soviet system.[113] In the succinct observation of one of Tina Rosenberg's informants: "Under communism . . . the future was certain; it was the past no one could be sure of."[114]

Totalitarian governments systematically seek to deprive their citizens of their memories, and work hard, by information control and disinformation, to keep researchers at bay. "What is horrifying in totalitarian regimes is . . . that there might remain nobody who could ever again properly bear witness to the past."[115] In such circumstances, outside scholars have a freedom that domestic scholars lack. Their studies may build up an intellectual capital that will be immensely valuable should the controls be relaxed, and peoples emerging into freedom wish to know where they have been.

The task of the outside scholar does not end with the emergence of democracy. Goldhagen attributes the basic integrity of domestic German scholarship on that country's past to the watchful eye of the international community and to the contributions of scholars outside Germany. This, he argues, has made it impossible for German scholars to write a "sanitized . . . history."[116] He goes as far as to argue that "all national histories should be internationalized,"[117] the rationale being that national histories are prone to self-flattery and taboos that a foreign scholar can more easily ignore.

In his recent book on French intellectuals in postwar France, Tony Judt also notes an advantage that accompanies outsider status: "A foreigner may . . . be predisposed to raise matters that would not immediately concern a French scholar," for example, citing his own research, the remarkable fact that the modern French philosophical tradition has minimal "concern with public ethics or political morality."[118] The advantage of being a scholar from far away, one not caught up in the conventional paradigms of the domestic society, inspired the Carnegie Corporation to select a Swedish social scientist, Gunnar Myrdal, to take charge of the research that led to the classic study *An American Dilemma.*

More generally, in a brilliant article written more than thirty years ago, the sociologist Robert K. Merton asserted the virtue of having both insiders and outsiders—although he admitted the ambiguity of both terms—employing their respective skills in the analysis of society. They complemented each other precisely because they commenced their inquiries from different vantage points.[119] Merton's rationale for the outsider role is especially pertinent for societies with limited intellectual autonomy for domestic (insider) scholars who are subject to taboos that put deeply divisive subjects or the major moral failures of previous generations off limits.

Yesterday's narratives of empire, of vanguard civilizations, of the white man's burden, of master races, of a Third Reich that was to last a thousand years, of a steady progression to the classless Communist future, and of the paternal exercise of a necessary wardship over indigenous peoples have one thing in common—they all lie in ruins.

The surviving subjects, the no longer voiceless, or successor generations in these grand visions and ruling ideologies have now emerged from the imperial and other closets in which they were hidden. Their emergence from the shadows comes with a desire to refashion the past—to have their stories included—sad, short, and unhappy as they often were. The recognition that they seek includes recognition of their suffering or that of previous generations. That recognition in itself is a component of justice. And furthermore, if we can explain why they were deprived of human dignity, their culture viewed as a dead end, or their lives treated as expendable, we will have provided a modicum of retrospective dignity to their lives and fates.

A comprehensive coming to terms with the past obviously requires much more than the writing of books or Royal Commission reports. It requires the active engagement of the powerful and the influential in apology and restitution and, where appropriate, punishment of the perpetrators if they are still alive, and much more, including the moral education of their own society. The focus of this chapter on the role of academics, on research, and on revising our understanding of what happened is not intended to mean that nothing more is required. However, without historical understanding informed by rigor and sensitivity, there is no past for us to come to terms with.

This does not mean that the powerful and the influential should not be studied, that our attitudes to the past should be monopolized by the unmarked graves of nameless victims, or that we should write as if the past contained nothing of which we should be proud. The world is too complicated to be classified in the simplified dichotomy of victims and oppressors. What we should aim for is a rounded portrait that includes the lives of those who held the command posts in societies where major oppression occurred as well as those who were victims.

We have made a beginning in coming to terms with the past—imperfect and compromised as it too often is. We have made some progress—both intellectual and political. This is an occasion for modest self-satisfaction.

NOTES

An early version of this lecture was delivered as the Walter S. Owen Lecture on March 23, 2000, in the Faculty of Law, University of British Columbia. Walter S. Owen was a prominent Vancouver lawyer, businessman, and philanthropist. His many honors and recognitions included president of the Canadian Bar Association (1958–1959), and lieutenant governor of British Columbia (1973–1978). Given his extensive interest and involvement in public policy issues, "Coming to Terms with the Past" seemed to be an appropriate way to honor his memory.

1. Robert Fulford, *The Triumph of Narrative: Storytelling in the Age of Mass Culture* (Toronto, Canada: House of Anansi Press, 1999), 48–49.

2. Cited in Eric Hobsbawm, *The Age of Extremes: A History of the World, 1914–1991* (New York: Vintage Books, 1996), 2.

3. Stéphane Courtois, "Introduction," in Stéphane Courtois et al., *The Black Book of Communism: Crimes, Terror, Repression*, trans. Jonathan Murphy and Mark Kramer (Cambridge, Mass.: Harvard University Press, 1999), 1.

4. Cited in Courtois, "Conclusion," in Courtois et al., *The Black Book*, 756.

5. François Furet, *The Passing of an Illusion: The Idea of Communism in the Twentieth Century* (Chicago: University of Chicago Press, 1999), 20.

6. Robert Conquest, *Reflections on a Ravaged Century* (New York: Norton, 2000).

7. Jürgen Habermas, *The Postnational Constellation: Political Essays* (Cambridge, U.K.: Polity Press, 2001), 45–48.

8. Courtois, "Introduction" in Courtois et al., *The Black Book*, 1.

9. International Theological Commission, *Memory and Reconciliation: The*

Church and the Faults of the Past (December 1999), at www.vatican.va/roman_curia/congregations/cfaith/cti_documents/rc_conc faith_doc_20000307_memory-reconcitc_en.html (accessed September 14, 2000).

10. For an incisive analysis of the Canadian case, see Matt James, "Redress Politics and Canadian Citizenship," in *Canada: The State of the Federation 1998/99: How Canadians Connect,* ed. Harvey Lazar and Tom McIntosh (Montreal, Canada: McGill-Queen's University Press, 1999), 247–81.

11. Timothy Garton Ash, *History of the Present: Essays, Sketches and Dispatches from Europe in the 1990s* (London, U.K.: Allen Lane, 1999), 294.

12. John Torpey, "The Past as Political Project," *Comparative and Historical Sociology, Newsletter of the ASA Comparative and Historical Sociology Section* 12, no. 2 (Spring 2000), 1.

13. Cited in Hobsbawm, *Age of Extremes,* 1.

14. Hobsbawm, *Age of Extremes,* 5.

15. Daniel Jonah Goldhagen, "Modell Bundesrepublik: National History, Democracy, and Internationalization in Germany," in *Unwilling Germans? The Goldhagen Debate,* ed. Robert R. Shandley (Minneapolis: University of Minnesota Press, 1998), 275.

16. V. G. Kiernan, *The Lords of Human Kind: European Attitudes to the Outside World in the Imperial Age* (Harmondsworth, U.K.: Penguin Books, 1972).

17. Hedley Bull, "The Revolt against the West," in *The Expansion of International Society,* ed. Hedley Bull and Adam Watson (Oxford, U.K.: Clarendon Press, 1985), 221, 227.

18. Augie Fleras and Roger Maaka, "Reconstitutionalizing Indigeneity: Restoring the Sovereigns Within," *Canadian Review of Studies in Nationalism* 27, no. 1–2 (2000): 114.

19. See John S. Milloy, *A National Crime: The Canadian Government and the Residential School System, 1879 to 1986* (Winnipeg, Canada: University of Manitoba Press, 1999), and J. R. Miller, *Shingwauk's Vision: A History of Native Residential Schools* (Toronto, Canada: University of Toronto Press, 1996).

20. See Milloy, *A National Crime,* and Miller, *Shingwauk's Vision.*

21. Peter Read, *A Rape of the Soul So Profound* (St. Leonards, NSW, Australia: Allen and Unwin, 1999).

22. Tina Rosenberg, *The Haunted Land: Facing Europe's Ghosts after Communism* (New York: Random House, 1995).

23. Cited in Karel Bartošek, "Central and Southeastern Europe," in Courtois et al., *The Black Book,* 451.

24. Rosenberg, *The Haunted Land,* xix.

25. Daniel Jonah Goldhagen, *Hitler's Willing Executioners: Ordinary Germans and the Holocaust* (New York: Knopf, 1996), 4.

26. Goldhagen, *Hitler's Willing Executioners,* 463; Robert R. Shandley, introduction to *Unwilling Germans?* ed. Shandley, 4–9, 13. See also the contributions to Geoff Eley, ed., *The "Goldhagen Effect": History, Memory, Nazism—Facing the German Past* (Ann Arbor: University of Michigan Press, 2000) for criticisms of Goldhagen's scholarship by American scholars.

27. Shandley, introduction to *Unwilling Germans?* 19.

28. Goldhagen, "The Failure of the Critics," in *Unwilling Germans?* 130–31, 134, 145, 147.

29. Goldhagen, *Hitler's Willing Executioners*, 23.

30. Goldhagen, *Hitler's Willing Executioners*, 267.

31. Daniel Jonah Goldhagen, "What Were the Murderers Thinking? Interview with Daniel Jonah Goldhagen by Rudolf Augstein," in *Unwilling Germans?* ed. Shandley, 157; see also Goldhagen, "The Failure of the Critics," in *Unwilling Germans?* ed. Shandley, 132, 134, 146; and Goldhagen, *Hitler's Willing Executioners*, 4, 468, 482.

32. Jürgen Habermas, "Goldhagen and the Public Use of History: Why a Democracy Prize for Daniel Goldhagen?" in *Unwilling Germans?* ed. Shandley, 263.

33. Charles S. Maier, *The Unmasterable Past: History, Holocaust, and German National Identity*, with a new preface (Cambridge, Mass.: Harvard University Press, 1997 [1988]).

34. Goldhagen, "Modell Bundesrepublik," in *Unwilling Germans?* ed. Shandley, 279.

35. Goldhagen, *Hitler's Willing Executioners*, 9.

36. Daqing Yang, "The Challenges of the Nanjing Massacre: Reflections on Historical Inquiry," in *The Nanjing Massacre in History and Historiography*, ed. Joshua A. Fogel (Berkeley: University of California Press, 2000), 134.

37. Iris Chang, *The Rape of Nanking: The Forgotten Holocaust of World War II* (New York: Penguin Books, 1998), 200.

38. Chang, *Rape of Nanking*, 13.

39. See Chang, *Rape of Nanking*, 4, 99–104, for analysis and discussion of the death toll.

40. Chang, *Rape of Nanking*, 89.

41. Chang, *Rape of Nanking*, 4. Chang's book is a catalogue of cruelties and atrocities. See especially chap. 4, "Six Weeks of Horror."

42. Chang, *Rape of Nanking*, x.

43. Chang, *Rape of Nanking*, 6.

44. See Roy L. Brooks, ed., *When Sorry Isn't Enough: The Controversy over Apologies and Reparations for Human Injustice* (New York: New York University Press, 1999), 87–151.

45. Chang, *Rape of Nanking*, 201.

46. See Chang, *Rape of Nanking*, 205–09 for textbook controversies, and 209–10 for academic cover-ups.

47. Joshua A. Fogel, "The Nanjing Atrocity and Chinese Memory" (paper presented at the "Justice, Memory and Reconciliation" conference, University of Toronto, February 16, 2000, mimeographed), 5.

48. Chang, *Rape of Nanking*, 11, 181–83.

49. Chang, chap. 10 in *Rape of Nanking*.

50. See Fogel, ed., *The Nanjing Massacre*, passim.

51. Chang, *Rape of Nanking*, 222. See also the excellent study by Ian Buruma, *The Wages of Guilt: Memories of War in Germany and Japan* (London, U.K.: Jonathon Cape, 1994).

52. Takashi Yoshida, "A Battle over History: The Nanjing Massacre in Japan," in Fogel, ed., *The Nanjing Massacre*, 106–10.

53. Howard W. French, "Japanese Call '37 Massacre a War Myth, Stirring Storm," *New York Times*, January 23, 2000. I am grateful to my colleague Peter Chamberlain for this reference. According to Fogel, "Deniers of the Nanjing Massacre have acquired the strength of numbers to ignore the facts, the photos, and the personal memoirs. Their concern is with Japanese national pride and self-confidence, not with redressing a historical wrong." Fogel, "The Nanjing Massacre in History," *The Nanjing Massacre*, 7.

54. Chang, *Rape of Nanking*, 47–50, 56–57, 123–24, and photos between 146–47. Dower, by contrast, argued that the rape of Nanking was not reported at the time. John W. Dower, *Embracing Defeat: Japan in the Wake of World War II* (New York: Norton, 2000). See also Fogel, "Nanjing Atrocity and Chinese Memory," *The Nanjing Massacre*, 3.

55. Dower, *Embracing Defeat*, 486, 505–7.

56. Dower, *Embracing Defeat*, 60, 475.

57. Martin Malia, "Foreword: The Uses of Atrocity," in Courtois et al., *The Black Book*, ix.

58. Malia, "Foreword: The Uses of Atrocity," in Courtois et al., *The Black Book*, x.

59. Courtois, "Introduction," in Courtois et al., *The Black Book*, 17.

60. Courtois, "Introduction," in Courtois et al., *The Black Book*, 28.

61. Malia, "Foreword: The Uses of Atrocity," in Courtois et al., *The Black Book*, xii.

62. Courtois, "Introduction," in Courtois et al., *The Black Book*, 30.

63. Malia, "Foreword: The Uses of Atrocity," in Courtois et al., *The Black Book*, xvii.

64. Furet, *Passing of an Illusion*, x.

65. Furet, *Passing of an Illusion*, ix.

66. Jean-Louis Margolin, "Cambodia: The Country of Disconcerting Crimes," in Courtois et al., *The Black Book*, 588.

67. Margolin, "Cambodia," in Courtois et al., *The Black Book*, 577.

68. Margolin, "Cambodia," in Courtois et al., *The Black Book*, 590.

69. Cited in Tony Judt, *Past Imperfect: French Intellectuals, 1944–1956* (Berkeley: University of California Press, 1992), 154.

70. Judt, *Past Imperfect*, 156.

71. Judt, *Past Imperfect*, 158.

72. Malia, "Foreword: The Uses of Atrocity," in Courtois et al., *The Black Book*, xi–xii.

73. Richard H. Crossman, ed., *The God That Failed* (Chicago, Ill.: Regnery Gateway, 1983 [1949]).

74. Furet, *Passing of an Illusion*, 446.

75. Malia, "Foreword: The Uses of Atrocity," x, and Courtois, "Introduction," 4, both in Courtois et al., *The Black Book*.

76. Malia, "Foreword: The Uses of Atrocity," in Courtois et al., *The Black Book*, xvii–xxviii.

77. Margolin, "China: A Long March into Night," in Courtois et al., *The Black Book*, 487.

78. Margolin, "China: A Long March into Night," in Courtois et al., *The Black Book*, 495.

79. Malia, "Foreword: The Uses of Atrocity," in Courtois et al., *The Black Book*, x.

80. Furet, *Passing of an Illusion*, 3.

81. Courtois, "Introduction," in Courtois et al., *The Black Book*, 11.

82. Courtois, "Introduction," in Courtois et al., *The Black Book*, 10.

83. Paul Hollander, *Political Pilgrims: Travels of Western Intellectuals to the Soviet Union, China, and Cuba, 1928–1978* (New York: Harper and Row, 1983), 160–67.

84. Hollander, *Political Pilgrims*, 166.

85. Hollander, *Political Pilgrims*, xviii.

86. Hollander, *Political Pilgrims*, xviii.

87. Simon Leys, *Chinese Shadows* (New York: Viking Press, 1977).

88. Hollander, *Political Pilgrims*, xxv.

89. Canada, *Report of the Royal Commission on Aboriginal Peoples* (hereinafter RCAP *Report*), 5 vols. (Ottawa: Canada Communication Group Publishing, 1996).

90. Paul Havemann, ed., *Indigenous Peoples' Rights in Australia, Canada, and New Zealand* (Auckland, Australia: Oxford University Press, 1999), and Ward Churchill, *A Little Matter of Genocide: Holocaust and Denial in the Americas, 1492 to the Present* (Winnipeg, Canada: Arbeiter Ring Publishing, 1998).

91. Ronald Niezen, "Recognizing Indigenism: Canadian Unity and the International Movement of Indigenous Peoples," *Comparative Studies in Society and History* 42, no. 1 (January 2000), 120.

92. That is, those who have an officially designated status as Indians, as opposed to others who might be of Indian descent but who lack such status in the eyes of the government.

93. Canada, RCAP *Report*, vol. 1, *Looking Forward, Looking Back*, 513.

94. Canada, RCAP *Report*, vol. 1, *Looking Forward, Looking Back*, 7–8.

95. Canada, RCAP *Report*, vol. 4, *Perspectives and Realities*, 17, 57, 307, 488.

96. Alan C. Cairns, *Citizens Plus: Aboriginal Peoples and the Canadian State* (Vancouver: University of British Columbia Press, 2000), 119.

97. Habermas, "Goldhagen and the Public Use of History," 272.

98. Habermas, "Goldhagen and the Public Use of History."

99. Goldhagen, *Hitler's Willing Executioners*, 483.

100. Shandley, introduction to *Unwilling Germans?* 20.

101. Gunnar Myrdal, *An American Dilemma: The Negro Problem and Modern Democracy*, 2 vols. (New York: Harper, 1944).

102. Chang, *The Rape of Nanking*, 13, 55, 220.

103. See in particular Vaclav Havel's two marvellous essays, "A Letter to Dr. Gustav Husak" and "The Power of the Powerless," in *Vaclav Havel or Living in Truth*, ed. Jan Vladislav (London: Faber and Faber, 1987) on the corruption of the spirit in totalitarian regimes, where public adherence devoid of real belief in vapid regime rhetoric is a civic duty.

104. Yoshida, "A Battle over History," in Fogel, ed., *The Nanjing Massacre*, 121.

105. Mark Eykholt, "Aggression, Victimization, and Chinese Historiography of the Nanjing Massacre," in Fogel, ed., *The Nanjing Massacre*, 14.

106. Milloy, *A National Crime*.

107. Malia, "Foreword: The Uses of Atrocity," in Courtois et al., *The Black Book*, xx.

108. Victor Klemperer, *I Will Bear Witness, 1933–1941: A Diary of the Nazi Years* (New York: Modern Library, 1999).

109. Chang, *Rape of Nanking*, 220.

110. Goldhagen, *Hitler's Willing Executioners*, 22.

111. Courtois, introduction to *The Black Book*, 30.

112. Courtois, introduction to *The Black Book*, 27.

113. Martin Malia, *The Soviet Tragedy: A History of Socialism in Russia, 1917–1991* (New York: The Free Press, 1994), 522–23.

114. Rosenberg, *The Haunted Land*, xv.

115. Paul Connerton, *How Societies Remember* (Cambridge, U.K.: Cambridge University Press, 1989), 15.

116. Goldhagen, "Modell Bundesrepublik," in *Unwilling Germans?* ed. Shandley, 277. See also Omer Bartov's perceptive discussion of the significance of outside interventions from *Schindler's List* to Goldhagen in making genocide "an inseparable part of German self-perception" in Bartov, "Reception and Perception: Goldhagen's Holocaust and the World," in *The "Goldhagen Effect,"* ed. Eley, 52 (n. 26 in this note section). See also Grossman, "The 'Goldhagen Effect,'" in *The "Goldhagen Effect,"* ed. Eley, 91–92 (see n. 26).

117. Goldhagen, "Modell Bundesrepublik," *Unwilling Germans?* ed. Shandley, 283.

118. Judt, *Past Imperfect*, 9.

119. Robert K. Merton, "The Perspectives of Insiders and Outsiders," in *The Sociology of Science: Theoretical and Empirical Investigations* (Chicago: University of Chicago Press, 1973).

3

Restitution and Amending Historical Injustices in International Morality

Elazar Barkan

The demand that nations act morally and acknowledge their own gross historical injustices is a novel phenomenon. Traditionally, realpolitik—the belief that realism rather then ideology or ethics should drive politics—was the stronghold of international diplomacy. But beginning at the end of World War II and quickening since the end of the Cold War, morality and justice are receiving growing attention as political questions. As such, the need for restitution to past victims has become a major part of national politics and international diplomacy.

The transition between 1989 and 1999 in the international arena has been dramatic. This transition includes not only the horrendous wars in Africa and Yugoslavia but also the liberation of Eastern Europe and South Africa and the return to democracy in many Latin American countries. Even these beneficial changes from a totalitarian regime or a dictatorship have been a painful experience for many countries. In several of these transitions, instead of revenge against the perpetrators, Truth and Reconciliation Commissions have tried to weigh culpability on pragmatic scales. Concurrently, as the so-called realism of the Cold War diminished, the United Nations, NATO, and individual countries struggle to define their own place in a world that is paying increased attention to moral values.

Previously, the fear of the unknown, the risk of a full confrontation with the Soviet Union, and the memory of Vietnam shaped the West's lack of response to human catastrophes. But the new moral frame in the nineties confuses observers and critics, and participants and politicians alike.[1] Instead of containment and security, the rhetoric and motivation underscored high morals. Nowhere was this confusion more pronounced than in the case of NATO's intervention in Kosovo in 1999. Was it an old-fashioned intervention by the West: imperialism under a new guise? Or was it a noble humanitarian effort to stand up to perpetrators of crimes against humanity? The lack of consistency in carrying out humanitarian policies makes favorable judgment harder. Yet the split among Western intellectuals, who are traditionally antiwar but were predominantly supportive of NATO over the Kosovo conflict, underscored this new complexity.

The novelty in the international emphasis on morality is that it has gone beyond accusing other countries of human rights abuses to include self-examination. The very countries and leaders who shaped the policies of a new internationalism—Bill Clinton, Tony Blair, Jacques Chirac, and Gerhard Schroeder—have all apologized and repented for gross historical crimes in their own countries and for policies that ignored human rights. (President George W. Bush's first international crisis over the downing of the American spy plane in Chinese territorial waters revolved around the question of whether the United States should apologize to China, and for what. The crisis was resolved with an apology, the meaning of which both sides continued to haggle over.) These actions did not wipe the slate clean and were not totally unprecedented. Yet the dramatic shift produced a new level of ethical introspection: moral issues came to dominate public attention and political discussion, and displayed the willingness of nations to embrace their own guilt. This national self-reflexivity is the new guilt of nations.

More often this issue is viewed through the prism of victimization. Ian Buruma has recently highlighted controversial aspects of the tendency to focus on identity through victimization in contemporary society. "What is alarming," wrote Buruma, "is the extent to which so many minorities have come to define themselves above all as historical victims." Not only does it "reveal . . . a lack of historical perspective," but it also "seems a very peculiar source of pride." Buruma does not negate the memory of suffering by numerous communities, but he is skeptical "when a culture, ethnic, religious, or national community bases its communal identity almost entirely on the sentimental solidarity of remembered victimhood. For that way lies historical myopia and, in extreme circumstances, even vendetta." The problem, as Buruma sees it, is that an identity rooted in victimhood "impedes understanding among people" and "cannot result in mutual understanding."

Victimization, Buruma is suggesting, is a growing industry because it enjoys public validation. He is obviously correct in his concern about its significance. Victimization, however, implies the existence of a perpetrator. By focusing on its effect on the victims, Buruma does not deal with the perpetrators, and he leaves the guilt component of the equation and therefore its effect on the identity of the perpetrator unexplored.

The growth of both identities—the victim and the perpetrator, both as subjective identities—is what informs this new space in national and international politics. In contrast to the potential risk of a morbid and autistic self-indulgence in victimization, the novelty in the discourse of restitution is that it is a discussion between the perpetrators and their victims. This interaction between perpetrator and victim is a new form of political negotiation that enables the rewriting of memory and historical identity in ways that can be shared by both. Instead of categorizing all cases according to a certain universal guideline, the discourse depends on the specific interactions in each case. Instead of seeing the increased role of victimization as a risk, the discourse of restitution underscores the opportunities and the ambivalence embedded in this novel form of politics.

Admission of responsibility and guilt for historical injustices by the perpetrators is in part a result of the relative strength of the political voice the victims can mount. The Roma people have only recently been emerging from their completely subaltern position; they are still quite a way from receiving an acknowledgment. But as predictions go, it is relatively safe to assume that increased attention to human rights in the European Union will lead to an apology and further restitution to the Roma in the future. The political valence of restitution is significant and particularly powerful in the post–Cold War years, but such compensation is neither omnipotent in resolving past injustices nor a panacea for inequalities.

Having recognized the new phenomenon, we may ask: How does a new insight into historical guilt change the interaction between two countries or between a government and its minority? How does this affect the relative power of the protagonists within a national framework and the potential resolution of historical disputes? We can explore the new threshold of morality in international politics through tracing the cases where perpetrators and their descendants have either formally embraced guilt or where they have become candidates for such an admission. Clearly, however, this is not to suggest that the new standard is implemented worldwide or that it is applied consistently in all cases.

What, then, is the legacy of the perpetrators in these situations? We may begin by generalizing to say that in those cases where the victim and the perpetrator are engaged in negotiating a resolution of historical crimes, the relative strength of the victims grows. While it is true that the whole process follows from the victims' relatively greater power in the first place, the process itself is crucial in giving it specific substance. This power—not to be found in their numbers or wealth, the traditional sources of power—comes from the greater attention given to human rights since World War II and, even more so, since the end of the Cold War. But how does this new voice (or strength) translate into concrete policies? Despite a new international moral frame, the standards clearly vary among groups even as far as the aspirations for justice go, let alone its manifestation.

What would constitute a fair restitution? This is at the heart of the political process. The results are often unsatisfactory to constituents of either party in the short run. Yet resolution of long-standing international disputes has become, in addition to improving the lives of the protagonists, a mark of the new international order and is viewed as such by both representatives of the relevant governments and the victimized groups involved. This is manifested in the rhetoric that justifies demands or policies by alluding to international developments. Restitution, reparations, and apology are all different levels of acknowledgment of past wrongdoing that, together, create a mosaic of recognition by perpetrators of the need to amend past injustices. Restitution refers to the integrated picture that this mosaic creates and is thus not only a legal category but also a cultural concept.

From this broader perspective, one may appropriately ask whether restitution for gross historical injustices, both internationally and in the domestic context, has become a significant trend in contemporary politics worldwide and, if so, in what way? What intrigues me is the willingness of the perpetrators to engage and accommodate the victims' demands. The restitution cases that I deal with involve no coercion, but rather evolve from the perpetrators' willingness to acknowledge their earlier misdeeds and the choice to compensate their victims or their descendants. As one looks closer at the various restitution cases, the global diversity in outcomes also becomes apparent. Some restitution debates involve cases in which the perpetrators do not accept responsibility for wrongdoing, and others in which the victims do not deserve consideration, still others in which the problem is "too little, too late."

Restitution plays a growing role in human rights activism, and it testifies to the increased attention being paid to public morality and the augmented efforts to amend past injustices. This phenomenon provides particular insights into national and international debates during the last generation about the extension of Enlightenment principles and human rights to peoples and groups previously excluded from such considerations and how such extensions potentially alter the very conceptualization of those principles and rights.

This particular view holds that while preserving individual human rights remains crucial, this in itself is no longer sufficient, because people cannot enjoy full human rights if their identity as members of a group is violated. This creates a modern dilemma: How can the Enlightenment principles of individual rights and justice be applied to minorities and to the traditional cultures of indigenous peoples, and what principles can be applied to resolve, or at least negotiate, the conflicts that arise when individual rights clash with those of a group? For example, governments do not generally recognize the communal legal identity of ethnic groups. However, by accepting a policy of restitution, governments implicitly or explicitly accept a mechanism by which group identity receives growing recognition.

A HISTORICAL OVERVIEW

To further explicate restitution as a cultural, political, and legal concept, I use it in contrast to enforced retribution—or "punishment"—and to the age-old custom of imposed war reparations. Traditionally, the winner imposed various payments on the loser. The Versailles Treaty (1919) postulated harsh terms for the losers. In public memory, the war indemnity levied on Germany in 1919 caused, or at least heavily contributed to, World War II. The wisdom of the Versailles terms was strongly criticized along *Realpolitik* lines and the perceived failure of the policies of vindictiveness. In 1945, learning from experience, the Allies did not impose reparations on Germany. Instead, the United States accepted the burden of rebuilding Europe and Japan and initiated the Marshall Plan. This introduced a novel factor into international relations: rather than holding to a moral right to exploit enemy resources, as had been done previously, the victor underscored future reconciliation and assisted its defeated enemies in re-establishing themselves.

In hindsight the policy is widely celebrated. It was within this context of nonvindictiveness that the modern concept of restitution was born. Germany, acting on vaguely comparable motivations of perceived international interests but also on its unique need to re-establish political and moral legitimacy, sought to repent for its sins under Nazism by reaching an agreement with its victims. With regard to this seminal case, a number of points deserve mention: First, the Germans paid compensation not to the winners, but to those they had victimized the worst, primarily the Jews. Next, the perpetrator compensated the victims of its own volition in order to facilitate self-rehabilitation. Third, this admission of guilt had to be done in concord with the victims. Fourth, the restitution agreement was formulated between West Germany and Israel, both "descendant" entities of the perpetrators and the victims. Finally, the idea of compensation, the rhetoric of guilt, and limited recognition and forgiveness were translated, through the legal medium of restitution, into new possibilities in international relations.

A generation after Germany began to pay restitution to Jewish victims, other victims of World War II called for reparations. The first case was concluded when, in the late 1980s, the American government compensated Japanese Americans interned in camps during the war. The agreement was particularly successful because it quantified a historical injustice and translated it into a specific sum acceptable to both the victims as compensation and to the government as an expense. The resolution quickly became a model for other groups who demanded justice. African Americans and other victims of the slave trade were quick to cite the agreement as a precedent for their own renewed claims.

Subsequently, other cases arose from the war, including among others Japan's refusal to acknowledge its own war crimes, the question of privatization and restitution in East Central Europe, and the dispute between Russia and Germany over the plundered art and cultural property. The last case is particularly interesting because of the conflicting moral considerations. Russia's 1992 disclosure of the "trophy art" in its possession—including numerous masterpieces, hundred of thousands of art objects, and a couple of million books—created the image of a new Ali Baba's cave. Initially, the political sentiments pointed to the need to return the plunder to Germany. But the negotiation over the next decade led to a dead end. This was partially due to the political muddle in Russia, but more so perhaps to moral ambiguities. While the plunder was illegal, restituting the objects to Germany would have left Russia poorer and with no compensation for its own lost cultural heritage, which Germany had destroyed previously. To make Germany the beneficiary of such a transaction was too confusing morally.

Another sphere of restitution cases resulted from the postcolonial condition. Together with the expansion of civil rights to minorities and women, a new willingness evolved to recognize the place of indigenous peoples in the modern nation. Here the extension of the principle of equality to groups previously denied such treatment has, first, expanded the notion of who deserves individual human rights and, second, reformulated these rights to include group rights.

During the 1960s the recognition that such rights must be extended to indigenous peoples grew initially in ex-British colonies, and then spread to Latin America. Indigenous demands for rights translated into a call for recognizing historical injustices and amending them or, in some cases, into a call for full or semisovereignty. In their struggle for legitimacy, indigenous peoples present a major challenge to the contemporary nation-state's self-perception as a just society and a unified sovereign nation, and many of these debates are conducted within the framework of negotiating restitution.

For example, legislation regarding Native American rights is influenced by the moral rhetoric of restitution and closely resembles the debates in Australia, New Zealand, and Canada. In all these countries, the indigenous individual is both a minority citizen and a member of an indigenous nation. Since the eighties a widespread expansion of indigenous rights has occurred. Negotiating property rights—land, economic resources, and cultural property—through restitution to indigenous peoples became the norm that defines the national conversation in these pluralistic societies. As the international community pays increased attention to group and individual rights, victims of imperialism—from Native Americans in the United States (and other ex-colonies) to numerous groups in the Fourth World—demand new rights as restitution. These rights run the gamut from exemptions from anti-gambling laws and casino licenses to mineral extraction, fishing treaties, and monetary compensation for traditional knowledge (at times through copyright legislation).

Philosophically and legally, the distinction between compensation for lost development rights and reparations for repression and victimization is significant, and historically these rights have unfolded differently. Courts are more likely to recognize actual damages for suffering than for rights that, had the situation been different, would have benefited the claimant. Take the Black Hills case in which the U.S. government owes the Lakota people hundreds of millions of dollars as determined by the courts in a conflict that has been debated since the 1860s.

It is one thing for the government to compensate them for the violence and for broken obligations; it is quite another to try to imagine what would have been the case had the violence not taken place and to compensate them for lost opportunities. Together these two types of claims have produced a new quilt of rights. While the rhetoric of restitution is gaining momentum, the practical demands face the difficulties of conflicting rights, of rival national identity claims, and of competition for resources.

The notion that group suffering deserves restitution evolved in the United States between the 1950s and the 1970s as part of the Civil Rights movement, including affirmative action. Although the changes were not framed in the language of restitution, they raised to public consciousness moral considerations that would inform a greater receptivity to minorities and a validation of the ethnic plurality of the nation. The growing legitimacy of group identity in competition with national identity became the basis of calls for domestic restitution. Demands for compensation based on shared culture, regardless of the actual blood relationship, present a new and growing challenge. As survivors and descendants of past wars, colonialism, and national disputes return to demand justice, the long list of restitution claims grows.

One of the most wide-ranging and most morally intriguing reparations cases is that of the descendants of slaves. In the United States, and more recently in other countries, the question of restitution for slavery has been reopened. Among the issues is the dilemma concerning the nature of the groups involved. Who are the victims and who ought to be compensated—descendants of slaves? all blacks? what of those of mixed race? In addition, who are the perpetrators: descendants of slave owners? all whites? the society in general? What is the relationship between the historical group that was enslaved and contemporary African Americans? between Southern slaveholders and current U.S. taxpayers? Have the groups been transformed in such a way that the injustices are no longer amendable? And, finally, which of the wide spectrum of injustices against the slaves ought to be restituted?

The demands were not new, but their impact has been dramatically more significant in recent years. It has reached a crescendo in 2001 as I write this. Will it be more successful in the future? I think so. It has become a mainstream demand for major African American politicians and activists. Various roads are explored, including litigation. Certain courts will likely open the door in a way that will force the government to intervene even before it can reach the Supreme Court. An analogous situation existed in the case of the German government, which coordinated the fund for slave labor in order to diminish the risk for German companies that were being sued in New York.

APOLOGY

One new measure of this public morality is the growing political willingness and, at times, eagerness to admit one's historical guilt. As a result of admitting their guilt, the perpetrators may expect to have a cleaner conscience and even a direct political payoff. Either way, the apology is evidence of the public's distress in carrying the burden of guilt for inflicting suffering and possibly of its empathy with the victims. For example, Queen Elizabeth has lately found herself apologizing around the globe: to the Maoris in New Zealand and the Sikhs in India. Despite a certain amount of mockery, mostly in the conservative London press or postcolonial electronic bulletin boards, there was little downside to her apologies.

In general, objections from the recipients come because they believe the apologies do not go far enough, not because they reject the notion of apologies in principle. Similar to the Maoris and the Sikhs, some among indigenous Hawaiians who received an apology from the American government on the centenary of their conquest (1993) cried "hypocrisy." The Clinton administration's apology risked little, yet provided most parties with a sense of accomplishment and virtue.

An apology does not mean the dispute is resolved but is, in most cases, a first step: part of the process of negotiation, but not the satisfactory end result. Often, lack of apologies, demands for apologies, and the refusal of them, are all pre-steps in negotiations—a diplomatic dance that may last for a while as well as a testimony to the wish and the need of both sides to reach the negotiation stage. Consider the debate over an official U.S. government apology for slavery. The calculus of apology involves addressing disagreements about how guilty the perpetrators were and about how much and for what their descendants should repent. Despite the often contentious debate this issue has provoked, the principle of apology is increasingly accepted. At the very minimum these apologies lead to a reformulated historical understanding that itself is a form of restitution and becomes a factor in contemporary politics and humanitarian actions.

Acknowledging responsibility has also become a liberal marker of national political stability and strength rather than shame. This acknowledgment is an attempt to recognize that nations have to come to terms with their own past, primarily with respect to responsibility for the others, their victims. In contrast, nondemocracies are less inclined to admit guilt because tribal ideologues and fundamentalists view the world through noncompromising lenses. Democracies are more open to such admissions, and while clearly not all democracies are eager to amend historical injustices, they are more likely to do so than nondemocracies. But the vague standard of restitution means that national cultural variations remain crucial.

JUDGING HISTORICAL INJUSTICES

In the case of the historical injustices discussed here, perpetrators or their descendants accept, or consider accepting, responsibility for actions that constituted gross atrocities. They do so for political and moral reasons: because they recognize that the historical injustices continue to impact not only the well-being and the identity of the victims but also their own identity as perpetrators. It should also be emphasized that in recognizing the most egregious historical injustices, only one layer of injustices is amended. In most cases the history of the protagonists is more complex, but other injustices, which are also part of its history, are ignored.

Despite the dissimilar temporality and rationality, there is an overlap between historical injustices and contemporary discrimination. This is to be expected since historical injustices are numerous, but redress is limited to the victims who continue to suffer the consequences of the original injustice but can mobilize sufficient political and moral leverage to effectively lay blame at the perpetrators' doorstep. The temporal distinctions remain significant nonetheless, especially where the current generation is unwilling to assume responsibility for past injustices.

In the court of public opinion, historical events are judged out of context and in light of contemporary moral standards. The public suspends a belief in cultural pluralism and ethical relativism, and based on local, provisional belief in contemporary superiority over previous generations, as well as growing egalitarianism, it views the past as a foreign, disdained culture. Thus, it may be willing to embrace certain cultural legacies, but in true buffet style, it chooses only the very appetizing dishes.

Similarly, the public tends to look at wars through lenses that see only heroes and villains, winners and criminals. History spares the public the need to make subtle choices, to recognize complex situations, or to see that good and evil inhabit the same space. Far enough from the events and out of context, there are no instances in which suffering will not animate sympathy or that destruction will not be denounced, often on both sides of the conflict.

Far from the pandemonium of war, the international public would be happy to take the moral high road. The presentist dilemma is whether such actions ought to be judged against the horror of the war or against some other global, abstract moral standard. These questions are particularly troublesome since the delegitimation of morality as such in public discourse.

The public, however, is not content with an abdication of moral responsibility, even if the alternative results conflict and confuse. This is part of a new, fuzzy neo-enlightenment morality that recognizes historical injustices despite the limitations of vague and provisional standards and that resolves them through negotiation. Democracies seem to prefer limited moral standards to the total abdication of responsibility. I argue that a quilt of these local cases comprises the global moral spectrum.

When the public judges historical events as crimes or injustices according to our contemporary moral values, the judgment is often anachronistic. Changing moral and cultural canons reclassify previous actions. At times, acts that had been viewed as "noble," even altruistic, by the general public have become injustices.

Consider the legacy of archaeological efforts to excavate ancient ruins and anthropological aspirations to "salvage" the culture of disappearing indigenous peoples. The heroic results of those efforts by "great (often) men" are housed in museums around the world. Over time, however, these actions have been re-evaluated as "appropriation" and "domination." Similarly, scientific efforts by physical anthropologists to study the remains of indigenous peoples have recently been reclassified as grave robbing.

Cultural property turns out to be a particularly appropriate medium for negotiating historical injustices. Cultural property embodies the group national identity. Specific cultural objects in every society bear the mark of that society's unique identity. Demands for restitution of objects and sites such as the Parthenon Marbles, the Benin Bronzes, Meso-American treasures, or indigenous sites of cultural significance go beyond the economic value of the objects because the group's identity is said to be invested in them. The international community increasingly recognizes these issues and attempts to formulate agreements to address cultural property as inalienable patrimony, the time limitations of historical injustices, and the place of the individual in a communal culture.

The United Nations Educational, Scientific, and Cultural Organization (UNESCO) now heads efforts to codify a series of international agreements about cultural property. The significance of cultural property increases not only for reasons of national identity but also because its control carries substantial economic consequences, including the future of tourism and museums. These discussions are particularly appropriate to a fuzzy moral logic, beginning from specific cases and generalizing to broader economic interests, culture, religion, and politics within and among rival societies.

CONCLUSION

Over the last two generations, the writing of history has shifted focus from the history of perpetrators to the history of victims. Focusing on the histories of everyday life has not surprisingly illuminated the ongoing victimization of large segments of humanity along the lines of gender, class, and race discrimination. As victorious histories of the elite and the rich are replaced by the lives of the conquered, the poor, and the victimized Other, the public is confronted by history as the territory of injustice.

In the democratization of historical memory, the public encounters its own identity over time, an identity that includes immoral acts, suffering, and oppression. Although the political system seems reluctant to take radical steps to heal contemporary injustices, it seems more willing to entertain the possibility of amending historical injustices.

The political calculus of restitution aims to privilege a moral rhetoric, to address the needs of past victims, and to legitimate a discussion about a redistribution of resources around the globe. A strong case for restitution would underscore a moral economy that would calculate and quantify evil and would place a price on amending injustices. Such a theory of justice would obviously suffer from all the shortcomings of utilitarianism that have been exposed over the last two hundred years. After all, who could quantify the costs of genocide? Yet the moral high ground has its own disadvantages. To maintain moral purity and claim that nothing can compensate for atrocities is surely more appealing, and selling the moral virtue of suffering for a few dollars is giving in to the perpetrators and encouraging future crimes.

In this context, one virtue the moral economy of restitution may offer is that it does not propose a universal solution but strives to evaluate conflicts in light of a vague standard and to be pragmatically mediated by the protagonists themselves. Even if from a historical global perspective a restitution agreement lets the perpetrators off the hook cheaply, the life improvement gained by the victims should not be underestimated.

In this case victims and perpetrators collaborate—searching for an exit from the bonds of history. This morality may have a particular cachet in our postcolonial world, where people's identity often includes their histories and sufferings. Descendants and survivors of peoples who were conquered, colonized, dominated, decimated, or enslaved may come to recognize that a new international standard enables them to establish new relations with the descendants of the perpetrators. Each new relationship is dependent not only on moral considerations but also on political and social power relations.

Beyond the moral framework, groups have to pursue their claims politically and persuade different constituencies of the justice of their claims.

Under such new circumstances, restitution may demonstrate that acting morally carries tangible and intangible political and cultural benefits. Yet we must temper our enthusiasm. Only against the poverty of the international community's inability to prevent or mitigate human disasters does restitution provide a beacon of morality. Its attractiveness results from presenting local moral solutions in a deeply immoral and unjust world. Restitution argues for a morality that recognizes an ensemble of rights beyond individual rights and privileges the right of peoples to reject external impositions and express their own agency by determining their own order of priorities.

As the language of restitution becomes central to negotiations over group rights, a door is opened to a potential redistribution of justice. A theory of conflict resolution based on restitution may illuminate the efforts by many nations and minorities to gain partial recognition and overcome conflicting historical identities through the construction of a shared past. Contemporary international discourse underscores the growing role of guilt, mourning, and atonement as part of a reconfiguration of national identity, including the national revival of indigenous groups on the verge of extinction or other historically victimized groups who do not enjoy full sovereignty.

NOTE

1. Ian Buruma, "The Joys and Perils of Victimhood," *New York Review of Books*, vol. 46, no. 6 (April 8, 1999), 4–9.

4

Reflections on Reparations

Roy L. Brooks

There is perhaps no more contentious an issue in international human rights today than the question of reparations. Innocent victims of human injustice claim a moral, if not a legal, right to obtain reparations from the perpetrator regime. Few governments have acceded to these demands, however. Some governments view reparations as a kind of moral shakedown, a cheap attempt to con the government out of large sums of money. Other governments, in a kind of official amnesia, dispute the historical record as represented by the victims. Still others view the claim for reparations as a threat to social harmony, and so subscribe to the policy of "let bygones be bygones." Adding to the complexity of the reparations question is the position taken by the victims themselves. Some will take nothing less than full monetary compensation, while others reject reparations altogether as little more than "blood money." It is quite possible that the drive toward reparations could founder on the shoals of internal discord among the victims themselves.

In this chapter, I shall not attempt to resolve these problems, but, rather, I shall address three fundamental questions about reparations that may help us better understand the manifold worldwide campaigns for reparations and, thus, move us closer to finding answers to the kinds of thorny problems mentioned earlier. The questions I should like to discuss are as follows: Do some societies have a natural proclivity to commit evil acts? Is it possible to construct a theory of redress? Are reparations the only form of redress?

DO SOME SOCIETIES HAVE A NATURAL PROCLIVITY TO DO EVIL?

My study of reparations claims[1] leads me to conclude that *all* societies have the capacity to do evil. No society holds a monopoly on the commission of human injustices, nor is any society exempted. To borrow from Max Frankel, "[T]here [is] a beast in each of us waiting to be unleashed by extraordinary fear, greed or fury."

Many of the most heinous acts can be attributed to the military gone amok during times of war. Examples include Japanese soldiers raping and torturing 300,000 civilians within a three-month period in Nanking, China, during World War II; American GIs slaughtering 504 women, children, and old men in four hours at the Vietnamese village of My Lai during the Vietnam War; and Argentine Navy officials throwing as many as 1,500 suspected leftist dissidents into the ocean from airplanes (the so-called death flights) during Argentina's Dirty War (1976–1983).

Most human injustices, however, can be tied directly to conscious political choice. Millions of Jews, Gypsies, and others were murdered as a result of Nazi policy before and during World War II. Millions of American blacks were killed and millions more enslaved under three centuries of American domestic policy. Thousands of Native Americans were killed and mistreated under similar policies. And millions of South African blacks were killed and subjugated by a ruling white minority through apartheid policies in South Africa.

Women seem to occupy a singularly precarious position during times of war. Women appear vulnerable to a broader range of human injustices than men. Not only are women victims of the same injustices as men (e.g., slavery, assault, torture, looting, and burning), but they are often singled out for additional sexual/reproductive brutalities (rape, sexual mutilation, forced prostitution, sterilization, impregnation, and maternity). Whenever there has been war (and to an alarming extent during times of peace), men sexually abuse women. Seen as an inevitability of war—a sort of "boys will be boys" extreme—rape is a historically well-documented war strategy that is highly effective for terrorizing the enemy.

In medieval times, unpaid soldiers' only "compensation" was the opportunity to rape and pillage. During the Crusades, the king conscripted women to follow behind the troops to provide sexual services on demand. Some reports estimate that Allied soldiers raped over 100,000 women in Berlin during the last two weeks of World War II. Also during World War II, approximately 200,000 Korean, Chinese, Filipino, Indonesian, and other women were forced into sexual slavery ("comfort women") for the Japanese military.

Catherine MacKinnon argues that rape during war is not just a harm that one enemy army does to another; it is one army enforcing domination over another and one gender enforcing domination over another. Rape occurs "among and between sides" and "the fact that these rapes are part of [a war] means that . . . women are facing twice as many rapists with twice as many excuses, two layers of men on top of them rather than one, and two layers of impunity serving to justify the rapes: just war and just life."[2] Perhaps this argument sheds some light on the otherwise unexplainable estimate by Joan Furey, former director of the Center for Women's Affairs at the Veterans Administration, that approximately half of the American nurses were raped by *American GIs* while serving in Vietnam.

Making matters worse, the international human rights community has largely ignored women's issues. "What happens to women is either too particular to be universal or too universal to be particular, meaning either too human to be female or too female to be human,"[3] MacKinnon contends. Mass rapes and other sexual assaults, long ago established as war crimes, are not prosecuted in war tribunals as often as other war crimes.

This sad state of affairs may be changing. The International Criminal Tribunal for the former Yugoslavia (ICTY) at The Hague convicted three Bosnian Serbs for raping and torturing Muslim women and girls in 1992 and 1993 during the Bosnian conflict. The February 2001 ruling made history by defining individual rape (as opposed to mass rape) as a crime against humanity separate and distinct from torture. In addition, the court extended the definition of "slavery" beyond slave labor to include sexual slavery.[4]

Despite this very important development, cultural barriers will likely continue to make rape a difficult crime to prosecute. Not only in the United States but in other countries as well, silence about sexual atrocities is the norm. Also, shame is routinely placed on victims of rape instead of on the perpetrators. For example, Muslim victims of mass rapes in the Bosnian conflict are considered soiled and unmarriageable in Muslim culture. Some traditional Muslims believe that killing or exiling rape victims is the only way for husbands and families to cleanse themselves of their family's shame.

Genocidal rape—mass rape for the purposes of eliminating unwanted ethnic groups from a territory—is a particularly egregious war crime that targets women. The Serbian rape of Bosnian women was implemented for this ghastly purpose. Many Serbians believe that a father's sperm carries the genetic makeup of his baby, which would mean that all babies conceived from the mass rapes are Serbian. Hence, Serbian rapes were designed to remove Bosnian Muslims from disputed territory and to populate remaining Muslim areas with Serbians.

In discussing the Bosnian conflict, I do not mean to suggest that the Serbs have a natural proclivity to commit acts of injustice. Atrocities were committed on all sides of the war. Nor do I mean to suggest that the Serbs are disposed to commit rape any more than other people. I use Serbia merely to illuminate the precarious position of women during times of armed conflict.

TOWARD A THEORY OF REDRESS

There are several conditions necessary for successful redress of human injustice. These conditions can be woven into a theory of redress, which, in my view, has four elements. The first is that the demands, or claims, for redress must be placed in the hands of legislators rather than judges. Legislators, quite simply, can do more than judges. In every nation of the world, the judiciary has the least amount of lawmaking authority of any branch of government. "If it be true that the Cherokee Nation have rights," Chief Justice John Marshall of the United States Supreme Court said in *The Cherokee Nation v. Georgia*, "this is not the tribunal in which these rights are to be asserted. If it be true that wrongs have been inflicted, and still greater are to be apprehended, this is not the tribunal which can redress the past or prevent the future."[5] This message is particularly instructive because it comes from a judicial tribunal that probably has more lawmaking power than any other judiciary in the world.

Courts do, however, play a useful role in the reparations movement worldwide. They can be and have been used to interpret and enforce extant rights—that is, laws handed down by the legislature or lawmaking authority. Sometimes the legislature will create a court or quasi-judicial body for the specific purpose of resolving redress claims. This happened in the United States with the creation of the now defunct Indian Claims Commission. But most of the time, the highest court in the land can only apply existing rights and remedies; it cannot create new ones.

Within the legislative realm, successful redress movements have been able to reach the hearts and minds of lawmakers and citizens alike. But clearly, the success of any redress movement has had a great deal more to do with the degree of pressure (public and private) brought to bear on the legislators—that is, with politics—than with matters of logic, justice, or culture. Political pressure, then, is the second condition necessary for successful redress. This redress element is a clear acknowledgment that not all meritorious claims succeed. Intuitions of public policy, the prejudices that legislators share with their constituencies, the willingness of political leaders to step forward and take political risks, and the simple exchange of favors have had a good deal more to do with the fate of redress than the merits of the claims. A good example of this was the campaign for reparations for the internment of Japanese Americans during World War II.[6]

Strong internal support is a third element of successful redress. The victims themselves must exhibit unquestioned support for the claims being pressed. Redress must be a top priority within the group or at least a vocal portion of the group. Internal cohesion may, however, be difficult to achieve when members of the group cannot agree on the form of reparations (or, more generally, the form of redress). This is particularly true when members of the group find redress of any kind to be morally objectionable, as little more than "blood money."

The "blood money" issue should, in my judgment, not get in the way of redress. While one must, of course, be sensitive to the concerns of the victims, I do not equate redress with blood money, and many victims who have actually received monetary redress do not either. True, a price cannot and should not be placed on the suffering exacted by the Holocaust, Japanese American internment, African American slavery, and the like. But when rights are ripped away, the victim or the victim's family is entitled to compensation, and much more.

Although the politics of redress typically overshadow the merits of redress, claims for redress must be meritorious if they are to have any prospect of success. There must be something of substance for lawmakers to promote. This requirement is the fourth and final element of my theory of redress. A meritorious claim is one that has the following factors: (1) a human injustice must have been committed; (2) it must be well documented; (3) the victims must be identifiable as a distinct group; (4) the current members of the group must continue to suffer harm; and (5) such harm must be causally connected to the past injustice.[7]

WHAT ARE THE FORMS OF REDRESS?

Paying reparations is not the only way a government can redress acts of injustice. Governments have, in fact, responded to human injustice claims in myriad ways. The list of responses is dizzying. Some governments have issued sincere apologies; others have not. Some have paid money to victims or their families; others have done so but without the issuance of an apology. And still others have invested money or services or both in the victims' community in lieu of compensating victims individually. Although the forms of redress are very diverse, conceptual categories do begin to emerge from a close study of them.

The template that emerges begins with a distinction between responses that are remorseful (some more so than others) and those that are not. Responses that seek atonement for the commission of an injustice are properly called *reparations*. Responses in which the government does not express atonement are more suitably called *settlements*. The latter can be analogized to their use in American law. Often a defendant corporation will settle a dispute by signing a consent decree in which it agrees to pay the plaintiff(s) a certain sum of money, but does not concede any wrongdoing. In fact, both parties stipulate the fact that the defendant has *not* violated any law. A settlement is less a victory than a compromise. It gives the victim a monetary award (not necessarily enough to cover actual losses) and gives the perpetrator a chance to end the dispute without a finding of liability. Usually, a reparation is easily distinguishable from a settlement by the presence or absence of an accompanying statement of apology.

Reparations and settlements can be subdivided into *monetary* and *non-*

monetary responses. Examples of the latter include amnesty, affirmative action, and municipal services from the construction of new medical facilities to the creation of new educational programs. Nonmonetary reparations or settlements can be more effective than cash in responding to the victims' individual or collective current needs.

Monetary or nonmonetary reparations and settlements can be directed toward the victims individually or collectively. A reparation or settlement directed toward the individual is intended to be *compensatory*—in other words, to return the victim to the status quo ante. One directed toward the group is designed to be *rehabilitative* of the community—in other words, the objective is to nurture the group's self-empowerment, to promote the community's cultural transformation, or to improve the conditions under which the victims live. "You could . . . try to help clean up the mess your grandpa made—like help me fix up my place, or help my cousin find a job."[8] That statement expresses the essence of rehabilitation.

Let me take a moment to try to fit this conceptual template over the better-known forms of redress and, in the process, raise some significant questions about redress. Germany has paid reparations (i.e., atonement) in the forms of individual compensation and community rehabilitation, the latter mostly to Israel. It has, in addition, paid more reparations (currently about 80 billion deutsche marks) than perhaps any other government in world history. Germany would seem to have created a successful program of redress. But has it? Have the compensating amounts been truly compensatory—in other words, sufficient to return the victim to the status quo ante? Have the Gypsies been included in the compensation structure? Is the compensation fund Switzerland has set up in response to its World War II injustices an admission of guilt or simply a settlement?[9]

Japan was ordered to pay a settlement (i.e., nonatonement money) to compensate several women exploited as sex slaves during World War II. This settlement, relatively small in amount, came by way of a judicial decree, an unusual source of redress, which was recently overturned by Japan's highest court.[10] However, Japan's parliament, the Diet, has provided for community rehabilitation through the "Asian Women's Fund." Because the Diet has not issued an apology and several prime ministers have, the question arises as to whether the Asian Women's Fund constitutes a reparation or a settlement? Another question concerns the propriety and effectiveness of community rehabilitation versus individual compensation.[11]

Japanese Americans and Aleuts have received a variety of reparations from the United States for forcible relocation and internment during World War II. Reparations were made monetarily and in-kind to both the individual and the group pursuant to the Civil Liberties Act of 1988. For example, twenty thousand dollars in compensation was allocated to each Japanese American victim. Nonmonetary individual compensation was given in the forms of a presidential pardon and restitution of status and entitlements lost due to discrimination. In addition, nonmonetary rehabilitation was offered in the form of certain educational programs. Was such a "generous" reparations package a unique achievement within the American political process? Should other American groups pressing similar claims (e.g., German Americans, Italian Americans, and African Americans) expect similar political success? Is the success of Japanese American redress tainted by the case of the Japanese Peruvians who, excluded from the Civil Liberties Act, were given only five thousand dollars each?[12]

Native Americans have received no dearth of governmental responses to their various claims for redress. All have been settlements rather than reparations. Also, most of the redress offered has been rehabilitative rather than compensatory. But the central question concerning the government's redress of Native American claims is whether it has in large part been unresponsive to these claims and result oriented.

For example, in 1946, Congress created the Indian Claims Commission, a quasi-judicial tribunal empowered to adjudicate Indian tribe lawsuits pending against the federal government. The Commission, which was dissolved in 1978, had authority to award monetary relief on any tribal claim, whether legal or "moral," that arose since 1776. Because it could only order monetary redress, the Commission was structurally precluded from offering redress for the most important Indian claim—the return of Indian lands. As Nell Jessup Newton observes, "The decision to equate justice with money . . . was the most serious flaw in the Commission's design and implementation."[13] Congress failed to incorporate in the Commission's enabling legislation the Indian view—the *victim's perspective*—of the relationship of people to land.

In addition to offering redress that failed to meet the expectations of the victims, the Commission's system of redress (both procedurally and substantively) seemed unabashedly result oriented. When necessary or convenient, the Commission ignored precedent or engaged in formalistic analysis, even with respect to moral claims. Worse, some decisions ordered forms of redress that were more harmful than helpful to Indian claimants. For example, many of the Commission's backers in Congress saw it as a means of terminating the tribal way of life and assimilating Indians into mainstream society. Most Native Americans deemed tribal termination and assimilation to be cultural genocide and, hence, more of an insult than a redress, let alone a reparation.[14]

In fairness, land-claim litigation before the Commission and other federal tribunals raised very difficult legal questions. Given the absence of records and the government's policy of removing tribes from their homelands, how could a court determine what land a tribe occupied two centuries ago? How does a court place a monetary value on land that everyone concedes belongs to a tribal group? Should a court determine value by the subsistence the land in question afforded the tribe prior to its taking (the so-called nuts-and-berries method of valuation) or should it determine value in a Euro-American fashion by appraising its worth to white farmers or miners who have taken over the land? As difficult as these questions are, they do not excuse or justify the government's handling of Indian claims.

African American claims for slavery and Jim Crow have not even merited an apology from the federal government of the United States. But redress has been provided to a very limited extent at the state level. For example, in 1994, the Florida legislature enacted the Rosewood Compensation Act to settle certain claims arising out of white violence that demolished the all-black town of Rosewood during a 1923 race riot. The settlement is both compensatory (actual proven losses are repaid) and rehabilitative (e.g., a scholarship fund is established for minority students, even those who are not direct descendants of the Rosewood families). But no apology is made.[15]

Recently, the Tulsa Race Riot Commission urged the Oklahoma legislature to appropriate reparations to the victims of what is considered the United States' bloodiest race riot, which took place in Tulsa, Oklahoma, in 1921.[16] Can African Americans live with a settlement rather than atonement, given how emotional the issues of slavery and Jim Crow are among some vocal members of the group? Is a state and local strategy more feasible than the failed national approach taken thus far? Is community rehabilitation more fruitful than individual compensation, especially in light of the privity problem (i.e., the fact that the actual victims of slavery have died)?[17]

South Africa has opted for reparations rather than settlement. A great deal of remorse exists in South Africa (perhaps more so among its political and intellectual leaders than the average citizens) over the injustices of apartheid. The government's Truth and Reconciliation Commission (TRC), which on July 31, 1998, ended two-and-a-half years of investigations into apartheid-related injustices, has provided reparations in the form of individual compensation and community rehabilitation. Similar forms of redress (e.g., affirmative action in employment) are being considered by other government entities. How effective these reparations will be in moving the country from a regime of racial oppression to one of racial justice and democratic process—what the South Africans call "reconciliation"—is difficult to discern at this time, only three years into the process.

But what seems clear even now is that although jobs have changed hands in the political sphere, little has changed or is likely to change in the employment area without affirmative action. Apartheid has given whites a built-in advantage—patterns of privilege and economic power have become entrenched—which cannot be eliminated simply by removing discriminatory laws from the books. What is required is a period of affirmative action before South Africans can begin talk about equality of opportunity. Unfortunately, affirmative action has yet to be fully implemented in South Africa.[18]

Reconciliation continues to be the overriding political imperative in South Africa, leaving its distinctive mark on the country's forms of redress. The dictates of reconciliation are what has made amnesty for the oppressors an acceptable, if highly unusual, form of redress. That is, within what Wilhelm Verwoerd calls the "transitional context"—the movement from apartheid to democracy—and *only* within this context, amnesty is seen as an essential ingredient of redress. Supporters of amnesty explain this point of view in several ways: First, amnesty creates conditions that lead to the validation of victims' stories, a correction of the historical record from the victim's perspective. It brings about a degree of disclosure that responds to the victims' "demand for rectification for wrongs done by the previous illegitimate state and other institutions. It can be argued that the justice system, with its primary focus on individual legal responsibility, is less suited to deal with this level of reparation than a Truth Commission—trying to get 'as complete a picture as possible of the nature, causes and extent' of gross human rights violations, placing the more wide-ranging moral responsibility of institutions like the state, the judiciary, the (security) police in the centre of the picture."[19]

Second, as an engine of disclosure, amnesty may be the only way to relieve victim suffering caused by not knowing what happened to loved ones who disappeared into the state's security establishment. Third, without amnesty, democratic government—the *real* reparation—will not be possible in a country like South Africa wherein every branch of the political establishment gave support to many gross human rights violations. Without amnesty, not only would there have been little unveiling of the truth and much collective amnesia among the perpetrators, but there certainly would not have been any forgiveness by the victims and, hence, no reconciliation and no democracy.[20]

There is perhaps another reason amnesty is offered as a form of redress in South Africa's transitional context. Some victims of apartheid committed politically motivated atrocities (let us call them victim perpetrators) and, hence, were in need of amnesty. Indeed, just prior to ending its public hearings, the TRC, headed by Archbishop Desmond Tutu, granted amnesty to four black South Africans who had beaten and stabbed Amy Biehl, a 26-year-old white American who was in South Africa to work on voter education, as she pleaded for mercy. Like so many whites who came before the TRC claiming they had killed, tortured, maimed, and raped as a means of exerting political pressure and who expressed what appeared to be genuine remorse for their injustices, these men walked out of the hearing immune from criminal or civil prosecution.[21]

Although I stand by my argument—that amnesty was intended to provide redress for victims of apartheid who had themselves committed atrocities in the struggle against apartheid—I should disclose that some South African officials have rejected the argument. In a private (but not confidential) discussion with me in Copenhagen in April 2001, both the South African Ambassador to Denmark, the Honorable Thembia M. N. Kubheka, a long-time member of the African National Congress (ANC), and Tseliso Thiipa-nyane, the head of research at the South African Human Rights Commission, argued that amnesty was not needed for victim perpetrators because the ANC had its own "internal mechanisms" for dealing with atrocities committed by its members.

I am not quite sure what that means; but I do know the following: (1) atrocities were committed by groups opposed to apartheid other than the ANC, most prominently the African People's Liberation Army (APLA), the military wing of the Pan African Congress (PAC); (2) the ANC, in its own statement before the TRC, confesses to the "adoption of armed struggle"; (3) many ANC members, including former President Nelson Mandela's ex-wife, Winnie, acknowledged their personal participation in murder and torture while the ANC was in exile; (4) the TRC granted amnesty to many victim perpetrators, including thirty-seven top ANC officials—one of whom was Thabo Mbeki, then deputy president of South Africa;[22] and (5) Alexander Boraine, vice chairperson of the TRC, at one time seems to have suggested that the existence of black-initiated human rights violations was a significant factor in the structuring of South Africa's peculiar form of redress.[23]

From this body of evidence, I draw the conclusion that, in addition to the usual arguments South African elites (Verwoerd, Archbishop Tutu, and the like) give in support of amnesty as a form of redress, black-initiated injustices provided another reason for this peculiar form of redress. Despite these manifold explanations, let us not lose sight of the main point: the deal in South Africa, even if tacitly understood, is that the oppressors get amnesty and the victims get compensation and rehabilitation as well as amnesty. All this is designed to lead to reconciliation and democracy, the real reparation.

CONCLUSION

Despite the many complex questions surrounding the reparations issue, one thing seems clear beyond peradventure: when a government commits acts of grave injustice against innocent people, it should make amends. This is as much a political as a moral assertion. Politically, remorse improves the national spirit and health. It allows a society to heal and move forward in the wake of an atrocity. This is a central lesson one takes from the people of Germany and South Africa as they have struggled to deal with the aftermath of Nazi crimes and apartheid, respectively. Germany, in fact, has made remorse and reparations for the crimes committed under the Nazi regime an inescapable point of reference for the nation even to this day. Likewise,

South Africa has made apology and reparations for apartheid an absolute precondition to moving forward democratically. If politics is nothing more than the naked exchange of favors, then reparations have something of value to offer to victims and perpetrators alike. This simple acknowledgment may give reparations a useful presence in the political arena.

NOTES

"Reflections on Reparations" was delivered at the conference, "Politics and the Past: On Repairing Historical Injustices," held at the Institute for European Studies, The University of British Columbia, Vancouver, B.C., Canada, on February 25, 2000.

1. See Roy Brooks, ed., *When Sorry Isn't Enough: The Controversy over Apologies and Reparations for Human Injustice* (New York: New York University Press, 1999).
2. Catherine MacKinnon, "Crimes of War, Crimes of Peace," *UCLA Women's Law Journal* 4 (1993): 59, 65.
3. MacKinnon, "Crimes of War, Crimes of Peace," 60.
4. *Prosecutor v. Dragoljub Kunarac, Radomir Kovac, Zoran Vukovic*, Cases No. IT-96-23-T & IT-96-23/1-T (March 22, 2001). For further discussion of the importance of this case, see Kevin Whitelaw, "A Verdict against Rape," *U.S. News & World Report* (March 5, 2001): 36.
5. *The Cherokee Nation v. Georgia*, 30 U.S. 1, 10 (1831).
6. On this campaign, see, e.g., Mitchell T. Maki, Harry H. L. Kitano, and S. Megan Berthold, *Achieving the Impossible Dream: How Japanese Americans Obtained Redress* (Urbana: University of Illinois Press, 1999); Leslie T. Hatamiya, "Institutions and Interest Groups: Understanding the Passage of the Japanese American Redress Bill," in *When Sorry Isn't Enough*, 190–200.
7. For a more detailed discussion, see Mari J. Matsuda, "Looking to the Bottom: Critical Legal Studies and Reparations," *Harvard Civil Liberties-Civil Rights Law Review* 22 (1987): 323, 362–97.
8. William Raspberry, "Don't Bother Saying You're Sorry," *San Diego Union-Tribune*, July 8, 1997, sec. B, p. 6 (quoting an African American cab driver).
9. On these issues, see Ian Hancock, "Romani Victims of the Holocaust and Swiss Complicity," in *When Sorry Isn't Enough*, 68–76; Hubert Kim, "German Reparations: Institutionalized Insufficiency," in *When Sorry Isn't Enough*, 77–80.
10. For a discussion of this ruling, see *San Diego Union-Tribune*, March 30, 2001, sec. A, p. 6.
11. For further discussion of these questions, see Roy Brooks, "What Form Redress?" in *When Sorry Isn't Enough*, 87–91.
12. See Maki, Kitano, and Berthold, *Achieving the Impossible Dream*; Hatamiya, "Institutions and Interest Groups," 190–200. For a discussion of the legal implications of the Civil Liberties Act, see *Jacobs v. Barr*, 959 F.2d 313 (D.C. Cir. 1992), cert. denied, 506 U.S. 831, discussed in *When Sorry Isn't Enough*, 206–16.

13. Nell Jessup Newton, "Indian Claims for Reparations, Compensation, and Restitution in the United States Legal System," in *When Sorry Isn't Enough*, 264.

14. See Lawrence Armand French, "Native American Reparations: Five Hundred Years and Counting," in *When Sorry Isn't Enough*, 244–45.

15. On this case, see Kenneth B. Nunn, "Rosewood," in *When Sorry Isn't Enough*, 435–37.

16. See Tim Talley, "Report Urges Race Riot Reparations," March 1, 2001, at www.agrnews.org/issues/112/nationalnews.html (accessed September 17, 2002).

17. On the privity question, see Boris I. Bittker and Roy L. Brooks, "The Constitutionality of Black Reparations," in *When Sorry Isn't Enough*, 374–89.

18. On the issue of affirmative action in South Africa, see Linda Human, "Affirmative Action as Reparation for Past Employment Discrimination in South Africa," in *When Sorry Isn't Enough*, 506–09.

19. Wilhelm Verwoerd, "Justice after Apartheid? Reflections on the South African TRC," in *When Sorry Isn't Enough*, 483.

20. Verwoerd, "Justice after Apartheid?" 482–83. See also Desmond Tutu, *No Future without Forgiveness* (New York: Doubleday, 1999).

21. See Brooks, "The Age of Apology," in *When Sorry Isn't Enough*, 11.

22. A court subsequently overturned the grant of amnesty to these officials because their TRC testimonies did not sufficiently indicate what each had done. See Brooks, "What Price Reconciliation?" in *When Sorry Isn't Enough*, 443–47.

23. See Alexander Boraine, "Alternatives and Adjuncts to Criminal Prosecutions," in *When Sorry Isn't Enough*, 469–74.

II

Reparations Politics:
Case Studies

5

Calculating Slavery Reparations
Theory, Numbers, and Implications

Dalton Conley

The possibility of paying reparations to black Americans as restitution for the legacy of slavery has made a recent comeback in the popular discourse. If and when this debate moves toward actual policy, there will be many details to be worked out on how to arrive at the "right" number. Implicit in each of these details is a set of assumptions not just about the meaning of race and the legacy of slavery but about how opportunity in America is structured by birth and background more generally. Putting these assumptions on the table is important if we are to have a fruitful debate about how to rectify inequities of the past.

HISTORICAL CONTEXT:
FORTY ACRES AND A MULE

With federal troops marching across Confederate territory, Union confiscation and seizure of "abandoned property" in the South was widespread. The total number of acres held by the Freedmen's Bureau, the administrating institution for confiscated property, has been estimated at 800,000 to 900,000 acres. Some of the Radical Republicans of the Committee of Fifteen on Reconstruction entertained designs to use these properties as the grist to provide freed slaves with the legendary "forty acres and a mule" as restitution for the slavery experience. Unfortunately for the ex-slaves, this promise of economic self-sufficiency was rhetoric that never came close to becoming law.

117

Instead, the lion's share of the total number of confiscated plantations went to white Northerners, who hired the former slaves to cultivate them, inaugurating the system of sharecropping that disadvantaged many African Americans for decades hence. Not only did former slaves fail to receive significant land or money as compensation for their toil, but after the Civil War, Jim Crow regimes in the South and racially biased policies elsewhere led to new institutional barriers to black economic progress. Is now the time to set these accounts straight—providing African Americans with the proverbial "40 acres and a mule" as compensation for the legacy of slavery?

CONTEMPORARY DEBATES

Today the issue has made another comeback.[1] Armed with precedents such as payments to Japanese Americans for internment during World War II and the claims of the Holocaust victims on Swiss banks, for example, the most recent discourse on slavery restitution is more legalistic in tone, and, as such, has been the most effective to date. For example, at least ten cities—including Washington and Chicago—have passed resolutions urging the federal government to take action on this issue.

A new California law requires insurance companies that do business in the state to research their past to determine whether they offered policies insuring slave capital. Aetna—one of the largest insurance companies in the United States—has issued an apology for having done just that. Editorials and feature stories calling for a serious examination of the reparations possibility have cropped up with increasing frequency. And perhaps most importantly, a group of prominent legal scholars, litigators, and advocates, such as Harvard law professor Charles Ogletree and TransAfrica's founder Randall Robinson, have declared their intention to bring class action suits against the government and corporations that benefited from America's "peculiar institution."

Even conservative pundits have argued for reparations as a method of abrogating societal responsibility to continue affirmative action policies in education and the labor market. As Charles Krauthammer wrote in *Time* magazine, "It's time for a historic compromise: a monetary reparation to blacks for centuries of racial oppression in return for the total abolition of all programs of racial preference.'"

With this increased volume has come increased noise about the topic. There are several important issues to sort out in this debate. Practical concerns like who will receive payments and how much they will amount to overlay directly onto larger theoretical issues about race and "ascription" (that is, assignment to a social status by virtue of birth). Had the proverbial 40 acres and a mule been reality rather than rhetoric, many of these issues would not have to be addressed. Back in the mid-nineteenth century, for example, payments could have been extracted from the seized properties of the Southern plantations, targeting most directly those who benefited from the chattel labor. Most important, payments could have been made directly to the victims of slavery, rather than their descendants. Fourteen decades later, it gets a lot more complicated.

HOW MUCH?

Perhaps the most direct reasoning for reparations is the payment of back wages for slave labor. This was the underlying rationale for calculations made back in the 1970s as part of the black power movement. One researcher used 1790–1860 slave prices as proxies for the value of slave capital. He then annuitized the prices into an income stream to which he applied compound interest, calculated since the slavery era. The figures he generated under different assumptions ranged from $448 billion to $995 billion at the time he wrote in the early 1970s. Merely adjusted for inflation, this would translate to a range of $2 trillion to almost $4 trillion today.[2]

This estimate happened to match the $400 billion sum that was being demanded around the same time by a prominent black separatist movement called the Republic of New Africa (RNA). The RNA, however, demanded this cash sum in addition to five southern states: Alabama, Georgia, Louisiana, Mississippi, and South Carolina (which the researcher estimated to be worth $350 billion at the time). If we were debating reparations to be paid directly to the ex-slaves themselves, we might follow this strategy of imputing a fair wage or splitting the profits made from the industries in which they toiled, adding on sums for pain and suffering and lost future earnings. Even if it were one generation later, we might be able to locate the heirs of the slaves and pay them as representatives of the estate.

However, the approach of estimating the value of slave labor and then spinning that forward to the present presents a number of difficulties when we are talking about six or more generations later. Using the compound interest approach only works when we assume an unbroken chain of birth from slave to the current African American population. There are issues of what to do with whites (and blacks) who immigrated to the United States well after slavery ended. (A majority of the white population is descended from people who arrived to these shores after 1870.) And what about the descendants of blacks who lived freely in the North during the antebellum period? Even more complicated is that some free blacks owned slaves themselves. And, of course, there is the issue of racial mixing. Does someone who is born to a white parent and a black parent end up canceling out on the issue; that is, is she reparations-tax exempt as well as not eligible to receive a payout?

IS SLAVERY A PROXY FOR RACE, OR IS RACE A PROXY FOR SLAVERY?

These latter concerns get to the larger issue of race in America acting as a proxy for descent from slaves and, therefore, entitlement to restitution. On the one hand, it is well known that Americans of all races have ancestors of various races. On the other hand, the way that race has long been classified in the United States, commonly known as the one-drop rule, suggests that whether accurate or not, African American racial identity should act as a proxy for slave descent since it is *socially* defined that way by the state. (The one-drop rule states that if it is determined that either parent of a child has any black "blood," the child is classified as black.) Or, to turn this question around, it might be reasonable to assume that slavery is acting as a stand-in for the sum total of oppression—economic and noneconomic—that blacks have experienced in America, both before and after 1865, starting with Jim Crow, onward to segregation in northern ghettos to job and housing discrimination, and so on. Are these not to be remedied through financial restitution as well?

One way of viewing this issue is to recognize slavery as an important institution on which this country's wealth was built. It bestows a legacy of economic development to some just as it bestows a stigma to those of African descent. Under this view, whether someone arrived in 1700 or in 1965 is not important—profits from slavery benefit all stakeholders in American society. The cash nexus of capitalism touches all of us; if you wear cotton blue jeans, if you take out an insurance policy from Aetna, if you buy or sell anything from anyone who has a connection to the industries that were built on chattel labor, then you have benefited from the "free" labor of the slave population. (These benefits extend beyond U.S. borders, of course, to our trading partners, and notably to the Africans who sold their neighbors into the middle passage.) Likewise, if you are black in America, regardless of when or how your ancestors arrived, you live with the negative legacy of slavery (and a disproportionately small amount of the profits).

In fact, there is a reasonable argument to be made that more or less all black-white inequality in contemporary America is a direct result of the institution of slavery. Under this paradigm, slavery stripped African Americans of their ethnic honor, which other groups in America enjoy. That is, part of the slavery experience was the erasure of identity based on national origin for black Americans, replaced by assignment to a stigmatized racial category. All other groups of Americans enjoy membership in a community that views itself as linked to a particular immigrant (or Native American) group and therefore to a particular nation of peoples.

During the slavery experience, this sense of nationhood was wiped out as slaveholders purposely mixed slaves of various tribal (read *national*) origins. This places African Americans at the bottom of the hierarchy of ethnic honor in the United States. This fact may combine with other stigmatizing aspects of slavery to make *all* black-white inequality today directly attributable to the historical slavery experience, whether or not particular individual blacks or whites had ancestors themselves that were in the United States before the time of abolition. This wider interpretation of the legacy of slavery would fall under a claim for "symbolic damages" or "group pain and suffering" in addition to back wages.

The benefit of extending the reparations argument to cover racial oppression in all forms up to the present day is that it provides a potentially simple way to calculate the right amount through property levels. One strategy is to use current property levels as a contemporary estimate of the long-run economic impact of slavery—both with respect to lost wages and as an institution with deleterious consequences after its abolition. Property values are often used as a direct measure of tort damages. If a chemical company spills its wares in my community, making my home unlivable, I am entitled to its full value (plus some amount for pain and suffering). Similarly, one could choose to view the wealth gap between blacks and whites as a result of slavery and its sequelae.

In fact, if there were one statistic that captured the persistence of racial inequality in the United States, it would be net worth—also known as wealth, equity, or assets. (If you want to know your net worth, all you have to do is add up everything you own and subtract from this figure your total amount of outstanding debt.) Overall, the typical white family enjoys a net worth that is more than seven times that of its non-white counterpart.

The wealth gap cannot be explained by income differences alone and, in this way, can be seen as conceptually distinct from "current" racial or class conditions. That is, while African Americans do earn less than whites, even when we compare black and white families at the same income levels, asset gaps remain large. For instance, at the lower end of the economic spectrum (incomes less than $15,000 per year), the median African American family has a net worth of zero, while the equivalent white family holds $10,000 worth of equity. Likewise, among the often-heralded new black middle class, the situation is not much better. The typical white family who earns $40,000 per year enjoys a nest egg of around $80,000. Its African American counterpart has less than half that amount.[3]

Why are these gaps so large, even among families with the same income levels? Some pundits—and many white Americans—believe that blacks perpetuate an oppositional culture that works to their own disadvantage. This culture manifests itself, they argue, in increased consumer spending at the cost of savings rates, in an anti-intellectual attitude in school and, more generally, in an oppositional relationship to mainstream social institutions, including the financial sector. Some theorists in this camp view this cultural stance as having had historical roots—that is, slavery and oppression—but as having now become self-perpetuating. Others see what they often call "underclass" behavioral patterns as genetically determined. The overwhelming majority of evidence, however, refutes these claims. Several studies have shown that black and white savings rates, for example, are indistinguishable. Surveys also show that blacks value education as much as, if not more than, whites.

In contrast to explanations that rely on behavior in the present, measures of wealth, more than other measures of socioeconomic status, capture long-term, multigenerational scars of prior inequality and are not easily erased by measures intended to guarantee equal opportunity or equal access. Most simply put, equity inequity is, in part, the result of the head start that whites have enjoyed in accumulating and passing on assets. In other words, it takes money to make money. Whites not only earn more now, they have always earned more than African Americans—a lot more. Wealth differences, in turn, feed on these long-term income differences.

Some researchers estimate that up to 80 percent of lifetime wealth accumulation results from gifts in one form or another from past generations of relatives.[4] These gifts can range from the down payment on a first home, to a free college education, to a bequest on the death of a parent. Over the long run, small initial differences in wealth holdings spin out of control, especially when combined with long-standing institutional barriers to black property accumulation ranging from the "black codes" of the nineteenth century to discrimination in the housing and credit markets that extended across the twentieth century up to the present. In other words, even if equal opportunity were finally here, wealth would be the last indicator to show it.

If we take the broad view that all wealth inequality between blacks and whites today is directly or indirectly a result of slavery, then there might be an argument to be made that whites should transfer 13 percent of their private wealth to blacks. Since the African American population is about 17 percent as large as the white population, this payment would close the gap. However, we may wish to preserve the analytic distinction between the earnings of the current generation and the legacy of injustice past (since we already have some policies in place to address current conditions—that is, affirmative action). Taking this approach, we would find that about half of the gap in wealth between whites and blacks is attributable to current income and demographic differences and would suggest a payment of white wealth half as large.

Another, more conservative approach is to use an upper-end estimate of intergenerational wealth stability to spin forward from the time of slavery to the present. Using the estimate mentioned earlier that 80 percent of our wealth can be attributed in one form or another to our parents' generation, we would find that after six generations after 1865 (assuming about twenty-two years per generation), about one-quarter (26.2 percent) of the distribution of wealth today is explained by the distribution of wealth at the time of emancipation (which would imply a transfer of 3.7 percent of private wealth).

Lowering the proportion of current wealth attributable to our ancestors or lowering the time frame of what we call a "generation" can lower this figure drastically. Correcting for this much of the gap would rectify only the wealth inequalities associated directly with slavery, not with Jim Crow, sharecropping, racial violence, housing segregation, or labor, educational and credit discrimination that has occurred since 1865.

WHAT IF, WHAT THEN?

Behind each of these numbers is a theoretical assumption (which includes the figure implicit in the present policy: zero). Behind each theoretical assumption is a rationalization for what is essentially an irrational political process. That said, numbers and logics still matter since they provide the grist for that political process.

Each year, Representative John Conyers Jr. (Dem.-Michigan) introduces a bill to establish a commission to examine the issue of slavery restitution to African Americans, and every year it goes nowhere. Even though in the current political climate reparations are a faraway dream of some activists, it is still worthwhile to go through the exercise of performing the calculations, if not for actual appropriations, at least for the light they shed on how race, history, and ascription matter in America.

What would it take to get from symbolic resolutions and theoretical calculations to a signed bill with appropriated funds? Reparations combine two policies that have been wildly unpopular in American political culture: taxes and group preferences. In fact, property taxes—the most logical mechanism by which wealth could be redistributed—are the least popular form of taxation even though they are generally more progressive than income or consumption taxes. Property tax revolts have occurred in political communities as diverse as Ronald Reagan's California (Proposition 13) and social-democratic Denmark. This is perhaps because private property has come to be seen as a natural right. So, if white resentment of affirmative action is strong and getting stronger, one can only imagine the backlash that would result from racially based wealth redistribution.

Reparations activists, therefore, would be wise to launder the money well. That is, the more that reparations could be paid out of general, existing revenue sources the less they would seem like a direct transfer from individual to individual. Of course, there is a tension between the size of reparations and the ability to finance them without a direct and obviously new tax.

But what if America did overcome the political obstacles to financing one of the aforementioned payment plans? What would be its effect? The answer, of course, depends on which plan we were to opt for and what you believe the effects of "money" are on life chances. For the sake of argument, let us assume we took the most radical option and completely equalized black-white wealth levels. Some research shows that when you compare blacks and whites who grew up in households with the same wealth levels, racial gaps in children's educational attainment evaporate. For example, my own study shows that when we compare African Americans and whites who come from families with the same net worth, blacks are, in fact, more likely to finish high school than their white counterparts and are just as likely to complete a four-year college degree.[5] This study also shows that racial gaps in welfare usage are eliminated when the impact of parental wealth is taken into account. However, the jury is still out on the race-wealth question with respect to a variety of other important indicators like health and life expectancy, test scores, occupational attainment, and even wealth levels themselves.[6]

If parental wealth levels in this scenario are truly causal—that is, it is not just that families who tend to have wealth also tend to have the skills that produce good students, for instance—then we should expect racial gaps in education to close in one generation. However, if it is not just parental wealth that matters for offspring but also other attributes such as parental education and race itself, then we are back to where we started from—an unlevel playing field in which we slowly accrete greater and greater inequalities over generations. In that case, the effect of slavery would continue to find wormholes through which to wiggle its way into the future. This possibility argues for a scenario in which we equalized black-white wealth levels and *also* kept in place affirmative action policies to address the lingering, indirect effects of what black racial status means in America.

Of course, no policies are born in a vacuum, and all policies generate unintended consequences. For example, windfall payments may reduce savings rates among the recipient population. They may also cause people to opt out of jobs they hold but do not like (this, of course, may be a good or bad thing). If large enough, reparations may even cause a big bump in consumer spending (again, a good or bad thing depending on the state of the economy and other fiscal policies).

Perhaps the most worrisome, however, is the question of how to turn a one-time payment into a stable and growing equity base for African American families. This is particularly an issue for the income poor (among which blacks are overrepresented) who have enormous, day-to-day financial pressures that might soak up the rising tide that reparations are intended to provide. Even more challenging is that as fast as progressives can think up ways to redistribute resources to underprivileged groups, the capital and credit markets are even faster at inventing ways to extract money from them.

Tax filing companies now offer "early" tax refunds for strapped individuals who need them right away—for a hefty percentage, of course. Predatory lenders target homeowners who may need cash for current expenses, draining their equity away. And check-cashing establishments—often called fringe banking—are the fastest growing sector of the banking industry. One can only imagine what kind of new financial industries would emerge if significant wealth redistribution were to occur. But it is at least equally important to try to envision what America would be like had the original promise of forty acres been more than just words—even if a century or two late.

NOTES

This chapter was originally published as "Forty Acres and a Mule: What If America Pays Reparations?" © 2002 by the American Sociological Association. Reprinted from *Contexts* 1, no. 3 (Fall 2002): 13–20, by permission.

1. See "Legal Scholars Debate Slavery Reparations," *Harper's* (November 2000), 37—51. Also see Randall Robinson, *The Debt: What America Owes to Blacks* (New York: Dutton, 1999).

2. Robert Browne, "The Economic Case for Reparations to Black America," *American Economic Review* 62 (1972): 39–46.

3. Melvin Oliver and Thomas Shapiro, *Black Wealth/White Wealth* (London, U.K.: Routledge, 1994).

4. See, e.g., Laurence J. Kotlikoff and Lawrence H. Summers, "The Role of Intergenerational Transfers in Aggregate Capital Accumulation," *Journal of Political Economy* 89 (August 1981): 706–32, and Franco Modigliani, "The Role of Intergenerational Transfers and Life Cycle Saving in the Accumulation of Wealth," *Journal of Economic Perspectives* 2 (1988): 15–40.

5. Dalton Conley, *Being Black, Living in the Red: Race, Wealth, and Social Policy in America* (Berkeley: University of California Press, 1999).

6. See, e.g., Dalton Conley, "Decomposing the Black-White Wealth Gap: The Role of Parental Resources, Inheritance and Investment Dynamics," *Sociological Inquiry* 71 (2001): 39–66. Also, Paul L. Menchik and Nancy A. Jianakoplos, "Black-White Wealth Inequality: Is Inheritance the Reason?" *Economic Inquiry* 35 (1997): 428–42.

6

War Compensation
Claims against the Japanese Government and Japanese Corporations for War Crimes

Laura Hein

REMEMBRANCE AND REDRESS

O ver the last decade, remembrance and redress for World War II actions have become major issues, both internationally and within Japan. In particular, the 1990s witnessed a concerted movement not only to institutionalize a critical narrative of Japanese acts during the war but also to pressure the Japanese government to officially repudiate those acts and to compensate wartime victims. This movement has included legal and educational efforts by women who were forced to provide sexual services to the Japanese military forces (the "military comfort women"), Asian men who were compelled to perform other kinds of slave labor, Chinese people subjected to chemical or biological experimentation, and Western POWs who were mistreated, starved, and forced to work in contravention of the Geneva Conventions on Prisoners of War. The increased effectiveness of these groups in bringing their cases to the public develops out of both domestic Japanese and international efforts to publicize and remember their horrible experiences.

These are people who suffered terribly at the hands of the Japanese during World War II. Some are women who were taken away by soldiers and impris-

oned for years, forced to provide sex to dozens of men every day. Their male
counterparts were assigned to back-breaking work on the skimpiest possible
rations. They were not safe from sadistic soldiers, and all have shocking tales
of gratuitous cruelty above and beyond their systematic torment. More fundamentally, their suffering was deemed inconsequential by the wartime Japanese and, all too often, by the leaders of other nations in the 1940s.

Their earlier attempts to collect redress over the last half a century were as
often stymied by their own governments as by the Japanese. The members
of these groups were frequently seen as less than human and, precisely for
that reason, once they captured sympathetic public attention, the moral
power of the tales they have to tell is enormous.

The underlying goal of all their efforts has been to win from the Japanese
government and people the recognition that those victimized are individuals
deserving of full human status, legally, socially, morally, and culturally. The
elderly victims also feel they are working to protect younger people from
the same cruel fate, as do their supporters. Their crusade is ultimately a
moral one for protecting human rights and international justice in the future
and, more pragmatically, for developing better tools for international
enforcement of those protections.

There are four main arenas in which demands for sustained remembrance
and redress about Japanese actions in World War II have appeared so far:
textbook reform, museum exhibits and memorials, metaphorical attempts to
institutionalize repudiation of the past through analogy and rhetoric, and
litigation for redress. After a brief discussion of the first three, this chapter
concentrates on the fourth strategy for redress. Rather than mutually exclusive strategies, these are complementary and overlapping ones, and many
activist groups have pursued all of them.

Textbooks and other school curricula have the imprimatur of the state and
are designed to socialize the next generation. Both those facts give textbooks
special significance as sites for official remembrance of the past. Activists for
textbook reform in Japan want Japanese, especially schoolchildren, to learn
about past Japanese wrongdoing. They hope both that this knowledge will
make future belligerence socially unacceptable and that young people will
fully understand the enormity of Japan's past crimes.

In Japan, the single most important figure in postwar textbook reform,
Ienaga Saburo, has used litigation as a tactic in this strategy. In a major innovation, he combined the two arenas of schools and courts. Between 1965 and
1997, Ienaga filed three major legal challenges to the Japanese Ministry of
Education's system of textbook "screening," which he attacked as censor-
ship. He hoped to change public opinion within Japan by encouraging discussion in school texts of such atrocities as the Nanjing Massacre. Ienaga and
his supporters saw the lawsuits over textbooks as one of many ways to insti-

tutionalize not only self-critical remembrance of the war but also more democratic and dissenting practices among the new generation of Japanese.[1]

Museum exhibits (especially those in national museums), memorials, annual days of remembrance, and other rituals of commemoration are another set of sites at which critics of Japan's wartime actions have insisted on including their narrative of the war and its meanings. The controversy over commemoration of the wrongs done by the Japanese during World War II has been an international struggle from the beginning. Far more than disputes over textbooks, this struggle increasingly involves private citizens, outside of as well as within Japan, who keep in touch with each other and publicize their positions through the World Wide Web. For example, the Global Alliance for Preserving the History of World War II in Asia, the leading North American–based coalition of activists demanding recognition of Japanese war crimes, has curated museum exhibits across North America and hosted virtual exhibits on its website.

The Global Alliance consists principally of professionals born in Taiwan, Hong Kong, and People's Republic of China (PRC) who now live in other countries. Moreover, when the Canadian parliament was considering a bill to establish an exhibit in the Canadian Museum of Civilization on crimes against humanity perpetrated during the twentieth century, the Canadian chapter of the Alliance campaigned successfully to add a section on Japanese war crimes.[2] Other recent controversies over war-related museum exhibits and memorials in Japan have occurred at the memorial to Korean atomic bomb victims at Hiroshima (the Showakan), a memorial to the war dead in Tokyo and an exhibit on the Battle of Okinawa in the Okinawa prefectural museum.[3]

Activists have also tried to institutionalize remembrance of Japanese atrocities by invoking parallels to the Nazi extermination of European Jews. Here again, the Global Alliance has pioneered educational efforts and also worked closely with the World Jewish Congress, the Simon Wiesenthal Center in Los Angeles, and the Canadian Jewish federation. Iris Chang's best-seller also made this imaginative connection in its title, *The Rape of Nanking: The Forgotten Holocaust of World War II*.[4]

These activists see the ubiquity of information on what they term "the European Holocaust" as a major reason why knowledge of that event is seared into international memory. That widespread consciousness, in turn, is in their view an important deterrent to future anti-Semitic actions. Activists working to publicize remembrance of the Nanjing Massacre state that "the constant reminders of the atrocities of Germany's Nazi regime are now recognized as a major preventive measure against the revival of Nazism in Germany" and see the reiteration of information itself as a key tactic in the task of establishing and institutionalizing the narrative of critical remembrance.[5]

This effort to call attention to the human rights violations committed by

Japan during World War II is most striking for the degree to which it is centered in North America and for the extent to which the goal is to establish a standard international moral judgment on the behavior of wartime Japan comparable to the one now prevailing with regard to Nazism. The internationalism of activists and their ties to advocates for remembrance and redress elsewhere enhance their effectiveness, a point to which I will return later. Moreover, this analogy operates simultaneously as a strategy for moral and legal persuasiveness, an intellectual category for organizing ideas, and a political tactic for gaining local power.[6] I should also note that the Japanese groups who most vociferously combat these efforts are also keenly aware of the debates over atrocities committed during World War II in Europe and of the arguments of the Holocaust deniers.

The activist movement supporting the plaintiffs' lawsuits for redress against Japan and publicizing their efforts is also notably international. Participants in the movement coordinate their efforts and operate globally. The Global Alliance for Preserving the History of World War II in Asia cooperated with the leading Japanese organization on these issues, the Japan War Responsibility Center (JWRC), or *Nihon no senso sekinin shiryo senta*, while the most internationally visible Korean group is the Korean Council for the Women Drafted for Sexual Slavery by Japan.[7]

The Global Alliance cooperated with the JWRC to organize a major conference in Tokyo, the "International Citizens' Forum on War Crimes and Redress: Seeking Reconciliation and Peace for the 21st Century," in December 1999. Together with an international feminist group, the Violence Against Women in War Network, all three organizations helped mount the Women's International War Crimes Tribunal on Japan's Military Sexual Slavery in December 2000. The Global Alliance and the JWRC both began their efforts in the late 1980s, and each has grown tremendously in the last few years.[8]

The adoption of critical war remembrance—in textbooks, national museums, public rhetoric, or elsewhere—is repudiation of the past and an attempt to create a sharp break between past and present. Demands for legal redress, such as reparations, are yet another strategy by which this struggle for control of remembrance takes place. The lawsuits are conceived of as both a form of witness to the past and a means of preventing its recurrence.

Defining legal redress as a strategy for control of remembrance has a number of implications. Foremost among them is recognition that demands for reparation—like all claims for remembrance—are forward-looking rather than backward-looking acts. While remembrance mobilizes the past and bases specific claims for redress on past actions, what is ultimately at stake is the present and future. This is why claims for redress for the distant past—for example, the era of legal slavery in the United States, which ended in

1865—have much in common politically with demands for redress to living people, although the precise legal issues differ.[9]

Politically speaking, the fight is over which aspects of the past are honored, accepted, or repudiated in the present. Similarly, most demands for redress for war crimes are primarily about forcing others to draw a bright line between actions of the past and the present, rather than primarily in hopes of achieving full restitution to the victims.

Second, demands for redress are really about claiming humanity in the present by demonstrating that this status was unjustly denied in the past. In other words, rather than reveling in the status of victimhood, plaintiffs use the charge that they were treated inhumanely to force a reevaluation of contemporary institutions so that their victimization and its lingering effects will end as soon as possible. This is true of all claims to commemorate and redefine the past, not just legal ones. The legal strategy of suing for redress is a claim for space at the table where future negotiations will take place. Like the museum collection and display issues discussed by Elizabeth Johnson and Ruth Phillips in this book, the real transformation achieved by these efforts involves rewriting the list of participants in such discussions rather than reaching a specific outcome in one museum display or one restitution settlement. When successful, the former "victims" have institutionalized themselves as individual people with legal clout in the future, comparable to that of other citizens.

This goal of establishing the right to negotiate over the future seems to me far from a politics of "sentimental solidarity of remembered victimhood" or of "historical myopia," as Ian Buruma put it, and from what Elazar Barkan has called, in his contribution to this book, the "morbidity of autistic self-indulgence in victimization." It is, rather, a shrewd mobilization of political support for victimized groups' claims to be treated as full human beings by means of reminders that that status was denied them in the past.[10]

LEGAL CLAIMS TO HUMANITY

The plaintiffs and their supporters in the redress suits against Japan have both benefited from, and contributed to, changing interpretations of international law in their attempts to enforce their status as individuals deserving protection from mistreatment. The key postwar legal transformation has been the growing consensus that individuals—not just states—have standing in international law. In addition, feminists have extended legal recognition of women's bodily integrity and redefined violations as crimes against their individual rights as people, rather than as affronts to the honor of their male relatives. These still-evolving legal developments are in part the product of political pressures applied by people who face discrimination today. This fact underlies the continuing relevance of these half-century-old stories.

One of the most important legal developments in this area has been the growing shift in reparations litigation toward compensating foreign individuals directly rather than the states of which they are citizens. Originally, reparations were thought of as entirely a matter between governments. Although other chapters in this collection explain that Germany began to pay reparations to individuals soon after World War II, in the Pacific region all parties thought of reparations in terms that were more traditional.

At the end of the war, the Allies all favored a major reparations program from Japan, which they saw as a method for the defeated aggressor nation to make amends to the countries it had ravaged during the war. Those payments went to national governments (including new postcolonial ones) to rebuild the physical infrastructure, and only very rarely to individuals. The Soviet Union literally dismantled factories and trucked them back to Siberia as reparations.

As the Cold War developed, however, despite the continuing Allied Occupation of Japan, U.S. policy on reparations changed, and the Americans began protecting Japan from reparations demands by other Allies in 1948. Before the end of the Occupation in 1952, it was clear that the United States would tolerate no restitution agreements that endangered Japanese economic development, even though all the Allies except the United States thought their economic development should take precedence over that of Japan.

The San Francisco Peace Treaty of 1952 did recognize Japan's responsibility to pay reparations to the governments in the areas Japan had invaded. But the treaty also stated that the amount of reparations would be worked out in a series of bilateral agreements between Japan and each of the other nations it had despoiled. The United States waived its right to reparations, as did the People's Republic of China (PRC), under pressure from the Americans.

Japan negotiated with the Philippines, Burma, Indonesia, and South Vietnam over the next decade to settle on relatively small reparations sums. When Japan resumed normal diplomatic relations with South Korea in 1965, the two countries also worked out a reparations arrangement, while the PRC agreed not to pursue reparations when it normalized relations with Japan in 1972. Japan has never negotiated reparations agreements with North Korea, an area devastated under Japanese rule. So, by 2001, there were still some outstanding legal issues related to state-to-state reparations, but most of the major players had established agreements resolving those claims at the national level.[11]

Most of the reparations accords disallowed legal claims by individuals against Japan. The official position of the Japanese government since that time has been that the San Francisco Peace Treaty protects the Japanese government from all future lawsuits brought by individuals. Generally, the courts of other nations have agreed. Both the U.S. and Japanese governments have continued to insist (as recently as December 1999) that this is the principle governing claims for reparations from the Japanese government.[12] Thus, most attempts over the last fifty years to bring suit against the Japanese government for enslaving POWs as workers or press-ganging local Asians into slave labor, for example, have been rejected either on the grounds that the plaintiffs had no standing or that the court had no jurisdiction in the matter—and only the legislature has the legal right to award compensation.

At least forty-six war redress suits have been filed in Japanese courts, many of which are still in litigation. Not all of them focus on forced labor. The plaintiffs in these suits include survivors of the 1937 Nanjing massacre, relatives of men who died in the biological and chemical warfare programs, former military sex slaves, Chinese injured after the war by ordnance (including chemical weapons) left behind, and former POWs and other slave laborers. Most of the outcomes so far have been disappointing to the plaintiffs.

Clearly, some of the most recent rulings demonstrate, however, that judges feel real discomfort about just dismissing the claims, given how much the plaintiffs had suffered at the hands of wartime officials. The growing confusion and angst revealed in these judgments suggest a shift in attitudes among jurists, although this change of heart has not yet been reflected in most of the rulings. In several of these cases, the judges seem to be begging the Diet to offer some compensation so that they will not be put in the position of denying all recompense to people who were deeply wronged.[13]

For example, in April 1998, the Shimonoseki branch of the Yamaguchi Prefectural Court ordered Japan to pay compensation to two former military comfort women because the Diet had failed to carry out its constitutional duty to enact an appropriate compensation law and therefore was liable for negligence. This is an interesting tack for two reasons: first, it suggests that the courts have an obligation to intervene if the legislature fails to shoulder its responsibility and, second, the court reasoned on the basis of domestic tort law rather than of international law. The court also agreed with the plaintiffs on the merits of the women's case, stating that "the comfort woman system was extremely inhuman and horrifying even [by] the standard of . . . the middle of the 20th century."[14] The Japanese government appealed, and the Tokyo District Court overturned this ruling on the grounds that individuals cannot sue nations under international law. The plaintiffs' lawyers plan to appeal to Japan's Supreme Court. These developments indicate that the hints of discomfort among Japanese judges remain as yet only suggestions of possible future legal changes.[15]

THE GROWING PRECEDENT FOR RECOGNIZING INDIVIDUAL STANDING IN INTERNATIONAL LAW

While the San Francisco Peace Treaty reaffirmed that Japanese reparations claims should be settled between states and laid out the parameters of liability for signatory governments, it also helped institutionalize the legal bases for future challenges by individuals. One of the conditions of the treaty was that the Japanese government explicitly accepted the verdict of the Military Tribunals for the Far East, also known as the Tokyo War Crimes Trials.

The Tokyo trials followed the Nuremberg precedent both chronologically and legally. They convicted major Japanese wartime leaders of crimes against humanity. The Tokyo trials also enlarged the scope of offenses by expanding the interpretation of "crimes against humanity" to include crimes of omission—that is, failing to prevent breaches of the conventional laws of war. Thus, for example, Matsui Iwane, who was in charge of the forces responsible for the Nanjing Massacre, was convicted and sentenced to death for failing to prevent the massacre.

The precedents set by the Nuremberg and Tokyo trials and by Japanese acceptance of their verdicts in the peace treaty later became the basis for innovative new claims against the Japanese government and against Japanese firms, enlarging the opportunities for individual claims for redress, particularly for human rights violations. By the 1990s, a new standard of international law was emerging, partially based on new laws but mostly derived from reinterpretations of older international law both pre-surrender and the Nuremberg/Tokyo laws. This development suggests that the official Japanese position that restitution is only a matter between states is increasingly incompatible with customary international law. The United Nations has played a particularly active role in establishing the idea that individuals have standing in international law and a right to claim enforcement of fundamental human rights and freedoms and restitution as well.[16]

As part of that broader effort, the former military comfort women and their attorneys have pioneered new legal strategies, particularly ones that emphasized their status as forced laborers. They have not only opened new territory recognizing individuals as having standing in international law, as noted in the preceding, but they have also contributed to evolving feminist legal theory.

The argument that their forced (sexual) labor was a crime against humanity also has encouraged other slave laborers, both civilians and POWs, to bring suit for redress for their forced labor. For example, in March 1995, the Federation of Korean Trade Unions requested that the International Labor Organization (ILO) rule that the comfort women were forced laborers, since they were not paid for their "work." The trade union federation then argued that that ruling should be extended to include male Korean wartime laborers. The ILO did rule as the federation wished in 1996, and its Committee of Experts did so again in 1997, strengthening the claim that all the workers were enslaved.[17] Neither the United Nations nor the ILO rulings are legally binding on Japan, but they are important indicators of changing international norms.

The ability of the military comfort women to mobilize international support and to get a hearing—in the courts of both law and public opinion—is also clearly due to another recent development: namely, the international sea change in attitudes toward sexual violence and toward the rights of women to bodily integrity. That shift was underscored by widespread horror at the massive numbers of crimes specifically directed at women as part of larger struggles in recent years, such as in Bosnia. The strength of international coalitions of feminists pushing for legal changes is also new, as are less harsh attitudes toward prostituted women in some parts of the globe.

The plaintiffs in the military comfort women suits have drawn on a century of international law to make their case. A major plank in their arguments has been that in 1925 Japan ratified three major international covenants relevant to the comfort women's case—the International Convention for the Suppression of the Traffic in Women and Children of 1921–1922, the International Agreement for the Suppression of the White Slave Traffic of 1904, and the International Convention for the Suppression of the White Slave Traffic of 1910.

The 1910 Convention, which was reaffirmed by the original signatories in the 1921 Convention, stated that "whoever, in order to gratify the passions of another person, has procured, enticed, or led away, even with her consent, a woman or girl under age, for immoral purposes, shall be punished." The 1921 convention not only condemned the traffic in women and children but also created rules for signatory states to prevent such trafficking. Japan's actions with respect to the comfort women appear to have been in clear violation of this accord.[18]

The Japanese government asserts that its activities in its colonial possessions were exempt from this convention, which only covers international relations and not activities that take place wholly within the boundaries of sovereign nations or empires. This was its position in the prewar and wartime years as well and partially explains why so many of the unfortunate military comfort women were Koreans.[19]

The fact that policymakers within the wartime Japanese government appear to have discussed interpretations of these conventions also suggests that they could be liable for conspiracy charges or another indictment that focuses on intent to commit a crime. To imagine that these government lawyers calmly analyzed international law so that they could determine who could or could not safely be kidnapped and tortured is chilling. Their wartime calculations also undercut the defensive argument that legal, coercive prostitution was normal and unremarkable for the era.

The North Korean government has argued that the annexation of Korea in 1910 was itself a crime, and therefore, since Korea was not legally part of Japan, the forcible recruitment of Korean women as comfort women should also be considered a crime under international humanitarian law. Others have argued that the Japanese government was not in violation of international law when Koreans were coerced into labor on the Korean peninsula, but that it was so as soon as any Koreans had been transported beyond Imperial Japan's borders.[20] Clearly, no consensus on these issues exists as yet, although the trend toward greater accountability is also obvious.

Claims of Japanese culpability rely on the assertion that the military comfort women are covered under the category of "white slavery," which the Japanese government rejects. Yet the Special Rapporteur for the UN Commission on Human Rights, Radhika Coomaraswamy, argued in her report on the subject in January 1996 that the government was wrong on this point. In her words, "The practice of 'comfort women' should be considered a clear case of sexual slavery and a slavery-like practice in accordance with the approach adopted by relevant international human rights bodies and mechanisms." She also argued that the term "military sexual slaves" was far more accurate than the euphemistic "comfort women."[21]

The two UN investigators on the comfort women case, Coomaraswamy and Gay McDougall, both concluded that Japan should be held liable for violating the 1929 Geneva Convention for the Amelioration of the Condition of the Wounded and Sick in Armies in the Field, which Japan agreed to honor in 1942. Article 3 of the Convention states that "prisoners-of-war are entitled to respect for their persons and honour. Women shall be treated with all consideration due to their sex."[22]

The investigators argue that this was the prevailing standard in international law at the time. More generally, the attorneys for the former military comfort women and other forced laborers have cited the Laws and Customs of War on Land Convention of 1907, which includes provisions protecting family honor and rights as well as the lives of persons. Family honor has been interpreted to include the right of women in the family not to be subjected to the humiliating practice of rape. This interpretation of "honor" is far more attractive to feminists who seek full legal protections for women than are older versions, which define female chastity as essential to the honor of male relatives and thus legitimate male actions that police women's behavior.

In a strategy that rhetorically better suits feminist goals, the comfort women and their lawyers also argued that acts of rape, forced prostitution, enforced pregnancy, or forced abortion—all attacks on women as women—are crimes against humanity rather than against honor. They base their arguments on the Nuremberg and Tokyo precedents.

Those precedents helped to expand international laws protecting individuals after World War II. Both the Nuremberg and Tokyo tribunals defined murder, extermination, enslavement, deportation, and other inhumane acts committed against any civilian population before or during the war as crimes against humanity. They also tried people for crimes that were only fully codified after the end of the war, using the argument that crimes against humanity were universal and timeless.

The International Law Commission of the 46th session of the UN and Special Rapporteur Coomaraswamy both argue that "there exists the category of war crimes under customary international law. The category overlaps with, but is not identical to, the category of grave breaches of the 1949 Geneva Conventions."[23] Others have argued successfully that the claims of those tribunals should be accepted because they merely codified existing customary law. The position staked out by such people as Radhika Coomaraswamy is still controversial and may or may not prevail fully in courts. Although change may be slow, however, it seems clear that the trend is toward greater recognition of individual rights by international law.

In 1968, in an important technical development, the UN championed the Convention on the Non-Applicability of Statutory Limitations to War Crimes and Crimes against Humanity, which mandated that international law precludes a statute of limitations for gross violations of human rights. That change made it possible for individuals to sue even if, under local laws, the statute of limitations had already been exceeded. (The statute of limitations in Japan is twenty years for civil claims and fifteen years for the most severe criminal claims, so legal avenues for redress for World War II–era events would by now have long since expired.)

The Japanese government has argued that it is not liable for any transgressions on the basis of postwar law, since those statutes were not in force during the war. Yet in 1993 the Secretary-General of the UN argued, in connection with the creation of the International Criminal Tribunal for the former Yugoslavia (ICTY), that rape, torture, enforced prostitution, and murder were already illegal under international customary law. Similarly, Coomaraswamy argued that "certain aspects of international humanitarian law are beyond any doubt part of customary international law and that States may be held responsible for the violation of these international humanitarian law principles even though they were not signatories to the particular convention."[24]

Law is still evolving on these issues. The Rome Statute of the International Criminal Court, adopted on July 17, 1998, criminalizes "rape, sexual slavery, enforced prostitution, forced pregnancy, enforced sterilization, or any other form of sexual violence of comparable gravity." Over eighty states have signed this convention, but Japan is not among them. This statute is not retroactive, so the court would not hear cases involving World War II–era crimes. But it is a sign that sexual slavery during war is more clearly demarcated as an international crime and suggests that methods and standards for prosecution and punishment of that crime will develop, further institutionalizing international legal norms criminalizing sexual slavery. Here, too, international understandings of the law seem to be moving in the direction of greater rights for individuals, especially women.[25]

In August 1999, the UN Subcommission on Human Rights rejected Japan's reasons for denying government compensation to women who were impressed as comfort women. The commission stressed that "governments are responsible for war crimes and other rights violations committed by their soldiers." Moreover, the governments "shall, if the case demands, be liable to pay compensation." Etsuro Totsuka, one of the lawyers for the plaintiffs, has said that this ruling undercut Japan's only substantial legal defense. The UN resolution was in part a response to the report by Gay McDougall, the American member of the UN panel, which denounced the military comfort system as the systematic war crime of sexual enslavement.[26]

SUITS AGAINST CORPORATIONS

Unlike national governments, corporations are not protected by treaty from lawsuits. For this reason, in recent years a number of former slave laborers have shifted the focus of their efforts to obtain redress from the state to corporations in both Japanese and foreign courts. This strategy is a major innovation and has already yielded results through out-of-court settlements. In April 1999, the steelmaker NKK Corp. agreed to pay reparations of about $33,000 to a South Korean man, Kim Kyong Suk, who not only was forced to go to Japan and work under grueling conditions for two years during the war but also was tortured after Korean workers protested a derogatory comment made by an NKK official at the plant. NKK did not admit legal liability but agreed to the settlement with Kim, who had sued for $81,000 and a public apology in 1991 in a Japanese court. Since then, the corporations Nippon Steel, Nachi-Fujikoshi, and Kajima have also settled with Korean or Chinese forced laborers, suggesting that the public relations nightmare of a lengthy lawsuit is a powerful political weapon, even though it has not yet been proven successful as a legal one.[27]

Globalization and the relatively new wealth of major German and Japanese corporations have created conditions allowing lawsuits in U.S. courts against the legally incorporated local subsidiaries of German- or Japan-based corporations. In other words, this legal innovation is based not only on the evolution of the law but also on that of the global economy. The most famous of these forced labor suits have been against German corporations, but Japanese firms have also been targets. Since 1999, the venues for lawsuits have expanded to include the United States, based on new legal strategies at both the state and national level.

A 1999 California law, written by state senator Tom Hayden, allows POWs to sue private corporations for compensation for the work they performed and for damages for inhumane working conditions; the law also extends the statute of limitations through January 1, 2010. It was directed against "the Nazi regime, its allies and sympathizers." Clearly, Japan was a major intended target, since the sponsors explained that they were motivated in part by irritation at the persistent failure of suits in Japanese courts against the Japanese government. The California legislature also adopted a companion resolution authored by then state senator Mike Honda (Dem.-San Jose) calling on the Japanese government to make a "clear and unambiguous apology" for war crimes committed by the military.[28]

As soon as the law passed, former POW Lester I. Tenney filed a lawsuit in Los Angeles Superior Court in August 1999 against Mitsui & Co. of Japan and New York as well as against Mitsui Mining Company. The Japanese government is not a party to this suit.[29] Three more former POWs, George Cobb, Frank Dillman, and Maurice Mazer, also filed suit in September 1999 against Mitsubishi. They had been pressed into slave labor in a copper mine in Akita Prefecture.[30]

The following month, about five hundred POWs, all survivors of the Bataan Death March, filed a nationwide class action suit in U.S. District Court in Albuquerque, New Mexico, against five corporations and their U.S. subsidiaries—Kawasaki Heavy Industries, Mitsubishi International Corporation, Mitsui & Co., Nippon Steel, and Showa Denko—claiming that they had been abused and exploited as slave labor. A change in federal law made those lawsuits easier to pursue; in 1996, Congress had passed an amendment that simplified procedures for plaintiffs to file under the Alien Tort Claims Act.[31]

The most recent developments have not favored the plaintiffs, however. A number of the California cases were consolidated and moved to federal court, where they were combined with others and eventually grouped into a huge class action suit involving twenty-five thousand former POWs or their survivors. In September 2000, U.S. district judge Vaughn Walker ruled against the plaintiffs on the grounds that the 1952 treaty had resolved all World War II–era claims for mistreatment, including those against corporations. His reasoning rested on the fear that the lawsuits had the potential to "unsettle half a century of diplomacy" between Japan and the United States, suggesting little distinction between the state and private firms in his mind. The U.S. Department of State had also asked the judge to dismiss the case on precisely those grounds.[32] The plaintiffs are appealing the ruling.

An important feature of the contemporary legal and commemorative environment is the cross-fertilization of the redress efforts against the Japanese government and firms with kindred movements elsewhere. The campaigns to win redress from Japanese firms for World War II–era actions are linked in a variety of ways to the ones for redress from European firms.[33] The plaintiffs in the cases in U.S. courts have been particularly encouraged by the out-of-court success of similar lawsuits against German corporations, which recently agreed to set up a joint compensation fund. Organizations such as the Simon Wiesenthal Center in Los Angeles have given legal and technical assistance to activists for war compensation from Japan. For example, the Wiesenthal Center petitioned the Justice Department to reverse a 1948 decision to grant amnesty to members of the infamous Japanese biological warfare Unit 731.

Plaintiffs have also used the victories regarding compensation to Holocaust survivors, both wins in lawsuits and out-of-court settlements, as precedents in their legal arguments. In fact, those cases, along with the American and Canadian payment of reparations and apologies to its resident Japanese noncitizens for internment during the war, have also been cited in at least one case to show a prevailing international norm for apologizing to and compensating individual foreign victims whose rights had been violated by the state during World War II.[34] And, in an even closer link, one group of ex-POWs, who filed suit in Los Angeles on December 7, 1999, at precisely 10:55 A.M. (the exact moment of the attack on Pearl Harbor in 1941), has retained Ed Fagan, the media-savvy lawyer who litigated a major class action suit against several Swiss banks.[35]

These political and legal efforts are already changing the global environment by making people everywhere more knowledgeable about Japanese wartime actions and establishing an international moral and (to a lesser degree) legal standard that individuals should be protected from certain forms of harm, even in time of war. Some of the wider implications of those efforts are only now emerging.

In Japan, the push to hold Japanese corporations accountable in U.S. courts is likely to encourage people to widen the scope of their thinking about war crimes and redress. Some Japanese, such as those working with the Japan War Responsibility Center, are systematically collecting new evidence of Japanese war crimes for the plaintiffs in those cases.[36] But, like their counterparts elsewhere, they are also using the developing global legal acknowledgment that individuals have the right to sue for war crimes and to reexamine the behavior of other states and corporations as well.

Professor Yasuaki Ōnuma, a perceptive and thoughtful analyst of legal issues, commented on the U.S.-based lawsuits that "it's very unfortunate that the matter has come to court. From a moral perspective, especially after we became an economic superpower, we could have and should have [passed] the domestic law to respond to the voices of the victims." But Ōnuma also decried "the tendency of the U.S. to settle every matter in a U.S. court and try to impose the effect of that decision globally. It has a self-righteous look. What will be the effect when there are claims from the Vietnamese or from Latin American countries who suffered from intervention by the United States? As a human rights activist, I personally understand the feelings of the victims. But as a lawyer, I see dangers."[37] Ōnuma fears that these efforts will lead to a conservative, nationalist backlash in Japan, out of frustration that only Japanese and German war crimes are being pursued.

Indeed, some of the same U.S.-based activists who seek redress from Japan also have leveled criticism at the United States. For example, in 1999 the Global Alliance added information on the case of Wen Ho Lee to its website and solicited money for his legal defense fund. The Alliance sees Lee's case as thematically linked to the efforts for redress from Japan because the U.S. government behaved like the Japanese in two respects: it established a hysterical tone of danger to national security and then took disproportionately harsh action against an individual, apparently because of his Chinese ethnicity.[38]

CONCLUSION

The cumulative effect of a decade of debate in Japan over the country's wartime past is hard to summarize. Certainly, the vast majority of Japanese are far better informed than they were before about the cruelties their soldiers perpetrated against others during the war. General interest magazines, professional journals, and newspapers publish spirited debates over what to make of these revelations. At this point, nearly all Japanese accept the claims that the Nanjing Massacre, for example, certainly occurred. Probably a substantial majority also acknowledge that the incident was a six-week orgy of torture (much of it sexualized) and murder of unarmed civilians. Most Japanese also recognize that failure to acknowledge and apologize for actions such as the Nanjing Massacre will hinder the development of better relations with Asia in the future. These attitudes explain the substantial movement in Japan over the last decade to reexamine and repudiate the war.

Yet many Japanese resent what they see as a global double standard. The former Allies have never had to explain and atone for their wartime behavior as have the former Axis powers. While all the major European and American states ran brutal colonial regimes, Japan's empire is remembered overseas as cruel and oppressive for its Japaneseness rather than for its imperial nature. As they see it, by framing the problem as one of *Japanese* brutality, Westerners are exhibiting precisely the same racism that had impelled the Japanese into a defensive strategy of imperial conquest a century ago. The issue for them is less whether the Japanese committed war crimes during World War II than whether other states have evaded punishment for comparable behavior. Many Japanese are convinced that they are being held to a far higher standard of wartime conduct than are the Americans, the British, the French, or the Dutch, and so, metaphorically, once again they face hostile encirclement by the Allied powers. That belief is the core around which a politics of resentment is forming and may grow strong.

Yasuaki Ōnuma, the legal scholar, is right that the process of articulating and enforcing an international moral standard will lead to increasingly precise charges of hypocrisy against those who do not examine their own past, whether these are nations or firms. U.S. citizens have led the attack against Axis war criminals and helped change global attitudes toward inhumane acts and policies during war. Yet the United States has its own dark wartime corners, during World War II and in more recent conflicts.[39] As both legal action and other forms of remembrance proliferate, Americans should expect that increasingly others will expect them to examine critically the U.S. wartime past.

There is now a small but highly vocal movement in Japan to rehabilitate the war as a noble nationalist project, one dedicated to ousting the racist Westerners from Asia. The arguments of those neonationalists are most successful when they show that foreign critics of Japan are far more forgiving of their own brutal wartime behavior than they are of Japan's. They have been less successful, however, when they have turned their attention to other Asians. The open contempt that contemporary Japanese right-wing nationalists have shown for the former slave laborers, especially the former military comfort women, has troubled many other Japanese.

The neonationalists are rejecting the proposition that they treat as equals people whom they still see as racial and gender inferiors. Their rage is fueled by a sense of diminished entitlement. Like the "angry white man" political phenomenon of the 1980s in the United States, which also occurred in the context of economic malaise, this is a plaintive backlash against changing social attitudes in the present.

In the last decade, groups long discriminated against in Japan—including Koreans, Ainu, Okinawans, outcastes, and women—have become far more vocal and insistent on their right to full citizenship. They have made significant progress too. Korean residents have fought for access to jobs in local government as teachers, postal workers, and civil servants, for example. Several major cities have changed their exclusionary policies recently. The resident Koreans, like the others, want full recognition as individuals deserving of human status.

The redress movement is thus not just an international legal effort but is also an important educational tool for problematizing and changing social attitudes within Japan. This is the main battle: whether or not the plaintiffs win their cases in court, they and their supporters have established themselves as vocal and effective contributors to contemporary Japanese debate. It seems unlikely that their stories, now that they are in the public realm, will soon be forgotten.

NOTES

1. See Laura Hein and Mark Selden, eds., *Censoring History: Citizenship and Memory in Japan, Germany, and the United States* (Armonk, N.Y.: M.E. Sharpe, 2000), especially the introduction by Hein and Selden and the essay by Nozaki Yoshiko and Inokuchi Hiromitsu, "Japanese Education, Nationalism, and Ienaga Saburo's Textbook Lawsuits," 96–126.

2. The website of the Global Alliance for Preserving the History of World War II in Asia is at www.sjwar.org (accessed July 25, 2002). This is an international federation of over forty organizations. See also the Canada Association for Learning and Preserving the History of World War II in Asia (ALPHA), at www.vcn.bc.ca/alpha/ (accessed July 25, 2001). Another important activist and research group is the Japan-based Japan War Responsibility Center, at www.jca.apc.org/JWRC/center/english/index-english.htm (accessed July 25, 2002). The Canadian exhibit has not yet been mounted but there is a World War II exhibit that discusses Japanese treatment of POWs. A virtual version is available at www.warmuseum.ca/cwm/tour/trnazeng .html (accessed February 10, 2001).

3. Laura Hein and Mark Selden, eds., *Living with the Bomb: American and Japanese Cultural Conflicts in the Nuclear Age* (Armonk, N.Y.: M.E. Sharpe, 1997). For the Korean memorial, see the essay by Lisa Yoneyama, "Memory Matters: Hiroshima's Korean Atom Bomb Memorial and the Politics of Ethnicity," in Hein and Selden, eds. *Living with the Bomb*, 202–31, and for the Tokyo museum, see especially Ellen H. Hammond, "Commemoration Controversies: The War, the Peace, and Democracy in Japan," in *Living with the Bomb*, 100–21. For the Okinawa case, see Gerald Figal, "Waging Peace on Okinawa," *Critical Asian Studies* 33, no. 1 (January–March 2001): 37–69.

4. Iris Chang, *The Rape of Nanking: The Forgotten Holocaust of World War II* (New York: Basic Books, 1997).

5. In addition to the citations in note 2, see "Basic Facts on the Nanjing Massacre and the Tokyo War Crimes Trial" on the website of the China News Digest, at museums.cnd.org/njmassacre/nj.html (accessed February 10, 2001).

6. I have argued this point at greater length in Laura Hein, "Savage Irony: The Imaginative Power of the Military Comfort Women in the 1990s," *Gender and History* 11, no. 2 (July 1999): 336–72.

7. See note 2 for JWRC website. The Korean Council website is at witness. peacenet.or.kr/kindex.htm (accessed September 17, 2002). There are a number of other Asia-based groups working on these issues, such as the Asia-Japan Women's Resource Center at www.aworc.org/org/ajwrc/ajwrc.html (accessed September 17, 2002).

8. Press release at Global Alliance website, at www.sjwar.org. See also VAWW-Net-Japan website, at www.hri.ca/partners/vawwnet/ (accessed September 17, 2002).

9. It is certainly harder to develop methods of calculating "just" compensation for injustices committed in the more distant past or to define who, if anyone, should stand in for the now-deceased direct perpetrators and victims. See Roy L. Brooks, ed., *When Sorry Isn't Enough: The Controversy over Apologies and Reparations for Human Injustice* (New York: New York University Press, 1999).

10. Ian Buruma, "The Joys and Perils of Victimhood," *New York Review of Books* 46, no. 6 (April 8, 1999): 4–8. See also Elazar Barkan, *The Guilt of Nations: Restitution and Negotiating Historical Injustices* (New York: Norton, 2000).

11. The Republic of China (Taiwan) actually waived reparations for the People's Republic of China (PRC) as well, and the claim that the Taiwan government spoke for all China in this matter has been a source of tension between Japan and the PRC. For reparations, see Chitoshi Yanaga, chap. 8 in *Big Business in Japanese Politics* (New Haven, Conn.: Yale University Press, 1968); Nancy Bernkopf Tucker, "American Policy Toward Sino-Japanese Trade in the Postwar Years: Politics and Prosperity," *Diplomatic History* 8, no. 3 (Summer 1984): 183–208; Aaron Forsberg, *America and the Japanese Miracle: The Cold War Context of Japan's Postwar Economic Revival, 1950–1960* (Chapel Hill: University of North Carolina Press, 2000), 70–72.

12. "Bill to Allow Suits against Japan Firms for Forced Labor," Kyodo News Service, November 9, 1999; George Nishiyama, "Japanese Industry Faces US Lawsuit," *Guardian* (London), December 9, 1999; Doug Struck and Kathryn Tolbert, "WWII Vets Revive Grievances with Japan," *Washington Post*, January, 19, 2000; BERNAMA, "176,000 Dollar Damage Suit by Dutch POWs, Woman Rejected," *The Malaysian National News Agency*, November 30, 1998.

13. Tong Yu, "Recent Developments: Reparations for Former Comfort Women of World War II," *Harvard International Law Journal* 36 (Spring 1995): 528; "High Court Nixes Redress Suit," *Japan Times*, December 21, 1999; "Court Rejects War Criminals' Payment Demand," *Yomiuri Shinbun English Edition*, July 14, 1998. This last case involved Koreans who had served as prison guards in the Japanese military, been convicted of war crimes, and then denied military pensions by the Japanese government after the war, unlike their Japanese counterparts. Here too the judge ruled against them but then commented that the law was unfair.

14. Etsuro Totsuka, "War Crimes Japan Ignores: The Issue of 'Comfort Women,'" November 30, 1999, at www.jca.apc.org./JWRC/center/english/Warcrime.htm (accessed September 17, 2002), and Hiromitsu Inokuchi and Yoshiko Nozaki, "Court Cases, Citizen Groups, and the Unresolved Issues of War: Updates and Brief Commentary," (n.d.), at www.jca.apc.org./JWRC/center/english/Courtcas.htm (accessed September 17, 2002). See also Etsuro Totsuka, "Translations: Commentary on a Victory for 'Comfort Women': Japan's Judicial Recognition of Military Sexual Slavery," *Pacific Rim Law & Policy Journal* 8 (January 1999): 47–61.

15. "Wartime Redress Suit Rejected," *Japan Times*, March 27, 2001.

16. Tong Yu, "Recent Developments"; Radhika Coomaraswamy, *Report of the Special Rapporteur on Violence against Women, Its Causes and Consequences, in Accordance with Commission on Human Rights Resolution 1994/45*, January 4, 1996, United Nations, Economic and Social Council, E/CN.4/1996/53/Add.1, 21; Gay McDougall, UN Sub-Commission on Prevention of Discrimination and Protection of Minorities, *Final Report on Systematic Rape, Sexual Slavery and Slavery-Like Practices during Armed Conflict*, August 12, 1998. This report confirmed all the Coomaraswamy findings and rebutted the Japanese government's claims that it was not liable "for grave violations of human rights and humanitarian law, violations that amount in their totality to crimes against humanity."

17. Coomaraswamy, *Report of the Special Rapporteur*, 18. See also Totsuka, "War Crimes Japan Ignores."

18. See, for example, the "Complaint by Korean Council for the Women Drafted for Sexual Slavery by Japan," available at witness.peacenet.or.kr/e_comfort/library/complaint/comp.htm (accessed September 17, 2002).

19. Yoshimi Yoshiaki, "Violations of International Law and War Crime Trials," chap. 5 in his *Comfort Women: Sexual Slavery in the Japanese Military during World War II* (New York: Columbia University Press, 2000). See also Tong Yu, "Recent Developments." Tong Yu describes this reading of the Convention as not only "inconsistent with the fundamental purpose of that article, which was to allow countries to eradicate such traffic," but also a "perverse" one. There were two other multilateral agreements prohibiting forced prostitution (1904) and slavery (1926) in the pre–World War II era. While Japan did not sign either one, their existence suggests that these prohibitions had "acquired the force of custom" before World War II.

20. Coomaraswamy, *Report of the Special Rapporteur*, 15–20. See also Won Soon Park, "Japanese Reparations Policies and the 'Comfort Women' Question," *Positions* 5, no. 1 (Spring 1997): 107–34.

21. I work through this linguistic issue in "Savage Irony." While I prefer the term "military comfort women" for educational purposes, there is an obvious advantage to the term "military sexual slaves" in this legal context. For the quotation, see Coomaraswamy, *Report of the Special Rapporteur*, 3.

22. Coomaraswamy, *Report of the Special Rapporteur*, 19; McDougall, "Final Report." See also Barry A. Fisher, "Japan's Postwar Compensation Litigation," *Whittier Law Review* 22, no. 35 (Fall, 2000): 35–46.

23. Coomaraswamy, *Report of the Special Rapporteur*, 15.

24. The International Tribunal is UN document number (S/25704). Coomaraswamy, *Report of the Special Rapporteur*, 15–19. Moreover, some (including the North Korean government) have argued that the act of military sexual slavery is a form of genocide and therefore falls under the 1948 Convention on the Prevention and Punishment of the Crime of Genocide, which is also invoked to show generally accepted norms of customary international law even before 1948. I personally don't find this logic convincing, but the Koreans link this policy to other Japanese efforts to eliminate Korean national identity, such as mandating Japanese language school curricula and forcing Koreans to change their names to Japanese ones.

25. Yasushi Higashizawa, "The Legal Strategy in View of Offending State: Current Situation on the Reparation and Punishment of the Responsible," at witness.peacenet.or.kr/symejapan2.htm (accessed September 17, 2002). In September 2000, fourteen rape and torture victims won a $745 million settlement (almost certainly uncollectible) from Bosnian Serb leader Radovan Karadzic on these grounds in a U.S. court. Elizabeth Amon, "Rape in Wartime: Letting the Victims Tell Their Stories," *National Law Journal*, September 18, 2000. See also Catharine A. MacKinnon, "Turning Rape into Pornography: Postmodern Genocide," *Ms.*, July/August 1993, 24–30.

26. *Global Alliance Newsletter*, September 1999, 6.

27. "NKK Pays 4.1 Million Yen to Wartime Laborer," *Japan Times*, April 7, 1999. Takagi quoted in Sonni Efron, "Pursuit of WWII Redress Hits Japanese Boardrooms," *Los Angeles Times*, January 10, 2000; "South Koreans Sue the State, MHI for Wartime Forced Labor," *Japan Times*, December 7, 2000.

28. Efron, "Pursuit of WWII Redress Hits Japanese Boardrooms." Honda is now in the U.S. Congress.

29. Ann W. O'Neill, "POW Files Suit for Compensation," *Los Angeles Times*, August 12, 1999. Tenney, aged 79, had worked in the Mitsui Miike coal mine under extremely harsh conditions. O'Neill notes: "Tenney claims that besides being regularly beaten and tortured, he suffered a broken nose, gashes on his face, knocked-out teeth, and sword and bayonet wounds to his shoulder and leg." Lester I. Tenney, "High Time Japanese Settled Up with Slave Laborers," *Houston Chronicle*, December 28, 1999.

30. K. Seana, "3 Former US POWs File Suit against Mitsubishi," *Kyodo News*, September 14, 1999; "Ex-POW Sues Nippon Sharyo in Forced Labor Case," *Kyodo News*, August 20, 1999.

31. Garry Pierre-Pierre, "Ex-POWs Sue 5 Big Japanese Companies over Forced Labor," *The New York Times*, September 15, 1999; Michael Dobbs, "Lawyers Target Japanese Abuses," *Washington Post*, March 5, 2000; Paul Abrahams, "Tokyo Grapples with Lawsuits for War Conduct," *Financial Times*, December 9 1999; Chalmers Johnson, "Japan Should Pay for Individuals' Suffering," *Los Angeles Times*, March 31, 2000, Op-ed.

32. Louis Sahagun, "Suit on WWII Slave Labor in Japan Voided," *Los Angeles Times*, September 22, 2000; "U.S. Judge Cites Treaty in Rejecting POW Suit," *Japan Times*, September 23, 2000.

33. Kazuo Ishii, "War Lawsuits against Japan on Rise in US," *Yomiuri Shinbun*, *English edition*, September 18, 1999.

34. These were the Japanese-born immigrants who were barred from becoming citizens because of their race, as opposed to their U.S. or Canadian-born children, who were also interned. See Totsuka, "War Crimes Japan Ignores."

35. The complaint was posted on the World Wide Web at www.japanesewwwi iclaims.com/default1.asp, but it appears that this URL is no longer accessible. See also Jonathan Levy, "The California Cure for Japanese War Crimes," *Flame*, no. 5 (Summer 2000), at www.flamemag.dircon.co.uk/levy_japanese_war_crimes.htm (accessed September 17, 2002).

36. In addition to their website, see their journal, *Sensō Sekinin Kenkyū*.

37. Struck and Tolbert, "WWII Vets Revive Grievances with Japan." Note also the link to another event being recast as a holocaust—the transatlantic slave trade. One of the lawyers for the California cases, Barry A. Fisher, told a Tokyo audience that "the Japanese were running no less than the biggest slave shipping operation since the middle passage, the African slave trade." Efron, "Pursuit of WWII Redress Hits Japanese Boardrooms."

38. The Global Alliance has also supported the redress efforts of about eighteen hundred Japanese Peruvians who were kidnapped from their homes during World War II and deported at U.S. government request from Peru to the United States, where they were incarcerated for the duration of the war. Most of them then were summarily deported to Japan in 1945, even though some were Peruvian citizens. Although the JACL supported an agreement in the Peruvian case worked out in a class action suit, *Mochizuki v. the United States*, which awarded five thousand dollars to each surviving plaintiff and an apology from the U.S. president, it "believes the amount of the settlement does not represent the degree of injustice the Japanese Latin Americans experienced." Japanese American Citizens League website, at www.janet.org/jacl

(accessed February 10, 2001). See also Manjusha P. Kulkarni, "Application of the Civil Liberties Act to Japanese Peruvians: Seeking Redress for Deportation and Internment Conducted by the United States Government during World War II," *The Boston Public Interest Law Journal* 5 (Winter 1996): 309.

39. The most recent revelations about disturbing American behavior during the Vietnam War—that of former Senator Bob Kerrey's involvement in a massacre of civilians—have led to very little re-evaluation. See Gregory L Vistica, "What Happened in Thanh Phong," *New York Times Magazine*, April 29, 2001: 50–68, 133.

7

Negotiating New Relationships
Canadian Museums, First Nations, and Cultural Property

Ruth B. Phillips and Elizabeth Johnson

THE GHOSTS OF HISTORY

C anadian museums are currently renegotiating their relationships with indigenous First Nations peoples. The roots of the issues being discussed, which range from shared authority over representation, to culturally appropriate treatment of objects, to the return and/or sharing of collections, lie deep in the histories of European contact with and colonization of the North American continent. In North American and (increasingly) European museums, there is a growing belief that successful resolutions of the often conflictual interests that are being articulated depend both on the acceptance of a pluralist ethics in the museum and on finer-grained understandings of the histories that lie behind collections. Most of these histories are informed by the long-standing assumptions held by colonizers and settlers that indigenous peoples were doomed to vanish. Their objects would, therefore, attain the status of relics and any notion of their return would be a moot issue.[1]

We begin with an illustrative anecdote. Around 1804 an army doctor named Edward Walsh, sitting in a British fort in the Great Lakes region, penned the following introductory passage to a book he never completed:

The tide of Emigration has lately flowed in on those colonies—wave impelling wave—so strongly that the natives have been literally pushed off their hunting

149

grounds and driven further into the Wilderness and have been obliged to resign and abandon those immense regions of which at no very remote period they were indisputed masters. . . . Their History is as mysterious as their fate is severe. Like the autumn leaves of their illimitable forests they are driven before the blast. They are gliding from the face of the Earth like guilty Ghosts, leaving no memorial, no record that they ever had existed.[2]

This example—one of many that could be quoted—is evidence of how early the impulse to record and collect emerged among educated Europeans and Euro-Americans who came in contact with indigenous peoples and of how immediate was their acceptance of the inevitability of the disappearance of these peoples as culturally distinctive groups. For two centuries and more, educated European and Euro-Canadians like Walsh collected and recorded in the belief that they were acting in the noble cause of preserving memory to investigate the great truths of universal history.[3]

In the largest sense, discussions of repatriation and other new forms of relationships being negotiated today by museums and First Nations differ from claims for restitution arising from oppressive events enacted by specific regimes over relatively short time periods. The historical conditions that fostered the eventual transfer to museums of the cultural property of indigenous North American peoples developed in the course of the establishment of settler societies during several centuries of European colonial expansion over Aboriginal territories. Many of the largest claims for return are therefore framed to redress appropriations that were enacted by whole societies in the course of decades and centuries.

Although situated within a history of dispossession and oppressive government policies, projects of collecting and recording were often (though certainly not always) pursued by the most humanitarian, liberal, and sympathetic individuals of their particular historical eras. Museums today are thus the repositories of the objects acquired by a number of different kinds of collecting projects, including early contact period curio collecting, missionary collecting, scientific ethnological collecting, touristic collecting of Native-made commoditized objects, and fine art collecting.

In this brief chapter, we cannot, of course, hope either to address fully the complexities of these processes or to provide a comprehensive survey of the repatriation requests and actions that have taken place. Rather, we will try to do three things: First, we will offer a more detailed account of the historical context out of which claims for the renegotiation and repatriation of cultural property have arisen. Second, we will move to a discussion of the post–World War II ethical and legal shifts that have shaped current repatriation issues and policies. Finally, we will illustrate how these shifts have produced fundamental changes in museum practices as well as repatriations of cultural property, using British Columbia as a case study.

The conclusion that we will draw is that repatriation negotiations should be understood not only as a struggle over ownership and a process for the return of cultural property but also as a mechanism for building new kinds of relationships between museums and First Nations based on the articulation of common interests in these materials. We argue that, at its most positive, repatriation negotiations open up the possibility of a "third way" to exorcise the ghosts of history.

THE LEGACY OF HISTORY

The 1996 *Report of the Royal Commission on Aboriginal Peoples* (RCAP *Report*) contains the most comprehensive and concise history of postcontact Native–settler relations in Canada written from an Aboriginal point of view. Its introductory section is entitled "The Ghosts of History." Unlike Edward Walsh, who wrote of "ghosts" in sentimentalist terms, the First Nations authors of the RCAP *Report* use the word to refer to a legacy of historical misunderstanding and misrepresentation. They define four phases of the relationship between native and nonnative peoples: the precontact period of mutual ignorance; the early contact period when a "rough equality" existed between invaders and indigenous peoples; the period of the empowerment of the settler society, of the dispossession of Aboriginal people and of assimilationist policies; and the current period of Aboriginal peoples' recovery and renegotiation of their relationships with non-Aboriginal people.[4]

The problems that must be dealt with today, the RCAP *Report* argues, arise from the third phase, a period that dates roughly from the third quarter of the nineteenth century until the middle of the twentieth century. During this period, in both the United States and Canada, the generalized expectation that indigenous peoples would disappear hardened into policies that implemented a campaign of social engineering designed to hasten the disappearance of First Nations communities by suppressing fundamental cultural practices and by facilitating the absorption of individuals into Euro-Canadian society.

The official policies of directed assimilation that were adopted in Canada have important historical roots in the successful lobbying projects of liberal and humanitarian factions in the United States. As Frederick Hoxie has shown, after the U.S. Civil War, abolitionists turned their attention to the "Indian problem," which had arisen as a result of the continuing westward expansion of white settlement into territories that had been reserved for Indians. Ranging themselves against those who believed in the physical extermination of Indians through war and starvation, liberals advocated a policy of enforced acculturation to Euro–North American religion, education, and economic and social arrangements.

Indians would be protected on reserves from those elements of settler society intent on their destruction until the civilizing project was completed. This was expected by many to be the work of a single generation. Disillusionment with the post–Civil War "peace policy" had led, in the United States, to more coercive, legislated attempts to accelerate assimilation through residential schooling, the dissolution of reserves, and enfranchisement. U.S. legislation, and especially the Dawes-Coke Bill of 1884 and the Dawes General Allotment Act of 1887, influenced Canadian legislation and particularly so in the case of the Indian Act of 1884.[5]

The litany of evils perpetrated by this oppressive piece of legislation is by now familiar to many Canadians. Confined to their reserves, Aboriginal people were deprived of a sufficient economic base. Under the Indian Act, status Indians were legally constructed as wards of the state, incapable of raising and educating their own children or managing their own lands and resources. Until 1960 members of reserve communities were not entitled to vote in federal elections nor, for much of that period, were they entitled to organize politically or to seek redress for their grievances from the courts.[6]

The act worked to prevent the survival of indigenous knowledge and culture by removing children to residential schools where they were forbidden to speak their own languages and where they were denied access to the traditional teaching of elders. It prohibited the observance of the Sun Dance, the Potlatch, and other centrally important ceremonial and ritual events. These measures caused the destruction of families through the enforced removal of small children from their parents.[7] Untold damage was done to these children by the physical and sexual abuse they suffered in residential schools and by the inadequate nutrition and medical care they were provided.[8]

It was, thus, in a period of impoverishment and extreme demoralization, when the Aboriginal population was at its lowest ebb, that the most extensive artifact collecting projects were carried out. These projects were informed by the same cultural evolutionist theories that justified the formulation of official policies of directed assimilation. In contrast to the majority of the objects that survive from the early contact period, which were acquired by gift or through trade between equal partners, the larger collections made during the "museum age" were collected for newly founded public museums.[9]

Both as research institutions and as sites of democratic public education, these new institutions placed tremendous emphasis on material culture, which was held by late-nineteenth-century anthropologists to hold important clues to the charting of the historical evolution of human societies. Wholesale removals of objects from First Nations communities to museums for preservation and study were central to the salvage ethnography that marked the era.[10] Within reserve communities, First Nations owners were induced to sell objects for a number of different reasons, including financial need, conversions to Christianity, conflicts between Christian and non-Christian factions, fear of thefts, the ever-present danger posed by house fires, and demoralization.

Two other important and roughly contemporary movements that are currently inadequately addressed in most repatriation negotiations also resulted in the eventual deposit of objects in museums. The first was the active and entrepreneurial commoditization of their art by First Nations producers. The origins of this trade go back to the early contact period in all parts of North America, but greatly expanded during the late nineteenth-century growth of tourism and increased economic dependence of First Nations on income from artisanal production.[11]

The second factor was the emergence of the paradigm of "Primitive Art" at the beginning of the twentieth century and the market for "authentic" older items it engendered. On the Northwest Coast, the popularity of touristic travel up the Inside Passage to Alaska during the last quarter of the nineteenth century further stimulated the production both of recognizable souvenir art and of less easily recognized replications of traditional arts made for sale to tourists, including argillite carvings, silver jewelry, baskets, and carvings.[12]

During the twentieth century many of these objects were purchased by or donated to museums. By the 1920s, the modernist "discovery" of "Primitive Art" during the first decade of the twentieth century had extended to Native North American objects.[13] Carved ritual masks and related objects are privileged within this paradigm, leading to the continuing circulation and retention in private and public art collections of some objects defined by originating communities as powerful, inalienable, restricted, or sacred.

Under the paradigm of scientific knowledge, museum curators assumed the virtually unfettered right to collect, look at, investigate, and interpret First Nations materials and human remains.[14] They displayed objects in museum collections to serve institutional mandates to inform the wider public about the cultures from which they came. The visible display of museum collections, especially when they involve objects that are normally private or seen only during ceremonies, has reinforced many First Nations people's feelings of powerlessness, inadequacy, and humiliation.

One of the contradictions that has characterized the museum's situation is that First Nations people have also expressed pride in seeing their objects displayed as things of significance and aesthetic value, preserved for future generations. These paradigms of art and science continue in varying degrees to inform contemporary museum and art gallery practices.

THE POST–WORLD WAR II PERIOD: THE EMERGENCE OF FRAMEWORKS FOR RESTITUTION

During the first half of the twentieth century, First Nations people resisted in a number of ways the oppressive laws under which they lived. In many communities the "underground" celebration of important ceremonies continued, but the enforced secrecy, the removal of objects from communities, the loss of knowledgeable people, and the disruption of traditional forms of education and training weakened artistic skills and interrupted the transmission of traditional knowledge.[15]

Students of contemporary First Nations cultural politics trace the origins of many current initiatives to the renewed First Nations political activism that followed World War II. Returning Aboriginal soldiers, having risked their lives for Canada and having had expanded experiences of travel, were unwilling to return to the status quo ante. The war also confronted Euro-Canadians with the horrific results of racism and made them more receptive to reform at home.[16]

In 1951 the Canadian government dropped from the Indian Act the prohibition against the Potlatch, the Sun Dance, and other First Nations ceremonies. Over the next several decades, Aboriginal people renewed long-standing fights for justice. One of the earliest and most important of the restitutions for past injustices in British Columbia was decided outside the courts but involved the government's acknowledgment of past illegality. Kwakwaka'wakw people had continued to hold potlatches after they had been declared illegal.

In 1921 high-ranking Namgis Chief Dan Cranmer held a potlatch. Christian converts informed the Indian Agent, who confiscated the people's regalia. In the trial they were made to choose between going to prison and relinquishing their regalia, a choice not sanctioned by law. The surrendered regalia was held by the Indian agent, who transferred some of it to the National Museum of Canada and sold other pieces to other museums. In the 1960s the people who had lost their regalia began the long process of pressuring the National Museum to return it on the grounds that it had been illegally confiscated. According to Gloria Cranmer Webster, "Our goal in having our treasures come home was to rectify a terrible injustice that is part of our history."[17]

According to a recent study by Donna McAlear, the return by the National Museum of Canada was agreed to in 1975 as a result of pressure put on the National Museum by the federal Department of Indian Affairs and Northern Development.[18] The return was made under the condition that the regalia be divided between the two principal Kwakwaka'wakw communities, not returned to the families who had owned it, and that cultural centers with museum standards be built to house and display the objects. The maintenance of these centers placed a new financial burden on the communities. Some contemporary Kwakwaka'wakw also say that the conditional return of their illegally confiscated regalia further damaged traditional observances by replacing hereditary forms of clan and lineage ownership and ceremonial display with the conventions of the Western public museum.[19]

Claims for control over cultural property have also been supported by the development of international and national declarations of human and indigenous rights and by the passage of national laws recognizing Aboriginal rights. In Canada, new multicultural policies began to be articulated in the 1970s in response to the large numbers of immigrants from non-European countries that began entering Canada after World War II. The pluralist ethics and political policies that resulted also increased support for First Nations rights by encouraging a shift toward acceptance of diversity.

THE TASK FORCE ON MUSEUMS
AND FIRST NATIONS

The ethical framework of equal human rights for all people has informed not only the aspirations of indigenous people but also the changing professional ethics and practices of museums. In the 1970s and 1980s, museums began to shift from virtually refusing to consider the possibility of repatriation under any circumstances to an acknowledgment that repatriation claims should be given serious consideration.[20]

In the United States, using an argument based on the principles of religious freedom and respect for human remains, Native Americans successfully lobbied the Congress to pass Public Law 101–601, the Native American Graves Protection and Repatriation Act, in 1990. Under this act all museums directly or indirectly receiving federal funds were given three years to complete inventories of their collections listing objects that fell under any of the following four categories: (1) human remains and associated funerary objects, (2) unassociated funerary objects, (3) sacred objects, and (4) objects of cultural patrimony. They were required to complete these inventories in consultation with tribal government, Native Hawaiian organization officials, and traditional religious leaders, to make them available to the relevant tribes, and to return items on request to known lineal descendants of the Native Americans or of the tribe or organization.[21] This law has resulted in substantial returns of human remains and associated burial objects as well as some objects in the other categories.

In Canada, in contrast to the United States, repatriation has rarely involved the intervention of the law but has taken place through a slowly evolving process that has been punctuated by several landmark events and specific cases, such as the return of the Kwakwaka'wakw potlatch collection already discussed. A Task Force on Museums and First Nations commissioned by the Canadian Museums Association (CMA) and the Assembly of First Nations (AFN), the largest national Native political organization, issued guidelines for new relationships between museums and First Nations in 1992. The task force was formed following a controversial boycott of a major Canadian exhibition of First Nations objects.[22] Its mission was "to develop an ethical framework and strategies for Aboriginal nations to represent their history and culture in concert with cultural institutions."[23] Composed of roughly equal numbers of Aboriginal and non-Aboriginal museum professionals and cultural workers, the task force also conducted extensive regional consultations with First Nations community members, elders, and other museum professionals.

The Task Force *Report* articulates a central principle of partnership and cooperation and asserts the shared interests of museums and First Nations in Aboriginal cultural materials. It also confirms the right of First Peoples to be fully involved in exhibitions, programs, projects, and the development of policies and funding initiatives related to their own cultures. The report recommends that museums and First Nations communities work collaboratively to correct past inequities, to increase the prominence of contemporary First Nations issues and arts in museums, and to represent more effectively the historical interrelationship of Euro-Canadian society and First Nations peoples. It articulates a principle of mutual respect for the different types of knowledge of First Nations and museum professionals, urges increased access to museum collections for Aboriginal people, and advocates increased government financial support of culturally-appropriate professional and technical training for First Nations people and other related initiatives. This funding has been only minimally provided to date.

The report also considers "the disposition of Aboriginal cultural patrimony including human remains, burial objects, sacred and ceremonial objects, and other cultural objects that have ongoing historical, traditional, or cultural import to an Aboriginal community or culture."[24] It recommends that human remains and associated burial goods be returned to legitimate First Nations claimants. It also mandates the return of illegally acquired objects to individuals or communities. With regard to other, legally acquired "sacred and ceremonial objects and of other objects that have ongoing historical, traditional, or cultural importance to an Aboriginal community or culture,"[25] the Task Force *Report* recommends that museums consider repatriation based on negotiations conducted on a case-by-case basis. It also presents three other options: the loan of materials for use in ceremonies or festivities, the creation of replicas for use by either museums or originating communities, and the development of systems of shared management of cultural property.[26]

The authors of the Task Force *Report* were careful to identify the reasons for the adoption of policy and guidelines rather than law:

There is a wide recognisation [*sic*] that concepts of ownership vary, therefore, a case-by-case collaborative approach to resolving repatriation based on moral and ethical criteria is favoured rather than a strictly legalistic approach. The "Native American Grave Protection and Repatriation Act," recently passed in the United States, was studied by Task Force members. While not ruling out the possibility of the creation of legislation in the future, it was agreed that it was preferable to encourage museums and Aboriginal peoples to work collabora-tively to resolve issues concerning the management, care and custody of cultural objects.[27]

In contrast to the United States, too, Canadian museums were not required to be proactive in inventorying their collections and informing First Nations communities about their holdings. Rather, the pattern has been for Canadian museums to comply with requests initiated by First Nations communities, families, and individuals for the return of human remains and associated burial goods. In keeping with the Task Force *Report*'s recommendations, many museums have shown themselves willing to return sacred objects, such as Plains medicine bundles, and objects of cultural patrimony, such as wampum.

The Task Force *Report* translated into policy the fundamental shift in museum ethics and practice that began in the postwar period.[28] Since the late 1980s (when task force regional working groups began), the report has come to be the foundation of professional museum practice in Canada.[29] Its rec-ommendation that museums consider not only the common law of property but also ethical principles and the needs of First Nations has resulted in the return of objects to which museums had title in strictly legal terms. In the years since the Task Force *Report* was issued there have been examples of the difficulty of adjudicating ownership as well as attempts to give the guidelines sharper teeth.

In 2000, for example, the Province of Alberta passed Bill 2, the First Nations Sacred Ceremonial Objects Repatriation Act. Whereas the Task Force *Report* recommended the repatriation of sacred and ceremonial objects, Bill 2 gives more force and definition to the task force's recommen-dation that museums consider the repatriation of sacred and ceremonial objects. Its preamble states the Crown's desire "to harmonize the role muse-ums play in the preservation of human heritage with the aspirations of First Nations to support traditional values in strong, confident First Nations com-munities" by providing specifically for the return to First Nations of "sacred ceremonial objects" (defined as items "vital to the practice of the First Nation's sacred ceremonial traditions") in the collections of the province's

two largest museums, the Provincial Museum of Alberta and the Glenbow-
Alberta Institute. Thus far, the law appears to have achieved its goal of "har-
monizing."

In 2001, however, newspapers across Canada reported on the dispute that
arose after a curator at the University of Winnipeg's Museum of Archaeology repatriated Ojibwa medicine objects originating among Manitoba
Ojibwa to the U.S.-based Three Fires Society, which also claimed them as
medicine objects necessary to the revival of Native spirituality. The descendants of the original owner of some of the objects have strongly objected to
their removal from the Museum, where they had been placed by his relative
to preserve them against destruction by Christian fundamentalists in his
community.[30]

Fundamental to these changes is the acceptance of the authority of originating peoples and the concomitant acceptance of limits on scholarly and
professional authority as museums strive to work as equal partners with First
Nations.[31] These changes permeate all aspects of museum practice and all
museum professions, and they necessitate ongoing negotiations and permission processes for acquiring informed consent at all stages of representation
and documentation. Exhibit text is attributed to named First Nations people
or curators, not, as previously, to anonymous, authoritative scholarly voices.

In the area of collections management, the goal is to identify First Nations
groups by their own preferred names. Museums are acknowledging that
many objects are known to be powerful and to consist of more than their
strict materiality, and that some objects require special care while others
should not be on public display. Conservators, for example, have come to
acknowledge that such care may necessitate offerings of food, or the burning
of sacred offerings within the museum, ideas that were previously anathema.
Conservation and collections management professionals also recognize that
it may be important to First Nations people to handle ancestral objects as
they care for them or study them. Museums' acceptance of this handling, not
normally permitted, is intended explicitly as redress of the injustices of the
colonial period and acknowledgment that First Nations people have special
rights in relation to their ancestral objects.[32] For the same reason, objects are
sometimes loaned for use in ceremonies, a procedure that is also questionable from the standpoint of orthodox museum practice.

The implementation of these changed practices is not simple and requires
sensitive and sometimes arduous negotiations and difficult day-to-day decisions. For example, which First Nations person or group is the appropriate
authority with respect to a particular object or objects is often not clear. People are often understandably reluctant to speak for others, which may leave
serious problems unresolved. For example, today the descendants of a historic First Nations community who now live in separate communities may

differ regarding the proper treatment of objects belonging to their common past.

THE TREATY PROCESS AND THE NEGOTIATION OF ABORIGINAL RIGHTS TO CULTURAL PROPERTY

The Canada Act of 1982, which repatriated the Canadian constitution from Britain, entrenched a notion of Aboriginal rights in Canadian law. During the 1980s federal and provincial governments resumed the process of settling outstanding land claims that had stopped in the 1920s. Although the primary focus of these negotiations has been land and resource rights, several Canadian Supreme Court decisions—especially the 1998 Delgamuukw decision, which accepted the principle of the fundamental interrelationship of land and other kinds of property, such as songs, privileges, oral traditions, and material objects—have supported the extension of Aboriginal rights to include rights in cultural property.[33]

The vast majority of the land in British Columbia was never ceded by treaty. Many land claims are currently in negotiation in British Columbia, a number of which include claims for the repatriation of cultural property held in federal and provincial museums. The first of these treaties, with the Nisga'a of northern British Columbia, received Royal Assent and became law in 2000. The agreement provides for the return of about three hundred objects, including one-third of the Nisga'a collection in the national museum, the Canadian Museum of Civilization, and a sizeable number from the provincial museum, the Royal British Columbia Museum. Another third of the national museum's collection will remain in shared ownership. A Nisga'a publication on the repatriation states: "Many of the artifacts are sacred, living objects we will be able to share with our children. Repatriation means bringing our ancestors home."[34]

Although nongovernment museums do not participate in treaty negotiations, the arguments for restitution based on Aboriginal rights to cultural property rather than on specific illegalities of acquisition under Canadian property law that are being made in the context of treaty negotiations are encouraging First Nations to approach nongovernment museums within the same framework.[35]

A statement on repatriation taken from the 1996 federally sponsored and First Nations–authored RCAP *Report* makes the First Nations position clear. Where the museum task force recommends several alternatives for addressing the issue of sacred objects and objects of cultural patrimony including return, loan, and special treatment within the museum, the RCAP *Report* states:

Aboriginal people are not calling for museums to divest themselves of all Aboriginal artifacts. In the AFN/CMA report, *Turning the Page*, there was general recognition that collections and the museums that care for them can contribute to public education and awareness of the contributions of Aboriginal people. In particular, items that have no sacred value, such as tools, can be kept and displayed with community consent. As well, objects that cannot be traced back to a specific family, community or nation of origin can remain in a museum's collection. Where repatriation is called for, however, museums must respect the wishes of the Aboriginal community.[36]

Statements such as this, which frame repatriation claims in terms of Aboriginal rights to cultural property, conflict with the case-by-case approach recommended by the Task Force on Museums and First Nations and with the common law of property.

THE MUSEUM OF ANTHROPOLOGY AT THE UNIVERSITY OF BRITISH COLUMBIA IN VANCOUVER

The impact of all these developments can be further illustrated by a brief summary of the experience of the Museum of Anthropology at the University of British Columbia (UBC) in Vancouver. From the early 1990s, the museum's guidelines have been based on the Task Force recommendations. Illegal alienation, such as the theft or sale of an object by someone who was not its legal and rightful owner, recently or in the past, provides perhaps the clearest grounds for a repatriation claim. The museum repatriated a ceremonial headdress to Mr. William Walker in 1995 because someone who did not have the right to sell it had sold it after the death of Mr. Walker's father. The repatriation was completed after the museum had determined, to the best of its ability and with Mr. Walker's consent, that there were no competing claimants.

The Museum of Anthropology has also accepted families' and communities' arguments that sacred and powerful objects in its collections are needed for the people's well-being. In 1997 the museum returned to the Pueblo of Zuni an Ahay:uda, or "war god," a sacred image considered by the Zuni to be "inalienable cultural property" and vital to the well-being of the Zuni people and the wider society. Similarly, the museum agreed in 1995 to a request made by the Jacks family of Tsey'cum, on Vancouver Island, for the return of powerful regalia from their winter ceremonies.

These materials could not be shown publicly in the museum, and the family argued that they are essential to the people's spiritual well-being. In both these cases, the recipients conducted ceremonies for the reintegration of the materials into their communities, and the Jacks family included museum staff in the ceremonial feast that was held in their longhouse. Furthermore, on those occasions, representatives of the Jacks family took seriously their responsibility to teach museum staff about the deep significance of the occasion and of the objects that were being returned.

The repatriation of human remains for the proper and respectful care enjoined by the Task Force *Report* is now commonly accepted. Although the Museum of Anthropology does not hold human remains in its own collection, the UBC Laboratory of Archaeology stores them in the museum's building. This is one of the reasons why the museum works with ritual specialists from local Coast Salish communities to hold a spiritual cleansing of the museum each year. The museum has also supported the return of human remains by the Laboratory of Archaeology to the Haida and other British Columbia First Nations.

These repatriations are the only ones completed by the Museum of Anthropology to date. Although several others are under discussion, relatively few claims have been made. However, like other museums, the Museum of Anthropology regularly receives requests from First Nations for information about its collections and archival holdings.

Thus far, this experience contradicts the alarms raised by some opponents of repatriation, who had feared that if repatriation were allowed, museums would soon be emptied of their collections. Although the reasons for the relatively small number of claims cannot be known with certainty, it is clear that some First Nations leaders have decided to address other, more pressing concerns for their people's welfare before initiating the return of cultural property. Equally, the repatriation of powerful objects can pose serious challenges to a community, since the recipients must have knowledge of how to reintegrate and care for them. The pressures of colonialism may have destroyed this traditional knowledge.

Clearly, many communities have come to accept the need to provide museum standards of preservation and protection for their objects, although these standards are very costly. Many British Columbia First Nations plan to build cultural centers embedded in the active life of the community that would also have museum-like functions, but so far financial resources for such projects have been lacking. Many First Nations people also perceive museums as authoritarian institutions that share an oppressive history with residential schools, churches, or prisons. Although some, like the Museum of Anthropology, have tried hard to make themselves approachable, it is difficult to overcome the discomfort many First Nations people inevitably feel when confronted with typical museum practices of ordering, regimentation, and security.

There is evidence, however, that when indigenous peoples and museums successfully establish new relationships of mutual trust, museums can serve useful purposes as repositories for information and cultural property, obviating temporarily or in the long term the need for repatriation. As elsewhere, a number of museums in British Columbia have entered into arrangements with First Nations for more flexible and mutually enriching arrangements regarding the location, movement, and use of objects. For example, the Simon Fraser University Museum of Archaeology helped the Saanich First Nation prevent the export of a stone bowl whose provenance was in its territories and now stores it on the band's behalf.[37] The Royal British Columbia Museum lends out certain ceremonial objects in its collection for use in potlatches.[38] For the past fifteen years, the Museum of Anthropology has served as a repository for several valued objects belonging to individuals, families, and a First Nations band.

One of the most serious impediments to repatriation is probably the need to demonstrate histories of ownership for objects being claimed from museum collections, many of which were sold on the curio market or collected as typological objects and were therefore poorly documented. An individual, a family, or a band council may bring repatriation claims forward. The museum and the claimant must determine that the person or group is the appropriate recipient and that there are no potentially competing claims. They must discuss the grounds for the claim, and the museum must decide whether or not to honor a claim for which there is an inadequate paper trail or which is made on grounds not covered in the Task Force *Report*.

Currently, the burden of proof lies on the First Nations representative making the claim, although the museum will make information from its records available. Very difficult questions may be raised in the negotiations. These include defining what is meant by "sacred," and what is meant by the "origin" of an object—the community where it was made, to which it was traded, or from which it was collected. Should an object be repatriated that was voluntarily and knowingly sold by its owner, because the societal context has now changed?

As a university museum, the Museum of Anthropology also has a mandate from the University of British Columbia to hold collections that are needed to support research and teaching, as well as obligations to donors who have given objects to the university on the understanding that they would remain in the museum. These sometimes conflicting mandates and ethical obligations must be negotiated where task force-mandated conditions for repatriation are not present. In such cases, other kinds of arrangements for sharing objects may be considered, such as long-term loans to community museums and cultural centers, where they exist, and loans of objects for use in ceremonies.

FUTURE CHALLENGES

Negotiations concerning both repatriation and authority over interpretation are now a regular part of the work of many Canadian museums. As we have suggested, many factors militate against global acts of restitution. Rather, there is an acceptance of the compelling need to engage in negotiations with First Nations representatives that will ensure not only that they have appropriate authority with respect to the care and interpretation of their ancestral materials but also that the return of these materials may, in some cases, take place.

For museum professionals, discussions with First Nations participants provide valuable opportunities to learn: to hear why cultural materials are so meaningful, to hear and bear witness to the anger and hurt carried by the people who no longer possess them, to hear why particular resolutions are appropriate or inappropriate because of the nature of the materials or the circumstances of their acquisition.

In confronting the legacy of the colonial period and trying to find ways to repair past injustices, new relationships with First Nations may be built. The challenge that museums and their staffs face, as individuals, as institutions, and as negotiators with First Nations representatives, is the resolution of the continuing imbalance in authority and in possession. Despite these inequalities, hope lies in the relationships that are being developed as negotiations take place. First Nations people have become an active, vital, and questioning presence in museums, definitively refuting the predictions of Edward Walsh and others that they would disappear, and sensitizing us to their distinctive cultural perspectives and to our place in their history.

NOTES

The authors are grateful to Rose Ellis and Gary Selinger for assistance in preparing this chapter. We also acknowledge our debt to our fellow members of the Repatriation Committee of the Museum of Anthropology at the University of British Columbia, to colleagues in other Canadian and American museums who are grappling with similar issues, and, particularly, to the members of First Nations communities who have been willing to share their perspectives and engage with us in discussion and negotiation. The opinions expressed in this chapter, reflect, however, only our own views.

1. Although indigenous peoples have been interested in negotiating repatriation with museums outside North America for some time, formal policies allowing the return of ethnographic collections and human remains are lacking. In January 2000 the British Museums and Galleries Commission issued a comprehensive guide for United Kingdom museums receiving repatriation requests. Entitled *Restitution and Repatriation: Guidelines for Good Practice*, it includes a useful set of case studies detailing requests for repatriation made in recent years by indigenous peoples and other claimants and the actions taken by the respective museums.

2. The manuscript, in the National Archives of Canada, is entitled *Notices of the Canadian Indians*, MG 19 F10. See Ruth B. Phillips, "Jasper Grant and Edward

Walsh: The Gentleman-Soldier as Early Collector of Great Lakes Indian Art," *Journal of Canadian Studies* 21, no. 4 (1986–1987): 56–71.

3. A child of the Scottish Enlightenment, Walsh, a humanitarian and a man of science, reacted to the threat of annihilation by inoculating Anishnabec gathered for a Midewiwin ceremony against smallpox. In gratitude he was presented with a rare shaman's headdress that he subsequently gave together with the small collection he had made to the "Chelsea museum."

4. Canada, Royal Commission on Aboriginal Peoples, *People to People, Nation to Nation: Highlights from the Report of the Royal Commission on Aboriginal Peoples* (Ottawa: Minister of Supply and Services, 1996): 5. The exact wording given in the summary volume of the report describes, first, the "time when [they] lived on separate continents and knew nothing of one another"; second, "Following the years of first contact, fragile relations of peace, friendship and rough equality were given the force of law in treaties"; third, "Then power tilted toward non-Aboriginal people and governments. They moved Aboriginal people off much of their land and took steps to 'civilize' and teach them European ways"; and, fourth, "Finally, we reached the present stage—a time of recovery for Aboriginal peoples and cultures, a time for critical review of our relationship, and a time for its renegotiation and renewal." The Report is discussed in some detail in Alan Cairns's contribution to this book.

5. See Frederick E. Hoxie, "The Campaign Begins," chap. 2 in his *A Final Promise: The Campaign to Assimilate the Indians, 1880–1920* (New York: Cambridge University Press, 1984), and J. R. Miller, "Owen Glendower, Hotspur, and Canadian Indian Policy," in *Sweet Promises: A Reader on Indian-White Relations in Canada,* ed. J. R. Miller (Toronto: University of Toronto Press, 1991), 326–27.

6. A 1927 amendment to the federal Indian Act that prevented Native people from raising money or hiring lawyers to pursue Indian land claims must also have discouraged First Nations people from seeking legal redress for illegal alienations of cultural property. On this legislation see Paul Tennant, *Aboriginal Peoples and Politics: The Indian Land Question in British Columbia, 1840–1989* (Vancouver: University of British Columbia Press, 1990), 111–12.

7. On the Northwest Coast, the seasonal calendar of European schooling was a particular problem because the most important ceremonial events occurred in the winter, when they were away.

8. See Celia Haig-Brown, *Resistance and Renewal: Surviving the Indian Residential School* (Vancouver: Tillacum Library, 1989).

9. See William C. Sturtevant, "Does Anthropology Need Museums?" *Proceedings of the Biological Society* 82 (1969): 619–50.

10. See Douglas Cole, *Captured Heritage: The Scramble for Northwest Coast Artifacts* (Vancouver: University of British Columbia Press, 1985).

11. For the commoditized trade see the essays on North America in Ruth B. Phillips and Christopher B. Steiner, *Unpacking Culture: Art and Commodity in Colonial and Postcolonial Worlds* (Berkeley: University of California Press, 1999); Ruth B. Phillips, *Trading Identities: The Souvenir in Native North American Art from the Northeast, 1700–1900* (Seattle: University of Washington Press, 1998); and Marvin Cohodas, *Basket Weavers for the California Curio Trade: Elizabeth and Louise Hickox* (Tucson: University of Arizona Press, 1997).

12. See Kate C. Duncan, *1001 Curious Things: Ye Olde Curiosity Shop and Native American Art* (Seattle: University of Washington Press, 2001); Robin K. Wright, *Northern Haida Master Carvers* (Seattle: University of Washington Press, 2001); and William McLennan and Karen Duffek, *The Transforming Image: Painted Arts of the Northwest Coast* (Vancouver: University of British Columbia Press, 2000).

13. See Christian F. Feest, "From North America," in *Primitivism in 20th Century Art: Affinity of the Tribal and the Modern,* ed. William Rubin, vol. 2 (New York: The Museum of Modern Art, 1984), 85–98.

14. See James Nason, "A Question of Patrimony: Ethical Issues in the Collecting of Cultural Objects," *Museum Round-Up* 83 (Fall 1981): 13–20.

15. See Margaret Seguin Anderson and Margorie M. Halpin eds., *Potlatch at Gitsegukla: William Beynon's 1945 Field Notebooks* (Vancouver: University of British Columbia Press, 2000).

16. Loretta Todd has documented the effect of the war in her film, *Forgotten Warriors* (National Film Board of Canada, 1997).

17. See Gloria Cranmer Webster, "The Potlatch Collection Repatriation," *University of British Columbia Law Review* 14 (1995), and "From Colonization to Repatriation," in *Indigena: Contemporary Native Perspectives,* eds. Gerald McMaster and Lee-Ann Martin (Vancouver: Douglas and McIntyre, 1992), 25–39; and Tina Loo, "Dan Cranmer's Potlatch: Law, Coercion, Symbol, and Rhetoric in British Columbia, 1884–1951," *Canadian Historical Review* 123, no. 2 (1992): 125–65.

18. *Repatriation and Cultural Politics: Australian and Canadian Museum Responses to First Peoples' Challenges for Cultural Property Ownership* (Ph.D. diss., Griffith University, Australia, 1999), 107–15.

19. Kim Recalma Clutesi, "Protecting Knowledge: Traditional Resource Rights in the New Millennium" (presentation in a panel on repatriation at a conference organized by the Union of B.C. Indian Chiefs, University of British Columbia, November 2000).

20. For an example of this fear see G. Ellis Burcaw, "A Museological View of the Repatriation of Museum Objects," *Museum Studies Journal* (Spring 1983): 8–11.

21. Jack F. Trope and Walter R. Echo-Hawk, "The North American Graves Protection and Repatriation Act: Background and Legislative History," *Arizona Law Society Journal* 24, no. 1 (Spring 1992): 35–74.

22. The exhibition was *The Spirit Sings: Artistic Traditions of Canada's First Peoples,* a blockbuster exhibition of early-contact period Native art organized by the Glenbow Museum in 1988 for the Calgary Winter Olympics. The boycott was initially called to protest sponsorship by an oil company drilling on land claimed by the Lubicon Cree, but rapidly broadened to encompass other issues around museums, representation, and cultural property. See, for example, Julia Harrison, Bruce Trigger, and Michael Ames, "Museums and Politics: The Spirit Sings and the Lubicon Boycott, *Muse* 6, no. 3 (1988): 12–16. For an account of the conference that led to the formation of the Task Force, see Valda Blundell and Laurence Grant, "Preserving Our Heritage: Getting Beyond Boycotts and Demonstrations," *Inuit Art Quarterly* (Winter 1989), 12–16.

23. Task Force on Museums and First Peoples, *Turning the Page: Forging New Partnerships between Museums and First Peoples* (Ottawa: Canadian Museums Association, 1992).

24. *Turning the Page,* 8.

25. *Turning the Page,* 9.

26. *Turning the Page,* 9.

27. *Turning the Page,* 5.

28. See Richard I. Inglis and Donald N. Abbott, "A Tradition of Partnership: The Royal British Columbia Museum and First Peoples," *Alberta Museums Review* 17, no. 2 (1991): 17–23; and Audrey Hawthorn, *A Labour of Love* (Vancouver: University of British Columbia Museum of Anthropology, 1993), 1–30.

29. See for example, *Canadian Museum of Civilization Corporation Repatriation Policy* (207), approved May 1, 2001; and Museum of Anthropology, University of British Columbia, *Guidelines on Repatriation of Canadian First Peoples' Cultural Materials Housed in MoA,* rev. ed. (2001).

30. Jennifer Brown, an ethnohistorian at the University of Winnipeg and an expert on the historical context of the objects concerned, has pointed out that the museum did not consult with the originating community or investigate competing claims—standard museum procedures in repatriation—before returning the objects. See Les Perreaux, "Native Leaders Want Artifacts Given to U.S. Group Returned: Questions Raised about Exporting Cultural Works," *National Post* (Canada), September 28, 2001, at 207.126.116.12/culture/native_news/m17685.html (accessed September 17, 2002).

31. See Nason, "A Question of Patrimony," 13–20.

32. See Miriam Clavir, *Preserving What Is Valued: Museums, Conservation, and First Nations* (Vancouver: University of British Columbia Press, 2002); and Elizabeth C. Welsh et al., "Multicultural Participation in Conservation Decision-Making," *WAAC Newsletter* 14, no. 1 (1992): 13–22.

33. For the extension of Aboriginal rights to cultural property see Catherine Bell, "Aboriginal Claims to Cultural Property in Canada: A Comparative Legal Analysis of the Repatriation Debate," *American Indian Law Review* 17, no. 2 (1992): 457–62, and "Repatriation of Cultural Property and Aboriginal Rights: A Survey of Contemporary Legal Issues," *Prairie Forum* 17, no. 2 (1992): 313–35; and Gii-dahl-guud-sliiaay, "Cultural Perpetuation: Repatriation of First Nations Cultural Heritage," *University of British Columbia Law Review* (1995): 183–201. See also Andrea Laforet, "Narratives of the Treaty Table" (paper presented to the Department of Anthropology, University of British Columbia, 1999).

34. Alex Rose, *Bringing Our Ancestors Home: The Repatriation of Nisga'a Artifacts* (New Aiyansh, B.C.: Nisga'a Tribal Council, 1997).

35. Catherine Bell and Robert Patterson, "Aboriginal Rights to Cultural Property in Canada," *International Journal of Cultural Property* (1999): 167–211.

36. Government of Canada, Royal Commission on Aboriginal Peoples, *Report of the Royal Commission on Aboriginal Peoples,* vol. 3, chap. 6, "Arts and Heritage," sec. 1, "Cultural Heritage" (CD-ROM, Canadian Government Publishing, 1997).

37. Agreements were drawn up whereby the Saanich Native Heritage Society has title to the bowl, but it is kept at the museum where it is subject to handling and other restrictions. It is loaned to the Society for use and will be returned to them upon request. See Diana Henry, "Back from the Brink: Canada's First Nations'

Right to Preserve Canadian Heritage," *University of British Columbia Law Review* (1995): 5–12; and Barbara Winter, "New Futures for the Past: Cooperation between First Nations and Museums in Canada," *University of British Columbia Law Review* (1995): 29–36.

38. See Inglis and Abbott, "A Tradition of Partnership."

8

Is Truth Enough?
Reparations and Reconciliation in Latin America

Sharon F. Lean

It is clear that no one is going to return to the imprisoned dissident his youth; to the young woman who has been raped her innocence; to the person who has been tortured his or her integrity. Nobody is going to return the dead and the disappeared to their families. What can and must be publicly restored [are] the victims' names and their dignity, through a formal recognition of the injustice of what has occurred, and, wherever possible, material reparation. . . . Those who clamor for social reparation are not asking for vengeance. Nor are they blindly adding difficulties to a historical process that is already by no means easy. On the contrary, they are promoting the personal and social viability of a new society, truly democratic.

—Ignacio Martín-Baro

Ignacio Martín-Baro, one of six Jesuit priests murdered by a government death squad in El Salvador on November 16, 1989, wrote the preceding in an essay on reparations shortly before his death. It was published posthumously by *Commonweal* and later reprinted in Neil Kritz's 1995 collection on *Transitional Justice*.[1] In this essay, he states clearly that reparations are a valid and important part of the process of national reconciliation following periods of severe repression and abuse of human rights. Martín-Baro argues that in such cases, while learning the truth about human rights violations is important, truth telling is not enough to cancel debts to the past in a manner that enables societies to renew social bonds among their citizens and move forward from their violent pasts. Some kind of compensation is needed as well.

The dilemma of how to promote national reconciliation after periods of systematic and severe human rights abuses committed during periods of authoritarian rule, military dictatorship, or civil war has been one of the most complicated issues to be dealt with in the negotiated transitions to democracy that have occurred throughout Latin America over the past two decades. The issues of reparation and reconciliation have become prominent because of the gravity of the harm that was done under the military dictatorships and also because of the demands of daily existence.

In many Latin American countries, with relatively small populations and a low degree of population dispersion, perpetrators and victims often come face to face in the course of their everyday lives. They therefore have a real and urgent need to find a way to coexist. The latter reality is highlighted poignantly in the introduction to the English language edition of *Uruguay: Nunca Más* (Never Again), the report of that country's nongovernmental truth commission, when it states: "Uruguay is a tiny country, there was no place to hide, and victims were coming upon their former tormentors almost every day in the streets in the middle of their daily rounds. . . . The problem became progressively more intense."[2]

Unlike some other cases in which reparations have been claimed, such as reparations for slavery in the United States or to indigenous peoples, where the harm is arguably too far removed for restitution to be made by the present generation, many of the cases being considered in Latin America have occurred within the past twenty years. The most distant cases go back no more than forty years.

Perhaps the most common mechanisms that societies have used in an effort to come to terms with the past are state and nongovernmental commissions of inquiry into the human rights violations that occurred. These truth commissions, through arduous and often dangerous work for those involved, investigate past abuses, and compile available evidence in a systematic manner about disappearances, torture, murder, and other rights violations. While truth commissions play an important fact-finding role in national reconciliation processes, current evidence suggests that the ability of truth commissions to put the past to rest by making it a matter of public record is illusory.

Indicative of the fact that truth commissions by themselves have been unable to bring closure is that years and even decades after some of the truth commissions' reports were published and amnesty agreements worked out, a rash of new trials addressing government-sponsored criminality has recently broken out in such countries as Chile, Argentina, and El Salvador. These trials can only be seen as ongoing efforts to settle with the past, to bring perpetrators to justice, and to punish them.

Thus far, however, it seems likely that many of these trials will end without conclusive punishment. In the most renowned case, that of former Chilean dictator Augusto Pinochet, after much legal maneuvering on both sides, both domestic and international courts ultimately spared the octogenarian on the grounds that he was medically unfit to stand trial. In the Florida trial of two retired Salvadoran army superiors who were in command at the time of the 1980 murders of three American churchwomen, the defendants were found not to be liable for wrongdoing.[3] At the same time, the government of El Salvador recently reopened an investigation of several high-ranking defense ministers for another of that country's most notorious crimes, the 1989 murders of six Jesuit priests (including Martín-Baro), a housekeeper, and her daughter.[4] In Argentina a number of military leaders who were first prosecuted for human rights abuses after an extremely complicated struggle to bring their cases to trial, then later pardoned, have now been brought to trial again on new charges involving violations against Spanish citizens and kidnapping children of the disappeared.[5]

While many are aware of the activities of truth commissions and of international efforts to bring the perpetrators of systematic abuses to justice in tribunals at home and abroad, few people are well acquainted with a third route being used in the Latin American reconciliation processes—namely, the provision of reparations. Reparations, already paid in some of the Latin American cases and reparations that are recommended, but not yet acted on as yet, are an important alternative mechanism for promoting reconciliation. As the number of cases in the Latin American context in which reparations have been paid increases, the precedent is set for many more such cases, not just in Latin America but in similar postauthoritarian contexts around the world as well.

Despite the growing incidence of claims for reparations in Latin America, very little published academic work deals specifically with this phenomenon. The growing body of literature on truth commissions includes some discussion of reparations, primarily with regard to truth commission recommendations concerning compensation of victims.[6] There is also an expanding body of work in the field of international law that touches on many of the key questions of transitional justice in the Latin America cases.[7]

This chapter offers a survey of reparations politics in Latin America. After defining terms, the first section of this chapter summarizes the human rights violations for which reparations have been made or considered. The second section compares the different bases on which claims are being made, the mechanisms by which claims are managed, and the types of measures that have been taken or are being considered—in particular, whether reparations are made to individuals or on a collective basis. A third section discusses one of the principal controversies around the subject of reparations in the Latin American cases, the emerging issue of transnational reparations claims. Finally, the chapter closes with some reflections about the potential of reparations to repair the injustices of Latin America's recent past.

REPARATIONS DEFINED

For the purposes of this chapter, reparations shall be understood as deliberate actions, both symbolic and material, that express acknowledgment of the state's responsibility for grave and systematic human rights violations by the state and other actors, including those under past regimes. Reparations are directed at repairing past injustices to the degree that this is possible. This definition has two key components. First, it singles out the role of states, because they have the key responsibility for making reparations. States and state agents have been the primary violators of human rights in Latin America, and they are appropriately the primary addressees of reparations claims. This is the position embraced by most truth commissions. For example, the "Rettig Report" of the Chilean National Commission on Truth and Reconciliation asserts that "the task of reparation requires conscious and deliberate action on the part of the state."[8] Although reparations can be made (and indeed have been made) by other types of actors, such as individuals and corporations, this chapter will focus on reparations by states, because these comprise the predominant forum for claims for reparations.

Second, the definition of reparations used here emphasizes the idea of restorative justice. As Walsh puts it, "Reparations are an attempt by the successor government to return the victims to their status quo ante."[9] At the same time, those recommending reparations acknowledge the impossibility of full compensation for the suffering that people have endured. The Guatemalan truth commission report, *Memory of Silence*, implicitly recognizes this fact when the authors write that "the state has the responsibility to institute economic, social, and cultural measures that partially compensate for the victims' losses and the harm they suffered."[10]

A final caveat: this chapter focuses specifically on reparations (and claims for reparations) for the grave and systematic human rights violations that occurred during periods of authoritarian rule and civil war in the 1970s and 1980s. In Torpey's typology, outlined in his contribution to this book, the claims considered in this chapter are "commemorative" reparations claims arising from state terrorism. The issue of reparations for injustices arising from colonialism in Latin America—for example, the claims by indigenous populations, such as the Mapuche people in Chile who were recently promised a $270 million development fund[11]—will not be considered here. The demands of indigenous populations for cultural recognition, full or partial political autonomy, and land encompass a somewhat different set of issues from the reparation claims for human rights abuses that I wish to consider.

AN OVERVIEW OF REPARATIONS CLAIMS IN LATIN AMERICA

This chapter discusses twelve countries in Latin America in which claims for reparations arising out of state terrorism have been publicly articulated. In

1991, Argentina set the Latin American precedent for making systematic reparations to victims of human rights violations following government participation in a "Friendly Settlement Procedure" before the Inter-American Human Rights Commission. The agreed-upon settlement, made law by Decree 70/91 in December 1991, included monetary compensation to victims of human rights violations that occurred during the Dirty War (1976–1983). In addition to Argentina, Latin American countries that are known to have provided reparations to victims of human rights violations include Chile, Brazil, Honduras, and Suriname. Chile, like Argentina, has made extensive reparations to families of murdered or disappeared persons. In Honduras and Brazil reparations have been paid to some families and individuals, and in Suriname the government provided compensation to one survivor and the families of six victims of a 1987 massacre by Surinamese soldiers, along with other community benefits.[12]

Other states have considered or are currently considering paying reparations for such atrocities. This latter group includes Bolivia (which ultimately did not pay reparations to victims of human rights violations or their families, but did prosecute and imprison a number of perpetrators of human rights abuses, including an ex-President), and Guatemala, El Salvador, and Uruguay.

In other countries (Mexico, Peru, and Paraguay), human rights organizations have long appealed to their governments for reparations to families of victims of state terrorism with no perceptible state response (despite, in Peru's case, a 1994 recommendation of the Inter-American Court of Human Rights that reparations be paid by the Peruvian government to three families of massacre victims). However, these types of claims in Peru and Mexico have recently begun to receive serious government attention. Peru's President Alejandro Toledo, elected to office in 2001, promised as part of his campaign platform to create a truth commission to investigate past human rights abuses. Similarly, in early 2001 in Mexico, President Vicente Fox proposed the creation of a citizen transparency commission to investigate abuses during the seventy-year tenure of the Institutional Revolutionary Party (PRI). Paraguay's government remains unresponsive to the issue.

Admitting the difficulty in quantifying human rights abuses, I summarize some information about the violations for which reparations are being claimed in table 8.1.[13] I stress that this is not intended to be a comprehensive list of human rights violations that have occurred, but rather a summary of the violations for which I have been able to ascertain that reparations have been or are being claimed, created for comparative purposes. Population figures are included to give a sense of the proportion of affected persons within a society and the day-to-day proximity of surviving victims and perpetrators.

It should be noted that the number of victims indicated in the Brazilian case is that documented by a clandestine nongovernmental effort,[14] and in

Honduras the number corresponds to a one-man judicial effort. The numbers are low in part because these cases do not reflect the same degree of available means for gathering evidence as in some of the other cases listed and in part because of the different degrees of repression across regimes.

During Argentina's Dirty War an officially documented total of 9,000 individuals were tortured, murdered, or "disappeared" at the hands of the state security forces; better estimates of the real totals reach 20,000 to 30,000.[15] In Chile between 1973 and 1990 (although most of the worst violations occurred during 1973–1974), over 2,000 people were killed, while many others were unlawfully detained, tortured, or forced into exile in the aftermath of the military coup led by Augusto Pinochet.[16] Prolonged arbitrary detention, rather than murder or disappearance, was the hallmark of both the period of authoritarian rule in Uruguay (1966–1985) and the Alfredo Stroessner dictatorship in Paraguay (1954–1991).

Table 8.1. Human Rights Violations for Which Reparations Have Been Claimed, by Country, Conflict, and Population

Country	Type of Conflict	Years	# of Victims	Population
Argentina	State terrorism	1976–1983	9–15,000 disappeared 30,000 imprisoned 500,000 exiled	35.8 million
Bolivia	State terrorism	1965–1982	155 disappeared 14,000 imprisoned 6,000 exiled	7.4 million
Brazil	State terrorism	1964–1979	136 disappeared	160.0 million
Chile	State terrorism	1973–1990	2–5,000 disappeared	14.6 million
El Salvador	Civil war	1980–1991	50,000 killed 22,000 h.r. violations	6.0 million
Guatemala	Civil war	1954–1996	160,000 killed 40,000 disappeared 50,000 h.r. violations	10.5 million
Honduras	Armed forces terrorism	1980–1993	184 disappeared	6.0 million
Mexico	State terrorism	1968–2000	Hundreds killed, disappeared	98.1 million
Paraguay	State terrorism	1954–1989	360,000 imprisoned 1 million exiled	4.8 million
Peru	Civil conflict	1980–1992	30,000 killed 5,000 disappeared 259 massacred	24.9 million
Suriname	Armed forces terrorism	1987	6 killed	0.4 million
Uruguay	State terrorism	1973–1985	164 disappeared 4,000 imprisoned	3.2 million

Disappearances, torture, and executions by government forces have been documented and denounced in Brazil, Honduras, Peru, and Suriname, though in much smaller numbers than in the Southern Cone cases. In Mexico, public outcry over relatively recent massacres of indigenous peasants galvanized attention to human rights abuses. In the first instance, government forces are known to have assaulted and killed twelve individuals in Aguas Blancas, Guerrero, in 1995. The second involves a case where paramilitary forces linked to the government killed more than forty civilians in Acteal, Chiapas, in 1997. Other cases now being raised by the human rights community in Mexico include the murder and disappearance of student demonstrators in Mexico City in 1968 and of hundreds of opposition politicians and journalists over the past thirty years.

In two cases, those of El Salvador and Guatemala, the violations of concern are those incurred in a context of civil war. After the signing of peace accords ended a twelve-year civil war in which over 50,000 people were killed, the United Nations truth commission in El Salvador received 22,000 denunciations of human rights violations, including extra-judicial executions, massacres, disappearances, and torture.[17] The report recently issued by the Guatemalan government's Commission for Historical Clarification, *Memory of Silence*, estimates 200,000 deaths in the course of that country's thirty-six-year civil war: an estimated 160,000 civilians were killed and another 40,000 disappeared.

According to the truth commission's investigation, 93 percent of these deaths and disappearances occurred at the hands of state military and police forces.[18] Over 80 percent of those affected in Guatemala were of Mayan descent. *Guatemala: Never Again*, a nongovernmental report compiled and published under the authority of the Archdiocese of Guatemala, documents 52,427 human rights violations and finds that military and paramilitary forces were responsible for nearly 90 percent of these. Guerilla forces are found to have been responsible for nearly 5 percent, and the responsibility for the rest remains undetermined.[19] In both the Salvadoran and Guatemalan cases, truth commission reports have recommended reparations for all victims and families of victims on both sides of the civil conflict.

REPARATIONS MEASURES AND
THE BASIS FOR CLAIMS

Reparation claims in the Americas are based on international law. At the same time, reparation practices in Latin America have contributed to the development of this body of law. The list of grave and systematic human rights abuses for which victims may be entitled to claim compensation under international law includes most of the violations recorded in the Latin American cases: the murder of or causing the disappearance of individuals; torture or other cruel, inhuman, or degrading punishment; prolonged arbitrary detention and, in the case of Guatemala, genocide.[20]

The American Convention on Human Rights, which was ratified by all the states in question and entered into force on July 18, 1978, establishes a right to reparations in international human rights law. Article 63(1) of the American Convention provides that if the Inter-American Court of Human Rights (IACHR) rules that a case has involved violations of the human rights and freedoms guaranteed by the Convention, the right or freedom that has been violated must be restored, the breach which led to the violation must be remedied, and the injured party must receive fair compensation.[21]

Another important international document that establishes a basis for reparations is the United Nations' *Draft Basic Principles and Guidelines on the Right to Reparation for Victims of Gross Violations of Human Rights and International Humanitarian Law*. This document was prepared by Special Rapporteur Theo van Boven for the United Nations Subcommission on the Prevention of Discrimination and Protection of Minorities. The draft principles, in preparation since 1988, use the Argentine and Chilean cases, as well as cases from other regions, as specific points of reference. The principles developed in this document maintain that states are obligated to provide full redress, including reparations for the consequences of grave and systematic human rights abuses and indemnification for damages, including but not limited to financial compensation.[22]

In cases in Latin America in which reparations have actually been paid, they are either the result of a ruling in a case brought by individuals to the IACHR (for example, Suriname and Honduras) or cases in which a state's legislative bodies have respected recommendations of official commissions of inquiry to varying degrees (as has been the case in Argentina and Chile). In Brazil, reparations payments were authorized by the legislature to compensate a small number of relatives of those disappeared individuals whose cases were documented by an unofficial, nongovernmental truth commission. Note that neither the IACHR nor the truth commissions have the power to enforce their recommendations or rulings.

In every case in which reparations have been made, it has ultimately been a governmental decision, either legislative or executive, that authorizes payments or other reparations measures. Table 8.2 summarizes the mechanisms through which reparations have been considered and the general measures that have been taken (or suggested) in the countries of interest.[23]

INDIVIDUAL OR COLLECTIVE REPARATIONS?

Table 8.2 illustrates the predominance of one particular trend in reparations measures in the Latin American cases. That is, reparations measures are over-

Table 8.2.   Reparations Mechanisms and Measures or Proposals, by Country

Country	Mechanism	Reparations Measures Taken/Proposals Made
Argentina	Govt. truth commission	$220,000 to 15,000 families of disappeared, $74/day of imprisonment to falsely detained or exiled, military service waivers
Bolivia	Govt. truth commission	None; ex-president and 50 other offenders tried and imprisoned
Brazil	NGO truth commission	$150,000 each to 136 families of disappeared
Chile	Govt. truth commission	$4,000–$6,000/year as pensions to 5,000 families of disappeared and executed persons, military service waivers, medical and educational benefits, tax waivers to exiled persons
El Salvador	UN truth commission	None to date; proposed reparations fund using 1% of international assistance
Guatemala	Govt. truth commission	None to date; proposals include apology, NGO truth commission, monument, community-based reparations
Honduras	Judicial investigation, IACHR case	$2.1 million to families of 19 of 184 disappeared persons
Mexico	Proposed government truth commission	None to date
Paraguay	NGO truth commission	None to date
Peru	IACHR case, proposed government truth commission	None to date; proposals include reparations to 3 families of 1986 massacre victims
Suriname	IACHR case	$450,000 to 37 beneficiaries, $4,000 for a community foundation, community school and health clinic reopened, public apology
Uruguay	NGO truth commission IACHR case	None to date; proposals include 1991 IACHR recommendation, payment unconfirmed

whelmingly directed toward individual victims or their survivors, rather than groups or communities. Reparations made to date in Latin America have taken a highly individualized and material form, such as payments or pensions to victims of certain human rights violations and their families. In some cases, they also include social welfare–type benefits such as medical care and scholarships or housing assistance. Family members of victims in Chile and Argentina have also been exempted from military service and in some cases individual debts have been forgiven.

Collective reparations are not the norm in the Latin American cases. Collective reparations vary widely and can include such measures as the creation of memorials, parks, staffing of community clinics, the establishment of foundations for national reconciliation, and even the introduction of human rights curricula into schools. Certain collective symbolic actions such as apologies, not necessarily treated as reparations measures, have been undertaken in some cases. Far more common as a claim and outcome of reparations efforts are public acts to clear the "good name" of victims, who had for years been falsely accused of subversion and other criminal acts. But in general, collective measures have been neglected.

Memorials, long proposed, are yet to be created. In Argentina, a 1996 proposal for a memorial museum at a former concentration camp, El Olimpo, created a controversial debate in the Buenos Aires City Council and ended in confrontation at the site between human rights activists and police in antiriot gear.[24] The proposal was ultimately rejected. In Uruguay, the Punta Carreta prison in Montevideo, where thousands of political prisoners were brutally and systematically tortured during the military dictatorship, is now the site of an upscale shopping mall, thwarting efforts to preserve the location as a place of public memory and memorial.[25]

The issue of individual versus collective reparations brings out an interesting aspect of reparation claims in Latin America. Why are collective measures of compensation so infrequent? Part of the reason for this is that most of the victims of human rights abuses in Latin America were not, at the time the violations were committed, part of a group sharing any common identity, with the exception of the cases in Guatemala and Suriname. In Suriname, the victims were all Saramaccan Maroons, an ethnic minority. In Guatemala, the report of the truth commission explicitly uses the term "genocide" to describe the atrocities because of the disproportionate number of Amerindian Mayan peasants affected by the violence.[26]

While it is true that the cases considered in this chapter (those arising from state terrorism, rather than colonialism) generally correspond to violations of individual rights rather than group rights and that it is more possible in this context to compensate individuals, there is no reason that the claims of individuals, especially when these are widespread, must be met exclusively with individualized remedies.

Another reason for the relative lack of attention to collective measures of reparation is that the legalistic mechanism by which reparations are determined, especially in the case of the interventions of the IACHR, pushes cases in the direction of individualistic remedies. Individual plaintiffs are named, and for cases before the IACHR and in cases of reparations passed by national legislative bodies, the burden of proof lies with the victims or their families. The government is rarely compelled to investigate the cases. Decree 70/91 in Argentina, for example, authorizes payment to persons who could prove they had been detained by executive order between 1976 and 1983, the period during which the military regime was in power. This has a limiting effect on the scope of reparations claims because of the difficulty in obtaining such evidence.

Another interesting factor that may contribute to the tendency toward individual reparations has to do with the politics of memory. At the time of the violations, most governments claimed that victims shared a group identity as leftist dissidents or "threats to national security." Defending the innocence of those who were persecuted by military dictatorships and government forces in the Central American civil conflicts depended on denying individual membership in political groups. The reports of truth commissions have taken pains to assert that victims of human rights violations were all sorts of people, from all walks of life, and of varied political persuasions.

The *Guatemala: Never Again* report states that "victims include members of the civilian population who were targeted whether or not they were politically active, or engaged in public, legitimate religious, community-based, labor or any other type of activities."[27] The *Uruguay: Nunca Más* report explains, "If at the beginning security forces concentrated on dismantling armed subversion, after the coup they extended their efforts to breaking up political organizations and labor unions, with the aim of dismantling society generally. Daily life was profoundly affected—any social interaction silenced, social organizations dissolved and professional organizations banned."[28] The *Nunca Más* report from Argentina reaches a similar conclusion—namely, that victims of human rights violations in that country were not part of any identifiable social group.

This stance may have begun to change recently. An observer of contemporary Argentina writes that "with the passage of time family members in Argentina have started to recognize and portray their disappeared relatives as social and political activists . . . , displacing the portrayal of the disappeared as 'victims.' . . . [T]his is a first and critical step in the process of recovering a memory of politics."[29] For claimants who have long denied group identity, collective reparations are less likely to be sought, considered, or delivered. By favoring individualized reparations claims, states may soften the degree of acknowledgment of the political sources of the violence.

The tendency to favor individualized over collective reparations measures has a further significance: First, the conditions created to specify who can seek redress and on the basis of what evidence may result in reparations only being paid in cases with limited numbers of documented victims. Where claims are limited, this may actually make it more likely that states will meet reparations demands, for economic reasons. The cases of Brazil, Honduras, and Suriname, where payments have been made to a small number of claimants, and the cases of Guatemala and El Salvador, where large numbers of claims have been documented but no reparations have been undertaken, certainly support this hypothesis.

More important, perhaps, at the same time that claims tend to be staked in individual terms, collective measures of reparation seem likely to be better received. Reparations are sometimes portrayed by opponents as divisive, in the sense that they may actually perpetuate strife by singling out beneficiaries in a manner that may be perceived as insulting, inadequate, or simply unfair—depending on one's perspective either more or less comprehensive than the situation might demand (see, for example, Phillips and Johnson's chapter on Canadian First Nations in this book). This view is not exclusively that of those who would be responsible for making reparations but may also be held by those who would potentially be receiving reparations.

Brandon Hamber and Richard Wilson have observed that "reparations . . . can aid closure but can also be viewed as problematical by some victims who may be uncomfortable with accepting what they perceive as 'blood money.'"[30] These authors note, in addition, that the act of accepting reparations for the "disappeared," when the facts about the disappearance and probable death of the missing individual have not been firmly established, means that families are in effect giving up hope that their loved ones might still be alive: "Reparations without truth make survivors feel that reparations are being used to buy their silence."[31]

One benefit of collective reparations is that they move away from the horrible calculus inherent in individual claims. How, after all, can you put a price on the life of a son or daughter, the use of a limb, or the theft of a grandchild? It goes without saying that fully adequate compensation is unachievable in all cases—it is impossible to bring back the dead, erase the physical and psychological damage inflicted on torture victims, or turn back time so that children can grow up in their biological families. Collective measures of reparation can have significance without undervaluing cases of individual harm done or forcing families to give up hope.

The potential of collective reparations is beginning to receive attention. In one of the most recent cases of Latin American reparations claims, the *Guatemala: Memory of Silence* report recommends collective reparations for collective violations (but not for victims of individual violations). Specifically, the report notes that in the case of collective violations, such as massacres of civilians in indigenous villages, the surviving members of the community should participate in defining the priorities of the reparations process.[32]

Collective reparations to the Saramaccan community affected by the massacre, including funds for a health clinic and school, were in fact part of the settlement recommended in the Surinamese case, the other case besides Guatemala in which victims were part of an ethnic group.[33] Nonetheless, for the reasons outlined in the preceding, collective reparations measures in general, not just for collective violations, merit greater consideration from states and courts than they have received to date.

TRANSNATIONAL REPARATIONS CLAIMS

Another type of reparations that has been called for periodically in the Latin American cases is what we might call transnational reparations— compensation to victims in one state from the government of another state deemed to share responsibility for the human rights violations that have occurred. The issue of transnational claims for reparations arose recently with the report of Guatemala's Historical Clarification Commission. The report not only recommends reparations for victims but also reform of the judicial and police systems; in addition, it details the role of the U.S. government in providing support to those responsible for human rights abuses in the form of training, weapons, and equipment for the Guatemalan armed forces.[34]

In view of the role of the CIA and other U.S. agencies in supporting repressive forces in Guatemala during the thirty-five-year civil conflict, political observers have raised the issue of U.S. responsibility to participate in reparations activities in Guatemala.[35] This argument gains in persuasiveness as more complete documentation of the U.S. role in Guatemala is slowly released to the public. We now know, for example, that during a congressional ban on military aid, the CIA funneled several million dollars each year to the notorious Guatemalan military intelligence unit G-2 and had on its payroll "informants" who have since been directly implicated in abuses including kidnapping and torture.[36]

Based on the release of some of this information and timed with a rare presidential visit to Central America, President Clinton made an official apology to Guatemalans in early 1999. Clinton acknowledged that what happened there was a terrible thing, that it never should have happened, and that the United States should not allow such a thing to happen in the future. But what is the meaning of such an apology? As one commentator has provocatively suggested, "If Clinton had crawled on his knees from the airport outside Guatemala City to the cathedral and fallen at the feet of the archbishop, that would have meant something."[37] The apology made by Clinton was not exactly an admission of guilt, and it represents at best only the smallest of possible steps toward addressing U.S. responsibility for redress and reparation in Guatemala or elsewhere.

Guatemala is not the only case in which transnational, and specifically U.S. responsibility for human rights violations has been discussed. Over a decade ago, the introduction to the English language edition of the *Brazil Nunca Mais* truth commission report noted that "of particular interest to Americans are accounts of official American participation in and knowledge about torture in Brazil, which make it quite clear that the United States played an active role in counterinsurgency training, and furthermore had covertly supported the 1964 military coup."[38] Lawrence Weschler has documented the influence not just of U.S. agencies, but also of the militaries of France and Argentina in training and supporting Uruguayan torturers. Weschler notes that the facts regarding several of the best-documented cases of the false imprisonment, torture, and murder of Uruguayan citizens are well established because they occurred in Argentina and are included in the Argentine truth commission report.[39] However, transnational reparations have not yet been paid in any of these cases.

There are two cases in which they have been paid, however. In Argentina, the fund established by the Forced Disappearance of Persons Law (24.411) provides for reparations to victims of illegal repression without a specific provision regarding nationality. In 1999, for the first time, this fund paid compensation to the widow of a victim from another country, former left-nationalist dictator General Juan José Torres of Bolivia. The Argentine government has acknowledged that Torres was kidnapped and killed as part of Operation Condor, a transnational repressive effort coordinated by authoritarian governments in the Southern Cone. Torres's widow was to be paid $224,000.[40]

The other example of transnational reparations worth noting is the five thousand dollars per person recently paid by the U.S. government to twenty-two hundred surviving Japanese Latin Americans who were forcibly kidnapped from their residences in Latin America, mainly Peru, and interned in U.S. camps during World War II. Interesting to note is the differential provisions for transnational reparations in this case as compared to reparations made to American nationals. Unlike the Japanese Latin Americans, Japanese Americans who had been interned were resettled, awarded twenty thousand dollars (four times the amount received by the Japanese Latin Americans), and received the reparations a decade earlier. The transnational case had a much slower and significantly less "generous" outcome.[41]

The transnational aspect of reparations claims also works in another way: claims may be filed in foreign courts against perpetrators for crimes committed in their countries against foreign nationals. The most widely known example of this type of transnational attempt to prosecute a responsible official for past abuses is the October 1999 arrest of former Chilean dictator Pinochet in Britain, on an extradition request from Spain, to stand trial for the murder of Spanish citizens in Chile. After much controversy in trying to determine whether the ex-dictator had diplomatic immunity (it was initially held by the Law Lords that he did not), and whether torture cases before 1988, when Britain enacted the Torture Convention, could be included in the extradition order (they were not), Pinochet was ultimately released as medically unfit to stand trial.[42]

Similarly, in the Salvadoran case mentioned earlier, the families of three American nuns and one layworker who were raped and murdered by members of the Salvadoran National Guard filed a wrongful death lawsuit in U.S. federal court against two of the perpetrators named in the UN truth commission report. Both are Salvadoran former army generals, now retired and living comfortably in Florida. The cases against the Salvadoran generals were eventually dismissed because the chain of command could not be proven. In July 2002, however, a federal jury in a civil lawsuit ruled that the two retired Salvadoran generals were responsible for acts of torture committed twenty years ago. They based their finding on the "command responsibility" doctrine, which holds commanding officers responsible for the actions of their troops.[43]

Although this type of action is beyond the scope of this chapter in that it focuses on punishing and obtaining damages from individuals rather than states, it is an important trend in current efforts to open transnational claims making. The significance for the consideration of reparations by states is this: if international trials become more frequent, as seems to be the trend, but continue to be unsuccessful in holding defendants accountable, future attention may refocus on seeking reparations from states.

THE VALUE OF REPARATIONS FOR RECONCILIATION IN LATIN AMERICA

To end this survey of reparations in Latin America, let us consider the value of reparations for reconciliation by addressing three of the most frequent objections raised in discussing reparations: (1) the claim that reparations are passive and are thus not sufficiently punitive, (2) the claim that reparations are controversial and exacerbate societal conflict, and (3) the assertion that no matter what measures are taken, reparations will always be insufficient to address the serious damage that has been done. Let us consider each of these points in turn, drawing on evidence from the Latin American cases.

First, what do the Latin American cases tell us about the reparations-versus-prosecution controversy? Authors writing in the field of international law most frequently embrace this position, which questions the punitive value of reparations. Jo M. Pasqualucci, for example, has argued that *de jure* and *de facto* impunity for violators of human rights effectively bar victims from appropriate redress and reparation: without prosecution and punishment, any reparations that might be made are illusory and incomplete.[44]

Other legal scholars and academics, such as Diane Orentlicher and Brian Walsh, believe that reparations can be of value, but like Pasqualucci they are still concerned that reparations cannot provide a strong deterrent to future violations.[45] These authors believe that criminal punishment is the most effective insurance against future repression. In Orentlicher's words, "if law is unavailable to punish widespread brutality of the recent past, what lesson can be offered for the future?"[46]

On the one hand, reparations are undoubtedly a more passive way of pursuing justice than prosecution. On the other hand, they may be more practical. Prosecution can be difficult if not impossible in these kinds of cases.[47] Among the difficult-to-rebut defenses that can be raised by rights abusers are lack of agency, necessity of action against subversion, self-defense, state of war, due obedience, expired statute of limitations, and the problem of selectivity of punishment.[48] Despite these drawbacks, however, some have argued that trials create a process of collective debate that is essential to democratization.[49] However, it seems that a similarly beneficial collective debate could also be generated around legislative processes or processes within special governmental human rights commissions to establish collective reparations measures.

Indeed, because of the individualistic nature of criminal trials, a process of reflection aimed at establishing collective reparations could actually be a more successful democratizing step. By moving beyond discussion of the guilt and innocence of individuals, such discussion could expand the scope of public debate to encompass and interrogate the political and social context that made the commission of human rights abuses possible.

Comparing the Latin American cases to those in Eastern Europe, Tina Rosenberg argues that trials should be a viable option in Latin America because the scope of societal complicity under authoritarian (as opposed to totalitarian) regimes is relatively narrow.[50] She believes that trials have a greater potential to address human rights violations in Latin America than in Eastern Europe, because there are fewer perpetrators in the Latin American cases. While it may be the case that a lower diffusion of responsibility for human rights abuses increases the chance of achieving justice through trials, there is reason for skepticism about the prospect of using trials effectively in Latin America.

Much depends on one's definition of what is diffuse. Carlos Nino, for example, believes that responsibility in most of the Latin American cases is diffuse, not narrow.[51] Though it may be the case that there was a lower degree of societal complicity in human rights abuses in Latin America than in Eastern Europe, in most cases and most countries in Latin America, the number of individuals involved is not so low as to justify Rosenberg's optimism about criminal trials.

A slightly different observation about the legacy of authoritarian regimes is important, however. This observation concerns the legacy of strong militaries and policing agencies often left behind by authoritarian regimes that undergo negotiated transitions to democracy. In many postauthoritarian cases, there is justifiable concern that the degree of posttransition civilian control over the military is insufficient to guarantee just trials.[52]

The reality of the current Latin American political context is that punishing the perpetrators is highly unlikely, for myriad reasons. Unlike reparations cases, which have greater potential to be addressed collectively, the norms of legal prosecution demand the singling out of individual plaintiffs and defendants. National judicial systems are gaining autonomy from political interference, but slowly. International legal recourse is available only after domestic attempts fail. (Cases cannot be referred to the IACHR until national venues have been exhausted.) Human rights violations are notoriously difficult to document, especially in the case of disappeared persons.

Finally, in cases where violence has been particularly widespread, specifically the civil war cases in Guatemala and El Salvador, a given individual may be legitimately considered to be both a victim and a perpetrator of rights violations, creating further complexity for already taxed judicial systems.

Thus, if it is true, as Hannah Arendt has written, that "men are unable to forgive what they cannot punish,"[53] and in light of the obstacles to prosecution just outlined, then both monetary and symbolic reparations may serve a useful purpose. Because of the recent vintage of the conflicts and abuses and the relatively concentrated nature of the populations involved, there is practical need for some measure of reparation. These are societies where past abuses grate on the nerves of everyday life. Victims and perpetrators, as groups and individuals, come into regular contact with each other and are often recognizable to each other. The undeniable fact that there are serious obstacles to justice—such as lack of punishment, impunity, and amnesties granted to rights violators—does not have to mean that the ugly truth about state terrorism in Latin America is a truth without consequences.

Second, what do these cases tell us about the potential for reparations to cause social turbulence? Despite a tendency among analysts and policymakers to label reparations as controversial or divisive by nature, in Latin America the reparations measures themselves have not been at the heart of the conflict as much as the truth commissions that recommend them. In fact, examination of the Latin American cases shows that controversy about reparations in this region is more likely to revolve around what states can "afford," how to verify victims' claims, and how to memorialize the victims appropriately, rather than around the issue of whether reparations should be made at all.

Truth commissions and trials are another story. In cases where reparations have been paid, this has resulted in little or no violence. Conversely, there is ample evidence that truth telling and prosecution are dangerous ventures. In Argentina, a December 1986 attempt to put perpetrators on trial provoked the violent takeover of a military garrison by some members of the military, a situation that was resolved only gingerly.[54] Similarly, in the three weeks after the truth commission report was first released in Chile, three people, including an opposition senator, were assassinated, and some ten thousand copies of the report were held back from distribution to allow political tensions to cool.[55]

Nearly ten years later, the 1999 international effort to try Pinochet provoked a series of contentious demonstrations and counterdemonstrations by Pinochet supporters and opponents throughout Chile. In Guatemala, Bishop Juan Jose Gerardi was murdered in 1998 shortly after his office released its "unofficial" truth commission report, *Guatemala: Nunca Más*. The violence may have its roots in the fact that truth commission reports and trials typically lead to real consequences (a reason, perhaps, that the U.S. Congress has been so reluctant to endorse a study on reparations for slavery). In the current logic of individualized reparations, trials and truth commissions are critical to the reparations process, due to their role in establishing which individuals are eligible for benefits.

Finally, we must consider the question of the impact that reparations can actually have on individual lives. A tendency to focus on acknowledgment of wrongs has led some people to argue that if truth is not enough, neither are financial reparations. Patricia E. Standaert typifies this view: "The mere transfer of funds is often seen as an inadequate remedy for the suffering inflicted by years of pain and terror. . . . Money, although it is seen as an acknowledgment of wrongdoing, does not close wounds or bring back a sense of dignity and respect to the individual."[56] In addition, other authors have raised concerns that not only is it impossible for reparations to restore victims to their former status, they often do not even make a significant impact on the financial situation of victims and their survivors (consider the five thousand dollar payment made by the United States to interned Japanese Latin Americans).

Hamber and Wilson, who bring a social-psychological approach to the study of reparations, have noted that "seldom will the amounts of money granted equal the actual amount of money lost over the years when a breadwinner is killed, and it is questionable whether the low levels of material reparations offered will dramatically change the life of the recipients."[57] However, these authors go on to argue that the transfer of material things between people has meaning beyond the cash value of the goods that are exchanged. The act of transfer, they argue, reflects a spirit of obligation.[58] Reparations, in this sense, can be understood to have meaning that transcends mere financial factors. Here, an appropriate example is the decision as part of reparations measures in Chile and Argentina to exempt survivors of human rights abuses and their immediate family members from mandatory military service.

Returning to financial considerations, other authors are less inclined to deny the material value of reparation. For example, Walsh espouses the view that "the pursuit of justice is incomplete without the appropriate compensation of the victims."[59] He points to the fact that in addition to physical and psychological damage, there was real economic harm done to the victims. People lost income and job tenure, were unable to finish high school and university careers, and were forced to give up land, home, and possessions. While physical and psychological damages are deserving of attention and concern, these may indeed be impossible to repair. Economic damages, however, can be concretely addressed. Walsh states, "Many victims and their families had to endure physical, psychological, and financial hardships, which continue long after the repressive regime loses power. Ignoring their needs is another inequity and undermines the pursuit of justice."[60]

Furthermore, in considering the value of reparations, we must consider the theory that underlies the justification for reparations. To judge the usefulness of reparations in restoring a society to a more stable state, we need to interrogate the goals we expect reparations to achieve. Reparations are unquestionably intended to address the needs of individuals and groups that have been victimized in the past, but they should also be understood as measures directed toward the future of a nation's citizenry. When the truth about the past is not enough, some measure of accountability is needed. As Mike Kaye has written, "Accountability is an essential prerequisite for a successful democratic transition. . . . [I]f past violations of human rights go unpunished it will undermine the rule of law and the new democratic institutions which are being built."[61] The payment of reparations to individuals— and perhaps even more effectively, the creation of collective reparations measures that benefit society more broadly—can demonstrate a government's interest in its citizens and their well-being, a desire for legitimacy, and a disposition to generate mechanisms for greater accountability. Indeed, as Elazar Barkan has argued in his contribution to this book, only those countries that wish to pursue these aims are likely to pay reparations at all.

Once the difficult work of truth commissions has been completed, reparations are an important measure of follow-through. Reparations indicate a state's acceptance of responsibility for the well-being of its citizens. Such compensation also validates the findings of truth commissions in a concrete way.[62] In cases where trial and punishment is not politically viable—and, perhaps more significantly, in cases where burden of proof requirements cannot at this time be fulfilled to the satisfaction of the courts—reparations such as money and social services, memorials, and other symbolic measures can serve as surrogates for the consequences some would like to see enacted.

Consider the distinction between the goal of retributive justice (which focuses on individual culpability) and restorative justice (which focuses on institutional reform). If democratizing Latin American governments will not or cannot seek the first at the present juncture, this does not mean that they should forgo the second. If we make this analytic distinction, and frame reparations as measures directed toward the achievement of restorative justice, we can also recognize more clearly that the provision of reparations does not prohibit the pursuit of retributive justice. Indeed, the seminal reparations cases from Latin America, Chile and Argentina, have shown this to be true. Relatively extensive reparations measures have been provided in both cases, yet these are two of the countries where retributive justice has been most actively pursued in recent times. In Latin America, reparations may no more be "enough" than the truth is; but, like truth-telling, they are a necessary step on the path to reconciliation.

NOTES

1. Ignacio Martín-Baro, "Reparations: Attention Must be Paid," in *Transitional Justice: How Emerging Democracies Reckon with Former Regimes,* ed. Neil Kritz (Washington, D.C.: United States Institute of Peace Press, 1995), 570.

2. Lawrence Weschler, Introduction to *Uruguay Nunca Más: Human Rights Violations 1972–1985,* by Servicio Paz y Justicia, trans. Elizabeth Hampsten (Philadelphia: Temple University Press, 1992), xxi.

3. David Gonzalez, "2 Salvadoran Generals Cleared by U.S. Jury in Nuns' Deaths," *New York Times,* November 4, 2000, A3.

4. Juanita Darling, "El Salvador to Reopen Murder Probe," *Los Angeles Times,* October 26, 2000, A12.

5. See "Argentine Political Crimes: Closing In," *The Economist* (November 6, 1999): 34.

6. The most authoritative works in this area are Priscilla B. Hayner, *Unspeakable Truths: Confronting State Terror and Atrocity* (New York: Routledge, 2001), and Kritz, ed., *Transitional Justice.* Also valuable are the online essay by Esteban Cuya, "Las Comisiones de la Verdad en América Latina," *KO'AGA RONE'ETA: A Journal of Human Rights* (1996): series iii, at www.derechos.org/koaga/iii/1/cuya.html (accessed January 2000), and the article by Mike Kaye, "The Role of Truth Commissions in the Search for Justice, Reconciliation and Democratization: The Salvadorean and Honduran Cases," *Journal of Latin American Studies* 29, no. 3 (October 1997): 693–717.

7. Dinah Shelton, *Remedies in International Human Rights Law* (Oxford, U.K.: Oxford University Press, 1999), and Kritz, ed., *Transitional Justice,* are important references in this area. For specific discussion of cases in the Americas, see Jo M. Pasqualucci, "The Whole Truth and Nothing But the Truth: Truth Commissions, Impunity, and the Inter-American Human Rights System," *Boston University Law Journal* (Fall 1994): 328–29, and Patricia E. Standaert, "Other International Issues: The Friendly Settlement of Human Rights Abuses in the Americas," *Duke Journal of Comparative & International Law* (Spring 1999): 519–43.

8. *Report of the Chilean National Truth and Reconciliation Commission,* trans. P. E. Berryman (Notre Dame, Ind.: Center for Civil and Human Rights, Notre Dame Law School, 1993): 837.

9. Brian Walsh, "Resolving the Human Rights Violations of a Previous Regime," *World Affairs* 158, no. 3 (1996): 112.

10. Committee for Historical Clarification, *Guatemala: Memory of Silence. Tz'inil*

Na Tab'al. Report of the Committee for Historical Clarification, Conclusions and Recommendations. English trans. (1999), at hrdata.aaas.org/ceh/report/english (accessed January 2001), Recommendations, point III.

11. See "Chile: Some Mapuche Sign Pact, Others Protest," *Weekly News Update on the Americas* 497 (August 8, 1999): 2; "A New Twist to an Old Tale," *The Economist* (September 4, 1999): 40.

12. David Padilla, "Reparations in *Aloboetoe v. Suriname*," *Human Rights Quarterly* 17, no. 3 (1995): 541.

13. Data in table 8.1 compiled from Pasqualucci, "The Whole Truth"; Priscilla B. Hayner, "Fifteen Truth Commissions," in Kritz, ed., *Transitional Justice*, 252–53; Margaret Popkin and Naomi Roht-Arriaza, "Truth as Justice: Investigatory Commissions in Latin America," in Kritz, ed., *Transitional Justice*, 262–89; David Pion-Berlin, "To Prosecute or to Pardon? Human Rights Decisions in the Latin American Southern Cone," in Kritz, ed., *Transitional Justice*, 82–103; Cuya, "Las Comisiones de la Verdad"; Human Rights Office, Archdiocese of Guatemala, *Guatemala Never Again*; and "Honduras: Death Squad Victims' Kin to Receive Funds," *Los Angeles Times*, February 24, 2000, A10. Population figures are from U.S. Department of State Background Notes: Western Hemisphere, January 20, 2001, at www.state.gov/p/wha/ci/ (accessed September 17, 2002).

14. For a description of the secret nongovernmental effort that produced the Brazilian truth commission report, see Lawrence Weschler, *A Miracle, a Universe: Settling Accounts with Torturers* (Chicago, Ill.: University of Chicago Press, 1998 [1990]).

15. Alison Brysk, "The Politics of Measurement: The Contested Count of the Disappeared in Argentina," *Human Rights Quarterly* 16, no. 4 (1994): 685–86. See also Cuya, "Las Comisiones de la Verdad en América Latina," at www.derechos .org/koaga/iii/1/cuya.html (accessed September 17, 2002).

16. Pasqualucci, "The Whole Truth," 328.

17. Pasqualucci, "The Whole Truth," 329.

18. Committee for Historical Clarification, *Guatemala: Memory of Silence*, Conclusions I.1–2, II.128.

19. Human Rights Office, Archdiocese of Guatemala, *Guatemala Never Again: Recovery of Historical Memory Project (REMHI), The Official Report of the Human Rights Office, Archdiocese of Guatemala*, abridged English translation (Maryknoll, N.Y.: Orbis Books, 1999), 289–91, 302.

20. Ellen Lutz, "After the Elections: Compensating Victims of Human Rights Abuses," in *Transitional Justice*, 555.

21. *American Convention on Human Rights*, OEA/Ser.L.V/II.82, doc. 6 rev. at 25 1992, at www1.umn.edu/humanrts/oasinstr/zoas3con.htm (accessed September 17, 2002). Also available online through document search at www.oas.org (accessed July 29, 2002).

22. United Nations, *Draft Basic Principles and Guidelines on the Right to Reparation for Victims of Gross Violations of Human Rights and International Humanitarian Law* (July 2, 1993), E/CN.4/sub.2/1993/8.

23. Data in table 8.2 compiled from Weschler, "Introduction"; Hayner, *Unspeakable Truths*, 314–17; Hayner, "Fifteen Truth Commissions," 225–61; Thomas Buer-

genthal, "The United Nations Truth Commission for El Salvador," in Kritz, ed., *Transitional Justice*, 319; Padilla, "Reparations in *Aloboetoe*," 544–45; Cuya, "Las Comisiones de la Verdad," and "Honduras: Death Squad Victims' Kin to Receive Funds," *Los Angeles Times*, February 24, 2000, A10.

24. Elizabeth Jelin, "The Minefields of Memory," *NACLA Report on the Americas* 32, no. 2 (September/October 1998): 26.

25. Jelin, "Minefields of Memory," 27.

26. On Suriname, see Padilla, "Reparations in *Aloboetoe*." On Guatemala, see "Guatemala: Pending Justice," *The Economist* (March 13, 1999): 46.

27. Human Rights Office, Archdiocese of Guatemala, *Guatemala Never Again*, 290.

28. Servicio Paz y Justicia-Uruguay, *Uruguay Nunca Más*, 284.

29. Inés Izaguirre, "Recapturing the Memory of Politics," *NACLA Report on the Americas* 31, no. 6 (May/June 1998): 29.

30. Brandon Hamber and Richard Wilson, "Symbolic Closure through Memory, Reparation and Revenge in Post-Conflict Societies," *Human Rights Working Papers* No. 5, April 24, 2000, at www.du.edu/humanrights/workingpapers/papers.htm (accessed September 17, 2002), 3.

31. Hamber and Wilson, "Symbolic Closure," 12–13.

32. Committee for Historical Clarification, *Guatemala: Memory of Silence*, Conclusions 111.10.

33. Padilla, "Reparations in *Aloboetoe*," 545–55.

34. David Holiday, "Reckoning in Guatemala," *The Nation* (March 22, 1999): 5.

35. See Holiday, "Reckoning in Guatemala," and Jo Marie Burt, "Time for a U.S. Truth Commission," *NACLA Report on the Americas* 32, no. 6 (May/June 1999): 5.

36. Kate Doyle, "Guatemala's Ghosts," *LASA Forum* 30, no. 2 (Summer 1999): 19.

37. Alexander Cockburn, "Regrets Only," *The Nation* (April 5/12, 1999): 9.

38. Joan Dassin, introduction to the English language edition, Archdiocese of São Paulo, *Torture in Brazil*, trans. Jaime Wright (New York: Vintage, 1986): xvi.

39. Weschler, *A Miracle, a Universe*, 118, 120, 129.

40. "Argentina Compensates Widow of Murdered Bolivian Leader," *Weekly News Update on the Americas* 513 (November 28, 1999): 4.

41. James Rainey, "U.S. Apologizes to Internees," *Los Angeles Times*, June 3, 1998, B1, B3.

42. Reed Brody, "The Pinochet Precedent: Changing the Equation of Repression," *NACLA Report on the Americas* 32, no. 6 (May/June 1999): 18–20.

43. James P. McGovern, "Silence on El Salvador," *The Nation* (September 20, 1999): 8; Manuel Roig-Franzia, "Torture Victims Win Lawsuit Against Salvadoran Generals," *Washington Post*, July 24, 2002, A1, at www.washingtonpost.com/ac2/wp-dyn?pagename = article&node = &contentId = A51496-2002Jul23&notFound = true (accessed September 17, 2002).

44. Pasqualucci, "The Whole Truth," 356.

45. Diane Orentlicher, "Settling Accounts: The Duty to Prosecute Human Rights Violations of a Prior Regime," in *Transitional Justice*, 375–416; Walsh, "Resolving Human Rights Violations," 117.

46. Orentlicher, "Settling Accounts," 377.

47. Carlos S. Nino, *Radical Evil on Trial* (New Haven, Conn.: Yale University Press, 1996) captures the difficulties of prosecution from an insider's perspective in this comprehensive discussion of the effort to put a limited number of human rights abusers on trial in Argentina.

48. Nino, *Radical Evil,* 164–85.

49. Nino, *Radical Evil,* 133.

50. Tina Rosenberg, *The Haunted Land: Facing Europe's Ghosts after Communism* (New York: Random House, 1995), 399.

51. Nino, *Radical Evil,* 124.

52. See Rosenberg, *The Haunted Land,* 391–95, for an elaboration of this position.

53. Hannah Arendt, *The Human Condition* (Chicago, Ill.: University of Chicago Press, 1958), 241.

54. Carlos S. Nino, "Response: the Duty to Punish Past Abuses of Human Rights Put into Context: The Case of Argentina," in *Transitional Justice,* 425–26.

55. Hayner, "Fifteen Truth Commissions," 236.

56. Standaert, "Friendly Settlement of Human Rights Abuses," 537.

57. Hamber and Wilson, "Symbolic Closure," 11.

58. Hamber and Wilson, "Symbolic Closure," 11.

59. Walsh, "Resolving Human Rights Violations," 116.

60. Walsh, "Resolving Human Rights Violations," 116.

61. Kaye, "The Role of Truth Commissions," 694.

62. Walsh, "Resolving Human Rights Violations," 115.

9

Moral Integrity and Reparations for Africa

Rhoda E. Howard-Hassmann

THE ARGUMENT FOR REPARATIONS

This chapter presents some very preliminary thoughts on reparations due to sub-Saharan Africa, including acknowledgment, apology, and financial compensation.[1] I am a political sociologist, a specialist in international human rights with a background in African studies. Focusing on the "factual" history of Africa, I consider the possibility of arguing a case for Western compensation for racial discrimination. I also consider the case for acknowledgment, apology, and compensation drawn from the need to recognize the *moral integrity* of Africans.

Moral integrity implies Africans' moral value and competence. From the point of view of universal human rights, the moral value of each individual African is equal to the moral value of any other human being, white or non-white, rich or poor. Moral competence is the capacity of any—or most (allowing for various forms of disability)—human beings to distinguish right from wrong and to make active decisions about moral issues. Acknowledgment of moral competence implies respect for the judgment of others, even when the observer disagrees with their conclusions.

Acknowledgment of the moral integrity of an individual requires acknowledgment of how that individual can be damaged or hurt by past wrongs. It also requires acknowledgment of the value to the individual of the community in which he or she lives and how destruction of that community can also constitute an individual wrong. Acknowledgment of moral integrity, then, requires that outsiders listen carefully to insiders' accounts of the wrongs they have suffered. In the case of Africa, this requires careful attention to accounts of wrongs suffered because of the slave trade, colonialism, neo-colonialism, and various forms of Western incursion into Africa in the present.

However, this need to respect Africans' accounts of their own histories does not require that the outsider suspend his or her own judgment. Trudy Govier argues that we do not always have to believe others' claims; rather, we can "take an interest, listen respectfully, and reflectively consider claims made by other people *without believing or accepting them.*"[2] When acknowledgment, apology, or compensation are at issue, one can legitimately apply a careful lawyer's or historian's consideration to the "facts." Historical evidence for the charges of collective or individual hurts should be pursued. The outsider is not required automatically to accept narratives and claims for reparations as truths. Nor is the outsider obliged to absolve from responsibility those from within the claiming community who are responsible for wronging each other. Claims for reparations for past wrongs require sympathetic and respectful hearing, but no automatic reparatory action.

What follows is my own very preliminary position on the question of reparations to sub-Saharan Africa. I have no legal training: this chapter does not argue in any way that there is a legal basis for reparation. The argument proceeds as follows:

1. The "factual" case for global financial compensation is unprovable, based as it is on a series of counterfactual assumptions of what "might have happened" in Africa had there been no slavery, colonialism, or neocolonialism.
2. The case for regarding the European incursion into Africa as a result primarily of racial discrimination is weak, but can be made.
3. Theoretically, rather than trying to calculate financial compensation from past historical relations, a better strategy would be to balance universal economic human rights with universal obligations to fulfill these rights; unfortunately, this is most unlikely to occur.
4. Regardless of the factual case for compensation, acknowledgment of past suffering is a necessary step to present recognition of the moral integrity of Africans.
5. Apologies are also a necessary step to recognition of the moral integrity of Africans, and the creation of an international moral community.
6. It may be possible to establish some bases for financial compensation to Africans, to be sought from, and payable by, governments, private corporations, and some private social institutions.
7. Even if there is no other reason for acknowledgment, apology, or com-

pensation, a realist view of international relations might wish to consider them as a foundation for trust-based relations between the West and Africa in the future.

QUESTIONABLE HYPOTHESES ABOUT COLONIALISM AND UNDERDEVELOPMENT

The Declaration of the African Regional Preparatory Conference for the World Conference against Racism, Racial Discrimination, Xenophobia, and Related Intolerance, held in Durban, South Africa, in September 2001, asks for historical justice.[3] The Declaration lays particular stress on the right to financial compensation; its recommendation no. 2 calls for "an International Compensation Scheme for victims of the slave trade, as well as [for] victims of any other transnational racist policies and acts."

Any attempts to calculate just compensation would encounter numerous obstacles, not least of which are incomplete knowledge and counterfactual assumptions about what "might have happened" in Africa had there been no periods of slavery, colonialism, or neocolonialism. The implied assumption is that, absent these incursions by the outside world, Africa "would have" developed in much the same way as the West has developed. This implication is manifested in many statements made by representatives of African governments at the Durban Conference. For example, Jakaya Kikwete of Tanzania "said that the slave trade and colonization of Africa in the nineteenth century are responsible in a big way for the poverty, underdevelopment, and marginalization that enveloped that continent.[4] This assumption is heavily influenced by the "development of underdevelopment" school of thought, popularized in the 1960s and 1970s, which attributes most African underdevelopment to its encounter with the West.[5]

I have myself contributed to this school of thought, with particular reference to Ghana.[6] In the 1970s I looked in my doctoral research for evidence that Ghana would have developed in its own right had it not been colonized by the British. Certainly, the evidence I found showed that the indigenous Ghanaian economy was profoundly changed by colonialism. The "development" of Ghana was definitely in the interests of British capital, from the stress on cultivation of cocoa to the detriment of other crops to the deliberate exclusion of African businessmen from the export-import trade with London.

In conducting this research, I was assuming that without European incursion, Ghana would have developed in a capitalist direction. This, however, was a counterfactual assumption. I could not show what might have happened in Ghana without British colonialism. Perhaps had Ghana been left alone, the economic outcome might simply have been the continuation of a subsistence-level peasant society. Ghana might have been simply undeveloped rather than underdeveloped. Perhaps, in another scenario of noncolonial development, the central Ashanti kingdom might have conquered even more of Northern and Southern Ghana (and parts of neighboring territories) than it had done prior to the British takeover. This might have resulted in a slave-based economy, trading items such as gold to other Africans and to Europeans in return for goods such as alcohol, tobacco, and guns, but not developing in a capitalist direction.[7] In Ghana and in other parts of Africa, without colonialism the result might have been agriculturally and technologically stagnant economies well into the twentieth century.

Thus, Africa might now be in a state of nondevelopment rather than of underdevelopment. Such non-capitalist development would not mean that Africa was in any way an uncivilized continent lacking culture, sophisticated forms of governance, moral structures, or laws. It would simply mean that, like China until the twentieth century, Africa had not adopted a capitalist path to development.

A second problematic assumption about development is found in the debate between external and internal models of Western development. The "development of underdevelopment" school of thought assumes that the West would not have developed without simultaneously underdeveloping its colonies; the wealth it acquired externally through empire caused its own internal development. The West's wealth was facilitated by the extraction of resources from the colonies, both human labor power and mineral and agricultural products. Therefore, the West, having profited by colonialism, owes financial compensation now to its ex-colonies.

This is a very contentious proposition. Other schools of thought suggest that internal changes in the West brought about capitalist growth. The evolution of internal markets, the changes in land-tenure arrangements, the stratification of society into different social classes with different roles in the productive process, and perhaps even the evolution of new cultural norms of savings and investment all seem to have contributed to the development of the rich Western European economies. Clearly, colonialism was not enough in and of itself to create a wealthy Western economy, as the economic decline of Spain despite its substantial colonial riches indicates.[8]

The "truth" about the role of colonialism in both underdevelopment and development is probably somewhere between these two schools of thought. One could therefore simply dismiss these academic debates as irrelevant to the current discussion of reparations, were it not for assumptions about redistributive benefits that, it is assumed, financial compensation would create. The assumption is that since the West stole from Africa in the past, then it should return what it stole now. Once the stolen wealth is returned, it can be used to remedy Africa's present poverty. It is not African social structure, or political relations, or class exploitation that causes its poverty: it is simply lack of a finite amount of wealth.

This is a mercantilist approach: There is a certain finite amount of wealth in the world, thus the more the West has, the less is available for others. Mercantilism assumes that once wealth is more equitably distributed, development is likely to occur in the poorer parts of the world. But in the West, development occurred as a consequence of capitalism. Capitalism is based on the presumption that increases in wealth will be generated by ever more efficient methods of production. Such increased efficiency in Africa would not necessarily be the result of monetary compensation, which could be squandered easily in temporary redistributive programs without any lasting effects on productive capacities.

These false assumptions about the relationship between colonialism and underdevelopment render problematic any call for material redistribution. Underdevelopment is not necessarily the consequence of colonialism; redirected development is an equally likely consequence. Externally generated wealth—from colonialism or from compensation—will not necessarily result in development. Redistribution of resources does not necessarily result in improvements in productivity.

The case for financial compensation is rooted in an assumption that compensation will render possible an improved African economy, but without concomitant changes in social and political relations, such an outcome will not necessarily transpire. Nor can it transpire without the entrenchment of principles of accountability and transparency in the administrative, legal, and governance institutions of African nations. Wealth alone is, and always has been, insufficient for development.

HISTORY AS RACIAL DISCRIMINATION

In preparatory documents for the World Conference, calls for reparations were justified on the grounds that the history of slavery and colonialism is a history of racial discrimination.[9] The Western incursions into Africa are not best described this way.

Slavery is not necessarily a matter of racial discrimination. Slaves are taken by those who share the slaves' "race," as well as by those who do not. Slavery was practiced in sub-Saharan Africa prior to the incursions of the Europeans. Slaves were taken in the conquest of one African society by another; disgraced individuals were also sometimes sold into slavery.[10] Moreover, the international slave trade involved exchanges not only between Europeans and Africans, but also between Arabs and Africans: the Arabs took about as many African slaves as were taken across the Atlantic.[11] Early relations between European slave buyers and African slave sellers were characterized by a fair degree of social equality. The trade in human beings was considered normal at the time, an era of very limited conceptions of humanity in "others." Indeed, the Nigerian historian Joseph Inikori argues that the reason Europeans first went to Africa for slaves was not because Africans were black, but because for political reasons white Europeans could no longer enslave each other.[12]

Thus, slavery cannot be attributed solely to prejudiced conceptions of race. Nevertheless, Europeans did harbor deeply rooted stereotypes of the "Moor," later the "black," as evil, uncivilized, violent, and dangerous.[13] Such assumptions undoubtedly facilitated both the slave trade and the later colonization of Africa. It was easier than it would otherwise have been to put down African rebellions—indeed, in some cases, to massacre tens of thousands of Africans at a time (as in the case of the Hereros of South West Africa)—if they were considered to be a lesser species of human being or indeed not human at all.[14]

The Europeans' assumption that they were actually bringing to Africa "Christianity, commerce, and civilization" also made it easier to colonize Africa. Ethnocentrism is not a uniquely European attribute, as we know from outbreaks of racism in decolonized countries since they received their independence.[15] Nevertheless, when combined with superior resources, ethnocentrism eases the process of colonization. Actions taken for pure self-interest can be justified in the name of helping the barbarians, the dehumanized Other, to become more like oneself.

The enterprise of colonialism, then, was greatly aided by racist perceptions, even if racism was not its prime cause. Neocolonialism may not be as dependent on racism as colonialism was. The term "neocolonialism" refers to the incursions of Western-based multinational corporations and financial institutions into Africa, along with international organizations of development management such as the World Bank. Even accepting for the sake of argument that their intentions and effects are neocolonial, such incursions need not be based on racism. The incentive to make profits knows no color; whether multinationals invest in Africa or not has to do with rational calculations of the profits to be made.

Similarly, the current stage of globalization is not necessarily based on racism. The NGO Forum at the World Conference in Durban maintained that "Globalisation is . . . inherently racist."[16] Yet, given the willingness of international capital to move its factories around the world and to hire its employees anywhere, one could argue that global capital is the antithesis of racism. Africa suffers from a lack of such international capitalist investment. If capitalists shy away from Africa, however, it is not because Africans are black, but because as human capital they suffer from lack of education, lack of skills, and poor health (not least AIDS). One might attribute some of this poor human capital to the structural adjustment programs encouraged by international financial institutions since the 1980s, which required governments to reduce their investments in education and health.[17] Again, though, it is not clear whether such programs were the consequence of racism so much as the consequence of economic theories that did not take into account the human costs of economic efficiency. The populations of the ex-Soviet bloc, who are predominantly white, suffered from similar "shock treatment" approaches to ameliorating Soviet-era economic inefficiencies.

The history of slavery, colonialism, and neocolonialism, therefore, cannot be attributed solely to racism. Indeed, this was acknowledged by the African Regional Preparatory Conference: "[The] slave trade, all forms of exploitation, colonialism and apartheid were essentially motivated by economic objectives and competition between colonial powers for strategic territorial gains, appropriation, control over and pillage of natural and cultural resources."[18] To attribute these historical processes to racism might be considered a politicized anachronism. Since international law prohibits racial discrimination, to rewrite African history through such a lens improves the chances for legal remedy. Yet it is perhaps unwise to try to view world historical and economic relations solely through the lens of racism. Such a lens obscures the many other causes of under- or nondevelopment, especially in Africa.

EXCURSUS: RESPECT FOR UNIVERSAL ECONOMIC RIGHTS

Any attempt to determine just financial compensation for the European incursion into sub-Saharan Africa would encounter irremediable obstacles, including a strong argument that since that incursion was not primarily motivated by racial discrimination, such compensation is not necessary. Nevertheless, the current suffering of the vast majority of Africans is so overwhelming that some effort must be made to recognize how that suffering has been caused by Africa's integration over several centuries into the world economy. One means would be to take seriously the obligation of all members of the world community to respect universal economic rights.

Article 28 of the Universal Declaration of Human Rights states that "everyone is entitled to a social and international order in which the rights and freedoms set forth in this Declaration can be fully realized." This implies, in its turn, that everyone has an obligation to ensure that such an order exists. The international consensus on economic rights does not require "proof" of the questionable counterfactual hypotheses just discussed. Rather, it requires attention to the needs of real human beings in the present.

By international law, everyone in the world is entitled to economic rights.

Whatever has happened to an individual, a group, or a nation in the past is irrelevant. The only matter of relevance is the current need for protection of economic rights. A world economic order based on individual economic rights would require all economic actors—whether states, private corporations, other organizations or individuals—to consider the effects of their actions on everyone's economic rights.[19]

Economic human rights are measurable and concrete. Minimum standards can be devised for diet, shelter, and health care; whether a state or a continent can provide those minimum standards can be ascertained. Economic human rights provide a standard of accountability by all states, Western or otherwise, to those affected by their policies. Past policies of a state become irrelevant, while its present policies must be geared to the promotion of economic rights.

Yet to ensure that all people, everywhere, enjoy their economic rights now is perhaps too idealistic a project to be considered. Whatever the normative power of the principle of universal responsibility, in practice states bear enforceable responsibilities only to their own citizens. Western citizens are unlikely to give up their privileged access to economic goods to help citizens of other countries. Most Westerners, like most people elsewhere, hold to a concentric circle theory of obligation that does not require them to sacrifice their own well-being for others.[20]

Thus, while theoretically elegant, the principle of universal promotion of economic rights is an unrealistic tool to assist Africans in remedying the past detrimental effects of their integration into the world economy, whether these effects were caused by racism or merely by the workings of the capitalist marketplace. The claim for financial compensation for racism substitutes as a political maneuver to obtain from the West some of the economic resources not otherwise attainable. This claim is based on the assumption that the responsibility for historical deprivations can be accurately and quantifiably attributed to the racist activities of external actors.[21] It is also based on the assumption that without such historical deprivations, Africa would be more developed (wealthy) than it is presently is.

I dispute these assumptions. Nevertheless, I believe there is a role for truth telling and acknowledgment in the current international system. Where the responsibility of the West—or of Western actors—for the circumstances in which Africans find themselves can be documented, there is also room for apology. A case can also be made for certain kinds of financial compensation by carefully delineated donors to carefully delineated recipients, even if a blanket apology by the West to Africa is inappropriate and even if there is no possibility for payment of blanket compensation by the West to Africa.

ACKNOWLEDGMENT AND MORAL INTEGRITY

There is a tendency in the Western world to attribute the dire economic straits in which Africans now find themselves to their own collective incapacities. Many Westerners believe that if Africans studied harder, worked harder, and obeyed the rules of rational economic behavior, their collective problems would be solved.[22]

Such comments deny the moral integrity of Africans. They imply that Africans, unlike Westerners, are incapable of recognizing the way to progress and general prosperity. They suggest that Africans are passive people, sitting under trees waiting for food to fall into their mouths. These stereotypes combine with ancient ideas that Africans are more sexually active than Europeans, less restrained and self-disciplined.

Racism against blacks in general, and Africans in particular, is still so strong in the Western world that some acknowledgment of the moral integrity both of individual Africans and of Africans as a collectivity is necessary. All peoples and all individuals are entitled to respect and a sense of dignity. This is not merely a platitude picked up from the Preamble to the Universal Declaration of Human Rights. It is difficult for any individual to function effectively without a sense of her or his own moral worth, a sense of self-respect. This is all the more so for individuals suffering from poverty and lack of educational opportunities and who are without any sense that the future might bring some relief. As Didjob Divungui Di-Ndinge, vice president of Gabon, said at the Durban Conference, "What Africa is asking for is not compassion, pity or charity. We are asking for recognition . . . of the dignity of its sons and daughters."[23]

White Westerners need to know, and to respect, the personal and collective stories of Africans. Only with such knowledge of personal and collective narratives can there be a real basis for collective empathy. To acknowledge the moral integrity of Africans as individuals—and of Africa as a civilization—requires acts by Westerners of empathic imagination, overcoming the racially denigrating stereotypes of their own collective history. This empathic imagination is not impossible to achieve, but it requires a constant humanizing of Africans—a constant awareness that, underneath the "different" black skin, cultural predispositions, and ways of living, there is a human soul.[24]

However, Westerners also possess moral integrity. They are not all racists, and their historical or their present relations with Africa are not and were not influenced only by racist perceptions or policies. Particularly in the postcolonial era, many Westerners involved in the social movements for economic development, human rights, and feminism have been trying very hard to rectify the results of past racist policies and to remedy current economic inequities. To paint all Westerners as stereotyping racists incapable of recognizing the humanity of Others does them a disservice and reduces the possibility of building an international moral community.

To further recognition of both Africans' and Westerners' moral integrity, some form of truth commission about European–African relations might be useful. This would not necessarily be a truth commission laying blame on individual perpetrators for discrete acts, as did the Truth and Reconciliation Commission in South Africa. It could, rather, follow the model of the 1967 International War Crimes Tribunal on U.S. involvement in Viet Nam, seeking to determine state responsibility for atrocities and injustices perpetrated against citizens of other states.

Such a truth commission would acknowledge the wrongs—whether intentional or not, whether caused by racial discrimination or not—inflicted on Africa by the Western world. A truth commission would also investigate the roles that the non-Western non-African world—that is, the ex-Soviet Bloc, China, and the Arab world—has played in Africa. For example, the tragedies in Ethiopia in the 1970s and 1980s were caused in part by the involvement of the Soviet Union.[25]

Establishment of a truth commission would also require that the truth be spoken about the responsibilities of Africans themselves for that continent's current dilemmas. Postcolonial African political leaders have much to answer for, from ill-conceived economic policies to intentional imprisonment and persecution of their critics and large-scale personal corruption.[26] To acknowledge the responsibility of African leaders for their continent's own fate is not to put a special onus on them because they are black; it is merely to show that, like political leaders elsewhere, they have their share of faults. In almost all new nation-states, similar large-scale personal corruption and political repression has occurred. This is a function of state and institution building, not of the peculiar characteristics of this or that racial or ethnic group.[27] Moreover, Africa is not a continent without an indigenous history: some, if not much of the current state of political chaos in some countries can be attributed to indigenous conflicts that must be overcome by Africans themselves.[28]

If the world community—a community inhabited by Africans as well as by others—does not require that Africans take responsibility for their actions, then in a backhanded way it denies them their own moral integrity. For example, despite everything that is known of the colonial history of Rwanda, as well as of the inaction of the United Nations, the United States, and France during the actual genocide of 1994, the burden of guilt for the genocide surely lies most directly on the Rwandans who instigated and promoted it. Africans, like Westerners—blacks, like whites—need to accept their own duties to others. The indigenous moral systems of Africa do not permit blatant disregard of others' rights. As many African scholars have maintained, checks and balances existed on the actions of rulers.[29]

Sorting out Western, non-Western but non-African, and indigenous responsibilities for Africa's current state of severe economic crisis is not possible in a manner that makes quantifiable financial compensation possible. No commission of inquiry could reach any more than a partial truth. Nevertheless, even such a partial truth might modify the perception that Africa's

current situation is all the "fault" of the Africans, as popular racist perceptions sometimes conclude. The findings of truth commissions can constitute
the bases for later writings of history and education. As South Africa's Truth
and Reconciliation Commission suggests, there is some value to a narrative
on which all sides agree.

The United Nations Draft Declaration for the Durban Conference laid
particular stress on the need for education, emphasizing "the importance
and necessity of teaching about the truth of the ... history of colonialism."[30]
Even if all that is accomplished by such a narrative is the acknowledgment
of a great historical tragedy, such acknowledgment might remove the burden
of belief from some African shoulders that one is personally inferior. Truth
telling, then, has a symbolic meaning. Truth commissions, history writing,
and educational curricula that sort out the responsibilities of African and
outside actors will help to acknowledge the moral integrity of Africans.[31]

A practical aspect of truth telling would be the establishment of a tangible
collective memory, which could be enhanced by the building of monuments
decrying racism and other forms of injustice. As the vice prime minister of
Luxembourg, Lydie Polfer, stated at the Durban Conference, there is a duty
to remember "the mechanisms which led to racism."[32] Ex-slave trading and
ex-colonial powers could contribute to the construction of such monuments;
for example, to the maintenance as museums of the slave forts of West Africa.
Such museums might also help in reconciliation by showing the responsibilities of all actors, not merely that of the colonial powers. Museums and monuments contribute to national myths, but they can also contribute to an
approximation of the "truth," neither minimizing nor exaggerating the roles
of any actors.

Truth telling, then, helps to sort out responsibilities. It allows for new
national truths, more accurate content in education, and collective memories
that show sorrow and reconciliation in national monuments. Truth telling
might also require a symbolic apology for the wrongs inflicted on Africa by
the West.

APOLOGY AND MORAL INTEGRITY

Perhaps recognition of the moral integrity of Africans by Westerners is
unnecessary from the African point of view. It is not clear whether racist
perceptions emanating from the West are influential in the formation of Africans' self-conceptions. Members of other groups that suffered discrimination, such as Jews, sometimes internalized a feeling of self-hatred and
contempt, a belief that the racist oppressor's derogatory views were correct.[33] Early black students of race relations such as Frantz Fanon suggested
there was similar self-hatred among blacks.[34] More reliable quantitative stud-

ies, however, have shown that African Americans have no less self-esteem than white Americans.[35]

Self-hatred may be even less common among black Africans, who at least live in their own communities, cities, and countries, ruled by people who are phenotypically and culturally much like themselves. Nevertheless, perhaps there is still a residual fear that whites really are superior. To learn one's own history properly and to have access to historical truths that explain the origins of one's own situation in a nonracist fashion is to be liberated from stereotypes, whether externally imposed or internally incorporated.

The African Regional Preparatory Conference called for an "explicit apology by the ex-colonial powers or their successors" for the human rights violations associated with the slave trade and colonialism.[36] An apology for racism serves the function of lifting from its victims the feeling that they were personally responsible for their fate. It tells them that others were responsible for that fate and that those others are finally willing to accept their responsibility. It restores moral equivalence between victims and perpetrators, if not actually giving the victims a deserved moral edge. It requires the perpetrators to demonstrate the depth of their apology through a continued attitude of respect, as well as through concrete actions.

Such an apology, however, must be sincere. It must show real contrition, remorse, and repentance.[37] The one who apologizes must "acknowledge the fact of wrongdoing, accept ultimate responsibility, express sincere sorrow and regret, and promise not to repeat the offense."[38] The apology cannot be perfunctory, a mere statement of acknowledgment of historical or contemporary fact without any sincere regret behind it. A sincere person suffers in apologizing: he knows he has done wrong, wishes he had not, and seeks to remedy the wrong he has done as best he can. As Olusegun Obasanjo, president of Nigeria, put it at Durban, "For us in Africa, an apology is a deep feeling of remorse, expressed with the commitment that never again will such acts be practised."[39]

To some Africans, advocacy of apology by a white person might sound like self-indulgent white liberal guilt. By way of analogy, one wonders what is the reaction of Australian Aboriginals to whites who sign "sorry books" to indicate their remorse for the treatment of Aboriginal people. Are such signatures merely viewed as aspects of a hypocritical "politics of gesture"?[40] It might do the apologizer more good than the group to which the apology is directed. Apologies, however sincere, could not remedy the extreme wrongs done to Africa over the five centuries since the advent of European colonialism and participation in the Atlantic slave trade. As such, they might be seen by some Africans to assuage white guilt without providing a concrete remedy.

Referring to apologies offered by individuals to each other within a culture, Nicholas Tavuchis argues that a sincere apology is "a potentially important cultural resource for tempering antagonisms and resolving conflicts."[41] Whether such a function can be performed across cultures is another matter. It is not clear whether people of European background and people of African background occupy the same moral universe, in the sense of a common space where an apology in either direction can have a reconciliatory effect. Within communities, trust tends to erode when there is little homogeneity and when there are weak or thin social networks.[42] One could expect even less trust where there is no community to begin with.

Govier argues that "in trusting another person, we confidently expect that he or she will do what is right for us."[43] Given the history of harms to Africa, perhaps Africans would not greet an apology by Westerners with trust; rather, suspicion and mistrust might continue to be their attitudes. According to James S. Coleman, trusting behavior can be defined as "actions that increase one's vulnerability to another . . . in . . . a situation in which the loss one suffers if the other (the trustee) abuses that vulnerability is greater than the gain one receives if the other does not abuse that vulnerability."[44] Given the history of African vulnerability to the West, an attitude of trust in Westerners might merely be regarded as foolish by many influential Africans.

Yet it would seem that a "thin," cosmopolitan world culture does now exist, in which actors are able to recognize whether others are sincere in their offer of an apology. Within that world culture, a sincere apologizer might be seen for what he or she is—someone who honestly regrets the actions of his state, his corporation, or his private institution and wishes to compensate for that action, at minimum in a moral sense. An apology is a "voluntary and humane means for reconciling personal and collective differences."[45] Apologies can function to create a moral community inside that cosmopolitan world culture. They might result in what the Secretary-General of the United Nations calls "racial reconciliation."[46] The distrust that seems still to characterize relations between the formerly colonized and the former colonizers—however politely and carefully concealed—might be somewhat tempered by statements of genuine regret for past actions. Such distrust might be more concretely tempered by actual compensatory measures, following the apology. As Roger Van Boxtel, a Dutch minister, said at Durban, "We express deep remorse about enslavement and the slave trade. But an expression of remorse is not enough. . . . It is important to implement structural measures that benefit the descendants of former slaves and future generations."[47]

FINANCIAL REPARATIONS

Just as it is impossible to determine once and for all Western, non-Western, and indigenous responsibility for Africa's current state of severe economic crisis, so it is also impossible to quantify definitively the amount of damage occasioned by the West, by other non-African actors, and by Africans themselves. The claim for financial reparations requires an unattainable knowledge of history. Nevertheless, it is possible to sort out different levels of responsibility on the part of different actors. Some of these actors can be shown to bear direct responsibility for depriving Africans of their human rights and can, therefore, be shown to bear a moral responsibility to compensate some Africans.

WHO SHOULD PAY COMPENSATION?

In discussing who bears the duty to compensate, one can consider a state's obligation to pay compensation to its own citizens and that state's obligation to pay compensation to the citizens of other states with which it has had relations. One can also consider the duty of private corporations to pay compensation. Finally, one can also consider the duty of other social institutions to pay compensation. In considering states' duties to compensate for racism, one confronts the problem of intergenerational responsibility, including intergenerational responsibility for underdevelopment. World history is full of terrible stories of conquest, mass murder, and genocide. Why try to compensate for that which is past? Almost everyone in the world is the descendant of some group that was conquered by some other group at some time, usually to the conquered group's detriment.

A conservative view might focus on rights to compensation of citizens or subjects of a state for acts that were illegal at the time they were committed. Such an approach would, for example, cover the Portuguese and Belgian enslavement of Africans in their own colonies, well into the twentieth century.[48] Such enslavement can be connected easily to racism. However, this conservative view would not accept that the colonial powers as a whole owe compensation for political conquest and the economic exploitation that was a normal consequence of such conquest, for those actions were not illegal at the time they were committed.

If the legal successors of slave buying, colonizing, or neocolonial states are to pay compensation, they need to sort out retroactive ideas of justice and law from what were considered principles of justice and law at the time these activities took place. They will also have to decide whether they are willing to compensate for activities not connected to racism. Neither conquest nor racism was illegal at the time that Africa was colonized, however reprehensible they may seem in retrospect.

Aside from the obligations of states, the movement for compensation includes suggestions that private corporations should compensate individuals for wrongs committed against them. Such wrongs would presumably include the human rights violations committed by private companies with investments in Africa, such as Shell Oil in the Ogoni region of Nigeria[49] or Canada's Talisman Oil Company in Sudan.[50] These are cases occurring in the present, for which there is real evidence of violations of national or international law. However, they might not need, or include, any evidence of racism per se, as opposed to the ordinary operations of international capitalism.

The case for compensating those who suffered under the activities of commercial firms during the period of colonialism would be more difficult to document. In Ghana, for example, the chocolate companies that still exist and that bought cocoa during the colonial period might be held accountable for monopolistic buying practices, which by undermining competition denied the cocoa growers the "fair price" they asked for.

Banks still in existence today might be expected to compensate for the preferential treatment they gave to Europeans over their African customers, as well as for their "gentlemen's agreements" in restraint of competition that might have benefited African customers.[51] Again, however, it would be difficult to evaluate which aspects of such exploitation were caused by or related to racism and which were merely aspects of the normal operation of the colonial economy. Monopolies in restraint of trade can be formed for purely commercial reasons. Bankers' preferences for European over African customers probably resulted from a combination of imperial interest, cultural misunderstanding, lack of collateral among Africans, and common racism.

The movement for reparations and financial compensation might look to private social as well as private economic institutions. For example, Makau Mutua has argued that the incursion into Africa of Christian missionaries violated Africans' collective right to enjoyment of their own culture.[52] Mutua's claim is similar to claims now being made by indigenous peoples in Canada that Christian missionaries destroyed their way of life by means of the forcible incarceration of Aboriginal children in boarding schools.

The question of whether the churches or the government should compensate indigenous peoples for such cultural destruction is presently under consideration. Nevertheless, there is a clear case for compensation. Indigenous parents did not have any choice as to whether to send their children to Christian schools: they were obliged to do so. In these schools, the children were forbidden to speak their own languages, often separated from their own opposite-sex siblings, and kept from their parents for ten months a year by force of geographic and climatic circumstance. Very large numbers of them were also subjected to physical and sexual abuse.[53] In 1998, the United Church of Canada officially apologized to Canada's indigenous peoples for its participation in this coercive residential school system.[54]

If similar violations of rights could be documented in Africa, then it would seem that a similar case for compensation could be mounted against Christian churches. On the other hand, if conversions to Christianity by Africans were voluntary, then the case for compensation would be much weaker. One could, perhaps, argue that the only path to education in colonial Africa was through Christian mission schools; thus, conversion could be deemed a quasi-coercive activity. Here one enters the sticky grounds of what constituted a coercive undermining of one's (retroactive) right to enjoy one's own culture and what conversely was mere social change engaged in voluntarily by individual Africans.

Compensation by social institutions such as Christian churches also raises the problematic point of whether religious conversion was, as such, a racist activity. Christians might argue the opposite: it was precisely their nonracist stance that impelled them to bring their view of the "Truth" to Africa. Just as Islam is, or sees itself as, a nonracist religion anxious to convert everyone in the world, so is Christianity. Both religions posit universal, nonracial, Truths.

WHO SHOULD RECEIVE COMPENSATION?

The preceding reflections on the question of who bears responsibility to compensate do not address yet another question: who should be compensated? Yet, as Michael Cunningham has argued, "Identification of the wronged is of particular potential significance if the matter of apology is to be linked to the matter of reparation or restitution."[55] In the case of the Jewish victims of the Holocaust (the prototypical bearers of rights to compensation), one rule that apparently has applied is that the living are entitled to compensation for direct wrongs, such as deprivation of property or incarceration in concentration camps. Also, the heirs of those murdered and those who survived are entitled in some instances to some compensation.

This principle of compensating the living also applies to other situations. In the current discussions regarding the compensation of African Americans for historical injustices, some suggest that the wrongs for which compensation should be sought are very recent ones, such as the denial of mortgages to black homebuyers or the denial of loans to black farmers.[56] Canada has compensated on both an individual and a collective basis the living survivors of its illegal internment of persons of Japanese descent during World War II, three-quarters of whom were Canadian born.[57]

Distinguishing between victims abused by their own states and victims abused by other states is useful. For example, Canada has not compensated the refugees from Europe who were interned on its territory early in World War II; at the time they were interned, these individuals were not Canadian citizens, but rather enemy aliens.[58] Surely, a country's obligation to its own citizens is greater than its obligation to outsiders. If the country violated laws that were extant at the time—either actual national laws or international laws—it has an obligation to its citizens or their descendants to compensate them for such violations.

In the case of Africa, though, except for a few *evoluées* and *assimilados* in the French and Portuguese colonies, no one was a citizen of the colonizing European power. The best claim that can be made here, then, is that legal subjects of colonizing powers may be entitled to compensation for acts that were illegal at the time they were committed. The problem still arises that many of the direct victims of colonial abuses (even assuming here that these abuses were caused by racism) are now dead. The other problem that occurs in Africa is that of compensating a whole society, indeed a whole continent, even if living victims of racism, colonialism, or neocolonialism can be identified.

At this stage in my meditations on the question of reparations to Africa, I am unable to make any useful suggestions as to who should be the recipients of compensation. I accept the argument that compensation to national governments would not always be a good solution, as in some situations such compensation would result in corrupt appropriation by individuals. Nevertheless, perhaps some accommodation could be reached, as in standard debt relief to the poorest countries. The Draft Declaration for the Durban Conference proposed debt relief, a special development fund, and improvement of access to international markets as reparations to "victims of slavery, the slave trade and colonialism and [to] their descendants."[59] Fear of corrupt appropriation is not sufficient to negate the idea of compensation to Africa.[60]

TRUTH TELLING AND TRUST-BASED INTERNATIONAL RELATIONS

Despite all the obstacles just discussed, acknowledgment of the responsibilities of the Western powers for the current tragic situation in Africa—at least in part—may be a necessary component of trust-based relations between Africa and other nations in the current century. Samuel Huntington has written of the possibility of international conflicts in the twenty-first century rooted in a "clash of civilizations."[61] Africa is too weak an actor on the world stage to be likely to instigate such a civilizational war. Nevertheless, some Muslim Africans quickly aligned themselves with Islamist extremists after the September 11, 2001, attacks on the United States; thus, they are already part of the worldwide movement toward civilizational resentment of the West.[62] Truth telling and acknowledgment of the responsibilities of all parties for Africa's underdevelopment might help defuse such resentment. So also might an actual apology. As Cunningham argues, an apology can draw a line under history, allowing the relevant political actors to "move on."[63] This might also establish moral equivalence between the actors. Once

Westerners (and other non-Africans) view Africans as equal partners in discussions of world affairs—in a moral, not merely a political sense—more rational decision making might occur.

For some analysts, trust is merely an interest-based social relationship. Both sides enter into a bargain based on mutual trust because each knows it is in the other's interest to adhere to that bargain.[64] In international relations, much trust is of this interest-based type. Between the former colonized and the former colonizing world, nevertheless, interest-based trust might not be adequate, the interests of the former colonizers not being sufficiently engaged in the rehabilitation of the former colonies. There needs to be a moral dimension to trust as well. In the African case, acknowledgment by both sides of moral responsibility for slavery and underdevelopment might improve the chances of building an international moral community in which the various sides trust each other in a relationship based on solidarity rather than merely on interest.

From the point of view of some embittered or angry Africans, perhaps such an international moral community is not a goal for which it is worth striving. Why, after so many centuries of slave trading and colonial, neocolonial, and capitalist exploitation, should any African feel part of a moral community that includes the West? Such an attitude is not entirely to be dismissed, however much one might rue it. On the other hand, some parts of international civil society already strive to acknowledge the moral equality of Westerners and Africans; for example, the international feminist movement has made enormous strides to overcome its origins among white Western women.

One might wish to dismiss those Africans who reject an international moral community as merely those who profit from promotion of an ideology of victimhood or a culture of complaint.[65] Such politics of resentment seem to permeate much of the international discussion of relations between the "Rest" and the West. Some commentators dismiss social movements seeking compensation—whether it be for African Americans, for Africans, or for any other group—as ways to perpetuate a group's underprivileged status instead of "getting on with it" and taking advantage of the opportunities available to anyone willing to work hard.[66] It would seem that the present cry for acknowledgment, apology, and compensation is the product of a developing social movement among persons of African origin, whether in the West or in the African continent itself. Social movements do not come from nowhere: they include interpreters who name injustices and define the sought-for solutions. A cynic might reject such namers of past injustices merely as moral entrepreneurs, carving places for themselves in the international community through invention of claims that did not previously exist.

A realist, however, might wish to take into account that the moral entrepreneurs of today are sometimes also present and future political leaders. If politics is an art, then in the twenty-first century it is in part the art of griev-ance. The Western world takes seriously the grievances of some people within its own boundaries. It ought to take equally seriously the grievances of those outside its boundaries whom it has conquered and exploited. Global political and economic relations in the twenty-first century will be more peaceful if all actors accept the idea of global justice. The historical hypothe-ses on which claims for reparations are based are certainly questionable; the moral weight of the claims is irrefutable.

NOTES

This is a slightly revised and updated version of an article previously published in George Ulrich, Lone Lindholt, and Louise Krabbe, eds. *Human Rights in Develop-ment Yearbook* (The Hague, Netherlands: Kluwer Law Publications, 2002). I am most grateful to Kluwer for permitting this republication. I am also most grateful to Joanna Quinn for the many conversations we have had about acknowledgment and apology over the past four years; to Anthony Lombardo for research assistance; and to the Social Sciences and Humanities Research Council of Canada for research funds. This chapter was revised after the World Conference against Racism, Racial Discrimination, Xenophobia, and Related Intolerance took place in Durban, South Africa, in September 2001, but before the final document from that conference was released. I did not attend the conference.

1. In using "reparation" as the encompassing term, I am following M. Cherif Bassiouni, "The right to restitution, compensation and rehabilitation for victims of gross violations of human rights and fundamental freedoms," United Nations, Com-mission on Human Rights, 56th session, E/CN.4/2000/62, January 18, 2000, 9–12.
2. T. Govier, "Trust and Testimony: Nine Arguments on Testimonial Knowl-edge," *International Journal of Moral and Social Studies* 8, no. 1 (Spring 1993): 31. Emphasis in original.
3. *Declaration of the African Regional Preparatory Conference for the World Conference against Racism, Racial Discrimination, Xenophobia and Related Intoler-ance,* WCR/RCONF/DAKAR/2001/L.1 REV 3 (January 24, 2001).
4. United Nations Press Release, "Acknowledgement of Past, Compensation Urged by Many Leaders in Continuing Debate at Racism Conference," RD/D/24 (September 2, 2001): 1.
5. See, for example, the influential book by the late Walter Rodney, *How Europe Underdeveloped Africa* (London, U.K.: Bogle L'Ouverture Publications, 1972).
6. Rhoda Howard, *Colonialism and Underdevelopment in Ghana* (London, U.K.: Croom Helm, 1978).
7. These were items in very high demand when Ghanaians started to trade with Europeans. See Howard, *Colonialism and Underdevelopment in Ghana,* 80.
8. Immanuel Wallerstein, *The Modern World-System II: Mercantilism and the Consolidation of the European World-Economy, 1600–1750* (New York: Academic Press, 1980), 179–85.

9. See, e.g., United Nations General Assembly, *World Conference against Racism, Racial Discrimination, Xenophobia and Related Intolerance: Conference Themes, Draft Declaration*, A/CONF.189/4, 20 August 2001, Article 15; and *WCAR [World Conference against Racism] NGO Forum Declaration*, September 3, 2001, Article 63, at www.racism.org.za/declaration.htm (accessed October 31, 2001).

10. Victor C. Uchendu, "Slaves and Slavery in Igboland, Nigeria," in *Slavery in Africa: Historical and Anthropological Perspectives*, ed. Suzanne Miers and Igor Kopytoff (Madison: University of Wisconsin Press, 1977), 124–27.

11. Adam Hochschild, "Human Cargo: A Study of the Little-Known Slave Trade in the Islamic World," review of *Islam's Black Slaves: The Other Diaspora*, by Ronald Segal (New York: Farrar, Strauss and Giroux, 2001), *New York Times Book Review*, March 4, 2001, 21.

12. Joseph E. Inikori, "The Struggle against the Trans-Atlantic Slave Trade: the Role of the State" (paper presented at the conference, "Fighting Back: African Strategies against the Slave Trade," Rutgers University, New Brunswick, N.J., February 16–17, 2001), 6–12.

13. V. Y. Mudimbe, *The Invention of Africa: Gnosis, Philosophy and the Order of Knowledge* (Bloomington: Indiana University Press, 1988), 44–97.

14. Horst Drechsler, "The Herero Uprising," in *The History and Sociology of Genocide: Analyses and Case Studies*, ed. Frank Chalk and Kurt Jonassohn (New Haven: Yale University Press, 1990), 230–48; and Jon Bridgman and Leslie J. Worley, "Genocide of the Hereros," in *Century of Genocide: Eyewitness Accounts and Critical Views*, ed. Samuel Totten, William S. Parsons, and Israel W. Charny (New York: Garland Publishing, 1997), 3–40.

15. A point made by Theodor Van Boven in his background paper on "United Nations Strategies to Combat Racism and Racial Discrimination: Past Experiences and Present Perspectives," E/CN.4/1999/WG.1/BP.7, February 26, 1999, sec. 3d.

16. *WCAR NGO Formula Declaration*, Article 123.

17. Rhoda E. Howard, "Communitarianism and Liberalism in the Debates on Human Rights in Africa," *Journal of Contemporary African Studies* 11, no. 1 (1992): 14.

18. *Declaration*, African Regional Preparatory Conference, 2001, Article 18.

19. On the emerging movement to hold private corporations accountable for human rights, see David P. Forsythe, *Human Rights in International Relations* (Cambridge, U.K.: Cambridge University Press, 2000), 191–213.

20. Rhoda E. Howard-Hassmann, "A Comfortable Consensus: Responsibility to Strangers," chap. 10 in her *Compassionate Canadians: Citizens Discuss Human Rights* (forthcoming).

21. For example, Daniel Tetteh Osabu-Kle claims that Africa is owed U.S.$100 trillion compensation. "The African Reparation Cry: Rationale, Estimate, Prospects, and Strategies," *Journal of Black Studies* 30, no. 3 (January 2000): 345.

22. This is not something I can document, but it is the kind of comment often made to me in casual conversation with "ordinary" people who are not scholars.

23. United Nations Press Release, "Opening Session of Conference General Debate Focuses on Addressing Legacy of Slavery, Colonialism," Plenary RD/D/19, 2nd Meeting (AM), 9–10.

24. For my argument that empathy is possible across the boundaries of "Otherness," see Rhoda E. Howard-Hassmann, "Identity, Empathy and International Relations," prepared for the book *Through the Eyes of Others: Cultural Encounters and Resistance in World Politics*, ed. Donald Puchala and Franke Wilmer, (forthcoming), available through McMaster University, Institute on Globalization and the Human Condition, Working Paper 00/2, April 2000, at www.humanities.mcmaster.ca/~global/wps.htm (accessed September 17, 2002).

25. Harold G. Marcus, "Ethiopia: History of Ethiopia and the Horn from 1600 to the Present," in *Encyclopedia of Africa South of the Sahara*, ed. John Middleton, vol. 2 (New York: Charles Scribner's Sons, 1997), 71.

26. Rhoda E. Howard, *Human Rights in Commonwealth Africa* (Totowa, N.J.: Rowman and Littlefield, 1986).

27. Rhoda Howard, "Evaluating Human Rights in Africa: Some Problems of Implicit Comparisons," *Human Rights Quarterly* 6, no. 2 (May 1984): 160–79.

28. Rhoda E. Howard, "Civil Conflict in Sub-Saharan Africa: Internally Generated Causes," *International Journal* 51, no. 1 (Winter 1995–1996): 27–53.

29. Kwasi Wiredu, *Cultural Universals and Particulars: An African Perspective* (Bloomington: Indiana University Press, 1996), 163–64.

30. United Nations General Assembly, World Conference on Racism, "Draft Declaration," Article 114.

31. For an assessment of the various functions of truth commissions, see Martha Minow, *Between Vengeance and Forgiveness: Facing History after Genocide and Mass Violence* (Boston, Mass.: Beacon Press, 1998), 52–90.

32. United Nations Press Release, "Acknowledgement of Past," 4–5.

33. Sander L. Gilman, *Jewish Self-Hatred: Anti-Semitism and the Hidden Language of the Jews* (Baltimore, Md.: Johns Hopkins University Press, 1986).

34. Frantz Fanon, *Black Skins, White Masks* (New York: Grove Press, 1967).

35. Judith R. Porter and Robert E. Washington, "Black Identity and Self-Esteem: A Review of Studies of Black Self-Concept, 1968–1978," in *Social Psychology of the Self-Concept*, ed. Morris Rosenberg and Howard B. Kaplan (Arlington Heights, Ill: Harlan Davidson, 1982), 224–34.

36. *Declaration*, African Regional Preparatory Conference, Article 27.

37. Michelle Parlevliet, "Considering Truth: Dealing with a Legacy of Gross Human Rights Violations," *Netherlands Quarterly of Human Rights* 16, no. 2 (June 1998): 172.

38. Nicholas Tavuchis, *Mea Culpa: A Sociology of Apology and Reconciliation* (Stanford, Calif.: Stanford University Press, 1991), vii.

39. United Nations Press Release, "Opening Session," 4.

40. Michael Cunningham, "Saying Sorry: the Politics of Apology," *The Political Quarterly* 70, no. 3 (1999): 285, 288.

41. Tavuchis, *Mea Culpa*, vii.

42. J. David Lewis and Andrew Weigert, "Trust as a Social Reality," *Social Forces* 63, no. 4 (June 1985): 980.

43. T. Govier, "An Epistemology of Trust," *International Journal of Moral and Social Studies* 8, no. 2 (Summer 1993): 157.

44. James S. Coleman, *Foundations of Social Theory* (Cambridge, Mass.: The Belknap Press, 1990), 100.

45. Tavuchis, *Mea Culpa*, 5.

46. Report of the Secretary-General, "Preparatory Process for the World Conference against Racism, Racial Discrimination, Xenophobia and Related Intolerance and Implementation of the Programme of Action for the Third Decade to Combat Racism," United Nations General Assembly, A/55/285, August 10, 2000, par. 28 (a).

47. United Nations, "Acknowledgement of Past," 15.

48. On Portugal, see John S. Saul, *The State and Revolution in Eastern Africa* (London: Heinemann, 1979), 28. On Belgium, see Adam Hochschild, *King Leopold's Ghost: A Story of Greed, Terror and Heroism in Colonial Africa* (Boston: Houghton Mifflin, 1998).

49. Sigrun I. Skogly, "Complexities in Human Rights Protection: Actors and Rights Involved in the Ogoni Conflict in Nigeria," *Netherlands Quarterly of Human Rights* 15, no. 1 (March 1997): 47–60; and Amos Adeoye Idowu, "Human Rights, Environmental Degradation and Oil Multinational Companies in Nigeria: The Ogoniland Episode," *Netherlands Quarterly of Human Rights* 17, no. 2 (June 1999): 161–84.

50. John Harker, "Human Security in Sudan: The Report of a Canadian Assessment Mission" (independent report prepared for the Minister of Foreign Affairs, Ottawa, January 2000).

51. Howard, *Colonialism and Underdevelopment in Ghana*, 206–19 on cocoa, 132–40 on banks.

52. Makau Mutua, "Returning to My Roots: African 'Religions' and the State," in *Proselytization and Communal Self-Determination in Africa*, ed. Abdullahi Ahmed An-Na'im (Maryknoll, N.Y.: Orbis Books, 1999), 169–90.

53. *Report of the Royal Commission on Aboriginal Peoples, Volume I: Looking Forward, Looking Back* (Ottawa: Minister of Supply and Services Canada, 1996): 365–82.

54. Douglas Todd, "United Church Apologizes for Abuse," *Vancouver Sun*, October 27, 1998; and Hollie Shaw, "United Church Apologizes for Residential School Abuse," *Canadian Press*, October 27, 1998.

55. Cunningham, "Saying Sorry," 287.

56. Jack Hitt et al., "Forum: Making the Case for Racial Reparations," *Harpers' Magazine* 301, no. 1806 (November 2000): 37–51.

57. Gerald L. Gall, Mary M. Cheng, and Keiko Miki, Advisory Committee to the Secretary of State (Multiculturalism) (Status of Women) on Canada's Preparations for the UN World Conference against Racism, "Redress for Past Government Wrongs" (January 2001): 2–4.

58. Eric Koch, *Deemed Suspect: A Wartime Blunder* (Toronto, Canada: Methuen, 1980).

59. "United Nations . . . Draft Declaration," Article 126.

60. Most of the issues I raise in this section are usefully addressed in United Nations Press Release, "Subcommission Continues Debate on Situation of Human Rights around the World: Subcommission Experts Discuss Reparations for Slavery, Colonization," Subcommission on the Promotion and Protection of Human Rights, 53rd Session, August 1, 2001.

61. Samuel P. Huntington, *The Clash of Civilizations and the Remaking of World Order* (New York: Simon and Schuster, 1996).

62. Rhoda E. Howard-Hassmann, "Culture and the Politics of Resentment in the Era of Globalization," prepared for a book to be edited by George Andreopoulos and W. Ofuatey-Kodjoe, available via Institute on Globalization and the Human Condition, McMaster University, Working Paper 00/4, December 2000, at www.humanities .mcmaster.ca/~global/wps.htm (accessed September 17, 2002).

63. Cunningham, "Saying Sorry," 289.

64. This is the type of trust that James S. Coleman seems to be discussing. See Coleman, "Relations of Trust," chap. 5 in *Foundations of Social Theory*.

65. The latter term is from Robert Hughes, *Culture of Complaint: A Passionate Look into the Ailing Heart of America* (New York: Warner Books, 1993).

66. David Horowitz, "Ten Reasons Why Reparations for Blacks Is a Bad Idea for Blacks—and Racist Too," *FrontPageMagazine.com*, January 3, 2001, at 206.183.2.199/ Articles/ReadArticle.asp?ID = 1153 (accessed September 17, 2002).

10

Wealth of Nations
Aboriginal Treaty Making in the Era of Globalization

R. S. Ratner, William K. Carroll, and Andrew Woolford

The situation facing First Nations peoples in twenty-first-century British Columbia is the culmination of political-economic processes that reach back to the mid-nineteenth century. In many ways, the story resembles developments elsewhere in Canada, in North America, and in other countries established through white-settler colonization; in other ways, the case of British Columbia is distinctive. In British Columbia as elsewhere, the political, economic, and social conditions in which most Aboriginal peoples live are "depressing and dehumanizing"—the result of a lengthy process of colonization, defined by Bill Lee as "the subordination of one people by another through destruction and/or weakening of basic institutions of the subjugated culture and replacing them with those of the dominant culture."[1]

Throughout Canada, First Nations have in the past century and a half lost the use of almost all the lands they once occupied and their political, religious, educational, and familial institutions have been profoundly weakened by the alienating practices of a colonial state whose claims to authority rest ultimately on the racist premise by which control of traditionally Aboriginal territory was initially secured. As B. Calliou and C. Voyageur put the matter, "Claiming the lands was seen as neither illegal nor immoral, because the Aboriginal occupants were neither people—they were heathens—nor legal owners of land."[2] Throughout Canada, the basic pattern of colonization involved an initial partnership between bourgeois European settlers and Aboriginal residents that was transformed as the developing capitalist economy rendered Indians less and less useful but also more problematic as possible barriers to accumulation. The "Indian Problem" was already recognized at mid-nineteenth century, and the proffered solution was for the state to secure by treaty legal title to Indian territory in exchange for promises of economic development and cultural security—promises that in the posttreaty era were perversely implemented as a project of assimilation.[3]

The history of colonization is also a history of Aboriginal resistance, but it was not until the release of the federal White Paper of 1969, which recommended full-scale integration of Aboriginal persons into mainstream Canadian society, that First Nations throughout the country became politically active in asserting claims to land and demands for self-government. Two decades later, after innumerable protests, court cases, lobbying efforts, and two major federal task forces, Weaver would write about the emergence of "a new paradigm in Canadian Indian policy"—a postcolonial project that attempts to construct an ethical relation between the Canadian state and its Aboriginal subjects, a framework that replaces paternalism and assimilation with concerns for "justice, adaptation, and workable inter-cultural relations."[4]

For Weaver, perhaps the most basic aspect of the "new paradigm" was the embrace of a "permanent organic relationship" between First Nations and the state, which means that "finality"—once and for all settlements of claims—is renounced in favor of a process of mutual adaptation with each party respecting the other's autonomy. What analyses of this kind ignore, however, are the capitalist economic practices, sanctioned by states, that cut against the grain of democratic communicative action as envisaged in the new paradigm and that present a new form of neoliberal colonization that subordinates Aboriginality not through political edict but through disciplines issuing from the world market. In concordance with neoliberal emphases on deregulation and devolution, the self-government offered within the new paradigm "focuses on reassigning powers and devolving administrative responsibilities to Aboriginal communities,"[5] ostensibly to open up new opportunities and jobs for Aboriginal peoples while removing their dependency on state programs.

Such pragmatic goals appeal to many Aboriginal leaders, some of whom are already positioned to gain financially from partnerships with corporations and banks keen to access the "natural and financial resources (in addition to human resources) that Aboriginal people control or will control in the near future."[6] Self-government in this neoliberal guise may deliver little more than the exchange of political discipline and dependency at the hands of the colonial state for the more totalizing discipline of the market. The already wounded moral economy of ecological communalism may be transformed, not into autonomous communities blending the traditional and the modern, but into a form of economy that "plays right into the consumptive commercial mentality shaped by the state corporatism that has so damaged both the earth and human relations around the globe."[7] The new paradigm may well be "new," but the newness it brings may not be very cheering for those interested in Aboriginal social justice. From this skeptical perspective, "recent concepts of self-government are a means to consolidate the transmission of capitalist values to the colonized peoples, to acquire the remainder of the land, and to subvert their own political economy and ontology."[8]

What is *distinctive* about contemporary British Columbia is, first, its late settlement and late industrialization; second, the heavy reliance that the regional capitalist economy has placed on resource extraction from the 1858 gold rush through the later twentieth-century tree harvests; and third, a polarized political history that in 1991 brought to power a reform-minded social-democratic administration, intent on implementing new paradigm approaches to Aboriginal–state relations. Let us consider each of these in turn.

First, as Paul Tennant points out, "the aboriginal past is closer in British Columbia than almost anywhere else on the continent."[9] Significant numbers of Europeans began to arrive only around the mid-nineteenth century, and in a departure from the practice of displacement that was implemented elsewhere, many Native communities were allowed to remain resident on traditional land, enabling the strong retention of historical memory—a cultural fund for continuing resistance.

Significantly, unlike the pattern in the rest of Canada, except for small parts of Vancouver Island that were ceded in the nineteenth century,[10] the provincial administration never secured treaty settlements with First Nations. Instead, with the expectation that disease-related demographic decline and cultural assimilation would gradually eliminate the Aboriginal population, the government of British Columbia soon after colonization came to assert, against the Royal Proclamation of 1763, that Aboriginal title had never existed in British Columbia and thus need not be extinguished.

By the closing decades of the twentieth century, this dubious legal argument would haunt a provincial state whose own legal claim to 93 percent of the province's land mass appeared increasingly tenuous when confronted with claims such as that of the Nisga'a, whose Tribal Council chairman, James Gosnell, declared in 1984:

> We are the true owners of British Columbia. The Indians across the province own everything—the rivers, the trees, the bugs, the animals. You name it. Subsurface rights, the air, the rain, the whole shot. That's what we mean when we say we have aboriginal title to the land.[11]

Second, the enormous land mass that comprises British Columbia is rich in forestry, mining, and fishing resources, which supported a complex Aboriginal material culture, particularly in the coastal region, before colonization and which provided substantial rents to both entrepreneurs and the state as capitalism took root and developed in the twentieth century. The extraordinary natural endowment meant that resource-based commodities could be produced at comparatively low cost, furnishing a basis for high profits as well as a flow of revenue to the state—so long as international demand was buoyant.

In the 1940s and succeeding decades, rising international demand for resource-based products funded both the growth of large corporations and the programs of a province-building government that supplied much of the infrastructure for capitalist development.[12] This accumulation strategy was entirely predicated on the state's providing business with cheap, reliable access to the land.

In the wake of the 1998 Delgamuukw decision in which Aboriginal title was recognized as a constitutionally protected collective right, Native claims to most of the province's land mass have come to directly challenge this accumulation strategy. Thus, the provincial government has understandably adopted the position that "the total land held by First Nations after treaty settlements are completed will be less than 5 percent of the province's land base," and that "fair compensation for unavoidable disruption of commercial interests will be assured" in all treaty negotiations.[13] But perhaps what best summarizes the desire to maintain a reliable accumulation base is the criterion, embraced by corporate business and both levels of government in the 1990s, of "certainty." As the federal government declared in a 1996 position paper on British Columbia treaty negotiations:

> Canada will not lose sight of the need to achieve certainty with respect to land and resource rights for Aboriginal people and other Canadians in order to preserve and encourage economic development possibilities for all Canadians.[14]

In a province where, despite recent diversification, industrial capital is still substantially reliant on access to land that is now credibly claimed by First Nations, and in an era in which global capital favors jurisdictions that offer friendly and secure investment climates, "certainty" on issues of land ownership and access becomes a crucial marker for successful political management.

The third distinctive feature of British Columbia—the province's polarized political history—has also flowed into the contemporary conjuncture of Aboriginal–state relations. In the early twentieth century, robber-baron entrepreneurs, closely aligned with the reigning political parties, established what Martin Robin has termed the company province.[15] The intense class struggles that accompanied this formation, particularly in the mining, forestry, and fishing/canning sectors, catalyzed a militant trade union movement whose radical politics infused both the social-democratic Canadian

Commonwealth Federation (CCF) and the Communist Party. However, until 1972 various configurations of right-wing parties formed an uninterrupted string of provincial governments that were as adamantly opposed to any form of negotiation with First Nations as they were to the claims of organized labor; and even the social-democratic New Democratic Party (NDP) government of 1972–1975 did not agree to negotiate with First Nations.[16]

It was not until the election of an NDP government in 1991 with a support base that included new social movements such as environmentalism and feminism that new paradigm thinking became an integral aspect of provincial policy and serious negotiation of Aboriginal claims began.[17] However, throughout the 1990s this commitment to good-faith negotiation and social justice was severely tested by the predominant tendency toward neoliberal globalization, of which the emergent discourse of certainty is an exemplar. The classic dilemma faced by all social-democratic governments—how to manage a capitalist state and sustain investor confidence while implementing reforms that at least in the short term conflict with business interests—was complicated by the increased pressures to sustain the conditions for an internationally competitive local economy, pressures that in recent decades have subverted attempts at social reform throughout the capitalist world system.[18] In this context, the new paradigm in Aboriginal–state relations becomes less an exercise in postcolonial democratic reform and communicative reason, and more a means for social control of the Aboriginal population—a hegemonic strategy that replaces the coercive paternalism of the Indian Act with forms of neoliberal self-governance within an accumulation regime that Elizabeth Rata has termed "neotribal capitalism."[19]

THE ADVENT OF THE BRITISH COLUMBIA TREATY PROCESS

In the mid-1980s, the period of economic downturn that evolved globally affected the resource-based economy of British Columbia in a drastic manner.[20] Deprived of a vibrant international export market for resources, industry and government in British Columbia became increasingly sensitive to the added costs and pressures placed on the resource sector by court injunctions filed by First Nations to halt development and by blockades that impeded resource company operations. Furthermore, First Nation legal challenges were beginning to achieve greater recognition of Aboriginal rights and title in the courtroom, and the Canadian public generally supported the resolution of First Nation land claims.[21]

Consequently, a task force was formed in December of 1990 to design a negotiation process specific to British Columbia. After six months of discussions involving government and First Nation representatives, the *Report of the British Columbia Claims Task Force* was produced, yielding nineteen recommendations that outline the creation of the British Columbia Treaty Commission (BCTC) and the British Columbia treaty process. The subsequent Treaty Commission Agreement of 1992 formalized the onset of the process—an official launching, as it were, of the new paradigm—and recognized British Columbia, Canada, and the First Nations Summit (a newly formed umbrella body representing the majority of First Nations and tribal groupings in the province) as the three "principals" to the negotiations. The BCTC was designated "keeper of the process" and charged with assisting the parties in overcoming the hurdles that stood in the way of treaty settlements.

At this stage, prospects for a new era in Aboriginal/non-Aboriginal relations were streaked with optimism as both the provincial and federal governments publicly endorsed key elements of the Aboriginal agenda. It appeared that Canada, British Columbia, and the First Nations were about to embark on a new relationship conditioned by mutual trust, respect, and understanding, in turn suggesting that the historical fate of Aboriginals in British Columbia might soon be reversed.

By June 1994, 41 First Nations chose to participate in the treaty negotiation process, the number peaking to 51 at 42 separate tables by 1998 (this composes 112 of the 197 bands in British Columbia and represents over 70 percent of the officially recognized "status Indians" in the province).[22] Some First Nations rejected the treaty process, arguing that only bilateral nation-to-nation negotiations—that is, between the First Nations and Canada, excluding the province—were appropriate, but a substantial majority viewed the treaty negotiations as a legitimate route to building just and equal relations between themselves and the other peoples of British Columbia and Canada. Since litigation and "direct action" were hardly conducive to conciliatory relations, most of the First Nations were now prepared to focus their efforts on treaty making as the best possibility for regaining control over their indigenous heritage and wealth. Treaty talks began in 1993, with settlements expected to value up to $10 billion in cash, land, and resources.

The enormous difficulty of conducting tripartite, multiple, and parallel negotiations had been at least partly anticipated by the British Columbia Claims Task Force in recommending the creation of the independent Treaty Commission to facilitate the complex process.[23] Fittingly, the Commission was not beholden to the three principals; their duties were to monitor, report, and advise on policy and procedures regarding the six-stage negotiation framework—from assessing the readiness of First Nations to enter the process once they had signified intent, to the implementation of ratified agreements.

The Commission began its work on April 15, 1993, by allocating start-up funds to those First Nations who decided to try the negotiation route. This initial distribution of funds proved immediately problematic since funding resources were inadequate and became more so as negotiations proceeded and more First Nations chose to participate in the process. Given that 80 percent of the annual funding is on a loan basis from the federal government, First Nations have been incurring serious debt levels over time, debts that may be either unpayable or likely to draw off any financial settlements won through negotiation. By 2000–2001, the Treaty Commission had already allocated a total of $151 million in negotiation support, $120 million of that total in loans.

The funding shortfall is only one of the many challenges that the BCTC has faced in attempting to ensure that all parties have what they need to negotiate on "an equal playing field" and work effectively toward agreements. While the diverse needs brought to the forty-two separate treaty tables can present a bewildering array, some core issues do tend to dominate the treaty-making discourse, with varying degrees of inflexibility and compromise on all sides.

OBSTACLES TO NEGOTIATIONS

Each of the forty-two negotiation tables faces its own *specific* challenges, ranging from issues of land selection to concerns about political representation for non-Aboriginal persons living on treaty settlement lands; however, there are also a number of *general* issues that concern most First Nations in the province, such as compensation, interim measures, and certainty. These province-wide issues are addressed at meetings of the three principals facilitated by the BCTC.

Compensation

Compensation refers to the demand by many First Nations that Canada and British Columbia provide recompense for infringements on Aboriginal title; that is, that a symbolic payment be made in return for the historic denial of First Nations' early use and occupation of traditional lands that were arbitrarily appropriated by the colonial government. The issue of a symbolic payment is contentious since it threatens the certainty sought by the non-Aboriginal governments by potentially exposing them to broad legal liability. For the non-Aboriginal governments, the liability implied by compensation would be especially problematic if treaty negotiations were to fail to reach final settlements and First Nations were then able to return to courts with the non-Aboriginal governments having publicly admitted fault.[24]

Consequently, and despite an agreement at the outset of the British

Columbia treaty process that any issue may be brought to the table by any of the three principals,[25] the federal and provincial governments have, to this point, refused to discuss the topic of compensation, preferring instead neutral terms such as "financial component" or "cash settlement" to refer to the money that will be transferred to First Nations through treaty settlements. For them, these latter terms are "forward-looking" in the sense that they do not fix settlements to specific transgressions or injustices, although they help to create agreements in which First Nations will discontinue claims for past infringements.[26]

However, for urban First Nations in particular, compensation has meaning beyond providing recognition of the wrongs committed by the governments of Canada and British Columbia against the First Nations of British Columbia. For these nations, the land and resources they could potentially claim have already been largely developed and exploited, leaving them with little foundation on which to build a local economy. Furthermore, based on the Memorandum of Understanding (MOU) on treaty cost sharing negotiated between Canada and British Columbia, any urban lands redistributed in the treaty are to be valued at current market prices.[27] In densely populated regions such as Vancouver, where the price of property is extremely high, the addition of a small parcel of land to a treaty settlement package could then account for a significant portion of the final agreement.[28] This has led some First Nations, such as the Musqueam—who have had much of their traditional territory swallowed by the city of Vancouver—to demand *quid pro quo* that lands lost should be compensated in a manner that reflects their current value.

Interim Measures

Interim measures were meant to be reached early in the negotiation process to ensure that the land and resources that First Nations claim through the British Columbia treaty process are not sold off or depleted prior to final agreement. The parties agreed at the beginning of the treaty process that interim measures would be put in place to demonstrate the commitment of the non-Aboriginal governments in establishing "just" and "fair" treaties.[29] However, such agreements have been slow in coming, and First Nations are becoming increasingly frustrated as they watch logging trucks roll by while they borrow funds to employ white lawyers to negotiate for what could in the end be nothing more than stumps.[30]

Four factors have contributed to the difficulty in arriving at interim measures. First, the original formulation of the MOU placed the onus for funding interim measures entirely on the shoulders of the province. Since the province's contribution to the final costs of a treaty was to provide the Crown lands required for settlement, any interim measures involving land or resources would represent a pre-treaty expense for the provincial government. The federal government, on the other hand, would be relieved of bearing these heavy costs until a final agreement was achieved since they were responsible primarily for paying the final cash settlement. The province protested this arrangement and, with the help of the BCTC, eventually managed to have the MOU amended so that the parties would share the costs of interim measures.

Second, the parties have had some difficulty arriving at consensus as to what the term "interim measures" should mean. Although the British Columbia Task Force *Report* provides a wide range of "interim" options, ranging from a moratorium on development in a particular region to comanagement and job-sharing strategies that would provide the First Nation an economic stake in industry activity on their traditional territory, the two non-Aboriginal governments and some business leaders have commonly assumed that interim measures, for First Nations, mean postponing business activity in the province until treaties are completed. This may be a willful misinterpretation on the part of non-Aboriginal government officials, providing them with an opportunity to delay completion of pre-treaty agreements that threaten some financial loss to government and/or business through measures such as revenue sharing on stumpage fees. Furthermore, interim measures are a politically unpopular policy in certain regions where non-Aboriginal resource workers would fear a loss of employment due to job sharing.

Third, until recently, the non-Aboriginal governments have argued that interim measures were in fact already in place. Despite First Nations' understanding that interim measures were about land and resources, the non-Aboriginal governments repeatedly insisted that monies provided to First Nations for treaty-related studies represent a form of interim measure.[31] First Nations vehemently deny this characterization, arguing that interim measures must provide some material benefit for their communities and their people. In reaction to these complaints, the non-Aboriginal governments devised the term "Treaty-Related Measures" to refer to pre-treaty agreements that provide funds to First Nations enabling them to gather information necessary for undertaking negotiations, as well as other arrangements that are triggered when certain stages of negotiation are reached.[32] However, the addition of this new term to the treaty lexicon has caused some confusion and is perceived by some to be "window-dressing" designed to distract First Nations in their push for "real" interim measures.

Finally, despite the persistence of First Nations in demanding interim measures and the recent support they have received from members of the business community who are pushing for nonmoratoria interim measures in hopes of achieving some short-term certainty for their investments, there has been only halting movement in implementing these agreements. This is in part because the complexity of these arrangements requires the non-Aboriginal governments to negotiate internally within their various ministries and departments, as well as with interested parties in local communities, to gain approval for any action taken or proposed.

Certainty

Certainty is the crux of treaty negotiations for the federal and provincial governments and cannot be easily separated from the issues of interim measures and compensation. Indeed, the hesitancy of the non-Aboriginal governments in meeting the demands of First Nations for interim measures and compensation stems from their risk-management preoccupations with the need for greater economic and legal clarity. To this end, a battery of legal and resource experts have been employed to weigh the potential long-term consequences of treaty making and to devise a language of certainty that will provide functional closure for the "Indian Problem" in British Columbia.

Also, certainty refers to a legal technique that is employed to define with a high degree of specificity the rights and obligations that flow from a treaty and to ensure that there remain no undefined rights outside of a treaty.[33] Before the British Columbia treaty process, Canada's Comprehensive Claims Policy pursued the goal of long-term certainty by requiring the First Nation signatory to "cede, surrender, and release" their Aboriginal rights and title. However, First Nations across the country find this phrasing offensive because it erases by an act of government much that is essential to Aboriginal identity—their tie to the land and the rights bestowed on them by the Creator. There are also pragmatic reasons for First Nations to reject this wording.

The harsh finality of this form of "certainty for government" could mean less certainty for First Nations. Should the treaty prove unsuccessful in developing economic security for First Nations and if non-Aboriginal governments continue their pattern of failing to meet their treaty obligations, then First Nations would have only the leg of their *treaty* rights on which to stand in future disputes since *inherent* Aboriginal rights would have been relinquished in the treaty-making process.

In the British Columbia treaty process, both non-Aboriginal governments—the provincial and the federal—have acknowledged that the traditional means of achieving certainty is no longer acceptable. The problem they now face is whether they can achieve certainty in a clear and comprehensive manner without the language of "cede, surrender, and release." This problem is amplified by the fact that many First Nations are reluctant to have certainty defined at the principals' level since they regard this as an affront to their individual autonomy. In theory, this could mean as many as forty-two different definitions of *certainty*, a situation for non-Aboriginal governments that would mean greater *uncertainty* since it would multiply the points at which the language of certainty could be challenged.

What certainty means for the provincial and federal governments is threefold. Most important for British Columbia, but also relevant to the federal government's concerns, is that treaties must provide the clarity of jurisdiction that is necessary for attracting both domestic and international investment capital. When questions arise as to who owns the land and who makes the rules with regard to that land, businesses are unable to feel ensured that their projects will not be disrupted by blockades, court injunctions, or other costly conflicts.[34] Indeed, these factors have, until now, helped produce what is commonly referred to as the "BC discount" that forces the government of British Columbia to devalue its land and resources in order to attract domestic and international investors.

Second, both non-Aboriginal governments desire that certainty provide mutually accepted rules for dealing with any conflicts that arise in the post-treaty relationship. This does not necessarily mean that all discussions between First Nations and non-Aboriginal governments will cease with regard to questions about land and resources, but rather that treaty mechanisms will be put in place that provide clear guidelines for resolving future disputes. Finally, the federal government, in particular, is seeking to protect its image through treaty negotiations. Canadian credibility on the international stage, not to mention its legitimacy in the domestic scene, depends on giving the perception of humane treatment of First Nations on the home front. If this image continues to be tainted, Canada risks losing some of its international clout in global politics.

ADAPTIVE STRATEGIES

In the shadow of these challenges, parties involved in and impacted by treaty negotiations are left with certain options in terms of how they may adapt to the global pressures on treaty making and the obstacles that stand in the way of settlement.

Corporate Adaptations

The economic stagnation and downturn of recent decades[35] have gravely affected the resource-based industries in British Columbia and elsewhere in Canada. Since these industries are particularly sensitive to fluctuations in the international marketplace, they rely on the state to provide them with secure access to land and resources, enabling them to price their goods at rates reflective of current market conditions[36] and assuring investors and developers that the risk on their investment is minimal.[37] However, a survey of representatives from British Columbia's forest products, oil and gas, and mining industries conducted by Price Waterhouse in 1990 suggests that the following factors continue to create *uncertainty* for major commercial operations: the unresolved question of who has rights and access to land and resources; the risk that production or shipment could be disrupted by court injunctions or blockades that would affect supplier reliability; and the possibility that treaty settlements may redistribute land without providing satisfactory financial compensation to affected companies.[38] These concerns have led many business leaders to cautiously support the British Columbia treaty process in the hope that *certainty* will be achieved.

However, the slowness of the process has moved business to develop strategies for ensuring that their interests are met. These strategies are geared toward ensuring the willingness of First Nations, who will have posttreaty powers of self-governance, to grant access to and receive rents from resource development companies wishing to continue extraction.[39] If First Nations were to implement conservationist policies, this would undo some of the benefits that certainty of ownership and jurisdiction would confer.[40] Therefore, industry has had to look toward more conciliatory approaches that create partnerships with First Nations and provide them with a stake in the status quo operation of the provincial economy.

One method toward achieving this end has been the creation and expansion of "Aboriginal Affairs" departments within larger organizations and across multimember, sectorally based groups. These departments, and the experts, lobbyists, and consultants they employ, are charged with the tasks of collecting information on Aboriginal-related issues (both treaty and nontreaty related), representing the organization or industry sector at consultation meetings, such as Treaty Negotiation Advisory Committee (TNAC) and the Regional Advisory Committees (RACs), and liaising with First Nations bodies to create a dialogue through which they can explore pre- and posttreaty arrangements that might be to their mutual benefit.[41]

This latter function of Aboriginal Affairs departments speaks to a broader adaptive strategy that is currently being employed by industry—building agreements with First Nations that permit business operations to continue prior to treaty, in exchange for the continued participation of First Nations in these business activities after the treaties are settled. Such agreements include joint ventures, employment, job-training programs, and other strategies that create partnerships between First Nations and industry.[42] Through these agreements, industry hopes to stem any protests or court injunctions that may adversely affect their business activities. More important, such arrangements serve the larger purpose of introducing and acclimatizing First Nations to the rationality of big business. They prepare First Nations for a market-oriented posttreaty environment, so that First Nations eventually compete among themselves to attract corporate investment and so that they, too, can ensure that local economic development persists and thrives.[43]

Government Adaptations

Earlier socioeconomic projects of national consolidation and Keynesian Welfarism in British Columbia have been superseded by the desire of the neoliberal state to strategically position the province within the global economy. These newer strategies of governance align with the goals of flexible and mobile global capital, providing First Nations with a modest reallocation of resources and a modicum of cultural recognition, in exchange for their economic assimilation.

Some First Nation chiefs have suggested that the slow pace at which treaty negotiations are moving is one tactic that governments have employed to achieve their goals. Blame for delays in the process have been placed separately on both the provincial and federal governments. The former is accused of not committing the human and material resources required for the consummation of treaties, while the latter is charged with operating through byzantine processes that sluggishly contend with treaty issues in protracted ways. Both governments defend the slow pace of negotiations, citing the complexity of these agreements and the length of time required to reach similar agreements in other locales (e.g., the Yukon and the Nisga'a).

Some First Nation leaders, however, have suggested that the two governments are intentionally orchestrating a laggard treaty process so they can create the appearance of addressing First Nation land claims while simultaneously thwarting the process. Furthermore, some suspect that the non-Aboriginal governments may be trying to improve their bargaining position by insidiously delaying settlements, causing First Nations to amass more debt and thereby compelling them to agree to less attractive terms.

The political caution exhibited by non-Aboriginal governments can also be attributed to their viewing modern treaties through the lens of neoliberal governance. The expense and difficulty of maintaining cumbersome regimes of regulation such as the Indian Act have led the Canadian state to explore options for governing and disciplining First Nations populations "at a distance," to use the governmentality vernacular.[44]

The non-Aboriginal governments are seeking to improve the machinery of regulation by "translating"[45] Aboriginal conceptions of autonomy and distinctness into forms of "self-governance" that are amenable to the political-economic objectives of industry and government. This is achieved by devolving to band and tribal councils more responsibility for everyday affairs on posttreaty lands[46]—the aforementioned new paradigm approach—while, at the same time, insisting that federal and provincial laws be given primacy in situations where conflicts between First Nations and government rule arise[47] and that pre-existing contracts with industry on treaty lands be upheld.[48]

On these terms, "self-governance" amounts to an ameliorative rather than transformative program: the government offers First Nations a "surface real-location"[49] of lands, resources, and governance power, without changing the status quo operation of the economy.[50] Such agreements would merely remove the regulatory machinery of the Indian Act in exchange for that of the market and provide little opportunity for First Nations to reclaim indigenous sovereignty.

However, the non-Aboriginal governments also need to position themselves so that they are not made irrelevant in the process of settling land claims. Their hesitancy to expedite treaty settlements could potentially lead to industries usurping governments' role and cutting their own deals with First Nations. This is already happening to some extent with the joint venture agreements that are arising across the province as businesses seek to ensure their continued immediate access to resources in First Nations traditional territory. The reasoning of the two non-Aboriginal governments for not perceiving these agreements outside of treaty as a threat is the assumption that First Nations will continue to negotiate treaties because they desire self-governance powers that businesses cannot offer.

For governments, pre-treaty arrangements between First Nations and industry then offer an opportunity for "capacity building" that will provide First Nations with experience in, and resources for, governing their populations in the future. In this sense, such deals can in fact serve as an introduction and socialization to the market economy.

Thus, the non-Aboriginal governments are likely to maintain a cautious approach to treaty making. Their primary concern remains building the long-term certainty required to attract both local and foreign investment to the region, and to fortify their legitimacy in the domestic and international arenas.

Aboriginal Adaptations

First Nations are not simply a blank slate on which non-Aboriginal governments and corporations will write the regulatory requirements of neoliberal capitalism. They have long resisted attempts at assimilation, and it is not likely they will just roll over and become good corporate citizens of the global economy. Nonetheless, the desperate social and economic circumstances on some reserves place pressure on First Nations leaders to think pragmatically about fostering economic development.

Many First Nations leaders argue that economic development does not necessarily entail the assimilation of Aboriginal persons to the logic of global capitalism. They claim it is possible for First Nations to actively participate in profit-driven enterprises without forsaking their community ethos. For example, to maintain their communal ideals, First Nations could redistribute the profit gained from market participation at the community level rather than having it solely benefit individual Aboriginal persons.[51] In this manner, First Nations would collectively combat the debilitating poverty that plagues many reserves. However, for this model to succeed, First Nations would have to find a means to resist the individualizing pressures of the market economy.

Quite often capital enters economically marginalized and desperate communities by first establishing a comprador bourgeois class fraction who are provided with personal economic gain in exchange for assisting in the exploitation of local individuals. If these patterns are played out on First Nations' post-settlement lands, it may not be possible for Aboriginal lifeworld cultural values to survive the maw of capital.

Thus in creating relationships in which First Nations and industry are "partners in development,"[52] First Nations cultures internalize capitalist values. First Nations in British Columbia have long managed to resist the assimilative snare of these values, but at the price of remaining largely marginalized from direct participation in the mainstream economy. Greater incorporation obviously fulfills a need—that of improving the everyday lives of First Nations people—but it is accompanied by the risks of a new form of colonization. Whereas colonization in the old economy employed physical and legal force to control First Nations and exploit their traditional lands, in this new colonization First Nations are disciplined by the need to compete in the economy in order to ensure continued benefits.

In this scenario the totalizing and individualizing force of the market system that has an impact on the lifeworld of First Nations is evident. Increased differentiation among First Nations peoples in terms of their abilities and their material rewards for employment threatens to exacerbate the already existing divide between the employed and unemployed on the reserves. A rewards-based system that privileges those advantaged enough to have had the opportunity to gain marketable skills or to access investment capital lends credence to merit-based ideologies of individualism that people employ to rationalize their personal advantage in an unequal world.

Until now, First Nations have ironically avoided high-grade economic colonization due to their marginalization from the mainstream economy. If treaties rectify this marginalization, it may be asked whether First Nations will be able to contain system pressures for economic integration and preserve distinct Aboriginal lifeworlds. Similarly, one can query whether doing business with big business in the era of globalization will make it possible for Aboriginal persons to share the fruits of industry and also retain or rediscover their Indianness.

DISCUSSION

While the outcome of such imponderables must, for now, remain an "empirical question," we may draw on the theoretical insights of Jürgen Habermas in order to consider the opportunities and pitfalls lurking within the current treaty making project. In his efforts to illuminate the problems and emancipatory potential of modern society, Habermas demarcates two main action spheres—"system" and "lifeworld"—which may help to explain the contradictions that arise in the attempts to invigorate Aboriginal cultures via negotiations conducted within the dominant economic order.[53] System refers to the forces of production and the impersonal "steering mechanisms" of money and power ("delinguistified media") pervading late capitalist society, whereas lifeworld refers to the shared cultural conventions, linguistic stock, and communicative interactions of people in their everyday social contexts.[54]

Ideally, the system and lifeworld function interdependently, with the lifeworld dependent on the material resources planned and generated by the system and with the system requiring appropriate socialization of individuals in the interactive milieu of the lifeworld. Habermas contends that societal evolution has reached the point where the structural imperatives of state and economy (i.e., the system) have encroached on and "colonized" the lifeworld, consequently undermining communicative rationality at the level of interpersonal exchange. Instrumental (means/ends) rationality has thus come to dominate all interactions, saturating modern life with impersonal motives of power, distorting and misrepresenting people's needs and normative expectations, and forcing them to regulate their lives in compliance with system imperatives that engender such social pathologies as alienation and anomie.

This "uncoupling" of system and lifeworld is particularly dire given that the lifeworld is normally the institutional anchor of the two, embedded as it is in cultural practices daily elaborated and reinforced by communicative interactions. Its diminishment paves the way for system reifications of social reality based on nonlinguistic media not in need of consensus. Thus, the impersonal steering mechanisms of money and power come to control the interpretation of everyday existence, resulting in "power-distorted communication" that subordinates the social creation of meaning to actions based on predetermined ends. Habermas' emancipatory formula is to decrease the instrumentalization that stems from interest-based rather than *communicative* motivations and to increase meaningful symbolic communication, thereby restoring the symbiotic balance between lifeworld and system processes.

Although late capitalism has obviously developed "one-sidedly" in ways that selectively steer communicative reproduction through the media of money and power—thwarting the potentially superior rationality that ostensibly resides in the speech acts of communicative action—nevertheless, Habermas argues that the system differentiation of modern society brings not only the reification processes that pathologize communicative rationality but also the very advances in evolutionary complexity that generate the material foundation for institutional recomposition of the lifeworld, setting the stage for successful rebalancing attempts. Thus, for Habermas, the colonization of the lifeworld is not a permanent, inevitable, or necessary feature of the logic of modernization. On the contrary, as Michael Pusey observes:

> [T]he modernization process releases an expanding potential for communicatively achieved agreement. . . . The ritually enforced and sacred social forms and practices of earlier societies are gradually secularized, and thus "liquefied", and opened to progressively more conscious communicative interaction and possible change."[55]

The specific locus of change, according to Habermas, is the "public sphere," newly resurrected in order to reduce power-distorted communication and foster rational discourse, enabling the creation of a more just, open, and free society.

Cursory as this account of some of Habermas' central ideas may be, we can see that they bear on the dilemmas facing First Nations as they engage in the treaty-making process under way in British Columbia. Suspending memory of 150 years of government neglect and arrogance, Aboriginals must now persuade themselves that systemic changes are conceivable and that change can be instigated by new self-reflective institutions composed of themselves and their former enemies. Of course, desperation fuels the urge to believe in this possibility, given that on the one hand Aboriginals suffer a chronic inability to access system processes, while on the other hand they experience an unrelenting impoverishment of their lifeworld.

Their precise dilemma is whether they can overcome their economic marginalization on reserves and in urban ghettos by gaining entry into the modern economy without subverting the communalistic premises of their lifeworld. This raises the pressing issue about whether the "public spheres" created to innovate formulas of both inclusion and autonomy are up to the task. A variety of such public spheres have been established to carry out this ambitious mandate,[56] but it remains to be seen whether the strenuous efforts at rational discourse will produce new solutions or whether the current deliberations will only usher in new forms of strategic domination.

For Habermas, the notion of rationality presupposes communication; reaching understanding is posited as the inherent telos of human speech. As Patrick Baert observes, Habermas' notion of rationality and truth is a *procedural* one that adheres to *procedures* for reaching knowledge rather than to any absolute foundation of knowledge (i.e., it is a consensus rather than a correspondence theory of truth).[57] Such radical proceduralism requires that all parties be included in fair, uncoerced, and dialogically engaged debate.

From this vantage point, achieving "communicative competency" depends on the realization of what Habermas calls the "ideal speech situation,"[58] one in which actors possess all the relevant background knowledge and linguistic skills to communicate without distortion. This hypothetical situation bears four recognizable characteristics (or validity claims) that specify the criteria for optimum dialogue and permit the "institutional unboundedness" conducive to the realization of undistorted communication:

1. Truth: The statements of speakers adequately portray realities in relation to the objective world;
2. Truthfulness: The speaker is sincere and authentic in the expression of intentions and feelings;
3. Understandability: Statements are appropriate or legitimate in a given situation in relation to shared norms and values;
4. Comprehensibility: The speaker uses language adequately enough to be understood. Affirmation, in dialogue, of these four validity claims means that debate is entirely guided by one principle: "The force of the better argument."

Whether these validity claims are, indeed, being honored within the treaty negotiations is a question that can offer reflection on the whole history of Aboriginal/non-Aboriginal relations; but in order to condense and highlight the most problematic aspects of the talks and demonstrate that such claims are being circumvented on all sides, we examine only a few difficulties associated with each validity claim.

Truth

Since establishing the "factual content" of rational discourse requires that all information relevant to an inquiry be at the disposal of participants, this situation can only exist if all affected parties have an equal right to enter the discussions and are, in fact, there or adequately represented. On the Aboriginal side, it cannot be said that the First Nations Summit is sufficiently inclusive of youth, women, and elders. The Summit is primarily a gathering of chiefs, who are usually males and, although charged with representing the concerns of their constituencies, who are often tempted, given the universal potential for human corruptibility, to prioritize the interests of lineage and family.[59] Also excluded from the treaty tables are representatives of the large nonreserve urban Native population, who do not accept that the chiefs speak for their interests.[60]

Perhaps more significantly, approximately 30 percent of the First Nations have chosen to boycott the negotiations. Most of these groups are associated with the Union of British Columbia Indian Chiefs, who argue that tripartite treaty negotiations are constitutionally illegal because, in their view, negotiations can only be sanctioned on a nation-to-nation basis (i.e., between First Nations and the government of Canada).[61] There is also a growing realization, as negotiations wend their way through various tables and advisory councils, that actual community groups have been peripheralized or simply defer to larger sectoral and commercial interests dominating the talks. Thus, the relative silence or complete omission of many voices from the Aboriginal constituency means that Summit decision making is neither consensual nor fully democratic and rational.[62]

From the government side, ascertaining the truth is less important than shaping the future, so questions of past injustices are continually subordinated to considerations of expediency. This nullifies the possibility of constructing a shared narrative of the past or present, skewing the discourse away from its own history.

A further problem in establishing truth is that the dissemination of news about the process is also subject to distorted communication, either by journalistic silence or by egregiously biased accounts that undermine the credibility of the negotiations. Obviously, the First Nations are more disadvantaged in this regard, having only restricted and episodic access to the mass media, and are constantly mulling over ways to inform the larger public, counter adverse publicity, and even get the media on board. While the treaty commission can internally monitor the portrayal of factual content and release its own accounts of what transpires, it has little impact on the wider repercussions of reports of the treaty-making process, so truth is perpetually at risk and rarely amenable to discursive closure.[63]

Truthfulness

On the question of whether the parties to treaty negotiations can be trusted not to deceive, there are grounds for skepticism on all sides. Although the First Nations, from the inception of the talks, claim to be engaged in a sacred process entered in good faith, their distrust toward government is based on a long history of colonization. On the other side, government officials see First Nations as "unrealistic" in their demands and entitlement claims, which, aggregated, span over 111 percent of the provincial land base. Moreover, the aim of delivering certainty, the cardinal motivation of the provincial government, is seriously compromised by the Summit's possibly disingenuous refusal to adopt any general positions that would bind First Nations at the separate treaty tables; thus, as previously noted, the task of negotiating roughly forty different definitions of certainty can itself prove a barrier to attaining certainty.

Accordingly, government negotiators come to the treaty tables with bottom-line positions, fixed mandates, or even no mandates,[64] conveying to First Nations the impression of a charade. The Summit reacts to government intractability with threats of litigation, blockades, and the resurrection of "War Councils"; the government responds, in turn, by threatening to suspend negotiations while litigation is pending, or to cut off loans that First Nations require for their continued participation in the treaty talks.

Another area drawing accusations of "insincerity" concerns the funding of interim measures. Governments are wary of granting interim measures prior to land settlements (in effect, holding the former hostage to the latter), and First Nations are outraged by the unprecedented granting of leases and licenses in perpetuity, which they regard as a scandalous theft of their resources, even while the treaty talks are ongoing. Although the provincial government has yet to place a moratorium on the transfer of Crown lands during the negotiations, some interim measures related to economic development and comanagement are under way. Even so, considerable discussion still centers on substantive issues that were already agreed to and inscribed in the 1991 Task Force recommendations.[65]

Another feature of the talks that may seem administratively innocuous has also contributed to distrust. Treaty protocols restrict First Nations from sharing detailed information about their own treaty tables with other First Nations; consequently, First Nations cannot negotiate in concert and are more vulnerable to government "divide and conquer" strategies. Whether insidiously motivated or not, deterrences to sharing information are not conducive to enlightened decision making.

In sum, though all parties profess interest-based (rather than positional) approaches that invite earnest dialogue, they envision, less publicly, a zero-sum gameboard. Governments view First Nations as recalcitrant and indifferent to their larger mandate to protect the interests of all Canadians, and First Nations fear that British Columbia and Canada are trying to slow down and thwart the treaty process.[66] In this dissimulating context, claims of sincerity are difficult to honor.

Understandability

Crucial to the negotiations is the claim of "moral rightness"—that one's statement is appropriate and legitimate within a given context. This raises a fundamental question—what is the process about? Is the purpose of treaty making about doing business, reconciliation, social justice, certainty, or all these objectives and perhaps more? Do the parties to the negotiations bring distinct and possibly nonconvergent goals: the federal government concerned primarily with offloading the cost of services (education, health, etc.), the provincial government seeking to obtain the clarity of jurisdiction necessary for attracting both domestic and international investment capital, and the First Nations wanting to enshrine Aboriginal rights and title?

Confusion about the primacy of guiding norms and values poses communicative difficulties for participants in the treaty negotiations. All would agree that the treaty talks represent, to some degree, a struggle for control of resources (the "wealth of nations"), but for Aboriginals, the struggle is cast in the mold of rights and title in order to guarantee the survival of their people, while for the governments of British Columbia and Canada, the process is largely about sustaining flexible and mobile capital, avoiding huge reparations payments, and ensuring a tax base for the provincial government. Many in government and some in First Nations view the treaty process as an economic opportunity to cash in on the global marketplace, with governments designing new paradigm forms of governance and ownership-management arrangements that incorporate Aboriginals into a grand business strategy without compromising vital corporate interests, while Aboriginal entrepreneurs look beyond small business joint ventures to independent forays in the primary sectors.

Alternatively, those Aboriginals who dwell on communitarian values, the revalorization of indigenous identities, and spiritual reclamation occupy another moral plane and to some extent are talking about completely different worldviews.[67] Thus, the moral pluralism imbricated in the fabric of treaty negotiations poses a formidable challenge to rational discourse, one complicated further by the individualistic stance of First Nations pursuing their specific challenges at the separate treaty tables, their interests embedded in values of family and nation not necessarily based on rational legitimation. All this gives rise to uncertain mandates, so it is no surprise that British Columbia and Canada negotiators are saddled with mandates that seem unresponsive to the state of negotiations and that the Treaty Commission must repeatedly urge the First Nations Summit to encourage its negotiators to come to the treaty tables with clear mandates.[68]

Underlying these communicative difficulties is the fact that the treaty talks engage different cultural heritages and traditions, some employing different modes of argumentation so that understanding may be impossible to achieve; also, understanding by itself does not imply consensus, which presupposes the former, but not the reverse. Nor, too, is it apparent, by the standards of a consensual theory of truth, on what evidentiary grounds (or other criteria) any achieved agreement can be said to represent "the force of the better argument."[69] In the most fundamental ways, therefore, claims of understandability readily elude the grasp of treaty participants.

Comprehensibility

Whether speakers use language intelligibly enough to be understood may not seem to qualify as a discursively redeemable validity claim, since, presumably, such claims would be honored once the statement were put differently. However, the very ability to argue validity claims (including the legal expertise needed to formalize or contest agreements) is socially constructed.[70] That parties to the negotiations clearly recognize this is evident in the constant wrangling over start-up funds and the ongoing loans/grants ratio—all of this falling under the rubric of "building capacity."

Although Summit delegates sometimes object to government stalling on the disparaging grounds of inadequate First Nations "capacity," there is ample realization that intelligibility cannot be achieved without increasing capacity. The fact that limiting funds starkly can control capacity illustrates that the parties taking part in the discussion are not necessarily "free and equal" but in need of a re-allotment of communicative skills. Within the vernacular of treaty talks, at stake would be the facility with which speakers grasp and utilize complex nuances in such antonymic terms as extinguishment versus certainty, compensation versus settlement trust, interim versus treaty-related measures, Aboriginal versus Crown title, and sovereignty versus self-governance. Even the notion of what a treaty means is part of a linguistic arsenal yet to be secured.[71]

Remedying the intelligibility deficit requires increased support for First Nations' preparatory work and education of constituents as well as increased funding for negotiating tables and for the treaty commission itself so that it can effectively monitor and communicate publicly about the complex details of the treaty process. Yet the provincial government has been reluctant to increase its share of the funding.[72] Hence, symptomatic of the ensuing frustration are the high levels of burnout and turnover, as well as threats of withdrawal or recourse to civil disobedience in order to maximize "uncertainty" and to force agreements.

Thus, comprehensibility in the treaty forum is an attribute to be earned and minimally requisite for establishing the grounds for a fruitful dialogue and the condition of good faith that may enable the talks to succeed. While the support and programming thus far provided acknowledges the challenges posed by fulfillment of this claim, government queasiness about continued and augmented funding suggests that they may be unwilling to stay the course (i.e., commit to an intelligible discourse).

CONCLUSION

In view of the foregoing analysis, it seems doubtful that good faith bargaining can endure at the treaty tables. The "strategic motivations" that define the various interest groups may pose insurmountable barriers to communicative reason, and the mere creation of new public spheres is no guarantor of collective social learning or an eventual convergence of system and lifeworld rationality. For First Nations, the concrete problem is the re-valorization of indigenous identity within the new policy paradigm. Undoubtedly, the devolution of governance is part of a neoliberal "hegemonic project"[73] to prepare and incorporate subordinate groups (e.g., First Nations) in a new accumulation strategy that emphasizes post-Fordist sensibilities and values. Such a strategy hints at a government revival of the assimilative philosophy in the 1969 White Paper (even allowing government to escape its fiduciary responsibilities in the name of Aboriginal self-government) or may otherwise point to a "citizens plus" approach[74] that de-prioritizes Aboriginal rights and title, thus bracketing the First Nations quest for sovereignty.

In either conception, indigenous interests can be readily appropriated into nonindigenous forms.[75] At worst, the construction of self-government under neoliberalism, which entrenches the values of private ownership and individualism, "is tantamount to cultural genocide"[76] and the state becomes a totalizing instrument[77] in re-subordinating the Aboriginal lifeworld and traditional subsistence economy to the forces of continued capital accumulation.

Unsurprisingly, one alternative that tempts those in a position to benefit is indulgence in "brokerage politics," entailing accommodations between elite groups that gratify some piecemeal First Nation interests while advancing the hegemonic project (particularly by restoring certainty), dispersing the costs of governance, and leaving unchallenged the logic of capitalist social relations. Yet it is not implausible to suggest a more optimistic scenario. Aboriginal resistances to the "new policy paradigm" may signify more than simple policy failures; indeed, they may represent sources of transformation in the form of rule. "Where governing at a distance appropriates pre-existing indigenous forms . . . the potential is created for a new level of complexity."[78] This suggests that the incorporation of indigenous forms is not unproblematic in stabilizing hegemony and that transformative possibilities may emerge out of the so-called Trojan horse effect. Accordingly, the dual consciousness often exhibited by First Nation individuals—aware of the "rules of the game" as defined by hegemonic neoliberalism, but also identifying with their traditional lifeworlds—connotes that Aboriginals may not experience joint ventures and economic participation in non-Aboriginal enterprises as incongruent with efforts to revitalize their own language and culture.

Here the issue would be the extent to which indigeneity and economic integration are compatible, so that neoliberal market assimilation can countenance political sovereignty and cultural differences, or whether the incorporation of First Nations into business's grand strategy precludes the pursuit of other First Nations goals. Certainly as Aboriginals gain control over traditional lands and resources, the possibility of *mutual* benefit between Aboriginal and non-Aboriginal entrepreneurs, without loss of indigenous integrity, is enhanced.[79] Current plans for the formation of a First Nations Financial Authority[80] that would enable band councils to raise money in domestic and international markets—borrowing against guaranteed future revenue streams, perhaps eventually using their collectively held land as collateral—would make it possible for First Nations to initiate their own economic development projects, conceivably furnishing a material basis for cultural revival.

In sum, and in keeping with the Habermasian vision, the current treaty negotiations may yet trigger the innovative learning responses that can broaden communicative horizons and clarify whether indigenization in the context of globalized capital is a viable formula for Aboriginal nationhood—ensuring both material wealth and political and cultural autonomy—or whether it portends a new form of cultural divestment and colonization.

NOTES

1. Bill Lee, "Colonization and Community: Implications for First Nations Development," *Community Development Journal* 27 (1992): 213.

2. B. Calliou and C. Voyageur, "Aboriginal Economic Development and the Struggle for Self-Government," in *Power and Resistance: Critical Thinking about Canadian Social Issues*, ed. Wayne Antony and Les Samuelson, 2nd ed. (Halifax, Nova Scotia: Fernwood Publishing, 1998), 6.

3. J. B. Waldrum, "Canada's 'Indian Problem', and the Indian's 'Canada Problem,'" in *Power and Resistance*, ed. Antony and Samuelson, 53–58.

4. Sally Weaver, "A New Paradigm in Canadian Indian Policy for the 1990s," *Canadian Ethnic Studies* 22, no. 3 (1990): 15.

5. G. A. Slowey, "Neo-Liberalism and the Project of Self-Government," in *Citizens or Consumers? Social Policy in a Market Society*, ed. D. Broad and W. Antony (Halifax, Nova Scotia: Fernwood Publishing, 1999), 118.

6. R. B. Anderson, "Corporate/Indigenous Partnerships in Economic Development: The First Nations in Canada," *World Development* 25 (1997): 1,490. As Tony Hall observes, the Assembly of First Nations (AFN), which endeavors to represent all Aboriginal communities, is itself a creature of the federal Indian Act, which creates the legal basis for its election of chiefs to the AFN. "Because of its structure, then, the AFN tends to represent that class in an increasingly stratified Indian Country who stand to gain the most from the delegation of power and money as the federal government attempts to escape its fiduciary responsibilities in the name of Aboriginal self-government" (Tony Hall, "Assembling the First Nations: The Class Struggle in Indian Country," *Canadian Forum* 76 [September 1997]: 6).

7. Taiaiake (Gerald) Alfred, *Peace, Power, Righteousness: An Indigenous Manifesto* (Don Mills, Canada: Oxford University Press, 1999), 114.

8. Slowey, "Neo-liberalism," 126.

9. Paul Tennant, *Aboriginal Peoples and Politics* (Vancouver: University of British Columbia Press, 1990), 3.

10. Arthur J. Ray, "Treaty 8: A British Columbia Anomaly," *BC Studies* 123 (Autumn 1999): 5. Treaty 8 covers northeastern British Columbia and was signed in 1899, forty years after the Douglas Treaties on Vancouver Island. Ray describes this treaty as an anomaly because it was signed after the provincial government had firmly entrenched its policy of not negotiating Indian land claims; however, the governments of Canada and British Columbia were compelled to negotiate in this region because Indians here and in northern Alberta were able to present a threat to mineral extractions, as many gold and other valuable deposits were discovered in this area near the end of the nineteenth century.

11. Quoted in Tennant, *Aboriginal Peoples and Politics*, 13.

12. Philip Resnick, "The Political Economy of B.C.—A Marxist Perspective," in *Essays in B.C. Political Economy*, ed. Paul Knox and Philip Resnick (Vancouver, B.C.: New Star Books, 1974), 7–9.

13. Quoted in Alfred, *Peace, Power, Righteousness*, 126–27.

14. Quoted in Alfred, *Peace, Power, Righteousness*, 122.

15. Martin Robin, *The Company Province* (Toronto, Canada: McClelland and Stewart, 1973).

16. Tennant, *Aboriginal Peoples and Politics*, 228.

17. Although the British Columbia treaty process in fact began under a Mulroney-led Progressive Conservative government federally and a Vander Zalm–led Social Credit government provincially, it was not until the provincial New Democratic Party (NDP) came to power that negotiations began in earnest.

18. Gary Teeple, *Neoliberalism and the Decline of Social Reform* (Toronto, Canada: Garamond Press, 2000).

19. Elizabeth Rata's study of the emergence of neotribal capitalism among the Maori people of New Zealand has some relevance to the case of First Nations in British Columbia, where land claims may eventuate in a similar capitalization of land, waters, and other resources as means of production effectively controlled by a new tribal bourgeoisie. "It is in the establishment and control of the tribal mode of regulation that the new tribal bourgeoisie has consolidated its privileged position as regulatory systems and ideological and economic relations are created that enable this class to appropriate the surplus value resulting from the commodification of the newly capitalized and recently legally recognized tribally-owned resources" (Rata, "The Theory of Neotribal Capitalism," *Review* 22 [1999]: 233).

20. William K. Carroll and R. S. Ratner, "Social Democracy, Neo-Conservatism and Hegemonic Crisis in British Columbia," *Critical Sociology* 16, no. 1 (Spring 1989): 29–53.

21. British Columbia Claims Task Force, *The Report of the British Columbia Claims Task Force* (Vancouver: British Columbia Land Claims Task Force, 1991).

22. A small executive group is elected every two years by the First Nations Summit (three task group members and two co-chairs of the quarterly Summit meetings) with a mandate to act on behalf of the Summit on general treaty matters, but *not* as representatives of individual First Nations who pursue negotiations with Canada and British Columbia according to their own unique needs and circumstances.

23. The commission consists of a full-time commissioner chair (appointed by the three principals) and four part-time commissioners—two appointed by the First Nations, and one each by the federal and provincial governments.

24. The Justice Department of the federal government has been adamant about not using the language of "compensation," since they feel it could be conflated with the form of "compensation" ordered after a court decision.

25. British Columbia Claims Task Force, *Report.*

26. A. C. Robertson, "An Overview of Treaty Negotiations before and after *Delgamuukw*," in *Beyond the Nass Valley: National Implications of the Supreme Court's Delgamuukw Decision*, ed. Owen Lippert (Vancouver, B.C.: The Fraser Institute, 2000), 141.

27. See Memorandum of Understanding, *Memorandum of Understanding between Canada and British Columbia Respecting the Sharing of Pre-Treaty Costs, Settlement Costs, Implementation Costs and the Costs of Self-Government* (June 21, 1993).

28. Many First Nations representatives suspect that the governments base their settlement offers on a *per capita* formula that provides $40,000 to $60,000 (in cash, land, and resources combined) per First Nation member. If such a formula does exist, and indications from offers made in the British Columbia Treaty Process thus far suggest that it does, this places severe limitations on the land demands of urban First Nations since any land they receive through a treaty will take up a significant proportion of their final settlement.

29. British Columbia Claims Task Force, *Report.*

30. Recently, as the newly elected liberal government in British Columbia has stalled the negotiation process, the parties at the negotiation tables have busied themselves by working on interim measures. Although these interim measures are often only of the "capacity building" variety, they are inspiring some optimism by providing First Nations with some on-the-ground, pre-treaty benefits. While governments and businesses were reluctant to agree to interim measures early in the British Columbia Treaty Process because they feared these agreements might preclude the competitive capitalization of resources, they have now become more inclined to accept interim measures so long as these agreements are designed to promote continued development and resource extraction as opposed to moratoria on economic activity.

31. Non-Aboriginal government negotiators further stress that such preliminary measures are necessary because many First Nations do not yet possess the governmental or economic capacity to make good on "real" interim measures.

32. Some non-Aboriginal government negotiators believe that stage-triggered interim measures are the only form that should be offered; otherwise, interim measures might serve as a disincentive to negotiations, since First Nations may feel less pressed to negotiate if they are already receiving economic benefits.

33. M. L. Stevenson, "Visions of Certainty: Challenging Assumptions," in the British Columbia Treaty Commission's *Speaking Truth to Power: A Treaty Forum* (Vancouver: British Columbia Treaty Commission, 2000).

34. KPMG, *Benefits and Costs of Treaty Settlements in British Columbia: A Financial and Economic Perspective* (Victoria: Government of British Columbia, 1996).

35. Robert Brenner, "The Economics of Global Turbulence: A Special Report on the World Economy, 1950–98," *New Left Review* 229 (May/June 1998): 1–2.

36. Steve Globerman, "Investment and Capital Productivity," in *Prospering Together: The Economic Impact of the Aboriginal Title Settlements in B.C.*, ed. Roslyn Kunin (Vancouver, B.C.: Laurier Institute, 1998), 145–46.

37. Paul Mitchell-Banks, "How Settlements Will Affect Access to Natural Resources," in *Prospering Together*, ed. Kunin, 133.

38. These issues are also of great concern to international investors. In interviews with government and business representatives, when asked about the importance of "certainty," a common anecdote recounted was of trade missions to foreign regions being entirely consumed by discussions of the land claims issue. Similarly, British Columbia Trade Commission (BCTC) representatives told of the many phone calls they received from potential investors concerned about the uncertainty of land ownership and regulation in the province.

39. Brian Scarfe, "Financing First Nations Treaty Settlements," in *Prospering Together*, ed. Kunin, 286.

40. Recently, Treaty 8 First Nations in northeastern British Columbia have threatened to disrupt oil explorations in the area based on concerns about the potential environmental impact of these operations. According to reports, the Ladyfern oil field in this region is the most significant Canadian oil find in a decade and could greatly increase the country's natural gas production. Through Treaty 8, the First Nations of northeastern British Columbia are to have consultation rights on any new developments on traditional lands; however, when the First Nations became bogged down by the number of applications for exploration and when some First Nations rejected explorations because they were to take place in traditional use areas or on sacred sites, the government overrode the First Nations and permitted exploration to continue nonetheless. One of the chiefs in the area has suggested that his band might be amenable to drilling if they were provided with true co-management powers as well as compensation for the damage done to traditional lands by the oil companies (Claudia Cattaneo, "B.C. Natives Threaten to Cap Massive Gasfield Development" *Financial Post*, August 7, 2001, at 207.126.116.12/culture/native_news/m14451.html (accessed September 16, 2002).

41. Ostensibly, such liaising activity is consonant with the "new paradigm" although driven, on both sides, by economic pressures and fears. Companies such as B.C. Hydro have been at the forefront in establishing relationships with Aboriginal communities. Their stated objectives in pursuing these relationships are "to maintain access to facilities on reserves within traditional territories and treaty settlement lands, to facilitate timely project licensing, and to maintain access to future land and resources in order to provide a continuous supply of electricity to our customers" (B.C. Hydro, "Aboriginal Relations Department Background," *BC Hydro* 2001, at www.bchydro.bc.ca/ard/background/background894.html (accessed September 17, 2002). In order to gain Aboriginal consent for the continuation of business activities in a posttreaty environment, B.C. Hydro has thus endeavored to create opportunities for "community economic development" in First Nation communities, "working together" with First Nations to create new business and investment opportunities.

42. Examples of already existing joint venture arrangements include: the Weyer-

haeuser Cooperative Agreement with five bands in the Merritt area, Qwa'eet Forest Products and Nicola Pacific Forest Products, Burns Lake Specialty Woods, and an Interfor Agreement with the Sechelt (Mitchell-Banks, "Natural Resources," 123).

43. Globerman, "Investment," 156.

44. See, for example, P. Miller and N. Rose, "Governing Economic Life," *Economy and Society* 19, no. 1 (February 1990): 1–31.

45. 45. Pat O'Malley, "Indigenous Governance," *Economy and Society* 25, no. 3 (1996): 310–11.

46. This includes making First Nations "accountable" for the monies they spend—an objective Canada is also trying to realize through its recent attempt to overhaul the Indian Act.

47. Christopher McKee, *Treaty Talks in British Columbia: Negotiating a Mutually Beneficial Future* (Vancouver: University of British Columbia Press, 1996).

48. In treaty negotiations, this is often phrased as maintaining "laws of general application." The Business Council of British Columbia (*The Nisga'a Agreement-in-Principle and the British Columbia Treaty Process* [Vancouver: Business Council of British Columbia, 1997], 1–2) has warned the provincial and federal governments that treaties should "not lead to the emergence of a chaotic, confusing, or inconsistent patchwork of governmental authorities and regulatory standards in British Columbia. There should be uniform, province-wide rules in areas such as environmental assessment and protection, forest practices, labor and employment laws, worker health and safety, and the regulation of transportation and utility industries, among others." As well, the Business Council also suggests that existing business contracts not be disrupted if at all possible, but, if they are, compensation should be provided to those who have had their business or economic interests affected. In general, the provincial and federal governments have sought to meet these demands when negotiating.

49. See Nancy Fraser, "From Redistribution to Recognition? Dilemmas of Justice in a 'Postsocialist' Age," in her *Justice Interruptus: Critical Reflections on the "Postsocialist" Condition* (New York: Routledge, 1997), 25.

50. The Nisga'a Final Agreement, reached outside of the British Columbia Treaty Process, provides many examples of the lengths to which government representatives may go to prevent treaty settlements from having a negative impact on the provincial economy. For instance, the forestry provisions of the Nisga'a treaty make the Nisga'a owners of forest resources on their lands. The Nisga'a can also set rules and regulate forest practices on their lands so long as these practices meet or exceed those of the provincial government. The treaty also requires the Nisga'a to follow provincial policies and rules of manufacturing. These rules prohibit the Nisga'a from exporting logs off their private lands—a potentially lucrative venture that requires low capital investment and provides high returns. If the Nisga'a engaged in this activity, however, it would likely displace many local manufacturers who are reliant on these logs (Mitchell-Banks, "Natural Resources," 119–23).

51. Royal Commission on Aboriginal Peoples, pt. 1 of *Report of the Royal Commission on Aboriginal Peoples*, vol. 2 (Ottawa: Royal Commission on Aboriginal Peoples, 1996).

52. F. Cassidy and N. Dale, *After Native Claims?: The Implications of Compre-*

hensive Claims Settlements for Natural Resources in British Columbia (Lantzville, B.C.: Oolichan Books, 1988), 29–31.

53. The discussion of Habermas' work draws mainly on *The Theory of Communicative Action*, vol. 1: *Reason and the Rationalization of Society*, trans. Thomas McCarthy (Boston, Mass.: Beacon, 1984), pt. 1, chap. 3, and *The Theory of Communicative Action*, vol. 2: *Lifeworld and System—A Critique of Functionalist Reason*, trans. Thomas McCarthy (Boston, Mass.: Beacon, 1987), pt. 6, chap. 4. As well, the explication of Habermas' concepts draws on the summary accounts and critical expositions provided by Jonathan H. Turner, *The Structure of Sociological Theory*, 6th ed. (Belmont, Calif.: Woodsworth Publishing, 1991); Patrick Baert, *Social Theory in the Twentieth Century* (New York: New York University Press, 1997); V. A. Malholtra, "Habermas's Sociological Theory as a Basis for Clinical Practice with Small Groups," *Clinical Sociology Review* 5 (1987): 181–92; Michael Pusey, *Jürgen Habermas* (New York: Tavistock Publications and Ellis Horwood Limited, 1987); R. A. How, "Habermas, History and Social Evolution: Moral Learning and the Trial of Louis XVI," *Sociology* 35, no. 1 (2001): 177–94; Alessandro Ferrara, "A Critique of Habermas's Consensus Theory of Truth," *Philosophy and Social Criticism* 13, no. 1 (1987): 39–67; James Bohman, "'System' and 'Lifeworld': Habermas and the Problem of Holism," *Philosophy and Social Criticism* 15, no. 4 (1989): 381–401; Albrecht Wellmer, "Reason, Utopia and the 'Dialectic of Enlightenment,'" in *Habermas and Modernity*, ed. Richard Bernstein (Cambridge, U.K.: Polity Press, 1995), 35–66; and Thomas McCarthy, translator's introduction to Jürgen Habermas, *The Theory of Communicative Action*, vol. 1 (Boston, Mass.: Beacon, 1984), vii–xxxix.

54. "As opposed to the lifeworld, which acts as a holistic normative background, systems act holistically as 'blocks of norm-free sociality'" (Bohman, "System and Lifeworld," 390).

55. Pusey, "Jürgen Habermas," 84.

56. The new arenas of dialogue created by the treaty-making process include the meetings of the British Columbia Treat Commission (BCTC) Commissioners, the First Nations Summit (FNS) itself, the principals' meetings that include high-level government bureaucrats, FNS representatives, and the BCTC Commissioners, the actual treaty tables (main and side), and the provincial Treaty Negotiation Advisory Council, as well as the regional and local advisory committees. Individual First Nations also have consultation mechanisms for guiding their negotiation mandates, which vary depending on resource capacity and the democratic leanings of the band leadership.

57. Baert, *Social Theory in the Twentieth Century*, 145.

58. The "ideal speech situation" assumes that speakers will have symmetrical chances to speak, that any speaker can call into question the assumptions and conceptual frameworks that govern the situation, and that attempts to dominate, or strategic motivations on the part of actors, will be cast aside. In this sense, the ideal speech situation represents "a 'counterfactual' ideal used to critically evaluate and compare actual situations and to critique distorted communication" (Baert, *Social Theory in the Twentieth Century*, 145).

59. As one interviewed chief described it, "The Summit enshrines bands; bands enshrine Chiefs; Chiefs enshrine male patriarchy. Native youth and women have no structured place in the negotiations."

60. The president of the United Native Nations (UNN), the main urban Native organization in British Columbia, now attends meetings of the Summit, but is ambivalent about the UNN's relation to it.

61. As an indication of the strategic interests at play, some of the First Nation abstainees are cautiously awaiting the outcome of negotiations at a few of the lead tables before committing to the treaty process.

62. Ironically, the exclusion of non-Aboriginal "ordinary citizens" from the negotiations serves as the justification for the new premier's proposed referendum on the provincial treaty negotiation mandate.

63. If this is in part the consequence of a "free, open society," containing democratic institutions such as the press, would Habermas have it any other way?

64. Mandates for agreements in principle are not given, even at times when treaty tables are ready for them, allegedly because the Treasury Board is not prepared to consider funding.

65. As one indication of the growing frustration with government dilatory tactics, Canada was censured in October 1999 by the United Nations for not moving forward with self-governance negotiations for First Nations people.

66. One "theory" is that by delaying settlements and thereby ratcheting up First Nations debt, governments may compel agreements on less attractive terms.

67. The notion that these worldviews are reconcilable was put, perhaps simplistically, by one chief who contended that the idea of the "hunt" can be reconceived as taking place in the city—in modern entrepreneurial fashion—organized around motives of fending for self and family, followed by sharing with others, including those in the community in which the "hunt" occurs.

68. This is not easy for the Summit to do, since it is based on a confederal model (i.e., maintaining the autonomy of all member Nations, but with an overarching objective). The very term "summit" implies a mere coordinating body.

69. We are indebted to Baert (Social Theory in the Twentieth Century, 147–49) for his thoughtful discussion of these latter points, which we feel to be confirmed by our observations of Summit proceedings. We must note, however, that Habermas' argument depends on the understanding that there are no evidentiary grounds for arriving at the "truth" outside of the uncoerced consensual process that serves as the sole criterion for ratifying the "force of the better argument." Of course, this does not simplify the problem of achieving agreement between participants.

70. Here we disagree with Baert's (Social Theory in the Twentieth Century, 144–45) interpretation, which sees intelligibility fulfilled within language use itself.

71. This would include, for example, making more intelligible the implications of the Delgamuukw decision in order to provide further clarity and guidance.

72. As one First Nations Task Force member said to the Aboriginal Affairs Minister at the June 2000 Summit gathering, "We're being treated now as supplicants who have to beg you for money in order to fight for what was taken away."

73. Bob Jessop, "Accumulation Strategies, State Forms, and Hegemonic Projects," Kapitalistate nos. 10–11 (1983): 89–111.

74. Alan Cairns, "Aboriginal Nationalism and Canadian Citizenship," Cité Libre (2000): 50–55.

75. Ross Poole, "Justice or Appropriation? Indigenous Claims and Liberal Theory," Radical Philosophy 101 (2000): 5–17.

76. Slowey "Neo-Liberalism," 116.

77. Peter Kulchyski, "Aboriginal Peoples and Hegemony in Canada," *Journal of Canadian Studies* 30, no. 1 (1995): 60–68.

78. O'Malley, "Indigenous Governance," 313.

79. R. B. Anderson, "Corporate/Indigenous Partnerships in Economic Development: The First Nations in Canada," *World Development* 25 (1997): 1,483–503.

80. *Vancouver Sun*, August 20, 2001, A10.

11

Victims of Genocide, Crimes against Humanity, and War Crimes in Rwanda

The Legal and Institutional Framework of Their Right to Reparation

Stef Vandeginste

Political transition from an authoritarian regime raises the issue of accountability for human rights violations committed by the previous regime. Various approaches have been adopted in specific cases, ranging from complete amnesty to criminal prosecution proceedings against a large number of the perpetrators of these violations.[1] Yet all too often, these approaches have focused mainly on the responsibility and sanctioning of the perpetrators of these criminal acts. With regard to the acts of genocide and other serious human rights violations committed in Rwanda in 1994, this is certainly the case in the trials before the International Criminal Tribunal for Rwanda (ICTR) and, at the national level, before the specialized chambers of the Rwandan High Court and national military tribunals. Questions arise, however, regarding the position of the victims in these proceedings. This chapter seeks to analyze the latter's position from a specific angle: their right to reparation and the legal and institutional framework that, at least theoretically, the Rwandan victims have at their disposal to demand the enforcement of this right.

THE NOTION OF REPARATION

Before tackling this problem in the Rwandan context, it is worthwhile high-lighting the increased attention being paid to the phenomenon of reparations internationally.

Reparation under International Law

Several human rights conventions provide for obligatory reparations by state parties vis-à-vis victims of violations of one of the rights guaranteed by the convention. For example, the Convention against Torture and Other Cruel, Inhuman, or Degrading Treatment or Punishment (which Rwanda has not yet ratified) stipulates that "each State Party shall ensure in its legal system that the victim of an act of torture obtains redress and has an enforceable right to fair and adequate compensation, including the means for as full reha-bilitation as possible" (article 14, par. 1). Similarly, the International Cove-nant on Civil and Political Rights, ratified by Rwanda in 1975, states that the state parties undertake "to ensure that any person whose rights or freedoms as herein recognized are violated shall have an effective remedy" (article 2, par. 3a) and "to ensure that the competent authorities shall enforce such remedies when granted" (article 2, par. 3c).

The notion of reparation is by no means standardized under current inter-national law. For some time now, however, the UN Commission on Human Rights has been examining this issue, in light of comments made by member states,[2] and seeks to elaborate a definitive version of the "Basic Principles and Guidelines on the Right to a Remedy and Reparation for Victims of Vio-lations of International Human Rights and Humanitarian Law."[3] Without going into the details of these principles, it may be useful to summarize the various forms of reparation proposed: (1) restitution (including the restora-tion of freedom, legal rights, social status, citizenship, employment, and goods); (2) compensation (for material damage and loss of income, as well as for physical or moral damage); (3) rehabilitation (including medical coverage and access to legal and social services); and (4) moral reparation ("satisfac-tion") and guarantees of nonrepetition (investigation of the facts, the full and public disclosure of the truth, apologies, public acknowledgment of the facts, acceptance of responsibility, legal or administrative sanctions against the per-petrators of these violations, commemoration of and homage to the victims, etc.). These principles face a rather uncertain future under international law, but this has not prevented them from being used already as a point of refer-ence for discussions of the subject, notably in the deliberations of the Prepa-ratory Commission for the International Criminal Court (ICC) concerning the issue of reparation under the ICC Statute.

Reparation in International Politics

Besides the attention being paid to the problem of reparation at the level of the UN, several movements and campaigns have been launched to claim some type of reparation (very often financial compensation) for all kinds of injustices committed in the more or less distant past. For these campaigns, often based on ethical arguments and political grounds, the legal responsibility of the state for acts that may have contravened either national or international law when they were committed seems less relevant than in a judicial setting. It suffices to mention as examples the campaigns of African Americans demanding compensation for damages inflicted as a result of slavery, of Americans and Canadians of Japanese descent who were interned during World War II, of some African states for ills associated with colonialism, and of Aboriginals in Australia (the "stolen generation" campaign). The most successful campaign to date has obviously been that of the Jewish survivors of the Holocaust of World War II (and their children). Some authors view this spread of reparations politics as the birth of a new moral order at the level of international relations.[4]

REPARATIONS IN THE RWANDAN CONTEXT

Before presenting the legal and institutional framework concerning reparation for the Rwandan atrocities, let me highlight some characteristics of the Rwandan context within which the various reparation efforts are taking place.

The Specific Context of Rwanda

First, the exceptionally destructive impact of the violations, not only at the individual level but also at the level of communities and of the society as a whole, is such that the very notion of reparation seems derisory. Such damage cannot be compensated, certainly not in the very strict sense of the term, which implies undoing all the consequences of the violation (*restitutio in integrum*).[5]

Second, the number of violations linked to the genocide and other crimes against humanity, as well as to war crimes, is exceptionally high. From a purely quantitative perspective, it is extremely difficult to organize criminal trials against the suspected perpetrators within a reasonable period of time. In his recent report on "The Question of the Impunity of Perpetrators of Human Rights Violations," Special Rapporteur Louis Joinet refers specifically to this problem in the Rwandan context: "The Special Rapporteur would like to draw attention to a number of particularly alarming situations for which he must admit he has no solutions to propose, though such situations—albeit largely for technical reasons—help to perpetuate impunity. How is it possible to combat impunity and ensure a victim's right to justice when the number of people imprisoned on suspicion of serious human rights violations is so large that it is technically impossible to try them in fair hearings within a reasonable period of time? Mention can be made of the case of Rwanda."[6]

As a consequence of the exceedingly high number of victims, there is a similar constraint with regard to reparation (specifically, monetary compensation) in the Rwandan case. This constraint is situated, first of all, at the level of principles. Should priority be given to measures promoting reconstruction and collective development, or should one, on the contrary, allocate limited financial resources primarily to compensate individual victims?

The same problem has been raised in the South African context.[7] This constraint is also apparent at the logistical and organizational levels. Even a simple inventory of the victims, as well as of the damage incurred in terms of human lives, material, and psychological damage and goods destroyed, would be an enormous undertaking. This is all the more true in a country where the public administration was almost completely destroyed.

Attention should, however, be drawn to a particular situation in which the large number of requests for compensation has not precluded the international community from setting up a mechanism for financial reparation. I refer here to the Compensation Commission created by the United Nations to process the requests for indemnification arising from damages incurred by individuals and enterprises following Iraq's invasion and occupation of Kuwait.[8] This exceptional case shows that where there is political will, a solution can be found to technical and logistical constraints.

Third, in the case of Rwanda, the just-mentioned political transition took place not only after the genocide but also after the military victory of the Rwandan Patriotic Front (RPF) rebellion. The supporters of this rebellion also committed serious human rights abuses, and the victims of these abuses were very numerous.[9] Recognizing the right of the latter to reparations, beginning with the simple recognition of their "status" as victims, will, quite obviously, be even more difficult than for the victims of the genocide. Here lies one of the major differences concerning transitional justice in Rwanda compared to that in South Africa. Under the criminal justice approach used in Rwanda, only the crimes committed by those persons with close ties to the former regime are to be prosecuted. In contrast, under the truth and reconciliation approach in South Africa, human rights violations committed by the former regime as well as by the former armed opposition were included in the process.[10]

REPARATION AT THE LEVEL OF THE INTERNATIONAL CRIMINAL TRIBUNAL FOR RWANDA

The Statute of the International Criminal Tribunal for Rwanda (ICTR), established in accordance with a resolution of the UN Security Council in November 1994, includes only a single reference to reparation: "In addition to imprisonment, the Trial Chambers may order the return of any property and proceeds acquired by criminal conduct, including by means of duress, to their rightful owners" (article 23, par. 3 of the statute). Strictly speaking, this article is referring to "restitution" rather than reparations in the broader sense of compensation for nonspecific harms. In none of the nine judgments passed to date (eight of which have been convictions) has the tribunal made use of its authority to order such restitution.

With regard to compensation for victims, article 106 of the ICTR Rules of Procedure and Evidence refers back to national justice systems: "(A) The Registrar shall transmit to the competent authorities of the States concerned the judgment finding the accused guilty of a crime that has caused injury to a victim. (B) Pursuant to the relevant national legislation, a victim or persons claiming through the victim may bring an action in a national court or other competent body to obtain compensation. (C) For the purposes of a claim made under Sub-rule (B) the judgment of the Tribunal shall be final and binding as to the criminal responsibility of the convicted person for such injury."[11]

These provisions are a very poor basis for victims to obtain (financial) reparation. The ICTR obviously deals with other elements of reparation, such as investigation of the facts and the sanctioning of individual perpetrators. Despite this limited framework, some initiatives have been launched within the ICTR to pay more attention to the issue of material reparation.

First, at the request of ICTR prosecutor Carla Del Ponte, the judges of the chambers of the first instance and appeal met in a plenary session in June 2000 and declared that "every judge subscribes to the principle that victims have to be compensated" and that "we took the view that we will have to approach the UN Security Council to amend the Statute to expand our jurisdiction so that we can adjudicate on compensation to victims."[12] Nevertheless, after several consultations, the president of the ICTR stepped back and announced to the UN Secretary-General that "the judges wholeheartedly empathize with the principle of compensation for victims, but, for the reasons set out below, believe that the responsibility for processing and assessing claims for such compensation should not rest with the Tribunal,"[13] as this would greatly hinder the proper functioning of the tribunal. In contrast to the ICTR Statute, article 75 of the Statute of the International Criminal

Court attributes more powers to the ICC to allow it to grant reparation to the victims. The government of Rwanda had also wanted the ICTR to consider allowing civil claimants to be involved in the trials and to have the power to award damages where it was found to be appropriate.[14]

Nevertheless, the judges of the ICTR are suggesting other compensation mechanisms for the victims, such as the creation by the Security Council of a new mechanism or a special fund through which the victims would be compensated on the basis of individual or collective claims, or even according to the needs of the community concerned. Similarly, the tribunal could eventually be endowed with new powers to order compensation from a special trust fund for those victims who appear as witnesses before it. It should be pointed out that, in a letter to the UN Secretary-General dated September 26, 2000, the president of the ICTR also requested a meeting of the Security Council to amend the ICTR Statute in order to allow it to award damages to another category of victims—namely, those persons unlawfully arrested or detained by the ICTR.[15]

Even more important for the victims in the field is an aid program for victims that was launched by the tribunal in September 2000. This initiative comprises the first phase of a broader aid program to the victims of the Rwandan atrocities, including legal advice, psychological counseling, physical reeducation, and financial assistance for resettlement.[16] The tribunal has also contributed 15 percent (or U.S.$52,000) of the total budget needed for the construction of twenty-three houses in the "Peace Village" in Taba. The first person sentenced by the tribunal, Jean-Paul Akayesu, is a former mayor of the commune of Taba. Five women's associations will implement the ICTR's aid program.[17] The aid program has been a rather controversial initiative. Several persons both within and outside the tribunal have questioned whether this type of activity is appropriate for a tribunal that was mandated to pursue and try perpetrators of international criminal offenses.

This controversy is obviously linked to the question of the identity of the tribunal itself and to that of the objectives of justice, reconciliation, and peace to which it is expected to contribute. The controversy is also linked to the problem of the practical implementation of the concept of reparation, which specifically arises in cases of massive violations that have implications surpassing individual victims. In such a context, should one give higher priority to those collective programs that favor vulnerable groups and that are future-oriented, or should one favor a more individual approach of financial compensation for damages incurred in the past?[18]

REPARATION AT THE LEVEL OF THE RWANDAN JUSTICE SYSTEM

Within the framework of the trials before the specialized chambers of the High Courts in Rwanda, victims may participate in the criminal proceedings as civil claimants. In addition, they may demand financial compensation for damages incurred as a result of criminal acts perpetrated by the accused person. By way of introduction to this second, national framework, I offer a brief overview of the relevant legislation and jurisprudence.

The Legislation

In principle, civil claims within the framework of genocide-related trials are regulated by the Code of Criminal Procedure (articles 16, 71, and 72) and the Code of Judicial Organization and Competence (articles 135 to 139). The Organic Law of August 30, 1996, on the Organization of Prosecution for Offenses Constituting the Crime of Genocide or Crimes against Humanity, committed between October 1, 1990, and December 31, 1994, also includes specific clauses concerning victims' representation in court, civil liability, and the creation of a Compensation Fund. The draft law concerning this fund will be addressed in the proceeding discussion.

In its deliberations on how to address the violence of 1994, the Rwandan legislature paid particular attention to the concerns of those victims least able to undertake legal actions on their own behalf. Hence, the law provides for the public prosecutor's office to represent minors and other disadvantaged persons lacking the capacity to represent themselves (article 27). Article 29, par. 2, authorizes human rights associations and, *a fortiori*, victims' rights organizations to represent victims before the courts.[19] Article 30, par. 3, allows the court to award compensation, at the request of the public prosecutor's office, to victims who at the time of the proceedings may remain unidentified.

The Organic Law of 1996 distinguishes between four categories of defendants depending on their level of responsibility. These levels of culpability range from the "masterminds"—that is, persons in positions of authority and persons leading and supervising the killings (category 1)—to those charged only with damaging and stealing property (category 4).[20] The Organic Law limits the civil liability of persons in categories 2, 3, and 4 to the criminal acts that they committed. On the contrary, for persons in the first category, their criminal responsibility goes hand in hand with a joint civil liability for all the damages caused all over the country as a result of their participation in criminal acts.

The law also provides for compensation awarded to victims as yet unidentified to be placed in a Compensation Fund, the creation and management of which are governed by a special law (article 32, par. 2). This fund, which should not be confused with the National Fund for Assistance to Survivors of Genocide and Massacres (NFASGM), had not yet been established at the time of writing.

By way of conclusion, one should note that, contrary to our findings concerning reparation at the level of the ICTR, the national legislation creates a framework that at least theoretically promotes the implementation of a right to reparation for victims. In the following section, I discuss the obstacles facing victims seeking compensation via this legal path.

Jurisprudence

By the end of 2000, nearly 5,000 persons had been tried by a specialized chamber of the High Court for acts of genocide. About 12 percent of those convicted received death sentences, 28 percent were condemned to life imprisonment, and 17 percent were acquitted. Yet according to the Ministry of Justice, as of the same date, the prison population stood at 116,000 persons, nearly 110,000 of whom had been arrested for genocide. The number of persons tried therefore represents a mere 4.5 percent of all detainees after four years of trials.[21]

An exhaustive analysis of the jurisprudence—even if it were possible to have access to the full set of records of all trials—falls outside the scope of this chapter. This section draws primarily on the analysis elaborated in April 2000 by the Civil Claimants Cell of the organization Attorneys without Borders and based on a study of 159 trials in different territorial jurisdictions of the country. Several observations can improve our understanding of the opportunities and constraints of this means of reparation:

1. Compensation was awarded in 50 percent of the cases; in 46 percent of the cases, the compensation was given to the civil parties, and in 8 percent of the cases to the Public Prosecutor's Office (thus, in 4 percent of the cases to both). In the latter cases, article 27 (favoring minors) or even article 30 (compensation to be placed in the aforementioned Compensation Fund for unidentified victims) is applied, or the decision is motivated by the argument that the compensation will be used to reconstruct the country.

2. No compensation was awarded in 50 percent of the cases. In 18 percent of the cases, the court separated the civil claim from the criminal prosecution (and, thus, discontinued it). The court did so mainly in cases in which the relevant certificates (identity cards, death certificates, etc.) were not presented or because the state, cited as being the responsible civil party, did not appear in court. In 32 percent of the cases, no victims at all participated in the criminal trials as civil claimants.[22] The victims must indeed overcome various problems in order to do so. For example, they need official documents certifying their direct relationship to the victim.

   According to a directive issued by the Ministry of Justice in late 1999, these certificates are to be issued free of charge. The victims must also overcome transportation difficulties. They lose a great deal of time as a result of postponed hearings. In some cases, they are justified in their fears of retaliation from relatives or others close to the detainees. Investigations conducted by the judicial police or the public prosecutor's office are often not sufficient to establish culpability, especially in cases of sexual violence.[23] All these constraints—in addition to the lack of actual enforcement of verdicts on compensation (a problem of which potential civil claimants are well aware)—undoubtedly explain why, in a third of all cases, no victims are involved in the trials as civil claimants.[24]

3. In only seven cases has the state been declared jointly liable with the accused. This civil liability of the Rwandan State for the damages caused by the former regime might seem odd but is very much in keeping with international and Rwandan domestic law. The letter from the Minister of Justice requesting all tribunals to "put on hold all files in which the Rwandan State is summoned to appear" is, hence, unacceptable.[25] Moreover, even for those damages caused by the participants in the rebellion organized by the RPF (which currently holds power in Rwanda), the Rwandan State could—legally speaking—be held civilly liable. In accordance with the "Draft Articles on State Responsibility" of the UN International Law Commission, "the conduct of an insurrectional movement which becomes the new government of a State shall be considered an act of that State under international law."[26] It is highly unlikely, however, that this principle will actually be implemented in the current political setting.

4. There is a striking lack of uniformity in the compensation awarded to victims, the total of which amounts to tens of billions of Rwandan francs. Compensation for the loss of a spouse ranges between 250,000 and 8,000,000 Rwandan francs (between about U.S.$600 and U.S.$18,000), while that for the loss of a child is between 250,000 and 11,000,000 Rwandan francs (between U.S.$600 and U.S.$25,000).

These differences are apparent not only across the various territorial jurisdictions, but among different courts within jurisdictions themselves. Furthermore, the verdicts are often not very convincing with regard to the civil element, rarely allowing for distinctions to be made between moral and physical compensation. Some courts base their decisions regarding compensation for the loss of income and moral compensation on the ministerial directive of September 14, 1987, which was adopted as guidance to settle disputes regarding traffic accidents.[27] Some commentators on the matter of compensation have proposed using lump sum amounts for certain types of damage.[28] This would no doubt ease the burden of assessment of losses and would also enhance the uniformity of the jurisprudence.

5. Compensation is awarded for the loss of a family member to civil parties with varying degrees of family ties (spouses, parents, and children, but also uncles, brothers-in-law, etc.). Compensation is also awarded for machete wounds, loss of income and honor, moral suffering, material loss, and the like, but in general those victims who have survived have been less likely to claim compensation for their own suffering.

6. In none of the cases analyzed were the civil verdicts actually enforced against the state or against those found criminally guilty, most of whom are effectively bankrupt: actual payments have yet to be made. This situation is obviously extremely discouraging and frustrating for the victims, and one can only hope that the creation of the Compensation Fund will remedy this problem. If not, it will be difficult for the victims to accept that justice has been done.[29]

Reparation and the *Gacaca* Tribunals

In an effort to augment the capacity of the justice system and to accelerate the legal proceedings in general, the Rwandan National Assembly adopted in early 2001 a law on the establishment of *gacaca* tribunals for the prosecution of the aforementioned categories 2, 3, and 4 of genocide suspects. This highly decentralized system, in which citizens are elected as lay judges and bring their fellow citizens to trial, is inspired by the traditional *gacaca*, or "front-yard justice," named after the place where, traditionally, family elders met with the (male) members of the local community to settle disputes. Once judges have been installed in office and trained, the almost eleven thousand *gacaca* tribunals will commence by classifying the detainees and trying those persons in categories 2, 3, and 4. The usual legal tribunals will still try defendants in the first category. The just-mentioned method of reparation, civil claimants participating in criminal trials, thus remains very pertinent. In the subsequent section, our analysis will be confined to future *gacaca* tribunals and reparation in this context.[30]

Given the unusual nature of the *gacaca* tribunals for rendering justice under the aegis of the state, the Rwandan legislature found itself compelled to clarify the extent to which those tribunals could make decisions regarding compensation. The following remarks, from a speech by the Minister of Justice in July 2000, summarize nicely the compromise that was worked out:

> The consultations with wide sections of the population . . . have led to two main and irreconcilable points of view on this [compensation] issue. On the one hand, it is recognised that fixing compensation is too complex an issue for *gacaca* tribunals, but, on the other hand, one is conscious of the need to clear up the disputes regarding reparation, while at the same time dealing with the events linked to the genocide and massacres in order to rapidly achieve social

harmony. The first point of view would see reparation being referred to the classical judge, who would only pass sentence when the criminal trial has finished, while in the second case, this would not be necessary. In order to reconcile these concerns . . . , one is considering restricting the role of the *gacaca* tribunals to making an inventory of the victims and the damages caused by the persons accused, while a special law would entrust a special Fund with the calculation of the amount of compensation to be awarded for the losses incurred on the basis of a scale determined by that same law.[31]

This arrangement, the legislature believed, would give legitimate weight to compensation in the framework of *gacaca* trials primarily charged only with determining guilt or innocence.[32]

With regard to the procedure for hearings before *gacaca* tribunals, both article 64 (in cases in which the procedure for confession and admission of guilt applies) and article 65 of the Organic Law of January 26, 2001, on the establishment of *gacaca* tribunals foresee the oral intervention of civil claimants who wish to make their case for compensation. The accused and, where relevant, other persons deemed civilly liable can then present their arguments against the civil claim. Next, the judges of the *gacaca* tribunals draw up a list of victims who suffered material losses or bodily harm and make an inventory of those losses. All judgments must indicate the amount of compensation to be awarded (article 67). The *gacaca* tribunal will determine the amount of compensation in accordance with the scales foreseen under the law regarding the creation of the Compensation Fund (see below). A copy of these verdicts indicating the identity of the victims, their losses, and the compensation is then transferred to the Compensation Fund, which will be mandated to implement this part of the verdict.

With respect to the civil liability of the state, the law dictates that "in return for the percentage of its annual budget that the State should earmark each year for the Compensation Fund in line with its acknowledgment of its role in the genocide, all civil actions aimed against the State should be declared inadmissible" (article 91, par. 3). It is even provided that past compensation verdicts rendered by the High Courts will be enforced in line with the scales fixed by the law on the Compensation Fund. This "legislative creativity" contradicts the fundamental principle of the Rule of Law regarding the authority of a legally binding judicial decision and the principle of *patere lequem ipse fecisti* ("you will respect the standard that you yourself have set"), and should therefore be reconsidered.

With this brief introduction, it should be clear that the issue of financial compensation under the *gacaca* "regime" will be highly dependent on the establishment, the proper operation, and especially the financial means placed at the disposal of the Compensation Fund. The system as it is proposed, however, seems to have the major advantage that the victim will receive a legal entitlement allowing him or her to obtain compensation, without the perpetrator necessarily having to be convicted at the criminal level (assuming that the law governing the establishment of the fund does not impose additional conditions). The problem of criminal evidence would therefore no longer play a role in the determination of compensation. Indeed, the perpetrator of the crime would not necessarily be charged or even identified in the process.

The law also offers some additional opportunities concerning other aspects of reparation (as elaborated earlier), especially regarding the investigation of the facts and restitution. Decentralizing the process of justice through use of the *gacaca* tribunals could facilitate access to justice (and not only in the literal sense of reducing problems and costs of transportation), lead to a stronger sense among the victims that "justice has been done," and enhance recognition of their status as victims.

In actual fact, survivors can participate in the *gacaca* tribunals in a number of different ways. Those who have reached the age of eighteen will automatically be part of the general assembly of the *gacaca* tribunals at the neighborhood level. They could be elected as judges in the tribunals (even if, of course, they would be barred from presiding over those cases in which they are civil claimants). They could also serve as witnesses or civil claimants. Clearly, just as is true for the success of *"gacaca* justice" in general, the feeling that "justice has been done" presumes a social and political context that encourages genuine and free participation on the part of the local population and freedom of expression for the different categories of victims (e.g., Tutsi victims of the genocide, Tutsi and Hutu victims of other crimes against humanity and war crimes, victims of unlawful pre-trial detention, and, in other cases, of torture and other inhumane treatment).[33]

Peter Uvin asks quite appropriately: "Will the *rescapés* [survivors]— people deeply traumatized by the violence inflicted upon them, and often still socially and politically marginal, especially in rural areas—have enough faith, in themselves and in the system, to participate, to speak out? Will the families of the accused, or the potentially accused, agree to participate in the proceedings given the stakes to them, their families, their community?"[34]

The population, including survivors of the genocide and other victims of massive human rights violations, will—always assuming the successful functioning of the *gacaca* tribunals—be actively involved in investigating the facts and establishing the truth about the events in question.[35] This outcome is very much in line with Principle 25b of the Basic Principles and Guidelines on the Right to a Remedy and Reparation for Victims of Violations of International Human Rights and Humanitarian Law (see the preceding).

With regard to the punishments handed down by the *gacaca* tribunals, the law provides that those found guilty of certain categories of crimes may have their prison terms commuted by half in exchange for community service.

This possibility is applicable to those convicted of the second category of accused who have confessed their guilt, as well as to all those convicted of crimes in the third category. Such commutation of sentences is optional; a convict is free to refuse it. The modalities for the execution of community service are to be set out in a presidential decree, but many think that such service will facilitate the gradual reintegration of prisoners into society. Some commentators even perceive this approach as a decisive step on the road toward reconciliation among Rwandans, assuming that the system is not transformed into a kind of *de facto* impunity and, at the other extreme, that it does not come to be identified with the *uburetwa* (forced labor) used by the former regime.[36]

The draft presidential decree on this matter foresees the creation of "Committees for Community Service" at the national, provincial, and local levels. These committees will decide on the placement of prisoners with a particular institution for their community service. The activities that such a host institution could propose as community service, which are to be carried out at a rate of sixteen hours per week (article 36), include "all types of administrative tasks; installation and maintenance work as well as caring for public buildings and other State assets such as public gardens, green areas, woods and forests; the construction of schools and community buildings; road construction and maintenance; crop cultivation to feed the prison population; the drainage of swamps . . . ; educational and motivational activities; first aid or personal care" (article 29).

For suspects in the fourth category, the organic law provides for them to render a compensatory payment for damage caused to the property of others, excluding the possibility of other criminal punishments (article 71).

The participation of the accused alongside the victims at the local level in a decentralized and less formal judicial process could also have the effect of collective reparation at the level of local communities. As one observer has argued, "The encounter between the perpetrators and the victims in a community-based communication space created by the *gacaca* tribunals seems to allow and to facilitate expression of the goal of justice on the part of those convicted as well as on that of the victims. . . . It is important to facilitate apologies and reconciliation, which are the acts of reparation in a symbolic sense."[37]

Under the ordinary justice rendered by state courts, the autonomy and security of judges have a considerable impact on the process of establishing the facts and on the popular acceptance of the justice rendered by the *gacaca* tribunals. A number of judges were victims of "a wave of arrests and suspensions" in the year 2000, according to a recent report by Attorneys without Borders.[38] The report rightly worries that "ingraining in the spirit of the population the idea that the verdicts passed by the courts are rather iniquitous or at the very least untrustworthy, as they do not meet the expectations of some persons, will definitely not help the *gacaca* tribunals. It seems essential to us that when one is seeking to set up an institution in which ordinary citizens will pass sentences that the population should respect, the principle of the authority of the judgements has to be upheld. If the sentence meted out on behalf of the State by a legally authorised official can be called into question outside the authorised channels, one may rightly fear that those handed down by an appointed citizen will have no authority whatsoever. Social peace is at stake with the use of the *gacaca* tribunals."[39]

REPARATION THROUGH FUNDS SPECIALLY EARMARKED FOR RWANDA

The Compensation Fund for Victims

As previously mentioned, the creation and operation of the Compensation Fund will be of utmost importance in ensuring proper financial compensation for the victims and the enforcement of their rights as acknowledged by the *gacaca* tribunals. This discussion of the fund is based on a draft version of the law from early 2001. According to the draft law, the aim of the fund is to effect "the payment, without any distinction according to whether the verdicts were rendered by the ordinary or the *gacaca* tribunals, of the funds collected for the purpose of compensating the victims of violations constituting crimes of genocide or crimes against humanity committed between 1 October 1990 and 31 December 1994, in accordance with the laws and in the general interest of the country" (article 2). The fund will be financed by annual contributions from the state budget according to a percentage fixed by the law governing state finances, voluntary contributions from foreign countries and donors, compensation paid following the verdicts handed down in the criminal genocide trials, donations, bequests and profit from community service works.

The draft law also defines the class of potential beneficiaries of the fund. Article 13 recognizes as beneficiaries the direct victims of the violations committed and also, in case of the death of the immediate victim, the following: the widow or widower, the children of the deceased, and his or her parents. Other eligible parties—second-generation descendants, the brothers and sisters, grandchildren, aunts and uncles—are only recognized in cases where none of the aforementioned can be found (article 14). Although it seems that articles 13 and 14 only recognize the eligible parties in cases where the immediate victim is deceased, this is contradicted by article 16 and annex C, which regulate compensation for reparation for moral damage, not only in case of the death of the victim but also in case of his or her permanent disability, in favor of the victim himself or herself as well as of his or her legally recognized beneficiaries.

For these different kinds of moral damage, a lump-sum compensation is to be determined. For example, the loss of a spouse will be compensated by a payment of Frw (Rwandan francs) 3,000,000 (or about U.S.$6,800), that of a child by Frw 2,000,000 (or about U.S.$4,500). In case of permanent disability (the extent of which must be certified by a medical certificate that the victims must submit to the tribunal), the sum is fixed according to the degree of disability of the victim, his or her age, and the category to which the beneficiary belongs. For example, a victim between the ages of eighteen and fifty-five with a disability grade of about 80 percent would receive a compensation of Frw 4,000,000 (or about U.S.$9,100) for himself or herself. Meanwhile, the spouse of a victim over fifty-five years of age with a 45 to 50 percent degree of disability would be entitled to Frw 275,000 (or about U.S.$625). With regard to material losses, article 15 provides compensation for lost income, to be determined by the *gacaca* tribunals on the basis of local norms and the assets currently held by the beneficiaries. For damaged or lost goods, compensation is fixed by the *gacaca* tribunals according to the scale established in annex A of the law. The annexes distinguish between food crop cultivation, fruit trees, industrial cultivation, enclosures, domestic animals, domestic possessions, and other furniture and buildings.

The draft law has taken into consideration the possibility that the amounts of compensation awarded will exceed the actual resources available. It treats this important topic in a rather enigmatic manner in article 18: "The Fund will pay the compensation awarded by the tribunals according to the scale established by its board in view of the amount of funds collected. Compensation can be made either in cash, or through actions and interventions undertaken for the direct benefit of the beneficiary or the survivors in general."

While remaining silent on the issue of compensation taking the forms laid down in the second sentence, the preamble illustrates a possible interpretation of the first phrase. The preamble raises the possibility that, in order not to risk the Fund's resources being depleted as a result of the large number of claimants, it will disburse compensation in four decreasing installments calculated on the basis of the available reserves. Some commentators had proposed that the Fund operate in a manner similar to a pension fund, with each victim receiving a monthly allocation calculated in terms of the total sum awarded, but this recommendation was not followed in the draft law.[40] Suffice it to say that given the limited resources that are available, there is likely to be some discrepancy between the amounts awarded and those actually paid out.

The National Fund for Assistance to Survivors of Genocide and Massacres

The Compensation Fund should not be confused with the National Fund for Assistance to Survivors of Genocide and Massacres (NFASGM),[41] whose aim and character is of a more humanitarian nature and whose activities (launched in June 1998) target the most economically disadvantaged victims of the atrocities. The NFASGM aims to establish the exact number of survivors, identify their principal needs, help them reintegrate socially, assist them to live using their own means, and ensure the follow-up of activities initiated for the benefit of survivors of the genocide.[42]

At the national level, the board of the NFASGM is made up of five members, three of whom are appointed by survivors' organizations. Its funds come from the following sources: 5 percent of the regular state budget; 1 percent of the annual salary of all salaried employees; contributions from self-employed persons, limited companies, and statutory bodies ranging from Frw 10,000 to Frw 200,000; and a variety of other sources (article 12). For the year 1999, the Fund is said to have spent a budget of Frw 4 billion (or about U.S.$9 million).[43] The victims benefiting from the fund are survivors of the genocide and the massacres "who are needy, especially orphans, widows and the handicapped" (article 14). A 1998 census identified 238,000 extremely disadvantaged survivors.[44] As an illustration of the "humanitarian" character of the fund, article 16 of the law explicitly states that "the fact of claiming or receiving compensation before the courts does not preclude the fund from providing assistance to survivors in need." In other words, judicial recognition of a victim's right to reparation is irrelevant to the fund's interventions.

The NFASGM's activities are centered on housing, education, health, and social reintegration. With regard to living conditions, the NFASGM has found that there are sixty thousand homeless families among the most needy survivors, and it plans to build five thousand houses per year. The Fund also subsidizes the costs of schooling for some thirty thousand pupils, most of whom are orphans, and supports income-generating activities of survivors by financing small projects. The Fund also provides support to survivors in the area of justice; these funds are disbursed in close consultation with Ibuka, the main genocide survivors' organization.[45]

The results of the NFASGM have not all been positive. Even the Special Representative of the UN Commission on Human Rights, usually extremely "diplomatic" in his reports on Rwanda, has written rather critically, "The Survivors' Fund [the NFASGM], a funding mechanism initiated by the Government to enable support to be channelled to survivors, has not been as successful in providing funds as had been hoped."[46] Limited human resources and experience, as well as the failure to implement an independent audit of its expenses (the audit commission foreseen by the law to monitor the utilization of the funds has still not even been put into place!), have led to the misappropriation and embezzlement of NFASGM funds, sometimes in conjunction with the local authorities. This corruption has only added to the victims' frustration. Furthermore, in some cases, the NFASGM's interventions—which usually respond to the most urgent needs—have at times been suspended for no apparent reason (e.g., the payment of school fees), or its work has gone uncompleted or is of poor quality (e.g., shoddy housing construction or misguided livestock purchases).[47] A study conducted by the Commission of National Unity and Reconciliation has shown that a large section of the population views the assistance provided by the NFASGM as being discriminatory to the extent that it benefits only the survivors and excludes other vulnerable groups.[48]

Conclusions Drawn

In order to create a genuine possibility of repairing the damages incurred by the victims—imperfect though it may be—through compensation, an exclusively judicial path is insufficient. A combination of various approaches is needed. Once the *gacaca* tribunals are operational, it will remain possible to undertake civil actions in the regular courts within the framework of the criminal trials of suspects in the first category. In addition, *gacaca* tribunals will draw up lists of victims, the damages they have suffered, and the compensation to which they are entitled. In combination with the actual payment by the Compensation Fund, this seems to be a promising approach to reparation.

Some advantages of this model include the active participation of the victims, the acknowledgment of their status as victims, the recognition of the damages they have incurred, the acknowledgment of their right to reparation independent of any sentencing of the perpetrator of a crime, the consistency and realism in the sums awarded, and the more than merely symbolic value of the amounts concerned. It also seems appropriate for both funds to continue operating in parallel, given their different nature and the disparate orientation of their activities. One aims to compensate the damage incurred in the past, while the other more generally seeks to create a better future.[49]

Some potential risks and shortcomings could nevertheless be decisive. First, financing for the Compensation Fund will remain a major constraint in the face of the expectations regarding compensation that have been created among the population.[50] Both the government and the associations for survivors of the genocide believe that those countries that bear some responsibility for the genocide as well as the United Nations should help finance the fund. If such contributions were forthcoming, they would indeed do a great deal to help meet the expectations that have developed. Second, proving that damages were incurred (more than seven years after the fact) will not be easy for the claimants, particularly in those cases where medical certificates are required to prove permanent disability. Next, the transparent and proper management of resources and the sanctioning of all forms of corruption pose enormous challenges. It will also be necessary to make the most ill-informed and destitute victims aware of the possibilities offered by the Fund and the *gacaca* tribunals.

Finally, there is a great risk of the unfair treatment of several different groups of victims, all of whom are—at least in theory—entitled to reparations. For example, no provision has been made for persons who have been illegally detained for several years in generally unacceptable conditions and who have subsequently been acquitted or released because their trials were dismissed.[51] Moreover, even if the victims of crimes committed by the RPF between October 1990 and December 1994 could, in theory, claim compensation without the individual perpetrators being sentenced, the political and military context would undoubtedly discourage them from doing so. To complicate the picture further, those Rwandan victims killed, tortured, raped, and otherwise subjected to gross violations of their human rights after 1994 (notably during the Rwandan invasion in eastern Congo) have no recourse to this mechanism at all.

REPARATION IN THE FRAMEWORK OF LEGAL PROCEEDINGS IN OTHER COUNTRIES

It is universally accepted that a state can exercise its jurisdiction within its own territory, which it does, for example, when prosecuting crimes. In criminal law, extraterritorial jurisdiction is recognized—to varying degrees in different countries—on the basis of the principle of active personality (linked to the nationality of the perpetrator of the crime), the principle of passive personality (linked to the nationality of the victim), and the principle of universal jurisdiction (linked to the gravity of the offense committed, which justifies a competence for all states, irrespective of where the crime has been committed or of the nationality of either the perpetrator or the victim). This explains why some countries besides Rwanda have launched criminal procedures or civil proceedings against those accused of genocide in Rwanda. I discuss such actions in the ensuing section, with no claim to offering an exhaustive treatment of the matter.

The United States: The Alien Tort Claims Act

During a visit to the United States by Jean-Bosco Barayagwiza, at that time the director of the Rwandan Ministry of Foreign Affairs, in May 1994—and,

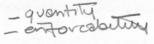
— quantity
— enforceability

hence, in the midst of the genocide then unfolding in the country—five Rwandans whose relatives had recently been massacred lodged a complaint against him.[52] They did so on the basis of the Alien Tort Claims Act (ATCA), until recently an obscure late-eighteenth-century law that allows federal courts in the United States to hear civil actions introduced by foreign petitioners following the violation of a rule of public international (customary) law.[53]

On April 8, 1996, two weeks after his arrest in Cameroon at the request of the ICTR and his transfer to Arusha, Tanzania (where his trial is now taking place), Barayagwiza was ordered to pay U.S.$105 million in compensation to the victims who had brought charges against him.[54] Judge John Martin of the U.S. District Court stated that Barayagwiza "engaged in conduct so inhuman that it is difficult to conceive of any civil remedy that can begin to compensate the plaintiffs for their loss or adequately express society's outrage at the defendant's actions. . . . This judge has seen no other case in which monetary damages were so inadequate to compensate the plaintiffs for the injuries caused by a defendant."[55]

To date, the five Rwandan victims have received nothing, which has been the result in most cases following proceedings based on the Alien Tort Claims Act. The inherent problems in its enforcement, the complexity of this particular case, and the time and money invested in the preparation of such cases makes it extremely difficult to use this mechanism in a context of multiple reparations claims. Nevertheless, this avenue for pursuing reparations does not seem totally useless, even in the absence of any criminal sentence.

Proceedings based on the Alien Tort Claims Act have important symbolic and moral value, for the law acknowledges the victims and their suffering and provides them with a forum for advancing their claims. It also deters perpetrators of violations from travelling to the United States, which, in turn, could have an impact on the political role they can play at the national and international level.[56]

Switzerland: A Military Tribunal

In April 1999, a trial was held before the cantonal military tribunal of Lausanne against Fulgence Niyonteze, a former mayor of the Mushubati commune (prefecture of Gitarama), on accusations of war crimes. Besides the seventy eyewitness reports gathered in Rwanda, the public prosecutor had summoned as witnesses eleven Rwandans, to whom the Swiss military court had guaranteed anonymity to help prevent reprisals against them. Seven Rwandans from the Mushubati commune also petitioned to undertake a civil action for compensation, thus linking the civil action to the criminal procedure. The tribunal, however, only upheld the claim of one of the seven plaintiffs. Two days after the opening arguments, the resident of the Mushubati commune who had petitioned for the civil action decided to withdraw his case because Swiss law rejects guarantees of anonymity in civil proceedings. On April 30, 1999, Niyonteze was convicted of war crimes and sentenced to life imprisonment. Slightly more than a year later, on May 26, 2000, the military appeals tribunal reduced his sentence to fourteen years imprisonment. Niyonteze's trial is historic in the sense that it is the first criminal trial resulting in the conviction of a direct perpetrator of the Rwandan genocide[57] by a national court other than that of Rwanda. At the level of reparation, however, no ruling was made on the compensation or the participation of victims in their capacity as victims (rather than as witnesses). It clearly highlighted the protection that victims might need if they are to appear as witnesses, as well as the problems they could face as witnesses when protective measures are introduced.[58] Another criminal trial was launched in Switzerland against Alfred Musema, but without any corresponding civil action. Musema was ultimately handed over to the ICTR and sentenced to life imprisonment in January 2000.[59]

Belgium: The Court of Assizes

Belgium is of particular interest to victims of the Rwandan massacres as a venue for pursuing reparations claims for two reasons: (1) more than many other countries, the legislation grants certain rights to the victims of violent crimes,[60] and (2) since 1993, Belgium has adopted legislation concerning universal jurisdiction with respect to criminal prosecution of serious violations of international humanitarian law.[61]

The first complaints had already arrived in the hands of the public prosecutor in Brussels in July 1994.[62] In March 1995, the investigating judge Damien Vandermeersch took up the mandate of investigating these complaints. After several missions of inquiry to Rwanda, a number of international arrest warrants were issued, including one for Colonel Théoneste Bagosora. As a consequence of these warrants, the university professor Vincent Ntezimana and the factory director Alphonse Higaniro were arrested at the end of May 1995.[63]

In November 1995, approximately twelve plaintiffs initiated a civil action against all three of the arrested men as well as against other possible defendants, giving the complainants access to the information contained in the prosecution's case file. Their involvement in the case facilitated access to information for the criminal investigators as well.

Several persons who have been arrested in Belgium have been handed over to the ICTR. According to article 7, par. 2, of the law of March 22, 1996, "Handing over a case to the Tribunal does not constitute an obstacle to the right of the civil party to claim reparation. The exercise of this right is suspended as long as the case is pending before the Tribunal."[64] This disposition is entirely in keeping with the impossibility of victims claiming compensation before the ICTR. In April 2001, a trial was opened against four accused (Vincent Ntezimana, Alphonse Higaniro, Sister Julienne Mukabutera, and Sister Consolata Mukangango), in the Court of Assizes (Crown Court) in Brussels. After two months of hearings and interrogations of over one hundred victims (many of whom traveled from Rwanda especially for the trial), the four were sentenced by the twelve members of the jury to terms of imprisonment ranging from twelve to twenty years.

The hearings regarding the amount of compensation to which the civil claimants are entitled was postponed at that time until October 2001. According to international private law, the amount of compensation must be determined in accordance with Rwandan law. The lawyers of the civil claimants also intend, however, to base their claims on international law and international human rights jurisprudence.

THE RESPONSIBILITY OF OTHER STATES

In December 1999, the Independent Inquiry into the Actions of the United Nations during the 1994 Genocide in Rwanda, headed by the former Swedish prime minister Ingvar Carlsson, presented its report concerning the failure of the United Nations to prevent and stop the genocide and the responsibilities of the different UN departments. The report recommends that the United Nations should acknowledge its share of the responsibility for not having done more to prevent or stop the genocide in Rwanda and that it should support efforts to rebuild Rwandan society after the genocide, paying particular attention to the need for reconstruction, reconciliation, and respect for human rights. Donors should bear in mind the importance of balancing and meeting the needs of survivors and returning refugees and other groups affected by the genocide.

The International Panel of Eminent Personalities to Investigate the 1994 Genocide in Rwanda and the Surrounding Events set up by the Organization for African Unity urged "all those parties that have apologized for their role in the genocide, and those who have yet to apologize, to support strongly our call for the secretary-general to appoint a commission to determine reparations owed by the international community to Rwanda."[65]

In reality, despite the observation that the responsibility (not only political but also legal) of several states and even of the United Nations could be at stake, the Rwandan State seems not to have initiated any judicial or other legal action. This is undoubtedly linked to Rwanda's interest in maintaining (even improving) diplomatic relations with Belgium and other donors. Rwanda has therefore restricted itself to requesting increased development cooperation, which could be beneficial to victims and survivors of the genocide.

CONCLUSION

I have tried to analyze the notion of reparation in the legal and institutional context of Rwanda. Without pretending to be exhaustive, I have shown how, at different levels (the ICTR, national courts, courts in third countries, and decentralized *gacaca* tribunals), as well as through judicial and nonjudicial mechanisms, several avenues for reparation are—or will soon be—available to victims of the genocide and massacres in Rwanda. Despite this theoretical availability, however, the first compensatory payments have still not been made. It is clear that the legal path, especially at the international level but also at the national level, is likely to lead to effective reparation only in isolated cases.

The creation of the Compensation Fund, which would operate in parallel to the *gacaca* tribunals, undoubtedly raises the highest expectations with regard to financial compensation for the majority of victims. I have also indicated other, nonfinancial means of reparation that have an important role to play in social reconstruction, as well as the humanitarian and collective efforts that could be of benefit to the victims. Finally, I also raised the difficult issues of competition and discrimination among victims, not only in their attempts to claim compensation, but also—and more importantly—with regard to achieving mere recognition of their status as victims.

These combined efforts, if and when they are successfully implemented, may lead to an increased feeling among certain groups of victims that justice has been done. But this effort of reparation should, unfortunately, be put in a context of an ongoing regional war and of ongoing grave human rights abuses. As a result of this violent context, the need for reparation in the future is rather increasing than decreasing, despite the current efforts at various levels.

NOTES

"Victims of Genocide, Crimes against Humanity, and War Crimes in Rwanda: The Legal and Institutional Framework of Their Right to Reparation" was translated by Christine Webster.

1. See Luc Huyse, *Young Democracies and the Choice between Amnesty, Truth Commissions, and Prosecutions* (Leuven, Belgium: Catholic University of Leuven, 1998), 3–12.

2. The UN member States were invited to submit their comments in resolution E/CN.4/RES/2000/41 of April 20, 2000, of the Commission on Human Rights.

3. The most recent version of these principles was an annex of the final report of Special Rapporteur Cherif Bassiouni (E/CN.4/2000/62 of January 18, 2000).

4. For a recent historical overview, see Elazar Barkan, *The Guilt of Nations: Restitution and Negotiating Historical Injustices* (New York: Norton, 2000); see also John Torpey, "'Making Whole What Has Been Smashed': Reflections on Reparations," *Journal of Modern History* 73, no. 2 (June 2001): 333–58.

5. For other approaches to the notion of reparation, see Yael Danieli, "Preliminary Reflections from a Psychological Perspective," in *Seminar on the Right to Restitution, Compensation and Rehabilitation for Victims of Gross Violations of Human Rights and Fundamental Freedoms*, ed. Theo van Boven et al. (Utrecht: Netherlands Institute of Human Rights, 1992), 196–213.

6. UN Commission on Human Rights, *The Question of the Impunity of Perpetrators of Human Rights Violations (Civil and Political)*, E/CN.4/Sub.2/1997/20, June 26, 1997, par. 48.

7. See for example, Catherine Jenkins, "After the Dry White Season: The Dilemmas of Reparation and Reconstruction in South Africa," *South African Journal of Human Rights* 16, no. 4 (2000): 415–85.

8. See, e.g., Marco Frigessi di Rattalma and Tullio Treves, *The United Nations Compensation Commission: A Handbook* (The Hague: Kluwer Law International, 1999).

9. Several corroborating sources confirm this; I limit myself here to a single reference from Human Rights Watch, *Leave None to Tell the Story* (New York: Human Rights Watch, 1999), 701–35.

10. For a comparative analysis, see Jeremy Sarkin, "The Necessity and Challenges of Establishing a Truth and Reconciliation Commission in Rwanda," *Human Rights Quarterly* 21, no. 6 (1999): 767–823.

11. In contrast to the ICTR Statute, the ICTR Rules of Procedure and Evidence have not been published, although they can be consulted at the ICTR website, at www.ictr.org (accessed August 2, 2002).

12. Fondation Hirondelle News Agency, "Judges Want Statute Changes to Compensate Victims, Improve Efficiency," June 30, 2000. This initiative was also taken up by the judges of the International Criminal Tribunal for former Yugoslavia (ICTY Press Release, September 14, 2000).

13. UN document S/2000/1198 of December 15, 2000, 3. For the ICTY, see the similar proposals made in the document S/2000/1063 of November 2, 2000.

14. Fondation Hirondelle News Agency, "Offensive du TPIR pour redorer son blason au Rwanda," September 27, 2000.

15. UN document S/2000/925 of October 6, 2000. Compare with article 85, par.1, of the Statute of the International Criminal Tribunal for Rwanda: "Anyone who has been the victim of unlawful arrest or detention shall have an enforceable right to compensation."

16. Fondation Hirondelle News Agency, "Le TPIR lance un programme d'aide aux victimes du génocide," September 26, 2000.

17. Namely, Avega-Agahozo, Asoferwa, Rwanda Women Network, Haguruka and Pro-femmes Twese Hamwe.

18. The distinction is akin to that between "commemorative" and "anti-systemic" reparations drawn by Torpey in "'Making Whole What Has Been Smashed.'"

19. "Victims acting either individually or through legally constituted associations for the defence of victims . . . may request the commencement of a public prosecution by submitting a written petition setting out the grounds for the prosecution to the Public Prosecutor of the competent jurisdiction. The status of civil party shall be given to the petitioner."

20. In accordance with article 9 of the organic law and despite the presumption of innocence enjoyed by those accused of crimes in category 1, their names have been published and are on the website of the Rwandan government. The list published in April 2001 comprised approximately 2,900 people. See at www.rwanda1.com/government/category1.htm (accessed August 2, 2002).

21. Source: unpublished report of the Centre de Documentation et d'Information sur les Procès de Génocide, a project of the human rights organization Liprodhor (Ligue Rwandaise pour la Promotion et la Défense des Droits de l'Homme).

22. During the first half of 2000, this percentage declined to 14 percent of the trials. See Avocats sans Frontières, *Justice pour tous au Rwanda: Rapport semestriel 2000. Janvier–Juin 2000* (Brussels and Kigali, January 2001): 37.

23. For more details see Martien Schotsmans, "Violences sexuelles pendant le génocide: les femmes réclament justice," *Le Verdict* 2, no. 4 (July 1999): 19.

24. For more details see Martien Schotsmans, "Les difficultés rencontrées par les victimes au cours des procès de genocide," *Le Verdict* 2, no. 3 (June 1999): 3.

25. Cited in Avocats sans Frontières, *Justice pour tous au Rwanda*, 18.

26. Article 10, par.1, of the Draft Articles on State Responsibility, adopted by the Drafting Committee of the International Law Commission of the United Nations (A/55/10, 2000).

27. Daniel Debeer, *Loi rwandaise du 30 août 1996 sur l'organisation des poursuites des infractions constitutives du crime de génocide ou de crimes contre l'humanité. Commentaire et Jurisprudence* (Kigali and Brussels: Alter Egaux, 1999), 74.

28. For example, see Theobald Gakwaya Rwaka, "Indemnisation des victimes du génocide: l'Etat doit éviter l'effet du boomerang!" *Le Verdict* 2, no. 4 (July 1999): 20.

29. Without going into too much detail, the Special Representative of the UN Commission on Human Rights, Michel Moussalli, appears to see a role for the donors in the enforcement of these verdicts ordering compensation (A/54/359 of September 17, 1999, par. 73).

30. For more details see, Stef Vandeginste, "Rwanda: Dealing with Genocide and Crimes against Humanity in the Context of Armed Conflict and Failed Political Transition," in *Burying the Past: Making Peace and Doing Justice after Civil Conflict*, ed. Nigel Biggar (Washington, D. C.: Georgetown University Press, 2001), 223–53.

31. Jean de Dieu Mucyo, "Des juridictions gacaca et de la réparation des dommages," *Le Verdict* 2, no. 17 (August 2000): 10.

32. Some amendments and updates have since been made, but the spirit of the law remains apparent in the speech cited.

33. See Jeremy Sarkin, "Promoting Justice, Truth and Reconciliation in Transitional Societies: Evaluating Rwanda's Approach in the New Millennium of Using Community-Based *Gacaca* Tribunals to Deal with the Past," *International Law Forum du Droit International* 2 (2000): 112–21.

34. Peter Uvin, *The Introduction of a Modernized* Gacaca *for Judging Suspects of*

Participation in the Genocide and the Massacres of 1994 in Rwanda (in the author's possession, June 2000): 8.

35. For an interesting analysis of the opportunities and constraints with respect to obtaining the truth through *gacaca* hearings, given the very specific cultural context of Rwanda, see Simon Gasibirege, *Conditions psychosociales d'efficacité de gacaca: contribution à la mise en œuvre effective du projet national des juridictions gacaca* (Butare: Université Nationale du Rwanda, 2000).

36. Alice Karakezi, *Juridictions Gacaca, lutte contre l'impunité et réconciliation nationale* (Butare: Centre de Gestion des Conflits, Université Nationale du Rwanda, 2000), 24.

37. Simon Gasibirege, *Résultats d'une enquête exploratoire sur les attitudes des membres des communautés locales et des prisonniers vis-à-vis de l'indemnisation des victimes des crimes de génocide et de crimes contre l'humanité* (Butare: Université Nationale du Rwanda, 2000), 10.

38. Avocats sans Frontières, *Justice pour tous au Rwanda*, 8.

39. Avocats sans Frontières, *Justice pour tous au Rwanda*, 9.

40. Theobald Gakwaya Rwaka, "SOS pour l'indemnisation des victimes du genocide," *Le Verdict* 2, no. 2 (May 1999): 7.

41. The NFASGM was created by law No. 02/98 of 22 January 1998, published in the *Journal Officiel* (February 1, 1998): 221.

42. Brochure in author's possession.

43. Venant Sinsebyimfura, "Le Fonds d'Assistance aux Rescapés du Génocide," in Avocats sans Frontières et Ministere de la Justice, Séminaire sur la réparation pour les victimes du génocide et des crimes contre l'humanité commis au Rwanda entre le 1er octobre 1990 et le 31 décembre 1994 (Kigali, Rwanda, 2000): 28.

44. Sinsebyimfura, "Le Fonds d'Assistance aux Rescapés du Génocide," 28.

45. Sinsebyimfura, "Le Fonds d'Assistance aux Rescapés du Génocide," 28.

46. Commission on Human Rights, *Situation of Human Rights in Rwanda*, E/CN.4/2001/45/Add.1, 21 March 2001, par. 38.

47. For an overview of survivors' experiences (positive and negative) with the NFASGM, see Martien Schotsmans, *A l'écoute des rescapés. Recherche sur la perception par les rescapés de leur situation actuelle* (in the author's possession, Kigali, Rwanda, 2000).

48. National Unity and Reconciliation Commission, *Nation-wide Grassroots Consultations Report: Unity and Reconciliation Initiatives in Rwanda* (Kigali, Rwanda, 2000): 8–9.

49. See also Uvin, *The Introduction of a Modernized* Gacaca, 23.

50. See Theoneste Muberantwari, "L'association IBUKA exige la mise en place d'un Fonds d'Indemnisation des Victimes du Génocide," *Le Verdict* 2, no. 1 (April 1999): 15.

51. For this group, financial compensation as well as a social reintegration program would be desirable (see Rwaka, "SOS pour l'indemnisation des victimes du génocide," 7. For a very interesting analysis of the problems (social and others) encountered by those accused of genocide and then released, see LIPRODHOR, *Problématique des libérations des accusés de génocide rwandais* (Kigali, Rwanda, July 1999).

52. Barayagwiza was also co-founder of the extremist CDR party, Coalition for the Defence of the Republic. He is also the author of the book *Le sang Hutu, est-il rouge?* (Yaoundé, Cameroon: 1995).

53. "The district courts shall have original jurisdiction of any civil action by an alien for a tort only, committed in violation of the law of nations" (28 USC § 1350, Alien Tort Claims Act).

54. See, among others, Fondation Hirondelle News Agency, "Court to Rule Tuesday on Barayagwiza's Lawyers, Request for Inquiry on Ngeze Prison Raid," February 5, 2001.

55. Cited in a Human Rights Watch Press Release, "Prosecutorial Incompetence Frees Rwandan Genocide Suspect," November 8, 1999.

56. For more details see Roger O'Keefe, "Civil Actions in US Courts in Respect of Human Rights Abuses Committed Abroad: Would the World's Oppressors Be Wise to Stay at Home?" *African Journal of International and Comparative Law* 9 (1997): 15–41.

57. Legally speaking, Niyonteze was convicted for war crimes (several serious violations of the Geneva Convention). In the absence of a specific norm under Swiss law, the tribunal deemed that it was not competent to rule on the charge of genocide.

58. For more details see L. Walleyn, "Bescherming van getuigen in procedures van misdaden tegen de mensheid," *Zoeklicht* 9, no. 28 (2000): 11–15.

59. Pierre-Serge Héger, "Détentions et poursuites judiciaires en Suisse," in *La justice internationale face au drame rwandais*, ed. Jean-François Dupaquier (Paris: Karthala Publishing, 1996), 189. For a commentary, see Cécile Aptel and Jamie A. Williamson, "A Commentary on the Musema Judgment Rendered by the United Nations International Criminal Tribunal for Rwanda," *Melbourne Journal of International Law* 1, no. 1 (2000): 131–48.

60. For specific information on the right to reparation, see Christine Van den Wyngaert, "The Compensation of Victims of Violent Crimes in Belgium," in *The Compensation of Victims of Violent Crimes,* ed. Desmond Greer (Freiburg im Breisgau: Max-Planck-Institut, 1996), 67–96.

61. Law dated July 16, 1993, modified by the law of February 10, 1999, regarding the prosecution of serious violations of international humanitarian law. For a commentary on the law, see, among others, A. Andries et al., "Commentaire de la loi du 16 juin 1993 relative à la répression des infractions graves au droit international humanitaire," *Revue de droit pénal et de criminologie* 74 (1994): 1,114–184.

62. Another approach would have been to initiate proceedings as civil claimants before an investigating magistrate. The chronological summary here is drawn from Marie-Anne Swartenbroeckx, "Détentions et poursuites judiciaires en Belgique," in *La justice internationale face au drame rwandais,* 144–67.

63. Vincent Ntezimana has discussed his experience in *La justice belge face au génocide rwandais: L'affaire Ntezimana* (Paris: L'Harmattan, 2000).

64. Law of March 22, 1996, concerning the recognition of the International Tribunal for Former Yugoslavia and the International Tribunal for Rwanda and collaboration with these tribunals (*Moniteur Belge,* April 27, 1996).

65. Recommendation 27 of the Report of July 7, 2000. The report was previously found at www.oau-oua.org/Document/ipep/ipep.htm, but it appears that this URL has not survived the recent transition from the Organization for African Unity (OAU) to the new African Union.

III

Judging the Past

12

Justice, History, and Memory in France
Reflections on the Papon Trial

Henry Rousso

O n October 31, 1997, three weeks after the beginning of the trial of
Maurice Papon for crimes against humanity, the Assize Court of Bordeaux began hearing from "witness-historians," with the American historian
Robert Paxton at the top of the list. At the end of his "deposition"—a statement on the politics of the Vichy regime between 1942 and 1944—the lawyer
for the defense, Jean-Marc Varaut, asked him, "Do you think that it is the
role of historians to testify at a trial?"[1] Paxton, who had already testified at
the 1994 trial of the former member of the *Milice*,[2] Paul Touvier, answered:

> I think that historians can have a role. My life would undoubtedly be simpler if
> I had refused. An historian is not an eyewitness. He does not judge. But he has
> a very precise role to play in a trial. I will take as an example the Touvier trial:
> historians testified and their role was not to talk about what they had seen but
> to provide a context, based on as complete a documentation as possible, in the
> light of which certain statements are no longer possible, just as certain explana-
> tions become clearer. Historians have the role of situating, of describing the
> context of facts; they have a genuine role and I have accepted it.[3]

Three months later, Robert Paxton responded in a more nuanced manner
to a journalist who posed essentially the same question: "Historians do not
pronounce on the guilt or innocence of an individual with respect to the
penal code. Historians are trying to understand the past, to make the past

intelligible. But you certainly do judge—this person did well, that one didn't do well."[4]

These few words—some said in court, others from a certain distance—show one of the dilemmas that confronted historians called to testify in a new kind of trial. In accepting the role of "expert witness," they ran the risk of confusing the boundaries between their scientific (historical) work and that of the court, between their interpretations and value judgments and those of the justice system, which had to deliver a sentence based on precise deeds attributable to a specific individual.

If they refused to testify, they ran the risk of being criticized for not wishing to take responsibility for a mission that had been assigned to them both by the justice system and by the pressures of public opinion—a mission that was, at first glance, that of giving the jurors all the available information about the Vichy period so as to avoid errors, anachronisms, or incomplete interpretations of events that they had been studying for a long time.[5]

It was the second time in France that in the space of only a few years historians were summoned as "experts" at a criminal trial. In both the Touvier trial and the Papon trial, what was at issue was the judgment of crimes committed against Jews during World War II. And in these two trials, the expertise solicited was neither of a technical nature, nor did it have a bearing on this or that precise point—as was the case, for example, in the trials linked to the Dreyfus Affair from 1898 on, when archivists and historians provided their expert opinions on the famous "bordereau."[6] At the Bordeaux trial, the expertise of historians, solicited at the initiative of the prosecution and civil parties in the case, aimed at the very heart of the case, namely, to determine the responsibility and the guilt of a high-level civil servant and, hence, those of the regime that he had served.

Historians were moreover particularly important and in a delicate position as the incriminating deeds harked back to a period during which none of the participants in the trial (with the exception of the accused himself and his few surviving victims) had lived. Historians were even more significant in this case, since the French justice system, as a public power, had made it known for some time that this trial, like the Barbie and Touvier trials, should be a great "pedagogical" event, a trial "for history and for memory."

The presence of historians at trials of this kind raised questions of method and scientific ethics. The difficulty was shown to be, above all, that of wanting to judge not only a man, but also a regime and an entire period, from a distance of more than half a century. Moreover, because the court relied on archival documents more than on direct eyewitnesses (of whom there were very few), it implicitly developed a form of "historical narrative" that appeared to be quite similar to that constructed by historians. In reality, however, this narrative was very far removed from the historian's narrative because by definition it had to submit to the dictates of a juridical reading in a case involving the penal charge of a crime against humanity. It also had to conform to any trial's strict juridical procedure, even if this was a trial of an exceptional nature.

All of this raised numerous questions: How does one reconcile a "judicial truth" with an "historical truth"? Can one view history in normative terms? Who, the judge or the historian, is most qualified to "render a legal judgment" on the past? To what degree is the case of Maurice Papon representative of the regime that he had served, and to what extent was his trial exemplary? What, finally, was the meaning of such a trial, not only with regard to basic justice and to the reparations due to the victims but with regard to France's collective memory, since that was the implicit target of this trial?

A SINGULAR DEFENDANT AND TRIAL

Of all those who have been indicted in France for crimes against humanity since the beginning of the 1970s, Maurice Papon was one of the most prominent, though less for his role during the war than for the exceptional career that he had afterwards. Before his extradition from Bolivia in 1983, and his trial in 1987, the former Nazi Klaus Barbie was known only to a few, who recalled his role as the former torturer of Jean Moulin, one of the leaders of the French Resistance. Similarly, the *milicien* Touvier, on the run since the end of the war, was even less known until, in 1973, he was the first charged with crimes against humanity, and the first Frenchman to be convicted of this crime in 1994. René Bousquet, the former general secretary of police in Pierre Laval's government under Vichy whose 1991 conviction, which came out of a much-awaited trial, had had a business career that was certainly brilliant but also rather discreet. Only the late revelation of his crucial role in Vichy's contribution to the "Final Solution"—and even more, the lasting ties that he had with François Mitterrand—made him into a well-known person before he was assassinated in 1993. After the war Maurice Papon, by contrast, had a career as a highly ranked civil servant. He was also a politician who moved in the highest circles.

In June 1942, Papon had been named secretary general of the prefecture of the Gironde, a relatively important post in that, under the Occupation, the local civil service administration played a vital role. As privileged relays of the Vichy regime throughout the entire territory of the country and above all in the occupied zone, prefects exercised great power at the local level as a result of the suspension of all elected representatives (deputies, mayors, etc.). On the front line in the implementation of policies of repression and persecution, they were the privileged interlocutors of the German military authorities and the German police, and thus the principal administrative wheels in the Vichy regime's collaboration with the Nazi regime (*collaboration d'État*).

At the time of Liberation, having acquired a reputation as an able technical administrator and priding himself on help given to the local resistance (the proof of which has never been formally supplied), Maurice Papon pursued his career and escaped sanction during the purge at the end of the war (*l'épuration*). In 1949, he was prefect of Constantine, in Algeria; and then, in 1954, secretary general of the Protectorate of Morocco. In March 1958, shortly before General Charles de Gaulle returned to power, he was named prefect of police in Paris, a key post that he occupied until 1967.

Under his authority, in the middle of the Algerian war, a violent repression of a demonstration of Algerians in Paris took place, which resulted in several dozen, perhaps several hundred victims (an episode about which there was lengthy questioning at the trial). He subsequently had a political career in the Gaullist movement and became Minister of Finance in 1978 in the centrist government of Raymond Barre. Then, in 1981, in the middle of the presidential campaign, the press, briefed by associations of former deportees, dredged up his role under the Occupation, thus launching a scandal that resulted in the Bordeaux trial.

In 1997, Maurice Papon was therefore neither an unknown emerging from the depths of the past, nor a contrite fascist, like Touvier. In spite of his past, he did not so much symbolize the Vichy regime as he did French high public office and the Gaullist Fifth Republic, whose legitimacy was rooted in the Resistance.

His political prominence aside, the trial was a major event for several reasons. Stretched over six months, it was the longest trial in the entire history of France. As a point of comparison, the trial of Marshall Pétain in July 1945 lasted three weeks. In contrast, the Papon trial opened after a judicial inquiry that lasted, in total, with striking ups and downs, close to fifteen years, a span of time that was outside of all known judicial norms. Moreover, never before had an accused been put on trial for deeds that had taken place so long ago. And never had an accused, remanded to a criminal court for such serious crimes, appeared freely. In sum, it was without question the first time, at least during peacetime and in a period of relative domestic peace, that a high civil servant, who had had such important administrative and political responsibilities, was put in the examination box for acts committed during the exercise of his duties and in conformity with the politics and policies of the government that he had served.

In this sense, the Papon trial was above all a trial of the Vichy administration and of its direct involvement in the extermination of Jews. It was implicitly the trial of the real and supposed inadequacies of the purge following the war, insofar as a large part of French public opinion, in particular younger generations, believed that those responsible for the Vichy regime had not been sufficiently judged or held accountable after Liberation.

Implicitly, it was also a trial that challenged a certain perception of the Occupation, which had won acceptance after the war and which prevailed into the 1960s, and that had sought to turn the page of history in the name of reconstituting national unity. In other words, the trial assumed a symbolic character because it questioned both the behavior of French elites during the Occupation and that of the majority of Frenchmen and Frenchwomen after the war. It was as much a trial of Vichy as a trial about memory and forgetting. To summarize, for reasons having to do with the particular circumstances of Maurice Papon's career, it was, at times, a trial about crimes committed by the French Republic during the Algerian War and, thus, a trial of a certain traditional conception of the state and of the idea of *raison d'État* ("reasons of state") in France.

THE PAPON TRIAL IN THE LONG HISTORY OF THE MEMORY OF VICHY

This trial strikes a prolonged chord in the still unfinished history of the difficult relationship that the French, like those in other countries that endured World War II, have had with their past since 1944–1945.

The essential element that made it possible, in addition to the two other trials that preceded it, was the application of the idea of the absence of a statute of limitations for crimes against humanity and for those crimes only. (In other words, crimes against humanity would not be subject to the same statutes of limitations as other crimes.) Foreign to French law, this juridical innovation was the result of a unanimous vote in the French parliament in December 1964 that followed the example of other European countries. Both the Left and the Right voted for this law without difficulty.

Originally it was not in any sense intended to reopen trials against French collaborators, who had benefited from amnesty laws in 1951 and 1953 and whose crimes, which stemmed from the charge of treason by virtue of the French penal code, should have lapsed at the end of twenty years. Never could deputies and senators, who included many former resisters, and who had been numerous above all in the Gaullist ranks voting for the laws of amnesty, have imagined that this law would open a new phase of the postwar purge, thirty years later.

What the French deputies feared at that moment was the risk of seeing Nazi war criminals (Germans) escape justice if such cases were barred from prosecution in the Federal Republic of Germany. For political and juridical reasons, the trials of Nazi criminals in France—Karl Oberg and Helmut Knochen, the head of the police and SS in Occupied France and his assistant—were suspended in the middle of the 1950s, and they were even set free in 1962 at the initiative of General de Gaulle. The French parliament feared that those under German jurisdiction (including Klaus Barbie, whose name was often invoked in the debates) who had exercised their terror in Occupied France would no longer be liable to prosecution by German courts. Hence the vote of this law, which stipulated in a single article: "Crimes against humanity, such as they are defined by the resolution of the United Nations of 13 February 1946, taking note of the definition of crimes against humanity such as they appear in the Charter of the International Tribunal of 8 August 1945, are by their nature not subject to a statute of limitations."[7]

Without its backers then perceiving all the implications, this law eventually shook France's legal traditions. It also marked a major turning point in the conception of the past in France's collective memory. This point merits emphasis because, for one part of public opinion in the 1990s, the notion of the absence of a statute of limitations seemed to go without saying, just as it seemed to go without saying that this juridical disposition would definitively solve all problems that arose less from enemy occupation than from the existence of the Vichy regime, and thus from the civil war that divided French society between 1940 and 1944.

If such was not the aim of this law, it nonetheless revealed the existence of two antagonistic conceptions of justice and of memory. It was voted by a generation that had lived through the war and that had, wrongly or rightly, considered it necessary at one and the same time never to forget Nazi barbarism and to make itself the advocate of Franco-German reconciliation and of reconciliation among the French themselves. But it was applied years later by and for generations who, in contrast, considered that the crimes committed, whether by the Germans or by the French, could not be forgotten in a fundamental sense, even if some had already been tried after the war on other grounds.

The law of December 1964 was thus, in its principle, a major change in the juridical and cultural approach to the past. For twenty-odd years, its effective application has raised other problems that reside in the very definition of "crimes against humanity," and above all in voluntary and involuntary distinctions that it introduced among different categories of victims of the German Occupation and Vichy. For reasons at once juridical, political, and moral, this law resulted in judicial procedures that targeted only crimes committed against Jews, to the exclusion of crimes committed against resisters. Even if certain legal decisions, notably one from France's highest court of appeals in 1985 just before the Barbie trial, formally permitted that crimes committed against resisters be taken into account, only the anti-Jewish policies of the Nazis and the complicity of Vichyites and collaborators in the matter were taken into account.

This state of affairs, which evidently resulted from the late awareness of the scope of the Jewish genocide, stirred up a number of polemics—and sometimes misunderstandings—in a country that always had the greatest difficulty assigning a clear status to all of the victims of the Occupation in the national memory. In the war's aftermath, in spite of official speeches concerning the "community of suffering," little by little a hierarchy of victims was established, at the summit of which figured the martyrs of the Resistance (approximately eighty thousand dead, shot, or who had died during deportation). The Jewish victims (seventy-five thousand men, women, and children) were not clearly set apart from others, nor specifically recognized as a distinct group.[8]

In contrast, from the 1980s, the deportation of Jews became the central element in all discussions of the war's past, a tendency that was reinforced by the very nature of judicial procedures that took into account only this aspect of the past. The "competition among victims" has thus been inverted in recent years in a country where a major portion of the population had suffered from Nazi Occupation, with the victims of the Resistance ceding first place to the Jewish victims.

In this regard the Papon trial demonstrates the spectacular evolution in France's collective memory in the last thirty years. While the question of European anti-Semitism in the 1940s—and even more that of French anti-Semitism—had been slighted, even ignored after the war, it has been the center of all debates about memory since the end of the 1970s, even becoming a recurrent element in French political debate, as it did in Germany and in other countries. It thus led to what one could call a "second purge," on bases and in a context obviously very different from those of the period following Liberation.

In fact, the procedures for crimes against humanity concerned only a single German (Klaus Barbie) and five Frenchmen in total, of whom only two were sentenced: besides Paul Touvier and Maurice Papon, between 1973 and 1991, René Bousquet, Jean Leguay (Bousquet's deputy in the occupied zone), and Maurice Sabatier, prefect of the Gironde (in the context of the case against Papon), were indicted, but all three died before the end of the preparation of cases against them.

Certainly no comparison can be made between this "second purge" and the immediate postwar purge, which lasted a whole decade, resulting in close to 130,000 trials and 1,500 legal executions (without counting the 9,000 to 10,000 of those who died in the "extra-judicial" purge).[9] Still, from the perspective of the symbolic importance of recent trials and taking into account the great impact they have had on public opinion, it is interesting to point out both the juridical and cultural differences between these two sets of events.

After the war, almost all the cases were initiated and launched by the state, by government officials who acted as attorneys. Very few resulted from complaints emanating from resisters or from victims. The objectives of the political purge (*épuration*)—a term that originally goes back to the French Revolution—were to "purify" the Nation and to legitimize the bases of the political and social reconstruction of the Republic. It was thus a national enterprise conducted in the name of *raison d'État* and carried out by governments who laid claim to the Resistance. Its aim was to punish the guilty as quickly as possible, to whitewash others, and then to turn a page in the civil war in ways that resembled past domestic conflicts (1848, the Commune, the Dreyfus Affair, etc.).

In contrast, *all* of the proceedings from 1973 on began as a result of complaints lodged by associations of former resisters and former deportees. They were the result of militant activity (in which Serge Klarsfeld played a determining role). They were the fruit of initiatives emanating from civil society and not from public action by the state. The latter sought, in contrast, at least in the beginning, to slow down the movement of certain dossiers (notably that of René Bousquet) before letting justice follow its course. These actions therefore did not occur because of a *raison d'État*, but because of a will to render justice to the victims, in the name of a "duty to memory" whose objective was the perpetuation of memory against all forms of forgetting, considered in this perspective as a new crime. In this sense, the Papon trial was a marker in the evolution of French society, not only with regard to its vision of the national past but with regard to the relationship between the state and civil society, or the growing significance of "communitarian" identities (religious, cultural, regional, etc.) in a country that has always in large part denied them.

The retrospective and repeated denunciation of the anti-Semitism of Vichy in these last fifteen years, notably by new generations, is also explained by the new and more conflictual relations that (many) French Jews have with the state and a certain rigid conception of *laïcité* and of the Republic. This trial is in this sense one symptom among others of a continuous process of desacralization of state authority and of traditional French national sentiment, an evolution that has to be understood in the context of the construction of a new European political space.

In the postwar trials, the question of anti-Semitism was of secondary concern (if it was not totally absent)—another great difference between the two purges. In reality, justice, power, and public opinion all then deemed that collaboration with the enemy was the major crime and that many of the crimes of an anti-Semitic nature and anti-Jewish persecutions had been, on the one hand, the direct result of the occupying power, and on the other had been committed in the context of a broader cooperation with the enemy. For example, in 1947, during his trial at High Court, when his accusers reproached him for having zealously applied anti-Semitic German and French measures, the first Commissioner General on Jewish Questions in Vichy,

the *maurrassien* Xavier Vallat, argued *in his defense* that he had acted by virtue of an anti-Semitic French ideology and not in the spirit of the enemy's
ideology. He thus sought to deny not his anti-Semitism, but only the accusa-
tion of collaboration.[10]

By contrast, the policy of Jewish persecution was the only crime cited
against Barbie, Touvier, and Papon, to the exclusion of all the other crimes
committed against resisters or against the civil population as a whole. This
"second purge" could thus give the impression that the question of the persecution of Jews had been as central in the reality of yesterday as it is today
on the moral plane, in the national and international memory, and in the
collective perception of the past. One of the major problems in this persecution, which was outside every known norm at the time, is that precisely neither the political elites who carried it out, as they carried out a more general
policy of repression against numerous categories of people, nor the French
people in general perceived the singular character of this racial persecution
at the time. If one part of French opinion reacted against the first deportations of Jews in the Spring of 1942, it was above all the the Service du Travail
Obligatoire (STO), which affected several hundreds of thousands of workers, leading to more massive reactions against the occupier in the beginning
of the year 1943.

Finally, the third difference is that in the trials of the immediate postwar
period, most of the accused were tried on the basis of their attitude toward
the enemy and for their lack of patriotism. The weight of foreign occupation
was therefore crucial. By contrast, in the recent trials—which had moreover
a "historical" and pedagogical goal—the question of the occupiers was
treated in a very ambiguous manner, if not neglected entirely. At the time of
Touvier's trial, for strictly juridical reasons, the prosecution wanted at any
cost to prove that the *milicien*, accused of the murder of seven Jewish hos-
tages in 1944, had acted under order of the Sipo-SD (*Sicherheitspolizei-
Sicherheitsdienst*) of Lyon.

In adherence to the London accord of August 8, 1945, French law held
that a lone French citizen could not be rendered guilty of a crime against
humanity. Such a crime could only have been committed by the Third Reich,
and a French national could only have acted in *complicity*.[11] Thus, the *milicien* Touvier had acted without any German order, in the context of the war
that the French *Milice* conducted, among others, against Jews. This contradiction was all the more flagrant because in the eyes of public opinion and
by virtue of the duty to memory in its French version, this trial purported
to show that the Nazis were not the only ones to persecute the Jews, and that
the French, beginning with the Vichy regime, had also committed this type
of crime, without submitting to pressure from the German occupier. This
was one of the most obvious contradictions in the Touvier trial—the first of
its kind against a French national and, it was thought, the last—between an

established historical truth, on the one hand, and an imposed judicial and juridical truth, on the other.

The Papon trial raised another type of problem. Not a single German witness testified, not even one of the German judges who had been charged with the trial of those responsible in the Sipo-SD operating in Bordeaux. In a general way, the impact of the Nazi Occupation—the fact that it was the occupier who decided on the very principle of Jewish deportation, was eliminated as a central concern, thus giving the impression that the Vichy regime, and more especially one of its functionaries, had had great autonomy of decision-making power in the matter, which was obviously not the case.

In this regard, the trial reflected existing representations of Vichy that, wishing to underscore the Pétain regime's own responsibility for the deportations, end by forgetting that the real source of power, in Occupied France, was in the hands of the Nazis, and that the Third Reich conceived of and willed the extermination of the Jews. The Vichy regime accepted and lent its support to this project for reasons having to do with a policy of state collaboration—which obviously does not diminish the criminal character of this policy or the overwhelming responsibility of an openly anti-Semitic regime.

In sum, the Papon trial (like the Touvier trial) resulted from a long evolution in public consciousness involving the gradual dissemination of the idea that justice must be the principal vector of memory, the most appropriate means to remember the crimes committed by Vichy. Despite all the difficulties that such trials raised, despite all the knowledge accumulated about this period over thirty years, despite the multitude of public debates centering on the creation of new national commemorations (among them that of July 16, adopted in 1993 to commemorate the Vél' d'Hiv roundup)[12]—despite all this, the Papon trial was perceived and accepted as a defining moment for the new perception of memory and of history in France.

Under these circumstances, the liberties taken with historical truth, with judicial rigor (the definition of a crime against humanity was modified three times in turn, before each of the trials) and with respect for legal procedures (attacks by certain lawyers on judges, lies proffered under oath by certain witnesses coming from both sides, etc.) were secondary considerations compared with the knowledge that France had been capable of looking its past in the face. Undoubtedly, apart from some observers (of whom Claude Lanzmann was one), few realized that the end of this trial was effectively a form of symbolic "closure." Having reopened the dossier of Vichy, once the verdict had been rendered (ten years of prison), the justice system had to close it—a situation that was not without its contradictions, because this very same justice system had been thought of, over the years, as a guardian of memory.

On the evidence, its capacity to sustain memory had one day to encounter the natural limits imposed on its mission, and because the dead cannot be judged, it was necessary for other vectors of memory to ensure a form of transition. In this respect, it is worth noting that the verdict in the Papon trial in no way closed the Vichy dossier in the political arena because at the very same time, as a result of pressure from the World Jewish Congress in particular, the question of the unlawful plundering of Jewish assets during the war came to the fore. Thus, in a few years, the demand for reparations came to take on a political dimension (recognition of crimes by the highest state authorities, the founding of new commemorative rituals), a juridical dimension in the form of trials, and finally a financial and material dimension. None of these is close to being resolved, given the technical complexity of the issues.

The first purge obeyed the constraints stemming from *raison d'État*, with its train of injustices and its inevitable imperfections. The second yielded to constraints stemming from another imperative: moral argument, embellished with the virtues of a duty to memory, but that is also no less problematic than the previous purge.

HISTORIANS AND THE LAW

Given these symbolic stakes, the presence of historians at the Papon trial (as at the Touvier trial) was not an insignificant problem. It constituted, inside an already exceptional event, something totally new in France, as much for legal history as for the historian's craft.

This summoning of historians to the halls of justice must be understood in a general context in which the academic language about the past, which is supposed to be incontestable and irrefutable, is increasingly frequent, particularly in everything that concerns the heritage of Nazism and World War II. This is almost always linked to the memory of Jewish extermination. This new genre of social demand emanates first from the public sphere, in the numerous commissions of official historians charged with resolving precise points of history: the commissions of the "fichier juif" of Vichy (created by the National Statistical Services, the SNS,[13] on the question of the use of statistical indexes of the Jewish population in France under the Occupation); on the plundering of "Jewish" property (commission Mattéoli on the aryanization of Jewish property in France); of the city of Paris on the question of real estate; and those formed by financial institutions, such as the Caisse des Dépots and Consignations, and so on.

This new genre of demand also comes from businesses or public and private institutions, such as the commission created by the Catholic Church of France to investigate the protection accorded to Touvier in Catholic circles,[14] to say nothing of the numerous less visible demands from associations of resisters, deportees, and isolated individuals. This is obviously an international phenomenon, but it had a relatively widespread and precocious development (at the beginning of the 1990s) in France.

This call to historians must also be placed in the context in which the general demands for "reparation" to compensate for past injustices and crimes have taken an increasingly formal turn—indeed, placing them in the domain of retroactive legislation. Thus it was in 1999 in this frame of mind that the French parliament "decided" that the massacre of Armenians was a genocide and a crime against humanity—a stance confirmed in 2001 by the Senate and adopted as a law that raised tremendous tensions with Turkey—or that the repression undertaken in Algeria, between 1954 and 1962, was a "war," and not an operation for the "maintenance of social order."

Without discussing here the basis for such decisions, it is necessary simply to keep in mind that public actions and forms of politics have gradually emerged that tended to give interpretations of the past (the recent and distant past) a formal, official, juridical character. Under these terms, historians became essential actors because they were assumed to have a kind of knowledge, a capacity for expertise, which is necessary for any public action of this type.

That being so, the historical expertise that was sought in the context of the Papon trial adhered to quite singular modalities. In normal times, juridical expertise, which has been the subject of numerous debates and reforms in France for more than a century,[15] was very strictly bounded by the code of penal procedure. Most of the time such expertise exists at a remove from the trial itself, at the level of judicial preparations, that is to say during preliminary investigations. It is translated most of the time into written reports and is thus subject to verification and eventually to refutations, which are attached or included in the judicial dossiers.

In the context of the Papon trial, nothing of this sort occurred. Most of the historians cited by the bar were not called (or only in very marginal ways were called) during the trial's preparation—that is to say at a time when they would have had the leisure to examine and judge the archival material that made up the core of the prosecution's case. They were cited as *witnesses* in the confines of criminal procedure, which requires that only the judges, the lawyers for the defense and for the civil plaintiffs, and those for the accused have access to the judicial dossier. This access is, in contrast, strictly prohibited to witnesses (even historian-witnesses), who must testify under oath without being able to use written notes—all procedure in criminal courts resting in this respect on the sacrosanct "oral character of argument."

In other words, the historians involved in the trial had no particular knowledge of the dossier, or hence of most of the archival materials concerning the prefecture of the Gironde, as almost all these documents had been unavailable for consultation for years because of the secrecy involved in the judicial investigation. Each of them spoke for several hours without being able to refer to notes or documents, even those of a very general nature. They testified, in other words, in a context that is quite removed from that in which historians normally work. As a result of this state of affairs, they found themselves in a very unnerving situation because they were at the mercy of retorts from the prosecution or from the lawyers, who themselves had at their disposal material from a dossier of several thousands of pages.

Only one academic, the political scientist Michel Bergès, had a thorough knowledge of the dossier. He was the one who had launched the Papon affair in 1980 and had helped associations of victims to bring suit on the basis of documents that he had found in the archives during his personal research on the matter. After helping the prosecution for a long time, Bergès changed his mind about the case, and found himself, in 1997, called by the accused, who hoped to use him as a counterwitness.

During his testimony, because the discussion focused not on generalities but on the Papon case properly speaking, he was violently attacked by the attorney general and the civil parties in the case, who even denied his capacities as a "historian" under the pretext that he was a political scientist.[16] Without passing judgment here on his personal positions, it is necessary to point out that Bergès was the only one of all the historians called to the bench to have directly treated the subject of how the prefecture of the Gironde functioned—that is, the precise facts that were being judged at Bordeaux. No other historian wished to address the subject or could have done so.

This raises other more important questions than those concerning formal methods and procedures in the use of historical expertise at trial: What is the nature of that expertise, its object, and its real objectives?

As the jurists tell it, there are, schematically speaking, two types of judicial expertise.[17] The first relates to the facts themselves, the conditions surrounding their existence, and objective elements, such as those gleaned through toxicology, biology, ballistic evidence, and so on. This type of expertise is based on the existence of more or less established and accepted scientific laws that the expert, under the authority of the investigating magistrate, has to apply to a particular situation, with a margin of error and uncertainty that must be assessed and highlighted. The second type of judicial expertise, of which psychiatric expertise is an example, concerns the author of the crime or infraction.

In the case of historical expertise, the "experts" were neither of the first nor of the second type. They could neither invoke reproducible general laws, nor were they really equipped to appreciate the *intentions* of the accused, his deepest motivations, and so on. Their only competence rested in their more or less thorough knowledge of singular facts, unique by definition, unless one argues that history obeys repetitive natural laws.

If one acknowledges the preceding, the only possible expertise that the historian could bring to bear was thus the painstaking analysis of the actions of the secretary general of the Gironde, using all the available archives and testimony, and reinserting it in the general context of the Occupation. That possibility was by definition precluded by the nature of penal procedure. This is where the major contradiction of this trial lies, since at the very beginning of the proceedings the historians were prevented from giving the only expert information that they could really be regarded as competent to render.

Their presence was thus justified for other reasons and other objectives. They were not asked to talk about the Papon case or even about what happened in Bordeaux between 1942 and 1944, but to evoke in the most general and broad way possible the "context" of the period of the Occupation.

The public prosecution, which took the initiative to bring historians into court, followed by the defense and the civil parties involved, implicitly asked most of them even to divide up the roles they would play among themselves. They thus, respectively, considered the general politics of Vichy (Robert Paxton), the ideology of the National Revolution and of anti-Semitism (Jean-Pierre Azéma), collaboration in public capacities (Philippe Burrin), the functioning of the civil service under Vichy (Marc Olivier Baruch), and so on. It was therefore a question of delivering a series of lectures on the subject in order to allow those judging the case to take a kind of crash course and to be initiated into the general history of the period.

This situation gave rise to problems of a very fundamental kind: is it possible for a historian to construct a historical context without first being questioned or without an a priori definition of the objective he is pursuing? A "context in and of itself" does not exist, outside of a field of questions. Every narrative and every historical argumentation is the result of a conscious and implicit choice, which puts an emphasis on this or that aspect, the function of the object that is sought, and which adapts itself gradually to the research as it goes on. This is almost a truism. But at Bordeaux, only the court was the mistress or master of prior questioning that was summed up in a question that was as simple as it was formidable: Was the accused guilty or not of the deeds of which he was accused as defined by the judicial texts in the case?

This dependence on an initial question that had not been formulated by the historians themselves was apparent in two essential points: On the one hand, few observers remarked on the absence among the themes "spontaneously" treated by the historians of a good account of the German authorities during the Occupation, of Nazi policies in France, or indeed of the history of the "Final Solution." On the other hand, no historian ventured to ask what acts of "resistance" on the part of certain Vichy functionaries could have meant in 1943–1944, with the approach of the Normandy Landing—a quite commonplace subject of inquiry and one that was a part of the investigation of Papon. In one case as in the other, even with a rigorous and nuanced discussion, to treat these questions could have helped the defense and hampered the prosecution.

Here one touches on the core of the problem in this kind of expert testimony. With the exception of certain historians who openly took the side of the accused, all the others, who were among the greatest specialists on the subject, undoubtedly feared that their testimony could come to the aid of Maurice Papon and could contribute to his acquittal or to the reduction of charges against him—a hypothesis that could hardly be excluded, at least at the beginning of the trial.

Whatever their competence and manifest good will, the historians could not express themselves in as complete freedom as they could have done in other settings. The symbolic weight of a criminal court and the pressure that weighed on them were certainly not of the kind to encourage distancing themselves from the object of their expertise. And as all had devoted their professional lives to explaining the crimes specific to Vichy, which had long been misunderstood or underestimated by public opinion, to contribute, if only in an imperceptible manner, to acquitting one who had become, for good or for ill, a living symbol was quite simply impossible or, at the very least, psychologically difficult.

There is a second problem inherent in exploring the historical context in such circumstances. Most of the time, historians go from the particular to the general, from the study of cases to the "big picture." However, even when they have attained a degree of knowledge sufficient to construct a global analysis—for example about the politics of the persecution of Jews by Vichy—they cannot go in the inverse direction, from the general to the particular, without an attentive examination of the particular case in question. In other words, what is true about the general case of Occupied France was not a priori the particular circumstances of the case in Bordeaux— something that could only be established by a *sui generis* examination. So, once again, only the court had the possibility of making comparisons between the general and particular cases, the historians being excluded from this crucial phase of historical interpretation.

The historians thus found themselves in a situation of having to provide a frame for a general reading, a sort of ideal type, without having been given the possibility to test the validity of this ideal type for the historical situation that was specific to Bordeaux in 1942–1944. It was at this level that the "competition" between judges and historians was the most evident. This does not mean that judges were necessarily in error, but it does raise a question regarding the extent to which historians were taken and used as instruments, in spite of themselves, in judicial stratagems that escaped them completely.

In the end, this type of expertise served above all to legitimize the supposed historical character of the trial more than to enlighten the court on

precise questions. The presence of the historians was even more indispens-
able since their task was to make up for the fact that most of the trial's actors
were not present during the period in which the events discussed had
occurred. The historians were the major guarantee that allowed one to affirm
that so delayed a trial was possible not only on an ethical level but also on a
technical level. This remains to be proved. The very important symbolic role
that the historians played, though it was very limited on a practical level, was
certainly one way to stress that historians are only depositories among others of knowledge of the past, which rests and must rest on a common good.
But their presence also showed all the limits and the contradictions in such
a trial.

NOTES

Translated by Caroline Ford from the French original of "Justiz, Geschichte und Erinnerung in Frankreich: Überlegungen zum Papon-Prozess," in Norbert Frei, Dirk
van Laak, Michael Stolleis, eds., *Geschichte vor Gericht: Historiker, Richter und die
Suche nach Gerechtigkeit* (Munich: C. H. Beck, 2000), 141–63.

1. Cited in *Le Procès de Maurice Papon, 8 October 1997–8 January 1998*, vol. 1
(Paris: Albin Michel, 1998), 317 (also see the daily *Le Monde*, November 2, 1997).
This work presents itself as a "stenographic report" of the Papon trial. But it has
no official character. In France, it is not customary for courts to provide an official
stenographic report of criminal trials. However, an exception has been made in trials
for crimes against humanity, which, in addition, have been filmed in their entirety—
and this is a new departure. But neither the official stenographic report nor the
recordings are in principle accessible (except with special permission) until after a
period of thirty years. In this sense, this volume is a convenient tool, but it is prudent
to verify its contents with other sources, including the reports on the trial by the
press. In this respect, among the numerous books written after the trial, one should
keep in mind that of the writer on judicial matters for the weekly *L'Express*: Eric
Conan, *Le Procès Papon: Un journal d'audience* (Paris: Gallimard, 1998); and that of
the daily *Le Monde*: Jean-Michel Dumay, *Le Procès Papon: La chronique de Jean-
Michel Dumay* (Paris: Fayard, 1998).
2. The *Milice* was a paramilitary organization of the Vichy regime. It consisted
of armed groups acting as a kind of anti-Communist and pro-Vichy extra police
squad—Translator's note.
3. Cited in *Le Procès de Maurice Papon, 8 October 1997–8 January 1998*, vol. 1,
317.
4. Interview with Elisabeth Bumiller, *The New York Times*, January 31, 1998.
5. Ten or so historians were "summoned to appear" in this trial. The academics
Robert Paxton, Jean-Pierre Azéma, Marc Olivier Baruch, Philippe Burrin, René
Rémond, Michel Bergès, as well as the writers and journalists Henri Amouroux, Jean
Lacouture, and Jean-Luc Einaudi agreed to testify. Several other historians refused
for diverse reasons, among whom were the writer Maurice Rajsfus (because his par-

ents had been deported), the German historian Eberhard Jäckel (who considered his work on France to be "too out-of-date"; cf. his interview with *Le Monde,* November 7, 1997), as well as the author of these lines, for the reasons in large part explained in this chapter (cf. also Henry Rousso, *La hantise du passé: Entretien avec Philippe Petit* (Paris: Textuel, 1998; to appear in an English translation as *The Haunting Past: History, Memory, and Justice in Contemporary France,* trans. Ralph Schoolcraft [University of Pennsylvania Press, 2002]).

6. Cf. on this point, Vincent Duclert, "Histoire, historiens et historiographie de l'Affaire Dreyfus (1894–1997)," in *La posterité de l'Affaire Dreyfus,* ed. Michel Leymaire (Lille, France: Presses Universitaires du Septentrion, 1998), 151–234, as well as Jean-Noël Jeanneney, *Le passé dans le prétoire: L'historien, le juge et le journaliste* (Paris: Seuil, 1998). (The *bordereau* was an unsigned document, purportedly written by Dreyfus, which was the principal evidence used to implicate and prosecute Dreyfus for espionage and high treason—Translator's note.)

7. Law of December 26, 1964 (*Journal Officiel* du 29 December 1964).

8. In the very abundant literature on the memory of the war in France, see Annette Wieviorka, *Déportation et Génocide: Entre la mémoire et l'oubli* (Paris: Plon, 1992); Pieter Lagrou, *The Legacy of Nazi Occupation: Patriotic Memory and National Recovery in Western Europe, 1945–1965* (Cambridge, U.K.: Cambridge University Press, 2000).

9. Cf. Henry Rousso, "L'épuration, une histoire inachevée," *Vingtième Siècle: Revue d'histoire,* no. 33 (January–March 1992): 78–105.

10. Cf. *Le Proces de Xavier Vallat présenté par ses amis* (Paris: Le Conquistador, 1948).

11. Cf. Eric Conan and Henry Rousso, *Vichy: An Ever-Present Past* (Lebanon, N.H.: The University Press of New England, 1998), 74–123.

12. The "Vél' d'Hiv roundup," which took place during July 16–17, 1942, was the most important roundup of Jews in Paris. In it, women and children were arrested for the first time; in total, about twelve thousand Jews were caught and held for several days at the Vélodrome d'hiver, a famous Parisian stadium popularly known as the Vél' d'Hiv, before being deported to Auschwitz.

13. Service national des statistiques, which after the war became known as the INSEE (Institut national de la statistique et des études économiques), the major French public agency for social and economic information.

14. René Rémond et al., *Paul Touvier et l'église* (Paris: Fayard, 1992).

15. Frédéric Chauveau, "Le corps, l'âme et la preuve. L'expertise médico-légale au XIXe siècle" (GERHICO, Université de Poitiers, Octobre 1998). On historical expertise, in addition to the works already cited, cf. also Yan Thomas, "La vérité, le temps, le juge, et l'historien," *Le Débat,* no. 102 (November–December 1998): 17–36; dossier "Vérité judiciaire, vérité historique."

16. *Le procès Papon,* vol. 2, no. 9 (January–April 2, 1998); see note 1, *Le procès Papon,* 112–35.

17. Cf. Pierrette Poncela, "Les experts sont formels," *Pouvoirs* 55 (1990): 95–106.

13

Overcoming the Past?

Narrative and Negotiation, Remembering, and Reparation: Issues at the Interface of History and the Law

Charles S. Maier

F aced with atrocities such as genocide and ethnic cleansing, systematic degradation or the planning of purposive war against populations, historians and lawyers share a certain fecklessness. They cannot prevent catastrophe; they intervene later as, in effect, ambulance chasers of history. They can record, they can adjudicate; at their best they can help in what Martha Minow and others have called restorative justice.[1] It could also be called restorative politics, because the process is one of contention among communities, and it seeks to recompose a common institutional and social framework for resuming everyday life without conflict. What I should like to explore are the challenges of that project, at least for historians, but perhaps for lawyers as well. In the present chapter, I would like to raise some related issues concerning history, memory, and restorative justice.

RETRIBUTION AND REMEMBERING

All the exercises of the historian or of truth commissions, or the trial of perpetrators, involve "re" words: retribution, reparation, remembering, recording, reconciliation. But none of these functions or roles can turn time

295

backward. We repair and remember because we cannot return. What community existed has been rent. All the "re" functions are designed to enable survivors to carry on life after the rending.

Retribution seems the most primeval claim of justice. Perpetrators should be punished, but the difficulties of punishment often appear daunting. Small fry can be prosecuted, while big fish escape. Erich Honecker flew off for cancer treatments; border guards at the Berlin Wall faced prison terms. Nonetheless, some progress may slowly be coming about. Milosevic, if not Karadzic, is on trial at The Hague. Still, trials must be highly selective, and the relatively few culprits must serve as proxy for a broader group of offenders. Complicity is diffuse, and it is impractical to try what may be close to an entire population. Providing proportionality of the punishment to the offense is also arbitrary. Rather than produce a general sense of contrition, trials may lead to further resentment and defiance. Today human rights activists praise Nuremberg, but for years after the trials there were serious questions as to their justice or their value as precedent or national pedagogy. And Nuremberg took place in a completely defeated land. In a country where civilians have merely displaced the military, trials may make settled civilian politics impossible and just introduce further cycles of violence. We know all the difficulties.

Remembering and commemoration are perhaps the easiest tasks to accomplish. The issue is not usually whether bad deeds will be remembered, but whether the wider society—outside the circle of survivors—makes the task of memory a wider public commitment. Part of public reconciliation involves nationalizing, so to speak, the task of memory. What the appropriate form of that public memory should be is eminently debatable. But the commitment is important. The hard question is sometimes how inclusive the memory work should be. Are the victims to be honored in their own right, as a particular community, or as examples of wider classes of victims? The temptation for the society that decides to honor those it killed or deprived of justice is to dilute the specificity of the act.

Richard Schroeder, an admirable clergyman dissenter who was active in the East German revolution of 1989, wanted to replace the proposed Holocaust memorial in Berlin with a column that read simply: "Thou shalt not kill." I think this was insufficient—perhaps if the column said, "Thou shalt not kill. We Germans erect this monument because we violated this commandment on a huge scale," one could be happier with it. The generalization of evil is a wonderful tactic: "We are all perpetrators; we are all victims," becomes its mushy endpoint.

RESTITUTION AND REPARATION

Restitution and reparation are different operations. Restitution is conceptually easier: a specific material good is restored to a previous owner. This does not mean that the operation does not sometimes threaten new forms of inequity. Are there not losses for the public weal if paintings are removed from a public viewing site to be returned to inaccessible private enjoyment? Should a handsome private villa that for several decades has found a new life as a kindergarten or communal facility be returned to descendants who have never seemed to need the asset?[2] In fairness, many private owners ask only for nominal recognition of earlier ownership and donate the property for public uses.

Reparation often seems more satisfactory than item-by-item restitution, but is a messier task conceptually. The claims for reparation are obviously multiplying. Reparation is, at one level, an impossible job; it can never be sufficient; it can never make up for what is really lost and irrecoverable, which is not a painting, or a villa, or a property as such, but a set of life chances. Whole possibilities for personal self-development, for personal relations, for professional fulfillment—if not life itself—have been taken away. It often seems obscene to put prices on such losses; claims for collective reparation, like demands for tort indemnification, are prefaced by the statement, "It's not the money, but. . . ." Nonetheless, no matter how crass it seems to talk money, bargaining for a material settlement has the virtue of bringing immeasurable damage and hurt back into the sphere of finite demands and satisfaction; it puts a price on the priceless loss.

The phrase is derived from Viviana Zelizer's imaginative discussion of the contradictory impulses in evaluating the cultural and social role of children: a tendency toward commodification and a counterimpulse toward what she terms sacralization.[3] Prices are placed on children even as the status of childhood and the love of children are declared to be beyond price. Many Israelis, including the more nationalist ones, did not want to accept German reparations, just as there was reluctance by some parents to accept money for the wrongful death of children. But the idea of large compensatory sums, precisely to demonstrate the priceless value of the lost child, came to prevail.[4]

"The process of rationalization and commodification of the modern world," Zelizer notes, "has its limits as money and the market are transformed by social, moral, and sacred values. . . . The sales value of an adoptive child or the economic value of the child at death are not determined only by ordinary utilitarian formulas, but depend on sentimental standards."[5] Yet reparation for historical wrongdoing usually has other dimensions: it is a negotiated sum, determined by agreement between historical plaintiffs and defendants, not by a jury's award. Reaching agreement must in effect desacralize the loss no matter what the protests of the victims or survivors.

That is precisely the point of the exercise: to remove the losses from the realm of the sacred, the never-to-be-forgiven, into the realm of the politically negotiated. Just the process of such negotiation indicates that communication is being resumed. The hitherto opposed parties—perpetrators and victims—are reaching across the gulf of historical hatred to resume a dialogue that will allow them to live together under some overarching rules of comity and coexistence. This involves what I have termed elsewhere "political reconciliation"—the institutional settlement that allows future political, commercial, and cultural interaction—if not the "spiritual reconciliation" of forgiving enemies.[6] Of course, the victims' groups claim simultaneously to have suffered a priceless loss; the perpetrators' representatives will question the appropriateness of the price tag under current conditions.

The process of bargaining becomes distasteful and sordid. The lawyers who mediate it appear as (and sometimes seem to act as) loathsome as caste societies think of tanners and waste handlers. But it is not just the litigation that soils the process. It *is* about money, even when both sides ritually protest that it is not about money. But making the priceless loss one that can be priced is precisely the value of the exercise.

In this process of materialist transformation, reparation, I believe, imposes a duty on those who accept payment as well as asking one of those who agree to make it. Those receiving reparation, in effect, must consent to a degree of closure: not closure on remembering or commemorating, but closure on material claims, assuming that all claims have been met and discussed and agreed on. We know that guaranteeing closure, above all in the menagerie of litigants that is the United States, is difficult in practice. But it does not seem an unreasonable request, if the settlement reached is indeed one that embodies free consent on both sides.

If reparation ultimately should be designed to compensate for lost life chances, then it need not take the form of cash payments. Even if one is sympathetic to the argument that American slavery deserves some form of reparation, it is precisely affirmative action, oriented toward the future, that seems to me the appropriate format. Conversely, the justification for continuation of compensatory preferences may best rest on their function as a sort of reparation that may temporarily collide with pure equal outcomes for the other groups in society.

RECORDING AND RECONSTRUCTING

Recording, or history writing, should be simple, but of course it is not. The report of a truth commission is not the same as a history. What a history must do is reconstruct the intentionality, the meaning of the violence that is recorded—the meaning for the perpetrators as well as for the victims.

Yes, the facts must be unearthed, sometimes literally, and, most crucial, they must be publicly acknowledged. A truth commission can satisfy itself with this goal. I personally do not think that private hearings make sense for this task: publicness should be a minimal condition. But the truth commission does not have to reconstruct the motivation of earlier perpetrators. Even if *"tout comprendre n'est pas tout pardonner,"* the truth commission does not have to understand everything. But the historian does have the additional task of making ugly violence plausible. Sustained political violence over time is usually committed within some mental framework: the conspirator often sees his or her victim as agents of a vast conspiracy (Communism, the Jewish world power, the outsiders "always out to get us") that must be combated.

What is the role that the lawyer, judge, or historian must accord to such an interpretation? In trials of political assassins, most notoriously perhaps in Weimar Germany, or even of lynch mob participants, judges have often taken into account the "patriotic" motivation of the defendants in assigning punishment. Liberals resent the practice, but the assignment of appropriate punishment often requires an assessment of motivation and character: although fanaticism or "conviction" perhaps should not mitigate the penalty, judges certainly respond to "depravity" with harsher punishments. However, from the outset the truth commission often trades amnesty for confession. The perpetrator who confesses (at least in South Africa) received amnesty for a mixture of confession and contrition. Since it cannot usually impose a penalty (in fact, the Truth and Reconciliation Commission [TRC] could and did refuse some amnesties for violence that transcended the political framework), it need not concern itself with the motives of the perpetrators.

It is the injury itself that must be acknowledged since often it has been denied or covered up. The truth commission imposes a radical break between the telling of events and explaining their occurrence or appeal. The historian has to go further, not necessarily in the collation of stories, but in assessing motivation and even in allowing for alternative narratives in his own account.

The historian's task is more akin to that of the judge than to that of the truth commission. The historian has to provide a narrative that "explains" or "accounts for," which means probing intentionality and worldviews. The historian rarely assumes a wholly determined framework, even if he or she wants to illuminate the constraints on actors. Thus, the historian presupposes choice and has to account for choice. He or she does not have to find an appropriate penalty for evil choices, but the weighing process is still akin to that of the judge.

According to Anthony Amsterdam and Jerome Bruner, among others, narrative and categorization are crucial to lawyering. Categories are extracted from narratives.[7] "Law lives on narrative," and "stories *construct* the facts that comprise them," the authors write.[8] But the lawyer's narrative is expected to be partisan, constructed only to persuade: being convincing is not necessarily the same as seeking the truth. Narrational logic presumes that there is not only one plausible story, but alternative stories; and although judges rely on narratives to convince themselves and their petitioners, they supposedly feel a duty to arrive at and to persuade their audience that they have gotten the right story. Even if alternative stories are possible, one of them must prevail in order to prescribe corrective remedies, whether it is a money payment, a restraining order, or an assigned punishment.

The historian, like the judge, has the duty of constructing a jurisprudential narrative—an Aristotelian exercise that, insofar as it deals with individual or collective actions, proceeds with a case-by-case sifting. Being jurisprudential, it is also "prudential"; the narrative does not set Kantian categories as the criterion for plausible human behavior, but relies primarily on contextualization to establish what constituted culpable or nonculpable or even praiseworthy action. And it presupposes weak and fallible creatures whose ethical commitments are fulfilled if they choose the mean and not the saintly or self-sacrificial course of action.

What makes the narrative persuasive? Perhaps it helps to invoke a mechanism like Adam Smith's concept of natural sympathy. The narrative is persuasive if, as readers, we can envisage ourselves following the protagonists' mental processes. The difficulty arises when deeds are truly atrocious. How though can such a deep understanding of the perpetrators be achieved when we write the history of the Holocaust?

Reflect on three recent narratives that may be familiar: Christopher Browning's *Ordinary Men*; Daniel J. Goldhagen's *Hitler's Willing Executioners*; and Arno J. Mayer's *Why Did the Heavens Not Darken?*[9] Each is beset by the challenge of explanation and interpretation, although each offers a different interpretation of behavior. For Browning, it is group camaraderie, the fear of being felt a coward, that leads ordinary men to extraordinary acts.

For Goldhagen, "ordinary" might be an appropriate term to characterize the actors as Germans, but ordinary cannot help explain their motivation, which must be an "eliminationist anti-Semitism." There is no mystery to the perpetrators' behavior. Along with other Germans, the SS were brought up to hate and fear Jews and to seek their physical slaughter. Hitler, in a sense, was their instrument.

Mayer, in contrast, suggests that he cannot understand the perpetrators' mentality. As a psychological problem, the murderous impulse is not explainable. Instead, it is the overarching, quasi-structural, centuries-long antagonism between Left and Right in Europe that culminates in an anti-Soviet crusade and an identification of the Jews with Bolshevism. The Jews are victims of ideological motivation.

In each case, the historian feels he has to account for a behavior that seems superficially inexplicable because of its cruelty and ferocity by describing a process that ordinary readers see as causally persuasive. The historian presumes that the reader is a rational creature who wants to be able to trace out the steps that lead to mass murder. For Browning the answer is, "You, too, might well have ended up a killer." For Goldhagen the answer is, "Were you a German, you, too, would probably have been programmed to kill Jews."

For Mayer the answer is, "It doesn't matter what you as an individual might think or want; given the fundamental political divisions of Europe, murdering the Jews and Soviets was a plausible and indeed recurrent outlet."

Each historian, in sum, feels the need to place the most inexplicable of events in a plausible story line. For Browning and Goldhagen the process involves the traditional Diltheyan process of *Verstehen*; for Mayer, a less psychological configuration of politics. In each case the reader is persuaded not that he or she would have been a killer, but that others easily could. Not all villainy is excusable—to the contrary!—but all villainy is contextual.

Historians, finally, face a narrative task that is in one respect more difficult than the judge's. The historian's public usually asks for a national or aggregating history. But nations are communities of winners and losers in the game of inequality. Sometimes they are communities of victims and victimizers (or their descendants) who have entered into long-term, indeed multigenerational, relationships. They share a common and intertwined history, but they also have separate histories as victims and victimizers.

How does the historian "do justice" to both sets of histories? "Synthesis" is the answer that is often given, and historians themselves bemoan the lack of historical syntheses. I think the diagnosis is misplaced. Synthesis is difficult in an era when new specializations open up and vast new reservoirs of testimony must be taken. But synthesis is also difficult when a society is sensitive to all its constitutive communities and their conflicting narratives. Ultimately, I fall back on a musical analogy. Historians can validly write "contrapuntal" history, with parallel story lines that are read horizontally, but maintain some determinate relation with each other. The independence of voices must be maintained even within a multivocal structure. Too frequent a harmonic coincidence is suspect.

RETRIEVING AND RECONCILING

Reliance on narrative obviously links the historian and judicial or quasijudicial efforts, such as truth commissions, to deal with the past, to overcome its legacies of hatred, and to seek political reconciliation. But return to reparation: Is there any inherent comparison between the activity of the historian and that of attempting reparation? To what degree does the establishment of a historical narrative about a past atrocity resemble the negotiation of reparations? To what degree must it be implicitly a political bargain? Is there any comparability between these two different ways of "overcoming" the past: historical remembrance and reparation? Reparation is a compact of offering and accepting, structured not around punishment or revenge, but around compensation, restoration, and "moving on." Is it fanciful to ascribe these qualities to history?

Consider briefly the role of "apology," which has also become a significant stake in restorative politics. History obviously provides the story of
why such compensation is appropriate. Tremendous political weight is now
assigned to the phrases, "We are sorry for," or—somewhat semantically different because it accepts more agency—"We apologize for. . . ." Not pronounced, the apology offends victims; pronounced, it offends the defenders
of a hegemonic narrative.

Unlike reparation, apology is not scalar; it is given or withheld. Calibrat-
ing it by its rhetorical form is possible, but only within limits. Its significance
consists less in its particular content than in the importance both sides attribute to its being granted or withheld. Curiously enough, although it involves
no cash (although it may preface a demand for reparations), it does not seem
to come cheap.

Like apology, historical versions of the past are often adversarial and
evoke great passions. Lest anyone think that they are politically charged
only for, say, German and Japanese war-guilt or genocide controversies,
recall the "revisionist" quarrel over Cold War origins during the 1960s and
1970s, which fundamentally split American academics and political commentators. Alternatively, consider the bitter disputes provoked by the "new historians"—no longer new, in fact—in Israel, who have largely supported the
narrative version of Arab expulsion in 1948. Like apologies (the bottom line,
in effect, of a historical narrative) and reparations, the historical past is a
stake in current politics. But must the historian surrender to a Thrasymachan
view of his or her craft, in which the narrative yields only to the right of the
stronger?

There is a predictable course to major historical controversies. Conflicting
historical narratives are often repeated and challenged across several iterations:
over time, for instance, the orthodox view of the Cold War was displaced by
the revisionist challenge, which in turn yielded to a less contentious post-
revisionism marked by a somewhat world-weary or avuncular rhetoric of
disdain for earlier stridency.

Historical controversies finally end, in fact, not when there is agreement
on one narrative; this is usually never achieved. They end where clarification
is reached on two or perhaps three basic stories, whose representatives
understand the issues that separate them (which is itself difficult) and agree
to live, so to speak, side by side. Such an agreement forms the basis of the
contrapuntal narrative that I described earlier; and the historian who aspires
to a truly national or multicommunal history must recapitulate both narratives with some effort at retracing the internal logic of each.

Yet it is less in contests over responsibility than in celebrations of once-
silent protagonists that history plays a role in reparation. Like reparations,
historical narratives are increasingly conceived of as compensatory. But not
in the sense that new stories merely contest the old and fix responsibility

for bad outcomes on those hitherto thought depicted as blameless. They are compensatory rather in that they introduce new agents who have hitherto been left in obscurity. Whether through the discovery of working-class spokesmen earlier silenced (in E. P. Thompson's phrase) by "the enormous condescension of posterity," or the attention paid to the subjects of postcolonial history, or even by dint of the now ritual obeisance to "race, class, and gender," which no young historian dares omit, writers of history strain to hear voices earlier assumed to be silent.

CONCLUSION

At the end, the projects of reparation, remembering, and reconciliation involve the right to tell histories and have them listened to respectfully—to be no longer voiceless in Gaza. How extraordinary that so much of our public energies, in so many of our societies, in the decades that bridge the end of the twentieth century, should have to be devoted to this revisiting of collective victimization and catastrophe. Such a dedication can be interpreted pessimistically—which has often been my own impulse—namely, as the result of our current incapacity to entertain transformative political projects for the future and hence to invest our collective resources in contesting the past. Or it can be seen, more optimistically, as the unfinished business left by the great dismantling of abusive political systems that has progressively taken place throughout much of the world at the end of the twentieth century. For any future understanding of this preoccupation, there will also be scope for contested narratives.

NOTES

Some of the ideas presented in this chapter were discussed at the symposium "Politics and the Past: On Repairing Historical Injustices," organized by John Torpey at the University of British Columbia in February 2000. The chapter printed here was discussed at the Columbia University Legal Theory seminar in April 2001.

1. Martha Minow, *Between Vengeance and Forgiveness: Facing History after Genocide and Mass Violence* (Boston, Mass.: Beacon, 1998), 81–82 and passim.
2. Cf., among other sources, Katie Hafner, *The House at the Bridge: A Story of Modern Germany* (New York: Scribner, 1995).
3. Viviana Zelizer, *Pricing the Priceless Child: The Changing Social Value of Children* (Princeton, N.J.: Princeton University Press, 1985).
4. Zelizer, *Pricing the Priceless Child*, 160–65.
5. Zelizer, *Pricing the Priceless Child*, 212.
6. See my essay "Zu einer politischen Typologie der Aussöhnung," *Transit* no. 18 (Winter 1999/2000): 102–17.

7. Anthony G. Amsterdam and Jerome S. Bruner, *Minding the Law* (Cambridge, Mass.: Harvard University Press, 2000), 12.

8. Amsterdam and Bruner, *Minding the Law*, 110–11.

9. Christopher Browning, *Ordinary Men: Reserve Police Battalion 101 and the Final Solution in Poland* (New York: HarperCollins, 1992); Daniel J. Goldhagen, *Hitler's Willing Executioners: Ordinary Germans and the Holocaust* (New York: Knopf, 1995); and Arno J. Mayer's *Why Did the Heavens Not Darken?* (New York: Pantheon, 1988).

Index

About the Contributors

Elazar Barkan chairs the Department of Cultural Studies and is professor of history and cultural studies at Claremont Graduate University, California. Among his books are *The Guilt of Nations: Restitution and Negotiating Historical Injustices* (2000), *The Retreat of Scientific Racism* (1992), and *Claiming the Stones, Naming the Bones: Cultural Property and Group Identity* (co-editor with Ronald Bush, 2002).

Roy L. Brooks is Warren Distinguished Professor of Law at the University of San Diego. He is the author of more than two dozen books on legal, political, and sociological topics, and the editor of *When Sorry Isn't Enough: The Controversy over Apologies and Reparations for Human Injustice* (New York University Press, 1999).

Alan Cairns is adjunct professor emeritus in the Department of Political Science at University of Waterloo. He taught at the University of British Columbia from 1960 to 1995. He has published on imperialism in Africa, Canadian federalism, the Canadian Charter of Rights and Freedoms, and Aboriginal issues. His *Citizens Plus: Aboriginal Peoples and the Canadian State* was recently published by UBC Press.

William K. Carroll teaches in the Department of Sociology and in the Interdisciplinary Graduate Program in Social and Political Thought at the University of Victoria, Victoria, B.C., Canada. He is currently editor of the *Canadian Review of Sociology and Anthropology*.

Dalton Conley is associate professor of sociology and director of the Center for Advanced Social Science Research at New York University. His research focuses on how socioeconomic status is transmitted across generations. He is author of *Being Black, Living in the Red: Race, Wealth and Social Policy in America* (California, 1999), *Honky* (Vintage, 2001), and, with Neil Bennett and Kate Strully, *The Starting Gate: Health and Life Chances across Generations* (California, forthcoming). He is also editor of *Wealth and Poverty in America* (Blackwell, 2002). His latest book is entitled *The Pecking Order: Which Siblings Succeed, Which Don't and Why* (Pantheon/Vintage, forthcoming).

Brenda Coughlin is a Ph.D. candidate in sociology at Columbia University and a research assistant at the Institute for Social and Economic Research and Policy. In research on U.S. congressional committee public hearings on organized crime, she examines the state's role in producing knowledge—especially knowledge of political and group identities as organized by racial ideologies and changing views of ethnicity.

Laura Hein is associate professor of Japanese history at Northwestern University. With Mark Selden, she has edited three volumes on various controversies over remembrance of World War II: *Living with the Bomb: American and Japanese Cultural Conflict in the Nuclear Age* (M.E. Sharpe, 1997), *Censoring History: Citizenship and Memory in Japan, Germany and the United States* (M.E. Sharpe, 2000), and *Islands of Discontent: Contemporary Okinawa, Japan, and the United States* (Rowman & Littlefield, in press).

Rhoda E. Howard-Hassmann is professor of sociology at McMaster University in Canada, where she is also associate director of that University's Institute on Globalization and the Human Condition. She has published widely on human rights in Africa and in Canada and on general theoretical and methodological issues to do with international human rights. Her chapter is the first publication emanating from her new research project on what the West owes Africa.

Elizabeth Johnson is an anthropologist specializing in the study of China. She is curator of ethnology at the UBC Museum of Anthropology, where she has been employed since 1979. Through her curatorial responsibilities and her teaching in the museum studies program, she works at the interface between museums and First Nations people.

Sharon F. Lean is a Ph.D. candidate in political science and a fellow at the Center for the Study of Democracy at the University of California, Irvine. Her research on democratization in Latin America explores the interdependent roles of international organizations and domestic social movements in defending citizens' political rights and fostering institutional accountability. She has an M.A. in social sciences from the Facultad Latinoamericana de Ciencias Sociales (FLACSO) in Mexico.

Charles S. Maier (born 1939) studied at Harvard and Oxford Universities, taught at Duke University, and since 1981 has taught modern European history at Harvard University, where he is a member and former director of the Center for European Studies. His books include *Recasting Bourgeois Europe* (1975), *In Search of Stability* (1987), *The Unmasterable Past* (1988), and *Dissolution* (1997). He is the editor of several other volumes and the author of many articles and book chapters and, among other eclectic interests, has written recently on the topic of collective memory and truth commissions.

Jeffrey K. Olick is associate professor of sociology at Columbia University, where he directs a university seminar called "Beyond History and Memory." He has published numerous articles on collective memory, German politics, and sociological theory; is editor of *States of Memory: Continuities, Conflicts and Transformations in National Commemoration*; and is completing a book on German memory titled *The Sins of the Fathers: Governing Memory in the Federal Republic of Germany*.

Ruth B. Phillips is director of the Museum of Anthropology and professor of art history and anthropology at the University of British Columbia. She has published in the areas of African and North American Native art history and museum history and theory. Her most recent books are *Trading Identities: The Souvenir in Native North American Art from the Northeast, 1700–1900* (University of Washington Press, 1999); *Unpacking Culture: Art and Commodity in Colonial and Postcolonial Worlds*, co-edited with Christopher B. Steiner (University of California Press, 1999); and *Native North American Art* (with Janet Catherine Berlo; Oxford University Press, 1998).

R. S. Ratner is professor of sociology in the Department of Anthropology and Sociology at the University of British Columbia, Vancouver, Canada. He has been studying First Nations and urban Aboriginal social movements for the last fifteen years.

Henry Rousso is senior researcher at the Centre National de la Recherche Scientifique (CNRS) in Paris and director of the Institute for the Study of Contemporary History. He has written several books on the history of memory, especially on the legacy of World War II. Among his works published in English are *The Vichy Syndrome: History and Memory in France Since 1944* (Harvard University Press, 1991); *Vichy: An Ever-Present Past* (with Eric Conan; University Press of New England, 1998); and *The Haunting Past: History, Memory, and Justice in Contemporary France* (University of Pennsylvania Press, 2001).

John Torpey is associate professor of sociology and European studies at the University of British Columbia. He is author of "'Making Whole What Has

Been Smashed': Reflections on Reparations," *Journal of Modern History* (June 2001). His most recent books are *Documenting Individual Identity: The Development of State Practices in the Modern World* (co-editor with Jane Caplan, Princeton University Press, 2001), and *The Invention of the Passport: Surveillance, Citizenship, and the State* (Cambridge University Press, 2000). He is writing a book about reparations politics that is to be published by Harvard University Press.

Stef Vandeginste is a legal researcher in the law department at the University of Antwerp, Belgium. His research covers the international right to reparation for victims of gross and systematic human rights violations. His writings in this area include a chapter on reparations in Luc Huyse, ed., *Democracy and Reconciliation in Post-Conflict States: A Handbook* (Stockholm: International IDEA, 2002) and, together with Marc Bossuyt, "The Issue of Reparation for Slavery and Colonialism and the Durban World Conference against Racism," *Human Rights Law Journal* (2002).

Andrew Woolford is assistant professor of sociology at the University of Manitoba. His doctoral dissertation at the University of British Columbia, "Between Justice and Certainty: Treaty Making in the Lower Mainland of British Columbia," analyzed the process of treaty negotiations in British Columbia.